The Original
U.S. CONGRESS
HANDBOOK

116th Congress Second Session 2019
Published Annually Since 1974

COLUMBIA BOOKS, Inc.
BETHESDA, MD

D0709629

THE ORIGINAL U.S. CONGRESS HANDBOOK™
PUBLISHED BY COLUMBIA BOOKS, Inc.
BETHESDA, MD

Acknowledgements the U.S. Congress, the U.S. Supreme Court, the White House staff, the Offices of the Governors, the U.S. Census Bureau and the Library of Congress.

Maps Map Resources

Pronunciations provided and copyrighted by inogolo.com

For information on obtaining photographs or data contact

Columbia Books, Inc.
1560 Wilson Blvd, Suite 825
Arlington, VA 22209
202.464.1662
www.columbiabooks.com and
www.uscongresshandbook.com
ISBN-10: 1-938939-86-7
ISBN-13: 978-1-938939-86-0

Managing Editor: Emma Griffin
Editorial Director: Duncan J. Bell

Printed in United States.

**Supreme Court photographs courtesy
of the Supreme Court Historical Society**

Publisher's cataloging in publication data
The Original U.S. Congress Handbook. - 116th Congress, Second Session (2019).

March 2019: State Version

TABLE OF CONTENTS

GUIDE TO STATE/LEGISLATOR PROFILES

Governor Title First name Surname (pronunciation)   Phone

Photo	Address1	Capital
	Address2	Population (Rank)
	Website	Area (Rank)
	Fax	
	Term Ends	State Map
	Lt. Governor	

U.S. Senators

U.S. Representatives

Title First name Surname (pronunciation)   Party-State-District   Phone

🐴 - Democrat and 🐘 - Republican

Names are displayed in red for Republican, blue for Democrat and green for Independent.

	Rm.	Web.	Fax
Photo	Bio. Birth Date • Birth City/State/Country • Professional Information • Military Service • Educational Institutions, Degrees and Years • Religion • Marital Status and Number of Children		
	Cmte. Committees		
	CoS.		LD.
	Sched.		PS.
	Dist Off. listing of state offices and phone numbers		

T: Percentage **Legend: Rm** - Room; **Web** - Website; **CoS** - Chief of Staff;
of the vote. **LD** - Legis. Dir.; **Sched** - Scheduler; **PS** - Press Sec.; **R** - Rank;
Elected Year **T** - Term; **M** - Married; **Se** - Separated; **D** - Divorced; **W** -
Next election year Widowed; **DP** - Domestic Partner; **S** - Single; **E** - Engaged; **ch**
(Senators only) - child/ren; **gr-ch** - grandchild/ren; **(CD)** - district office staff
member

Above positions are a description of the staffer's role and function. Actual job titles may vary.

Ethics Guidelines for Lobbyists and Non-Lobbyists

The US House and US Senate prohibit a registered lobbyist from giving 'anything of value' to Members, officers or employees of the House or Senate. . This prohibition applies as well to reimbursing a non-lobbyist employee of a registered lobbying entity for 'anything of value' given to a covered legislative branch person. Further, the gift rules restrict to $100 per calendar year (and $49.99 maximum per occurrence) the value of any gift received by a Member, officer or employee of the Congress from a non-lobbyist, citizen advocate.

There are exceptions to the gift restrictions (citizen advocates) and gift ban (lobbyists).

Notwithstanding the rules and the exceptions, both the House and Senate Ethics Committees instruct Members and staff:

- NOT to accept any gifts that are linked to an official action (referred to as a "quid pro quo")
- Not to solicit a gift from anyone with business before Congress
- Not to allow third parties to pay for gifts, travel or entertainment for a Member or staffer, unless it is clearly permitted as an exception to the ban on gifts from lobbyists and lobbying entities
- Some Members have established stricter rules for their office staff in order to ensure that impermissible gifts are not accepted by those employed in that office.

As indicated above, there are exceptions to the gift rules. Some of the more common exceptions are listed below. Note that this list is not exhaustive.[2]

Gifts of nominal value, including food and drink of nominal value, not as part of a meal. Generally, items valued at less than $10 are allowed, as are certain specific items: "greeting cards, baseball caps, or T-shirts" (which may cost more than $10). Food and drink, not as part of a meal, are allowed for attendance at receptions.

Home state/district items. Products that are made or produced in the state or district represented by a member of Congress, , and are displayed or available to members, staff and visitors, at no cost, at the Member's office are allowed.

Attendance and meals at widely attended events are exempt from the gift rules as long as the following conditions exist: the event must include at least 25 people who are not "from the Hill" (i.e. congressional members and staff) who may be from a specific industry or have a specific interest, the invitation to the event must be from the event sponsor, and the event must be related to a member or staffer's official duties. A sporting or recreational event does qualify under the exception for a "widely attended event" and free tickets / food at such an event would not be permissible.

Personal friendship allows a member or staffer to accept a gift from a lobbyist , provided there is a history of friendship, including the exchange of gifts between the congressional member/staffer and the person giving the gift, and provided that the gift is paid with personal funds and not reimbursed or deducted as a business expense by the one giving the gift. And, of course, the gift cannot be in exchange for or related to any official action.

Items given by federal, state or local government refer to gifts that are paid for directly by any of the three levels of government. These cannot be paid for by an outside source and then given by a federal, state or local government. In addition, the House and Senate rules are different insofar as defining certain entities as 'agencies of the federal government' under the gift rules.

[1] This information should not be relied on as complete legal advice. Please contact legal counsel if you need further guidance.

[2] A full listing of the exceptions under the gift rule is available in the Lobbying Compliance Handbook: A Practitioner's Guide to HLOGA, published by Columbia Books, Inc.

Meals and transportation in the course of a site visit: the exception (specific to the House) allows a House member or staffer to accept a meal and local transportation to / from a site being visited by the House member/staffer, even if the source is a lobbying registrant.

Lobbyists and lobbying entities must certify compliance with the gift rules: Adhering to the gift rules is of prime importance. Registered organizations and individual lobbyists are required to file the LD-203 report semiannually, on which lobbyists and registrant organizations must certify under penalty of perjury that they did not knowingly violate the House and Senate gift rules by providing gifts and/ or travel to a Member, officer or employee of the House or Senate.

Congressional Demographics

Breakdown by Gender

- Male (75.84%)
- Female (24.16%)

Breakdown by Ethnic Group

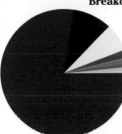

- White/Caucasian (77.45%)
- Black/African American (9.61%)
- Hispanic/Latino (7.02%)
- Asian/Pacific American (2.03%)
- Other (1.29%)
- Not Specified (0.92%)
- Indian/Native American (0.74%)
- Two or More Ethnicities (0.55%)
- Hawaiian/Pacific Islander (0.37%)

Breakdown by Marital Status

- Married (83.73%)
- Single (7.95%)
- Divorced (5.55%)
- Not Stated (0.74%)
- Widow (0.74%)
- Widower (0.55%)
- Not Specified (0.55%)
- Separated (0.18%)

Breakdown by Religion

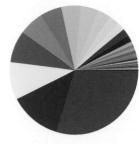

- Catholic (29.76%)
- Baptist (12.94%)
- Protestant - Unspecified Christian (9.43%)
- Methodist (7.95%)
- Jewish (6.1%)
- Presbyterian (5.36%)
- Lutheran (4.99%)
- Episcopalian (4.81%)
- Unspecified/Other (3.14%)
- Christian - Non-Denominational (2.59%)
- Evangelical (2.03%)
- Mormon (1.85%)
- Not Known (1.66%)
- African Methodist Episcopal (0.92%)
- Church of Christ (0.74%)
- Greek Orthodox (0.74%)
- Hinduism (0.74%)
- Islam (Muslim) (0.55%)
- Anglican (0.37%)
- Assembly of God (0.37%)
- Buddhism (0.37%)
- Congregationalist (0.37%)
- Seventh-Day Adventist (0.37%)
- Christian Reformed Church (0.18%)
- Church of the United Brethren in Christ (0.18%)
- Disciples of Christ (0.18%)
- Eastern Orthodox (0.18%)
- Nazarene (0.18%)
- None (0.18%)
- Pentecostal (0.18%)
- Unitarian (0.18%)
- United Church of Christ (0.18%)
- Wesleyan (0.18%)

2019 Legislative Calendar

JANUARY 2019
S	M	T	W	T	F	S
		1	2	3	4	5
6	7	8	9	10	11	12
13	14	15	16	17	18	19
20	21	22	23	24	25	26
27	28	29	30	31		

FEBRUARY 2019
S	M	T	W	T	F	S
					1	2
3	4	5	6	7	8	9
10	11	12	13	14	15	16
17	18	19	20	21	22	23
24	25	26	27	28		

MARCH 2019
S	M	T	W	T	F	S
					1	2
3	4	5	6	7	8	9
10	11	12	13	14	15	16
17	18	19	20	21	22	23
24	25	26	27	28	29	30
31						

APRIL 2019
S	M	T	W	T	F	S
	1	2	3	4	5	6
7	8	9	10	11	12	13
14	15	16	17	18	19	20
21	22	23	24	25	26	27
28	29	30				

MAY 2019
S	M	T	W	T	F	S
			1	2	3	4
5	6	7	8	9	10	11
12	13	14	15	16	17	18
19	20	21	22	23	24	25
26	27	28	29	30	31	

JUNE 2019
S	M	T	W	T	F	S
						1
2	3	4	5	6	7	8
9	10	11	12	13	14	15
16	17	18	19	20	21	22
23	24	25	26	27	28	29
30						

JULY 2019
S	M	T	W	T	F	S
	1	2	3	4	5	6
7	8	9	10	11	12	13
14	15	16	17	18	19	20
21	22	23	24	25	26	27
28	29	30	31			

AUGUST 2019
S	M	T	W	T	F	S
				1	2	3
4	5	6	7	8	9	10
11	12	13	14	15	16	17
18	19	20	21	22	23	24
25	26	27	28	29	30	31

SEPTEMBER 2019
S	M	T	W	T	F	S
1	2	3	4	5	6	7
8	9	10	11	12	13	14
15	16	17	18	19	20	21
22	23	24	25	26	27	28
29	30					

OCTOBER 2019
S	M	T	W	T	F	S
		1	2	3	4	5
6	7	8	9	10	11	12
13	14	15	16	17	18	19
20	21	22	23	24	25	26
27	28	29	30	31		

NOVEMBER 2019
S	M	T	W	T	F	S
					1	2
3	4	5	6	7	8	9
10	11	12	13	14	15	16
17	18	19	20	21	22	23
24	25	26	27	28	29	30

DECEMBER 2019
S	M	T	W	T	F	S
1	2	3	4	5	6	7
8	9	10	11	12	13	14
15	16	17	18	19	20	21
22	23	24	25	26	27	28
29	30	31				

Federal Holiday   House not in session
Senate not in session

U.S. SENATE LEADERSHIP

Republican Party   53   Democratic Party   45   Independent   2

A senator must be at least 30 years old, a U.S. citizen for nine years, and a resident of the state in which he or she is elected. Each state sends two senators to serve six-year terms. They are elected on a rotating schedule, with one-third of the Senate being elected every two years.

THE LEADERSHIP

Senate Majority Leader
Mitch McConnell (R-KY)   The Capitol S-230   **202.224.3135**

Senate Majority Whip; Assistant Majority Leader
John Thune (R-SD)   The Capitol 208   **202.224.2321**

Senate Republican Conference Chairman
John A. Barrasso (R-WY)   HSOB 307   **202.224.2764**

Senate Minority Leader
Charles E. Schumer (D-NY)

Senate Minority Whip
Dick Durbin (D-IL)

Senate Democratic Conference Secretary
Tammy Baldwin (D-WI)   HSOB 717   **202.224.5653**

THE OFFICERS

President of the Senate
Mike Pence

President Pro Tempore
Chuck Grassley   The Capitol 126   **202.224.3744**

Secretary of the Senate
Julie E. Adams

Sergeant at Arms and Doorkeeper of the Senate
Michael C. Stenger

Senate Majority Secretary
Laura Dove

Senate Minority Secretary
Gary Myrick

Senate Parliamentarian
Elizabeth C. MacDonough

Chaplain of the Senate
Barry C. Black

THE SENATE OFFICE BUILDINGS

When addressing correspondence to Members of the Senate, use the following abbreviations for office buildings. No street address is required. The Senate ZIP code is 20510.

S	Senate north side of Capitol Building
DSOB	Senate Dirksen Office Building
	Constitution Avenue and First Street NE
HSOB	Senate Hart Office Building
	Constitution Avenue and Second Street NE
RSOB	Russell Senate Office Building
	Constitution and Delaware Avenues NE

SENATE ELECTION INFORMATION

As set forth in Article I, Section 3 of the Constitution, Senators are divided into three classes so that one-third may be elected every second year:

Class I - Senators whose next election occurs in 2024:

Democrats (21)	Republicans (10)	Independents (2)
Baldwin, Tammy (D-WI)	Barrasso, John A. (R-WY)	King, Angus S. (I-ME)
Brown, Sherrod C. (D-OH)	Blackburn, Marsha (R-TN)	Sanders, Bernie (I-VT)
Cantwell, Maria (D-WA)	Braun, Mike (R-IN)	
Cardin, Ben L. (D-MD)	Cramer, Kevin J. (R-ND)	
Carper, Tom R. (D-DE)	Cruz, Ted (R-TX)	
Casey, Bob (D-PA)	Fischer, Deb (R-NE)	
Feinstein, Dianne (D-CA)	Hawley, Josh (R-MO)	
Gillibrand, Kirsten E. (D-NY)	Romney, Mitt (R-UT)	
Heinrich, Martin T. (D-NM)	Scott, Rick (R-FL)	
Hirono, Mazie K. (D-HI)	Wicker, Roger F. (R-MS)	
Kaine, Tim M. (D-VA)		
Klobuchar, Amy (D-MN)		
Manchin, Joe (D-WV)		
Menendez, Bob (D-NJ)		
Murphy, Chris S. (D-CT)		
Rosen, Jacklyn S. (D-NV)		
Sinema, Kyrsten (D-AZ)		
Stabenow, Debbie A. (D-MI)		
Tester, Jon (D-MT)		
Warren, Elizabeth A. (D-MA)		
Whitehouse, Sheldon (D-RI)		

Class II - Senators whose next election occurs in 2020:

Democrats (12)	Republicans (21)	Independents (0)
Booker, Cory A. (D-NJ)	Alexander, Lamar (R-TN)	
Coons, Christopher A. (D-DE)	Capito, Shelley Moore (R-WV)	
Durbin, Dick (D-IL)	Cassidy, Bill (R-LA)	
Jones, Doug (D-AL)	Collins, Susan M. (R-ME)	
Markey, Ed (D-MA)	Cornyn, John (R-TX)	
Merkley, Jeff A. (D-OR)	Cotton, Tom B. (R-AR)	
Peters, Gary C. (D-MI)	Daines, Steve (R-MT)	
Reed, Jack F. (D-RI)	Enzi, Mike B. (R-WY)	
Shaheen, Jeanne (D-NH)	Ernst, Joni K. (R-IA)	
Smith, Tina (D-MN)	Gardner, Cory S. (R-CO)	
Udall, Tom S. (D-NM)	Graham, Lindsey (R-SC)	
Warner, Mark R. (D-VA)	Hyde-Smith, Cindy (R-MS)	
	Inhofe, James M. (R-OK)	
	McConnell, Mitch (R-KY)	
	Perdue, David A. (R-GA)	
	Risch, James E. (R-ID)	
	Roberts, Pat (R-KS)	
	Rounds, Mike (R-SD)	
	Sasse, Ben (R-NE)	
	Sullivan, Dan S. (R-AK)	
	Tillis, Thom R. (R-NC)	

Class III - Senators whose next election occurs in 2022:

Democrats (12)	Republicans (22)	Independents (0)
Bennet, Michael F. (D-CO)	Blunt, Roy D. (R-MO)	
Blumenthal, Richard (D-CT)	Boozman, John N. (R-AR)	
Cortez Masto, Catherine M. (D-NV)	Burr, Richard M. (R-NC)	
Duckworth, Tammy (D-IL)	Crapo, Mike D. (R-ID)	
Harris, Kamala D. (D-CA)	Grassley, Chuck (R-IA)	
Hassan, Maggie (D-NH)	Hoeven, John H. (R-ND)	
Leahy, Patrick J. (D-VT)	Isakson, Johnny (R-GA)	
Murray, Patty (D-WA)	Johnson, Ron H. (R-WI)	
Schatz, Brian E. (D-HI)	Kennedy, John N. (R-LA)	
Schumer, Charles E. (D-NY)	Lankford, James P. (R-OK)	
Van Hollen, Chris J. (D-MD)	Lee, Mike (R-UT)	
Wyden, Ron (D-OR)	McSally, Martha E. (R-AZ)	
	Moran, Jerry (R-KS)	
	Murkowski, Lisa A. (R-AK)	
	Paul, Rand (R-KY)	
	Portman, Rob J. (R-OH)	
	Rubio, Marco (R-FL)	
	Scott, Tim E. (R-SC)	
	Shelby, Richard C. (R-AL)	
	Thune, John (R-SD)	
	Toomey, Pat J. (R-PA)	
	Young, Todd C. (R-IN)	

U.S. HOUSE OF REPRESENTATIVES LEADERSHIP

Democratic Party   239   Republican Party   199

A representative must be at least 25 years old, a U.S. citizen for seven years, and a resident of the state in which he or she is elected. The U.S. Census determines each state's allocation of the 435 representative seats, and each state legislature determines congressional district boundaries in that state. Every state has at least one representative, and all representatives are elected every even-numbered year.

Delegates and commissioners represent the U.S. territories, commonwealths and the federal district. Although they may not vote on the House floor, they can vote on legislation in their committees.

THE LEADERSHIP

Speaker of the House
Nancy Pelosi (D-CA)   The Capitol H-232   **202.225.0600**

House Majority Leader
Steny H. Hoyer (D-MD)   The Capitol H-107   **202.225.3130**

House Majority Whip
James E. Clyburn (D-SC)   The Capitol H-329   **202.225.0197**

House Republican Conference Chairman
Liz L. Cheney (R-WY)   LHOB 1420   **202.225.5107**

House Republican Policy Committee Chairman
Gary J. Palmer (R-AL)   CHOB 207   **202.225.4921**

House Minority Leader
Kevin McCarthy (R-CA)   The Capitol H-204   **202.225.0100**

House Minority Whip
Steve J. Scalise (R-LA)   The Capitol H-148   **202.225.3130**

House Democratic Caucus Chairman
Hakeem S. Jeffries (D-NY)   LHOB 1420   **202.225.1400**

THE OFFICERS

Clerk of the House
Cheryl Johnson

House Sergeant at Arms
Paul D. Irving

House Chief Administrative Officer
Philip G. Kiko

Chaplain of the House
Patrick Conroy

THE HOUSE OFFICE BUILDINGS

When addressing correspondence to Members of the House of Representatives, use the following abbreviations for office buildings. No street address is required. The ZIP code for the House is 20515.

CHOB	Cannon House Office Building	
	First Street and Independence Avenue SE	
FHOB	Ford House Office Building, 300 D St. SW	
H	House-south side of Capitol Building	
HB	House Basement-northwest side of Capitol Building	
LHOB	Longworth House Office Building	
	New Jersey and Independence Avenues SE	
RHOB	Rayburn House Office Building	
	South Capitol Street and Independence Avenue SW	

NOTES

SENATORS - 116th Congress

REPRESENTATIVES - 116th Congress

INDEX OF LEGISLATORS BY RANK

STATE/LEGISLATOR PROFILES

STATE/LEGISLATOR PROFILES - 116th Congress

ALABAMA

⚑ Governor Kay Ivey ("EYE"-vee)   p 334.242.7100

600 Dexter Avenue
Montgomery, AL 36130
Website alabama.gov
Fax 334.353.0004
Term Ends 2023
Lt. Governor
Will Ainsworth, **R**

C: Montgomery
P: 4,887,871 (24)
A: 50,645.39 mi^2 (28th)

U.S. Senators
Richard C. Shelby, **R**
Doug Jones, **D**
U.S. Representatives
01 / Bradley R. Byrne, **R**
02 / Martha Roby, **R**
03 / Mike D. Rogers, **R**
04 / Robert B. Aderholt, **R**
05 / Mo Brooks, **R**
06 / Gary J. Palmer, **R**
07 / Terri A. Sewell, **D**

⚑ Sen. Doug Jones (joanz)   D-AL-Jr.   p 202.224.4124

Rm. RSOB 326 **Web.** jones.senate.gov   **f** 202.224.3149
Bio. 05/04/1954 • Fairfield, AL • Univ. of Alabama, B.S.,
1976; Samford Univ. Cumberland School of Law (AL)
Cumberland School of Law, J.D., 1979 • Methodist • M.
Louise F. Jones, 3 ch ; 2 gr-ch **Cmte.** Aging • Armed
Services • Banking, Housing & Urban Affairs • Health,
Education, Labor & Pensions
CoS. Dana G. Gresham   **LD.** Mark Libell
Sched. Olivia Chartier   **PS.** Heather Lynn Fluit
Dist. Off. Birmingham 205.731.1500 • Dothan 334.792.4924
• Huntsville 256.533.0979 • Mobile 251.414.3083 •
Montgomery 334.230.0698

R: 90 **T:** 1st 50%
Elected Year: 2017
Next Election: 2020

⚑ Sen. Richard C. Shelby (SHELL-bee)   R-AL-Sr.   p 202.224.5744

Rm. RSOB 304 **Web.** shelby.senate.gov   **f** 202.224.3416
Bio. 05/06/1934 • Birmingham, AL • U.S. Representative;
Attorney • Univ. of Alabama, B.A., 1957; Univ. of Alabama
School of Law, LL.B., 1963 • Presbyterian • M. Annette
Nevin Shelby, 2 ch ; 2 gr-ch **Cmte.** Appropriations •
Banking, Housing & Urban Affairs • Environment & Public
Works • Rules & Administration
CoS. Dayne Cutrell   **LD.** Morgan Carter Ulmer
                               PS. Blair Taylor
Dist. Off. Birmingham 205.731.1384 • Huntsville
256.772.0460 • Mobile 251.694.4164 • Montgomery
334.223.7303 • Tuscaloosa 205.759.5047

R: 4 **T:** 6th 64%
Elected Year: 1986
Next Election: 2022

⚑ Rep. Robert B. Aderholt (A-dur-holt)   R-AL-04   p 202.225.4876

Rm. LHOB 1203 **Web.** aderholt.house.gov   **f** 202.225.5587
Bio. 07/22/1965 • Haleyville, AL • Municipal Court Judge
• Birmingham-Southern College (AL), B.A., 1987; Samford
Univ. Cumberland Law School (AL), J.D., 1990 • Methodist •
M. Caroline McDonald Aderholt, 2 ch **Cmte.** Appropriations
CoS. Brian Rell   **LD.** Mark E. Dawson
Sched. Chris Lawson   **PS.** Carson Clark (CD)
Dist. Off. Cullman 256.734.6043 • Gadsden 256.546.0201
• Jasper 205.221.2310 • Tuscumbia 256.381.3450

R: 45 **T:** 12th 80%
Elected Year: 1996

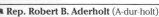

ALABAMA

🏛 Rep. Mo Brooks (brooks)   R-AL-05   p 202.225.480

Rm. RHOB 2246   **Web.** brooks.house.gov
Bio. 04/29/1954 • Charleston, SC • State Legislator; County
Commissioner • Duke Univ. (NC), B.A., 1975; Univ. of
Alabama School of Law, J.D., 1978 • Christian Church •
M. Martha Brooks, 4 ch ; 8 gr-ch   **Cmte.** Armed Services •
Science, Space & Technology
CoS. Mark Pettitt   **LD.** Tiffany Noel (CD)
Sched. Madison Engelking   **PS.** Clay Mills
Dist. Off. Decatur 256.355.9400 • Florence 256.718.5155 •
Huntsville 256.551.0190

R: 154   **T:** 5th 61%
Elected Year: 2010

🏛 Rep. Bradley R. Byrne (burn)   R-AL-01   p 202.225.493

Rm. CHOB 119   **Web.** byrne.house.gov   **f** 202.225.056
Bio. 02/16/1955 • Mobile, AL • Duke Univ. (NC), B.A., 1977;
Univ. of Alabama School of Law, J.D., 1980 • Episcopalian •
M. Rebecca Dukes, 4 ch ; 2 gr-ch   **Cmte.** Armed Services •
Education & Labor
CoS. Chad Carlough   **LD.** Mitch Relfe
Sched. Jordan Howard   **PS.** Seth Morrow
Dist. Off. Mobile 251.690.2811 • Summerdale 251.989.266

R: 245   **T:** 4th 63%
Elected Year: 2013

🏛 Rep. Gary J. Palmer (PALL-mur)   R-AL-06   p 202.225.492

Rm. CHOB 207   **Web.** palmer.house.gov   **f** 202.225.208
Bio. 05/14/1954 • Hackleburg, AL • Univ. of Alabama,
B.S., 1977 • Presbyterian • M. Ann Cushing, 3 ch   **Cmte.**
Select Committee on the Climate Crisis • Transportation &
Infrastructure
CoS. William Smith   **LD.** Cari Fike
Sched. Camille Smith   **PS.** Elizabeth Hance
Dist. Off. Birmingham 205.968.1290 • Clanton
205.280.6846 • Oneonta 205.625.4160

R: 276   **T:** 3rd 69%
Elected Year: 2014

🏛 Rep. Martha Roby (RO-bee)   R-AL-02   p 202.225.290

Rm. CHOB 504   **Web.** roby.house.gov   **f** 202.225.891
Bio. 07/26/1976 • Montgomery, AL • New York Univ.,
B.M., 1998; Samford Univ. Cumberland School of Law (AL)
Cumberland School of Law, J.D., 2001 • Presbyterian • M.
Riley Roby, 2 ch   **Cmte.** Appropriations • Judiciary
CoS. Mike Albares   **LD.** David Allen
Sched. Kate Hollis   **PS.** Emily Taylor-Johnson
Dist. Off. Andalusia 334.428.1129 • Dothan 334.794.9680
Montgomery 334.262.7718

R: 178   **T:** 5th 61%
Elected Year: 2010

🏛 Rep. Mike D. Rogers (RAH-jurz)   R-AL-03   p 202.225.326

Rm. RHOB 2184   **Web.** mikerogers.house.gov   **f** 202.226.848
Bio. 07/16/1958 • Hammond, IN • Jacksonville State Univ.
(AL), B.A., 1981; Jacksonville State Univ. (AL), M.P.A., 1984;
Birmingham School of Law (AL), J.D., 1991 • Baptist • M.
Beth Rogers, 3 ch   **Cmte.** Armed Services • Homeland
Security
CoS. Christopher Brinson   **LD.** Whitney Verett
Sched. Alexis Barranca   **PS.** Shea Miller
Dist. Off. Anniston 256.236.5655 • Opelika 334.745.6221

R: 82   **T:** 9th 64%
Elected Year: 2002

🏛 Rep. Terri A. Sewell (SOO-wull)   D-AL-07   p 202.225.266

Rm. RHOB 2201   **Web.** sewell.house.gov   p 202.226.956
Bio. 01/01/1965 • Huntsville, AL • Selma High School (AL)
A.B., 1982; Princeton Univ. (NJ), A.B., 1986; Oxford Univ.
(England), M.A., 1988; Harvard Univ. Law School (MA), J.D.,
1992 • Protestant - Unspecified Christian • D. Theodore
Dixie   **Cmte.** Permanent Select on Intelligence • Ways &
Means
CoS. Cachavious English
Sched. Perry Hamilton   **PS.** Jackie McGuinness
Dist. Off. Birmingham 205.254.1960 • Montgomery
334.262.1919 • Selma 334.877.4414 • Tuscaloosa
205.752.5380

R: 181   **T:** 5th 98%
Elected Year: 2010

ALASKA

⚑ Governor Mike Dunleavy (DUHN-lee-vee) p 907.465.3500

Office of the Governor, P.O. Box 110001
Juneau, AK 99811
Website alaska.gov
Fax 907.465.3532
Term Ends 2022
Lt. Governor
Kevin Meyer, **R**

C: Juneau
P: 737,438 (49)
A: 570,640.61 mi² (1st)

U.S. Senators
Lisa A. Murkowski, **R**
Dan S. Sullivan, **R**
U.S. Representatives
01 / Don Young, **R**

⚑ Sen. Lisa A. Murkowski (mur-KOU-skee) R-AK-Sr. p 202.224.6665

Rm. HSOB 522 **Web.** murkowski.senate.gov **f** 202.224.5301
Bio. 05/22/1957 • Ketchikan, AK • Attorney; State
Representative • Georgetown Univ. (DC), B.A., 1980;
Willamette Univ. College of Law (OR), J.D., 1985 • Roman
Catholic • M. Verne Martell, 2 ch **Cmte.** Appropriations •
Energy & Natural Resources • Health, Education, Labor &
Pensions • Indian Affairs
CoS. Mike Pawlowski **LD.** Garrett Boyle
Sched. Kennis Brady (CD) **PS.** Karina Borger
Dist. Off. Anchorage 907.271.3735 • Fairbanks
907.456.0233 • Juneau 907.586.7277 • Ketchikan
907.225.6880 • Soldotna 907.262.4220 • Wasilla
907.376.7665

R: 20 **T:** 3rd 44%
Elected Year: 2002
Next Election: 2022

⚑ Sen. Dan S. Sullivan (SULL-lih-vuhn) R-AK Jr. p 202.224.3004

Rm. HSOB 302 **Web.** sullivan.senate.gov **f** 202.224.6501
Bio. 11/13/1964 • Fairview Park, OH • Harvard Univ., Bach.
Deg., 1987; Georgetown Univ. Law Center (DC), J.D., 1993;
Georgetown Univ. Law Center (DC), M.S., 1993 • Roman
Catholic • M. Julie Fate, 3 ch **Cmte.** Armed Services •
Commerce, Science & Transportation • Environment &
Public Works • Veterans' Affairs
CoS. Larry Burton **LD.** Erik Elam
Sched. Avery Fogels **PS.** Mike Anderson
Dist. Off. Anchorage 907.271.5915 • Fairbanks
907.456.0261 • Juneau 907.586.7277 • Ketchikan
907.225.6880 • Soldotna 907.283.4000 • Wasilla
907.357.9956

R: 81 **T:** 1st 48%
Elected Year: 2014
Next Election: 2020

⚑ Rep. Don Young (yung) R-AK-01 p 202.225.5765

Rm. RHOB 2314 **Web.** donyoung.house.gov **f** 202.225.0425
Bio. 06/09/1933 • Meridian, CA • State Legislator; School
Teacher • Army 1955-57 • Yuba Junior College (CA), A.A.,
1952; California State Univ., Chico, B.A., 1958 • Episcopalian
• M. Anne Garland Walton, 2 ch ; 14 gr-ch ; 1 great-gr-ch
Cmte. Natural Resources • Transportation & Infrastructure
CoS. Pamela Day **LD.** Alex Ortiz
Sched. Paula Conru **PS.** Zack Brown
Dist. Off. Anchorage 907.271.5978 • Fairbanks
907.456.0210

R: 1 **T:** 24th 53%
Elected Year: 1973

ARIZONA

⚑ Governor Douglas A. Ducey (DOO-see) p 602.542.4331

1700 W. Washington St.
Phoenix, AZ 85007
Website az.gov
Fax 602.542.7601
Term Ends 2023

C: Phoenix
P: 7,171,646 (14)
A: 113,593.91 mi² (6th)

ARIZONA

U.S. Senators
Kyrsten Sinema, **D**
Martha E. McSally, **R**
U.S. Representatives
01 / Tom O'Halleran, **D**
02 / Ann L. Kirkpatrick, **D**
03 / Raul M. Grijalva, **D**
04 / Paul A. Gosar, **R**
05 / Andy Biggs, **R**
06 / David Schweikert, **R**
07 / Ruben Gallego, **D**
08 / Debbie Lesko, **R**
09 / Greg Stanton, **D**

♀ Sen. Martha E. McSally (mik-SA-lee)   R-AZ-Jr.   p 202.224.2235
Rm. DSOB B40D **Web.** mcsally.senate.gov   **f** 202.228.2862
Bio. 03/22/1966 • Warwick, RI • National Air War College,
Mast. Deg.; United States Air Force Academy, B.S., 1988;
John F. Kennedy School of Government, Harvard Univ.,
M.P.P., 1990 • Christian Church • S. **Cmte.** Aging • Armed
Services • Banking, Housing & Urban Affairs • Energy &
Natural Resources • Indian Affairs
CoS. Justin Roth   **LD.** Pace McMullan
Sched. Alana Wilson   **PS.** Katie Waldman
Dist. Off. Phoenix 602.952.2410 • Tucson 520.670.6334

R: 95   **T:** 0th
Elected Year: 2019
Next Election: 2020

♀ Sen. Kyrsten Sinema (SIH-nih-muh)   D-AZ-Sr.   p 202.224.4521
Rm. HSOB 825B-C **Web.** sinema.senate.gov
Bio. 07/12/1976 • Tucson, AZ • Brigham Young Univ. (UT),
Bach. Deg., 1995; Arizona State Univ., M.S., 1999; Arizona
State Univ. Law School, J.D., 2004; Arizona State Univ., Ph.D.,
2012 • None • S. **Cmte.** Aging • Banking, Housing & Urban
Affairs • Commerce, Science & Transportation • Homeland
Security & Government Affairs • Veterans' Affairs
CoS. Meg Joseph   **LD.** Michael Brownlie
Sched. Jamie Lynch   **PS.** John LaBombard
Dist. Off. Phoenix 602.598.7327

R: 93   **T:** 0th 50%
Elected Year: 2018
Next Election: 2024

♂ Rep. Andy Biggs (bigz)   R-AZ-05   p 202.225.2635
Rm. LHOB 1318 **Web.** biggs.house.gov
Bio. 11/07/1958 • Tucson, AZ • Brigham Young Univ. (UT),
B.A., 1982; Univ. of Arizona Rogers College of Law, J.D.,
1984; Arizona State Univ., M.A., 1999 • Mormon • M. Cindy
Biggs, 6 ch **Cmte.** Judiciary • Science, Space & Technology
CoS. Deborah Mazol   **LD.** Kate LaBorde
Sched. Tina Seideman   **PS.** Daniel Stefanski
Dist. Off. Mesa 480.699.8239

R: 297   **T:** 2nd 59%
Elected Year: 2016

♀ Rep. Ruben Gallego (gah-YEH-go)   D-AZ-07   p 202.225.4065
Rm. LHOB 1131 **Web.**
   rubengallego.house.gov
Bio. 11/20/1979 • Chicago, IL • Harvard Univ., A.B., 2004 •
Catholic • M. Kate Gallego **Cmte.** Armed Services • Natural
Resources
CoS. David Montes   **LD.** Nathan R. Schelble
Sched. Allison Childress   **PS.** Christina Carr
Dist. Off. Phoenix 602.256.0551

R: 262   **T:** 3rd 86%
Elected Year: 2014

▣ Rep. Paul A. Gosar (go-SAR) R-AZ-04 p 202.225.2315

Rm. RHOB 2057 **Web.** gosar.house.gov **f** 202.226.9739
Bio. 11/27/1958 • Rock Springs, WY • Creighton Univ., B.S.,
1981; Creighton Boyne School of Dentistry (NE), D.D.S., 1985
• Roman Catholic • M. Maude Gosar, 3 ch **Cmte.** Natural
Resources • Oversight & Reform
CoS. Thomas Van Flein **LD.** Rory Burke
Sched. Leslie Foti **PS.** Melissa Brown
Dist. Off. Gold Canyon 480.882.2697 • Kingman
928.445.1683 • Prescott 928.445.1683

R: 164 **T:** 5th 68%
Elected Year: 2010

▣ Rep. Raul M. Grijalva (gree-HAHL-vah) D-AZ-03 p 202.225.2435

Rm. LHOB 1511 **Web.** grijalva.house.gov **f** 202.225.1541
Bio. 02/19/1948 • Tucson, AZ • Pima County Supervisor;
Member, Tucson Unified School Board • Univ. of Arizona,
B.A., 1986 • Roman Catholic • M. Ramona Grijalva, 3 ch
Cmte. Education & Labor • Natural Resources
CoS. Amy C. Emerick **LD.** Kelsey H. Mishkin
Sched. Cristina Villa **PS.** Geoff Nolan
Dist. Off. Avondale 623.536.3388 • Somerton 928.343.7933
• Tucson 520.622.6788

R: 79 **T:** 9th 64%
Elected Year: 2002

▣ Rep. Ann L. Kirkpatrick (kirk-PA-trik) D-AZ-02 p 202.225.2542

Rm. CHOB 309 **Web.** kirkpatrick.house.gov
Bio. 03/24/1950 • McNary, AZ • State Legislator • Univ. of
Arizona, B.A., 1972; Univ. of Arizona James E. Rogers College
of Law (AZ), J.D., 1979 • Roman Catholic • M. Roger Curley,
2 ch **Cmte.** Agriculture • Appropriations
CoS. Carmen Frias **LD.** Christian K. Walker
Sched. Matt Lubisich **PS.** Abigail O'Brien
Dist. Off. Sierra Vista 520.459.3115 • Tucson

R: 248 **T:** 4th 55%
Elected Year: 2018

▣ Rep. Debbie Lesko (LEH-skoh) R-AZ-08 p 202.225.4576

Rm. LHOB 1113 **Web.** lesko.house.gov **f** 202.225.6328
Bio. 01/01/1959 • Univ. of Wisconsin - Madison, B.B.A.
• Christian Church • M. Joe Lesko, 3 ch **Cmte.** Homeland
Security • Judiciary • Rules
CoS. Abby Gunderson- **LD.** Matthew Simon
Schwarz
Sched. Regan Delaney **PS.** Heather K. Smith
Dist. Off. Glendale 623.776.7911

R: 341 **T:** 2nd 56%
Elected Year: 2018

▣ Rep. Tom O'Halleran (o-HA-lur-uhn) D-AZ-01 p 202.225.3361

Rm. CHOB 324 **Web.** ohalleran.house.gov **f** 202.225.3462
Bio. 01/24/1946 • Chicago, IL • Catholic • M. Pat O'Halleran,
3 ch ; 3 gr-ch **Cmte.** Agriculture • Energy & Commerce
CoS. Jeremy J. Nordquist **LD.** Xenia Ruiz
Sched. Charlie Burgin **PS.** Cody Uhing
Dist. Off. Casa Grande 520.316.0839 • Flagstaff
928.286.5338 • Tucson 928.304.0131

R: 327 **T:** 2nd 54%
Elected Year: 2016

▣ Rep. David Schweikert (SHWY-kurt) R-AZ-06 p 202.225.2190

Rm. LHOB 1526 **Web.** schweikert.house.gov **f** 202.225.0096
Bio. 03/03/1962 • Los Angeles, CA • Scottsdale Community
College (AZ), A.A., 1985; Arizona State Univ., B.S., 1988;
Arizona State Univ., M.B.A., 2005 • Roman Catholic • M.
Joyce Schweikert, 1 ch **Cmte.** Ways & Means
CoS. Katherina Dimenstein **LD.** Katherine Duveneck
Sched. Ashley Sylvester **PS.** Grace White
Dist. Off. Scottsdale 480.946.2411

R: 179 **T:** 5th 55%
Elected Year: 2010

ARIZONA

↪ Rep. Greg Stanton (STAN-tuhn) D-AZ-09 p 202.225.9888

Rm. CHOB 128 **Web.** stanton.house.gov
Bio. 03/08/1970 • • Marquette Univ. (WI), B.A., 1992;
Univ. of Michigan Law School, J.D., 1995 • Catholic • M.
Nicole Stanton, 2 ch **Cmte.** Judiciary • Transportation &
Infrastructure
CoS. Seth Scott **LD.** Tracee Gross Sutton
Sched. Ashley Zafaranlou **PS.** Nicole Pasteur
Dist. Off. Phoenix 602.956.2463

R: 417 **T:** 1st 61%
Elected Year: 2018

ARKANSAS

↪ Governor Asa Hutchinson (HUH-chin-suhn) p 501.682.2345

State Capitol, Room 250 **C:** Little Rock
Little Rock, AR 72201 **P:** 3,013,825 (34)
Website arkansas.gov **A:** 52,035.35 mi^2 (27th)
Fax 501.682.1382
Term Ends 2023
Lt. Governor
Tim Griffin, R

U.S. Senators
John N. Boozman, R
Tom B. Cotton, R
U.S. Representatives
01 / Rick A. Crawford, R
02 / French Hill, R
03 / Steve Womack, R
04 / Bruce Westerman, R

↪ Sen. John N. Boozman (BOAZ-muhn) R-AR-Sr. p 202.224.4843

Rm. HSOB 141 **Web.** boozman.senate.gov **f** 202.228.1371
Bio. 12/10/1950 • Shreveport, LA • Optometrist • Univ. of
Arkansas, O.D., 1972; Southern College of Optometry (TN),
O.D., 1977 • Baptist • M. Cathy Marley Boozman, 3 ch ; 2 gr-
ch **Cmte.** Agriculture, Nutrition & Forestry • Appropriations
• Environment & Public Works • Veterans' Affairs
CoS. Toni-Marie Higgins **LD.** Mackensie Burt
Sched. Holly Lewis **PS.** Sara Lasure
Dist. Off. El Dorado 870.863.4641 • Fort Smith
479.573.0189 • Jonesboro 870.268.6925 • Little Rock
501.372.7153 • Lowell 479.725.0400 • Mountain Home
870.424.0129 • Stuttgart 870.672.6941

R: 48 **T:** 2nd 60%
Elected Year: 2010
Next Election: 2022

↪ Sen. Tom B. Cotton (KAH-tuhn) R-AR-Jr. p 202.224.2353

Rm. RSOB 124 **Web.** cotton.senate.gov **f** 202.228.0908
Bio. 05/13/1977 • Dardanelle, AR • Harvard Univ., A.B.,
1998; Harvard Univ. Law School (MA), J.D., 2002 • Methodist
• M. Anna Cotton, 2 ch **Cmte.** Armed Services • Banking,
Housing & Urban Affairs • Intelligence • Joint Economic
CoS. Doug Coutts **LD.** Joe Kristol
Sched. Joni Deoudes **PS.** Caroline M. Tabler
Dist. Off. El Dorado 870.864.8582 • Jonesboro
870.933.6223 • Little Rock 501.223.9081 • Springdale
479.751.0879

R: 74 **T:** 1st 57%
Elected Year: 2014
Next Election: 2020

ARKANSAS

🏛 Rep. Rick A. Crawford (KRAW-furd)   R-AR-01   p 202.225.4076

Rm. RHOB 2422 **Web.** crawford.house.gov   **f** 202.225.5602
Bio. 01/22/1966 • Homestead Air Force Base, FL • Army 1985-89 • Arkansas State Univ., Jonesboro, B.S., 1996 • Baptist • M. Stacy Crawford, 2 ch **Cmte.** Agriculture • Permanent Select on Intelligence • Transportation & Infrastructure
CoS. Jonah Shumate   **LD.** Ashley Shelton
Sched. Courtney Handey   **PS.** Sara Robertson
Dist. Off. Cabot 501.843.3043 • Jonesboro 870.203.0540 • Mountain Home 870.424.2075

R: 157   **T:** 5th 69%
Elected Year: 2010

🏛 Rep. French Hill (hill)   R-AR-02   p 202.225.2506

Rm. LHOB 1533 **Web.** hill.house.gov   **f** 202.225.5903
Bio. 12/05/1956 • Little Rock, AR • Vanderbilt Univ. (TN), B.S., 1979 • Roman Catholic • M. Martha Hill, 2 ch **Cmte.** Financial Services
CoS. A. Brooke Bennett   **LD.** Dylan Frost
    PS. Steven D. Smith
Dist. Off. Conway 501.358.3481 • Little Rock 501.324.5941

R: 266   **T:** 3rd 52%
Elected Year: 2014

🏛 Rep. Bruce Westerman (WES-tur-muhn)   R-AR-04   p 202.225.3772

Rm. CHOB 209 **Web.** westerman.house.gov   **f** 202.225.1314
Bio. 11/18/1967 • Hot Springs, AR • Univ. of Arkansas, B.S., 1990; Yale Univ. (CT), M.S., 2001 • Southern Baptist • M. Sharon French, 4 ch **Cmte.** Natural Resources • Transportation & Infrastructure
CoS. Vivian Moeglein   **LD.** Jefferson Deming
Sched. Madeline Bryant   **PS.** Rebekah Hoshiko
Dist. Off. El Dorado 870.864.8946 • Hot Springs 501.609.9796 • Ozark 479.667.0075 • Pine Bluff 870.536.8178

R: 284   **T:** 3rd 67%
Elected Year: 2014

🏛 Rep. Steve Womack (WOE-mak)   R-AR-03   p 202.225.4301

Rm. RHOB 2412 **Web.** womack.house.gov   **f** 202.225.5713
Bio. 02/18/1957 • Russellville, AR • Mayor of Rogers, AR • Arkansas Army National Guard, 1979-2009 • Russellville High School (AR), B.A., 1975; Arkansas Tech Univ., B.A., 1979 • Southern Baptist • M. Terri Williams Womack, 3 ch; 2 gr-ch **Cmte.** Appropriations • Budget
CoS. Beau Walker   **LD.** Geoffrey Hempelmann
Sched. Madison Nash   **PS.** Alexia Sikora
Dist. Off. Fort Smith 479.424.1146 • Harrison 870.741.6900 • Rogers 479.464.0446

R: 186   **T:** 5th 65%
Elected Year: 2010

CALIFORNIA

🏛 Governor Gavin Newsom (NEW-sum)   p 916.445.2841

State Capitol Building, Suite 1173   **C:** Sacramento
Sacramento, CA 95814   **P:** 39,557,045 (1)
Website ca.gov   **A:** 155,779.03 mi^2 (3rd)
Fax 916.558.3160
Term Ends 2023
Lt. Governor
Eleni Kounalakis, **D**

CALIFORNIA

CALIFORNIA

U.S. Senators
Dianne Feinstein, **D**
Kamala D. Harris, **D**

U.S. Representatives
01 / Doug LaMalfa, **R**
02 / Jared W. Huffman, **D**
03 / John R. Garamendi, **D**
04 / Tom McClintock, **R**
05 / Mike C. Thompson, **D**
06 / Doris O. Matsui, **D**
07 / Ami Bera, **D**
08 / Paul J. Cook, **R**
09 / Jerry McNerney, **D**
10 / Josh Harder, **D**
11 / Mark J. DeSaulnier, **D**
12 / Nancy Pelosi, **D**
13 / Barbara J. Lee, **D**
14 / Jackie Speier, **D**
15 / Eric M. Swalwell, **D**
16 / Jim Costa, **D**
17 / Ro Khanna, **D**
18 / Anna G. Eshoo, **D**
19 / Zoe Lofgren, **D**
20 / Jimmy Panetta, **D**
21 / T.J. Cox, **D**
22 / Devin G. Nunes, **R**
23 / Kevin McCarthy, **R**

24 / Salud Carbajal, **D**
25 / Katherine L. Hill, **D**
26 / Julia Brownley, **D**
27 / Judy Chu, **D**
28 / Adam B. Schiff, **D**
29 / Tony Cardenas, **D**
30 / Brad J. Sherman, **D**
31 / Peter Aguilar, **D**
32 / Grace F. Napolitano, **D**
33 / Ted W. Lieu, **D**
34 / Jimmy Gomez, **D**
35 / Norma J. Torres, **D**
36 / Raul Ruiz, **D**
37 / Karen R. Bass, **D**
38 / Linda T. Sanchez, **D**

39 / Gilbert Cisneros, **D**
40 / Lucille Roybal-Allard, **D**
41 / Mark A. Takano, **D**
42 / Ken S. Calvert, **R**
43 / Maxine Waters, **D**
44 / Nanette Diaz Barragan, **D**
45 / Katherine Porter, **D**
46 / Lou Correa, **D**
47 / Alan S. Lowenthal, **D**
48 / Harley E. Rouda, **D**
49 / Mike Levin, **D**
50 / Duncan D. Hunter, **R**
51 / Juan C. Vargas, **D**
52 / Scott H. Peters, **D**
53 / Susan A. Davis, **D**

☙ Sen. Dianne Feinstein (FINE-stine)　　　D-CA-Sr.　p 202.224.3841

Rm. HSOB 331 **Web.** feinstein.senate.gov　**f** 202.228.3954
Bio. 06/22/1933 • San Francisco, CA • Mayor (San Francisco, CA) • Stanford Univ. (CA), Bach. Deg., 1955 • Jewish • M. Richard C. Blum, 1 ch; 3 stepch **Cmte.** Appropriations • Intelligence • Judiciary • Rules & Administration
CoS. David A. Grannis　　　**LD.** Joshua Esquivel
Sched. Chesna Foord　　　**PS.** Tom Mentzer
Dist. Off. Fresno 559.485.7430 • Los Angeles 310.914.7300 • San Diego 619.231.9712 • San Francisco 415.393.0707

R: 5 **T:** 5th 54%
Elected Year: 1992
Next Election: 2024

☙ Sen. Kamala D. Harris (HAIR-iss)　　　D-CA-Jr.　p 202.224.3553

Rm. HSOB 112 **Web.** harris.senate.gov　**f** 202.224.2200
Bio. 10/24/1964 • Oakland, CA • Howard Univ. (DC), Bach. Deg. • Baptist • M. Douglas Emhoff **Cmte.** Budget • Homeland Security & Government Affairs • Intelligence • Judiciary
CoS. Rohini Kosoglu　　　**LD.** Clint Odom
Sched. Michelle L. Rothblum　　　**PS.** Chris Harris
Dist. Off. Fresno 559.497.5109 • Los Angeles 310.231.4494 • Sacramento 916.448.2787 • San Diego 619.239.3884 • San Francisco 415.355.9041

R: 86 **T:** 1st 62%
Elected Year: 2016
Next Election: 2022

⚑ Rep. Peter Aguilar (ah-GEE-lar) D-CA-31 p 202.225.3201
Rm. CHOB 109 **Web.** aguilar.house.gov f 202.226.6962
Bio. 06/19/1979 • Fontana, CA • Univ. of Redlands, B.R.E.,
2001 • Roman Catholic • M. Alisha Aguilar, 2 ch **Cmte.**
Administration • Appropriations
CoS. Becky T. Cornell **LD.** Stephanie Cuevas
Sched. Danielle Giulino **PS.** Parker Dorrough
Dist. Off. San Bernardino 909.890.4445

R: 251 **T:** 3rd 59%
Elected Year: 2014

⚑ Rep. Nanette Diaz Barragan (BAIR-uh-guhn) D-CA-44 p 202.225.8220
Rm. LHOB 1030 **Web.** barragan.house.gov
Bio. 09/15/1976 • San Pedro, CA • Univ. of California, Los
Angeles, B.A., 2000; Univ. of Southern California, J.D., 2005
• Catholic • S. **Cmte.** Energy & Commerce • Homeland
Security
CoS. Robert Primus **LD.** Mike Stoever
Sched. Clarissa Rojas
Dist. Off. Carson 310.831.1799 • San Pedro 310.831.1799 •
South Gate 310.831.1799

R: 295 **T:** 2nd 68%
Elected Year: 2016

⚑ Rep. Karen R. Bass (bass) D-CA-37 p 202.225.7084
Rm. RHOB 2059 **Web.** bass.house.gov f 202.225.2422
Bio. 10/03/1953 • Los Angeles, CA • California State
Univ. - Dominguez Hills, B.S., 1990 • Baptist • D., 2 ch (1
deceased); 4 stepch **Cmte.** Foreign Affairs • Judiciary
CoS. Caren Street **LD.** Janice Bashford
Sched. Lauren Radice **PS.** Zachary Seidl
Dist. Off. Los Angeles 323.965.1422

R: 153 **T:** 5th 89%
Elected Year: 2010

⚑ Rep. Ami Bera (BAIR-uh) D-CA-07 p 202.225.5716
Rm. LHOB 1727 **Web.** bera.house.gov f 202.226.1298
Bio. 03/02/1965 • Los Angeles, CA • Univ. of California,
Irvine, B.S., 1987, Univ. of California, Irvine, M.D., 1991 •
Unitarian • M. Janine Bera, 1 ch **Cmte.** Foreign Affairs •
Science, Space & Technology
CoS. Chad Obermiller **LD.** Kelvin Lum
Sched. Emma Bruce **PS.** Jack Miller
Dist. Off. Sacramento 916.635.0505

R: 196 **T:** 4th 55%
Elected Year: 2012

⚑ Rep. Julia Brownley (BROWN-lee) D-CA-26 p 202.225.5811
Rm. RHOB 2262 **Web.** f 202.225.1100
juliabrownley.house.gov
Bio. 08/28/1952 • Aiken, SC • Mount Vernon College, B.A.,
1975; American Univ. (DC), M.B.A., 1979 • Episcopalian •
D., 2 ch **Cmte.** Select Committee on the Climate Crisis •
Transportation & Infrastructure • Veterans' Affairs
CoS. Lenny Young **LD.** Sharon Wagener
Sched. Jonathan **PS.** Samantha Greene
Cousimano
Dist. Off. Oxnard 805.379.1779 • Thousand Oaks
805.379.1779

R: 198 **T:** 4th 62%
Elected Year: 2012

⚑ Rep. Ken S. Calvert (CAL-vurt) R-CA-42 p 202.225.1986
Rm. RHOB 2205 **Web.** calvert.house.gov f 202.225.2004
Bio. 06/08/1953 • Corona, CA • Real Estate Agent;
Restaurateur • Chaffey Community College (CA), A.A.,
1973; San Diego State Univ., B.A., 1975 • Protestant -
Unspecified Christian • D. **Cmte.** Appropriations
CoS. David Kennett **LD.** Rebecca Keightley
  PS. Jason Gagnon (CD)
Dist. Off. Corona 951.277.0042

R: 24 **T:** 14th 57%
Elected Year: 1992

CALIFORNIA

✎ Rep. Salud Carbajal (KAR-bah-HAHL)   D-CA-24   p 202.225.3601

Rm. LHOB 1431 **Web.** carbajal.house.gov   **f** 202.225.5632
Bio. 11/18/1964 • Moroleon, Mexico • Univ. of California,
Santa Barbara, B.A., 1990; Fielding Univ. (CA), Mast. Deg.,
1994 • Catholic • M. Gina Carbajal, 2 ch **Cmte.** Agriculture
• Armed Services • Transportation & Infrastructure
CoS. Jeremy Tittle   **LD.** Nancy Juarez
Sched. Erin Sandlin   **PS.** Mannal Haddad
Dist. Off. San Luis Obispo 805.546.8348 • Santa Barbara
805.730.1710 • Santa Maria 805.730.1710

R: 301   **T:** 2nd 59%
Elected Year: 2016

✎ Rep. Tony Cardenas (KAR-deh-nahss)   D-CA-29   p 202.225.6131

Rm. RHOB 2438 **Web.** cardenas.house.gov   **f** 202.225.0819
Bio. 03/31/1963 • Pacoima, CA • Univ. of California,
Santa Barbara, B.S., 1986 • Christian Church • M. Norma
Cárdenas, 4 ch **Cmte.** Energy & Commerce
CoS. Miguel A. Franco
Sched. Devin Kolb   **PS.** Bryan Doyle
Dist. Off. Panorama City 818.221.3718

R: 200   **T:** 4th 81%
Elected Year: 2012

✎ Rep. Judy Chu (choo)   D-CA-27   p 202.225.5464

Rm. RHOB 2423 **Web.** chu.house.gov   **f** 202.225.5467
Bio. 07/07/1953 • Los Angeles, CA • Univ. of California,
Los Angeles, B.A., 1974; California School Professional
Psychology, Los Angeles, M.A., 1977; California School
Professional Psychology, Los Angeles, Ph.D., 1979 •
Unspecified/Other • M. Michael Eng **Cmte.** Small Business
• Ways & Means
CoS. Linda Shim   **LD.** Sonali Desai
Sched. Alyssa Giammarella   **PS.** Benjamin Suarato
Dist. Off. Claremont 909.625.5394 • Pasadena
626.304.0110

R: 145   **T:** 6th 79%
Elected Year: 2009

✎ Rep. Gilbert Cisneros (siss-NAIR-roess)   D-CA-39   p 202.225.4111

Rm. CHOB 431 **Web.** cisneros.house.gov
Bio. 02/12/1971 • Los Angeles, CA • George Washington
Univ. (DC), B.A., 1994; Regis Univ., M.B.A., 2002; Brown Univ.
(RI), M.A., 2015 • Catholic • M. Jacki Cisneros, 2 ch (twins)
Cmte. Armed Services • Veterans' Affairs
CoS. Nicholas Jordan   **LD.** Emma Norvell
Sched. Annie Campbell   **PS.** Michael Quibuyen
Dist. Off. Placentia 714.329.7467

R: 356   **T:** 1st 52%
Elected Year: 2018

♟ Rep. Paul J. Cook ("cook")   R-CA-08   p 202.225.5861

Rm. LHOB 1027 **Web.** cook.house.gov   **f** 202.225.6498
Bio. 03/03/1943 • Meriden, CT • Southern Connecticut
State Univ., B.S., 1966; California State Univ., San Bernardino,
M.P.A., 1996; Univ. of California, Riverside, M.A., 2000 •
Roman Catholic • M. Jeannie Cook, 2 ch **Cmte.** Armed
Services • Natural Resources
CoS. John A. Sobel   **LD.** Tim Itnyre
Sched. Bert Johnson   **PS.** Michael Fresquez
Dist. Off. Apple Valley 760.247.1815 • Yucaipa
909.797.4900

R: 205   **T:** 4th 60%
Elected Year: 2012

✎ Rep. Lou Correa (ko-RAY-ah)   D-CA-46   p 202.225.2965

Rm. LHOB 1039 **Web.** correa.house.gov
Bio. 01/24/1958 • Los Angeles, CA • California State Univ.
(Fullerton), B.S., 1980; Univ. of California, Los Angeles,
J.D., 1985; Univ. of California, Los Angeles, M.B.A., 1985 •
Catholic • M. Esther Reynoso Correa, 4 ch **Cmte.**
Homeland Security • Judiciary
CoS. Laurie Beth Saroff   **LD.** Emilio Mendez
Sched. Julia Kermott   **PS.** Andrew Scibetta
Dist. Off. Santa Ana 714.559.6190

R: 303   **T:** 2nd 69%
Elected Year: 2016

Rep. Jim Costa (KAHS-tuh) D-CA-16 p 202.225.3341

Rm. RHOB 2081 **Web.** costa.house.gov **f** 202.225.9308
Bio. 04/13/1952 • Fresno, CA • State Legislator • California
State Univ., Fresno, B.S., 1974 • Roman Catholic • S. **Cmte.**
Agriculture • Foreign Affairs • Natural Resources
CoS. Juan E. Lopez **LD.** Jared Feldman
Sched. Elina Karapetyan **PS.** Tammy Johnson
Dist. Off. Fresno 559.495.1620 • Merced 209.384.1620

R: 91 **T:** 8th 58%
Elected Year: 2004

Rep. T.J. Cox (kahks) D-CA-21 p 202.225.4695

Rm. LHOB 1728 **Web.** cox.house.gov
Bio. Walnut Creek, CA • Univ. of Nevada, Reno, B.S.;
Southern Methodist Univ. (TX), M.B.A. • M. Kathleen
Murphy, 4 ch **Cmte.** Agriculture • Natural Resources
CoS. Francois Genard **LD.** Jared Henderson
PS. Drew Godinich
Dist. Off. Selma 559.257.9037

R: 358 **T:** 1st 50%
Elected Year: 2018

Rep. Susan A. Davis (DAY-vuhs) D-CA-53 p 202.225.2040

Rm. LHOB 1214 **Web.** susandavis.house.gov **f** 202.225.2948
Bio. 04/13/1944 • Cambridge, MA • San Diego Broad of
Education, Member; Member, State Assembly • Univ. of
California, Berkeley, B.S., 1965; Univ. of North Carolina,
M.A., 1968 • Jewish • M. Dr. Steve Davis, 2 ch ; 3 gr-ch
Cmte. Administration • Armed Services • Commission
Congressional Mailing Standards • Education & Labor
CoS. Lisa Sherman **LD.** Ian Staples
Sched. Ashley Campbell **PS.** Aaron Hunter
(CD)
Dist. Off. San Diego 619.280.5353

R: 66 **T:** 10th 69%
Elected Year: 2000

Rep. Mark J. DeSaulnier (deh-SOAN-yay) D-CA-11 p 202.225.2095

Rm. CHOB 503 **Web.** desaulnier.house.gov **f** 202.225.5609
Bio. 09/31/1952 • Lowell, MA • College of The Holy
Cross (MA), B.A., 1974 • Roman Catholic • D., 2 ch
Cmte. Education & Labor • Oversight & Reform • Rules •
Transportation & Infrastructure
CoS. Betsy Arnold Marr **LD.** Sarah Jackson
Sched. Bambi Yingst **PS.** Aimee Wall
Dist. Off. Richmond 510.620.1000 • Walnut Creek
925.933.2660

R: 259 **T:** 3rd 71%
Elected Year: 2014

Rep. Anna G. Eshoo (EH-shoo) D-CA-18 p 202.225.8104

Rm. CHOB 202 **Web.** eshoo.house.gov **f** 202.225.8890
Bio. 12/13/1942 • New Britain, CT • San Mateo County
Board of Supervisors; Chief of Staff, CA Assembly Speaker
• Canada College (CA), A.A., 1975 • Roman Catholic • D., 2
ch **Cmte.** Energy & Commerce
CoS. Matthew McMurray
Sched. Noor Shah **PS.** Michael Brady
Dist. Off. Palo Alto 650.323.2984

R: 26 **T:** 14th 75%
Elected Year: 1992

Rep. John R. Garamendi (gair-uh-MEN-dee) D-CA-03 p 202.225.1880

Rm. RHOB 2368 **Web.** garamendi.house.gov **f** 202.225.5914
Bio. 01/24/1945 • Camp Blanding, FL • State Legislator; Lt
Governor (CA) • Univ. of California, Berkeley, B.A., 1966;
Harvard Business School (MA), M.B.A., 1970 • Christian
Church • M. Patricia Wilkinson Garamendi, 6 ch ; 10 gr-ch
Cmte. Armed Services • Transportation & Infrastructure
CoS. Bradley Bottoms
Sched. Tessa Browne **PS.** Eric Olsen
Dist. Off. Davis 530.753.5301 • Fairfield 707.438.1822

R: 146 **T:** 6th 58%
Elected Year: 2009

CALIFORNIA

⚲ Rep. Jimmy Gomez (GO-mehz)　　　D-CA-34　p 202.225.6235

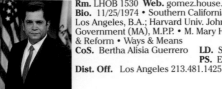

Rm. LHOB 1530 **Web.** gomez.house.gov　**f** 202.225.2202
Bio. 11/25/1974 • Southern California • Univ. of California, Los Angeles, B.A.; Harvard Univ. John F. Kennedy School of Government (MA), M.P.P. • M. Mary Hodge **Cmte.** Oversight & Reform • Ways & Means
CoS. Bertha Alisia Guerrero　**LD.** Samuel Negatu
　　　　　　　　　　　　　　PS. Eric Harris
Dist. Off. Los Angeles 213.481.1425

R: 337　**T:** 2nd 73%
Elected Year: 2017

⚲ Rep. Josh Harder (HAR-dur)　　　D-CA-10　p 202.225.4540

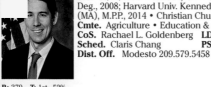

Rm. CHOB 131 **Web.** harder.house.gov
Bio. 08/01/1986 • Turlock, CA • Stanford Univ. (CA), Bach. Deg., 2008; Harvard Univ. Kennedy School of Government (MA), M.P.P., 2014 • Christian Church • M. Pamela Harder
Cmte. Agriculture • Education & Labor
CoS. Rachael L. Goldenberg　**LD.** Adela Amador
Sched. Claris Chang　　　**PS.** Jenna Behringer
Dist. Off. Modesto 209.579.5458

R: 379　**T:** 1st 52%
Elected Year: 2018

⚲ Rep. Katherine L. Hill (hill)　　　D-CA-25　p 202.225.1956

Rm. LHOB 1130 **Web.** katiehill.house.gov　**f** 202.226.0683
Bio. 08/25/1987 • Aberdeen, TX • California State Univeristy Northridge, B.A., 2008; California State Univeristy Northridge, M.P.A., 2014 • Unspecified/Other • M. Kenny Hill
Cmte. Armed Services • Oversight & Reform • Science, Space & Technology
CoS. Emily Burns　　　**LD.** Graham Kelly
Sched. Rebecca Kahn　**PS.** Kassie King
Dist. Off. Palmdale 661.839.0539 • Simi Valley

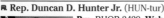

R: 381　**T:** 1st 54%
Elected Year: 2018

⚲ Rep. Jared W. Huffman (HUF-muhn)　　　D-CA-02　p 202.225.5161

Rm. LHOB 1527 **Web.** huffman.house.gov　**f** 202.225.5163
Bio. 02/18/1964 • Independence, MO • Univ. of California, Santa Barbara, B.A., 1986; Boston College Law School (MA), J.S.D., 1990 • Protestant - Unspecified Christian • M. Susan Huffman, 2 ch **Cmte.** Natural Resources • Select Committee on the Climate Crisis • Transportation & Infrastructure
CoS. Ben D. Miller　　　**LD.** Logan Ferree
Sched. Iliana Madrigal (CD)　**PS.** Alexa Shaffer
Dist. Off. Eureka 707.407.3585 • Fort Bragg 707.962.0933 • Petaluma 707.981.8967 • San Rafael 415.258.9657 • Ukiah 707.671.7449

R: 212　**T:** 4th 77%
Elected Year: 2012

⚲ Rep. Duncan D. Hunter Jr. (HUN-tur)　　　R-CA-50　p 202.225.5672

Rm. RHOB 2429 **Web.** hunter.house.gov　**f** 202.225.0235
Bio. 12/07/1976 • San Diego, CA • Businessman; Military Officer • Marine Corps 2001-2007 • San Diego State Univ., B.A., 2001 • Baptist • M. Margaret Hunter, 3 ch
CoS. Rick Terrazas　　　**LD.** Reed Linsk
Sched. Olena Nalivkina　**PS.** Meghan Badame
Dist. Off. El Cajon 619.448.5201 • Temecula 951.695.5108

R: 133　**T:** 6th 52%
Elected Year: 2008

⚲ Rep. Ro Khanna (KAH-nuh)　　　D-CA-17　p 202.225.2631

Rm. CHOB 221
Bio. 09/13/1976 • Philadelphia, PA • Univ. of Chicago (IL), A.B., 1998; Yale Univ. Law School (CT), J.D., 2001 • Hinduism • M. Ritu Ahuja, 2 ch **Cmte.** Armed Services • Budget • Oversight & Reform
CoS. Pete Spiro　　　**LD.** Chris Schloesser
Sched. Nandini Narayan　**PS.** Heather Purcell
Dist. Off. Santa Clara 408.436.2720

R: 318　**T:** 2nd 75%
Elected Year: 2016

CALIFORNIA

🏵 Rep. Doug LaMalfa (luh-MAL-fuh) R-CA-01 p 202.225.3076

Rm. CHOB 322 **Web.** lamalfa.house.gov
Bio. 07/02/1960 • Oroville, CA • Butte College (CA), A.A., 1980; California Polytechnic State Univ., San Luis Obispo, B.S., 1982 • Evangelical • M. Jill LaMalfa, 4 ch **Cmte.** Agriculture • Transportation & Infrastructure
CoS. Mark Spannagel   **LD.** Colleen McGowan
Sched. Meredith Kroft   **PS.** Parker Williams
Dist. Off. Auburn 530.878.5035 • Chico 530.343.1000 • Redding 530.223.5898

R: 219 **T:** 4th 55%
Elected Year: 2012

🏵 Rep. Barbara J. Lee (lee) D-CA-13 p 202.225.2661

Rm. RHOB 2470 **Web.** lee.house.gov   **f** 202.225.9817
Bio. 07/16/1946 • El Paso, TX • Congressional Aide; Social Worker • Mills College (CA), B.A., 1973; Univ. of California, Berkeley, M.S.W., 1975 • Baptist • D., 2 ch ; 5 gr-ch **Cmte.** Appropriations • Budget
CoS. Julie Little Nickson   **LD.** Emma Mehrabi
Sched. Christopher   **PS.** Nissa Koerner
   Livingston
Dist. Off. Oakland 510.763.0370

R: 57 **T:** 12th 88%
Elected Year: 1998

🏵 Rep. Mike Levin (LEH-vin) D-CA-49 p 202.225.3906

Rm. LHOB 1626 **Web.** mikelevin.house.gov
Bio. 10/20/1978 • Inglewood, CA • Stanford Univ. (CA), B.A., 2001 • Catholic • M. Chrissy Levin, 2 ch **Cmte.** Natural Resources • Select Committee on the Climate Crisis • Veterans' Affairs
CoS. Kara van Stralen   **LD.** Jonathan Gilbert
Sched. Mark Foley   **PS.** Eric Mee
Dist. Off. Dana Point 949.281.2449 • Oceanside 760.599.5000

R: 389 **T:** 1st 56%
Elected Year: 2018

🏵 Rep. Ted W. Lieu (loo) D-CA-33 p 202.225.3976

Rm. CHOB 403 **Web.** lieu.house.gov   **f** 202.225.4099
Bio. 03/29/1969 • Taipei, Taiwan • Stanford Univ. (CA), B.S., 1991; Stanford Univ. (CA), B.A., 1991, Georgetown Univ. Law Center (DC), J.D., 1994 • Roman Catholic • M. Betty Lieu, 2 ch **Cmte.** Foreign Affairs • Judiciary
CoS. Marc A. Cevasco   **LD.** Corey Jacobson
Sched. Harshitha Teppala   **PS.** Jenna Bushnell
Dist. Off. Los Angeles 323.651.1040 • Manhattan Beach 310.321.7664

R: 270 **T:** 3rd 70%
Elected Year: 2014

🏵 Rep. Zoe Lofgren (LAHF-gruhn) D-CA-19 p 202.225.3072

Rm. LHOB 1401 **Web.** zoelofgren.house.gov **f** 202.225.3336
Bio. 12/21/1947 • San Mateo, CA • Attorney; Immigration Law Professor • Stanford Univ. (CA), B.A., 1970; Santa Clara Univ. Law School (CA), J.D., 1975 • Lutheran • M. John Marshall Collins, 2 ch **Cmte.** Administration • Judiciary • Science, Space & Technology • Select Committee on the Modernization of Congress
CoS. Stacey E. Leavandosky
Sched. Angela Nguyen (CD) **PS.** Peter Whippy
Dist. Off. San Jose 408.271.8700

R: 41 **T:** 13th 74%
Elected Year: 1994

🏵 Rep. Alan S. Lowenthal (LO-wuhn-thall) D-CA-47 p 202.225.7924

Rm. CHOB 108 **Web.** lowenthal.house.gov **f** 202.225.7926
Bio. 03/08/1941 • New York, NY • Hobart College (NY), B.A., 1962; Ohio State Univ., M.A., 1965; Ohio State Univ., Ph.D., 1967 • Jewish • M. Deborah Malumed, 2 ch; 1 gr-ch **Cmte.** Natural Resources • Transportation & Infrastructure
CoS. Tim Hysom   **LD.** Chris Gorud
Sched. Rufino Bautista (CD) **PS.** Keith Higginbotham
Dist. Off. Garden Grove 714.243.4088 • Long Beach 562.436.3828

R: 220 **T:** 4th 65%
Elected Year: 2012

CALIFORNIA

⋆ Rep. Doris O. Matsui (mat-SOO-ee) D-CA-06 p 202.225.7163

Rm. RHOB 2311 **Web.** matsui.house.gov **f** 202.225.0566
Bio. 09/25/1944 • Poston, AZ • Deputy Assistant, President
Clinton; Deputy Director, Public Liaison; Television
Executive; Civic Leader • Univ. of California, Berkeley,
B.A., 1966 • Methodist • W., 1 ch ; 2 gr-ch **Cmte.** Energy &
Commerce
CoS. Kyle Victor **LD.** Kristen Donheffner
Sched. Mckinley Krongaus **PS.** Hannah Blatt
Dist. Off. Sacramento 916.498.5600

R: 105 **T:** 8th 80%
Elected Year: 2005

⋆ Rep. Kevin McCarthy 1SG (muh-KAR-thee) R-CA-23 p 202.225.2915

Rm. RHOB 2468 **Web.** **f** 202.225.2908
kevinmccarthy.house.gov
Bio. 01/26/1965 • Bakersfield, CA • Small Business Owner
• California State Univ., Bakersfield, B.A., 1989; Univ. of
California, Bakersfield, M.B.A., 1994 • Baptist • M. Judy
McCarthy, 2 ch
CoS. James Min **LD.** Kyle Lombardi
Sched. Alex Gourdikian **PS.** Matt Sparks
Dist. Off. Bakersfield 661.327.3611

R: 117 **T:** 7th 64%
Elected Year: 2006

⋆ Rep. Tom McClintock (muh-KLIN-tahk) R-CA-04 p 202.225.2511

Rm. RHOB 2312 **Web.** mcclintock.house.gov **f** 202.225.5444
Bio. 07/10/1956 • Bronxville, NY • State Legislator • Univ.
of California, Los Angeles, B.S., 1978 • Baptist • M. Lori
McClintock, 2 ch **Cmte.** Judiciary • Natural Resources
CoS. Chris Tudor **LD.** Steve Koncar
Sched. Hannah Cooke **PS.** Jennifer Cressy
Dist. Off. Roseville 916.786.5560

R: 136 **T:** 6th 54%
Elected Year: 2008

⋆ Rep. Jerry McNerney (mik-NUR-nee) D-CA-09 p 202.225.1947

Rm. RHOB 2265 **Web.** mcnerney.house.gov **f** 202.225.4060
Bio. 06/18/1951 • Albuquerque, NM • Engineer • Univ.
of New Mexico, B.S., 1973; Univ. of New Mexico, M.S.,
1975; Univ. of New Mexico, Ph.D., 1981 • Roman Catholic
• M. Mary McNerney, 3 ch **Cmte.** Energy & Commerce •
Science, Space & Technology
CoS. Nicole Damasco **LD.** Rishi Saghal
Sched. Trevor Jones **PS.** Nikki Cannon
Dist. Off. Antioch 925.754.0716 • Stockton 209.476.8552

R: 118 **T:** 7th 57%
Elected Year: 2006

⋆ Rep. Grace F. Napolitano (nah-poe-lee-TAH-no) D-CA-32 p 202.225.5256

Rm. LHOB 1610 **Web.** napolitano.house.gov **f** 202.225.0027
Bio. 12/04/1936 • Brownsville, TX • Member, State
Assembly; Mayor (Norwalk, TX) • Roman Catholic • M.
Frank Napolitano, 5 ch (5 from previous marriage); 14 gr-
ch ; 2 great-gr-ch **Cmte.** Natural Resources • Transportation
& Infrastructure
CoS. Daniel Chao **LD.** Joe Sheehy
Sched. Joseph Ciccone **PS.** Jerry O'Donnell
Dist. Off. El Monte 626.350.0150

R: 60 **T:** 11th 69%
Elected Year: 1998

⋆ Rep. Devin G. Nunes (NOO-nehz) R-CA-22 p 202.225.2523

Rm. LHOB 1013 **Web.** nunes.house.gov **f** 202.225.3404
Bio. 10/01/1973 • Tulare County, CA • State Director, USDA
Rural Development • College of the Sequoias (CA), A.A.,
1993; California State Polytechnic Univ., B.S., 1995; California
State Polytechnic Univ., M.S., 1996 • Roman Catholic • M.
Elizabeth Tamariz Nunes, 3 ch **Cmte.** Joint Taxation •
Permanent Select on Intelligence • Ways & Means
CoS. Jilian Plank **LD.** Ian Foley
Sched. Jennifer Morrow **PS.** Jack Langer
Dist. Off. Clovis 559.323.5235 • Visalia 559.733.3861

R: 81 **T:** 9th 53%
Elected Year: 2002

ⁿ Rep. Jimmy Panetta (puh-NEH-tuh) D-CA-20 p 202.225.2861
Rm. CHOB 212 **Web.** panetta.house.gov f 202.225.6791
Bio. 10/01/1969 • Washington, DC • Monterey Peninsula
College (CA), A.A., 1989; Univ. of California, Davis, B.A.,
1991; Santa Clara Univ. (CA), J.D., 1996 • Catholic • M.
Carrie Panetta, 2 ch **Cmte.** Agriculture • Budget • Ways &
Means
CoS. Joel Bailey **LD.** Matthew J. Manning
Sched. Stephanie Mulka **PS.** Sarah Davey
Dist. Off. Salinas 831.424.2229 • Santa Cruz 831.429.1976

R: 328 T: 2nd 81%
Elected Year: 2016

ⁿ Rep. Nancy Pelosi (puh-LO-see) D-CA-12 p 202.225.4965
Rm. LHOB 1236 **Web.** pelosi.house.gov f 202.225.8259
Bio. 03/26/1940 • Baltimore, MD • Chairman, California
State Democratic Party; Public Relations Consultant • Trinity
College (DC), A.B., 1962 • Roman Catholic • M. Paul F.
Pelosi, 5 ch ; 9 gr-ch
CoS. Robert Edmonson
Sched. Pearl Mangrum
Dist. Off. San Francisco 415.556.4862

R: 11 T: 17th 87%
Elected Year: 1987

ⁿ Rep. Scott H. Peters (PEE-turz) D-CA-52 p 202.225.0508
Rm. RHOB 2338 **Web.** scottpeters.house.gov
Bio. 06/17/1958 • Springfield, OH • Duke Univ. (NC), B.A.,
1980; New York Univ. Law School, J.D., 1984 • Lutheran • M.
Lynn Gorguze, 2 ch **Cmte.** Budget • Energy & Commerce
CoS. Daniel Zawitoski **LD.** Sterling McHale
Sched. Hannah Stern **PS.** Martha Spieker
Dist. Off. San Diego 858.455.5550

R: 226 T: 4th 64%
Elected Year: 2012

ⁿ Rep. Katherine Porter (POR-tur) D-CA-45 p 202.225.5611
Rm. LHOB 1117 **Web.** porter.house.gov
Bio. 01/03/1974 • Des Moines, IA • Yale Univ. (CT), B.A.,
1990, Harvard Univ., J.D., 2001 • Episcopalian • D., 3 ch
Cmte. Financial Services
CoS. Amanda Fischer **LD.** Brieana Marticorena
Sched. Elizabeth Murray **PS.** Jordan Wong
Dist. Off. Irvine 949.236.7207

R: 403 T: 1st 52%
Elected Year: 2018

ⁿ Rep. Harley E. Rouda Jr. (ROO-duh) D-CA-48 p 202.225.2415
Rm. RHOB 2300 **Web.** rouda.house.gov
Bio. 12/10/1961 • Columbus, OH • Univ. of Kentucky, Bach.
Deg., 1984; Capital Univ. School of Law, J.D., 1986; Ohio
State Univ., M.B.A., 2002 • Christian - Non-Denominational •
M. Kaira Sturdivant Rouda, 4 ch **Cmte.** Oversight & Reform
• Transportation & Infrastructure
CoS. Emily Crerand **LD.** Andrew Noh
Sched. Caroline Bovair **PS.** Zach Helder
Dist. Off. Newport Beach 714.960.6483

R: 409 T: 1st 54%
Elected Year: 2018

ⁿ Rep. Lucille Roybal-Allard (ROY-buhl-A-lurd) D-CA-40 p 202.225.1766
Rm. RHOB 2083 **Web.** roybal f 202.226.0350
allard.house.gov
Bio. 06/12/1941 • Boyle Heights, CA • Member, State
Assembly; Public Relations and Fundraising Executive •
California State Univ., Los Angeles, B.A., 1965 • Catholic
• M. Edward T. Allard III, 2 ch ; 2 stepch ; 9 gr-ch **Cmte.**
Appropriations
CoS. Victor Castillo **LD.** Josh Caplan
Sched. Christine Ochoa **PS.** Benjamin Soskin
Dist. Off. Commerce 323.721.8790

R: 31 T: 14th 77%
Elected Year: 1992

CALIFORNIA

Rep. Raul Ruiz (roo-EES) — D-CA-36 — p 202.225.5330
Rm. RHOB 2342 **Web.** ruiz.house.gov **f** 202.225.1238
Bio. 08/25/1972 • Zacatecas, Mexico • Univ. of California, Los Angeles, B.S., 1994; Harvard Univ., M.P.P., 2001; Harvard Univ., M.D., 2001; Harvard Univ., M.P.H, 2007 • Seventh-Day Adventist • M. Monica Ruiz, 2 ch (twins) **Cmte.** Energy & Commerce
CoS. Tim Del Monico **LD.** Erin Doty
Sched. Lauren Heasley **PS.** Ross Arnett
Dist. Off. Hemet 951.765.2304 • Palm Desert 760.424.8888
R: 229 **T:** 4th 59%
Elected Year: 2012

Rep. Linda T. Sanchez (SAN-chez) — D-CA-38 — p 202.225.6676
Rm. RHOB 2329 **Web.** lindasanchez.house.gov **f** 202.226.1012
Bio. 01/28/1969 • Orange, CA • Union Official; Attorney • Univ. of California, Berkeley, B.A., 1991; Univ. of California School of Law, Los Angeles (JD), J.D., 1995 • Roman Catholic • M. James M. Sullivan, 1 ch ; 3 stepch **Cmte.** Ways & Means
CoS. Lea Sulkala **LD.** Melissa Kiedrowicz
Sched. Juan Rangel **PS.** Alexander Nguyen
Dist. Off. Norwalk 562.860.5050
R: 85 **T:** 9th 69%
Elected Year: 2002

Rep. Adam B. Schiff (shihf) — D-CA-28 — p 202.225.4176
Rm. RHOB 2269 **Web.** schiff.house.gov **f** 202.225.5828
Bio. 06/22/1960 • Framingham, MA • State Senator; U.S. Attorney, Los Angeles • Stanford Univ. (CA), B.A., 1982; Harvard Univ. Law School (MA), J.D., 1985 • Jewish • M. Eve Sanderson Schiff, 2 ch **Cmte.** Permanent Select on Intelligence
CoS. Jeff Lowenstein **LD.** Joe Jankiewicz
Sched. Christopher Hoven **PS.** Patrick Boland
Dist. Off. Burbank 818.450.2900 • Los Angeles 323.315.5555
R: 71 **T:** 10th 78%
Elected Year: 2000

Rep. Brad J. Sherman (SHUR-muhn) — D-CA-30 — p 202.225.5911
Rm. RHOB 2181 **Web.** sherman.house.gov **f** 202.225.5879
Bio. 10/24/1954 • Los Angeles, CA • Harvard Law Instructor; CPA • Univ. of California, Los Angeles, B.A., 1974; Harvard Univ. Law School (MA), J.D., 1979 • Jewish • M. Lisa Kaplan Sherman, 3 ch **Cmte.** Commission Congressional Mailing Standards • Financial Services • Foreign Affairs • Science, Space & Technology
CoS. Don MacDonald **LD.** Lauren Wolman
Sched. Maggie Pillis **PS.** Arya Ansari
Dist. Off. Sherman Oaks 818.501.9200
R: 53 **T:** 12th 73%
Elected Year: 1996

Rep. Jackie Speier (speer) — D-CA-14 — p 202.225.3531
Rm. RHOB 2465 **Web.** speier.house.gov **f** 202.226.4183
Bio. 05/14/1950 • San Francisco County, CA • State Legislator; Attorney • Univ. of California, Davis, B.A., 1972; Univ. of California Hastings College of Law, J.D., 1976 • Roman Catholic • M. Barry Dennis, 2 ch **Cmte.** Armed Services • Oversight & Reform • Permanent Select on Intelligence
CoS. Josh Connolly **LD.** Molly Fishman
Sched. Kate Adams **PS.** Tracy Manzer
Dist. Off. San Mateo 650.342.0300
R: 127 **T:** 7th 79%
Elected Year: 2008

Rep. Eric M. Swalwell (SWALL-well) — D-CA-15 — p 202.225.5065
Rm. CHOB 407 **Web.** swalwell.house.gov **f** 202.226.3805
Bio. 11/16/1980 • Sac City, IA • Univ. of Maryland - College Park, B.A., 2003; Univ. of Maryland School of Law, J.D., 2006 • Christian - Non-Denominational • M. Brittany Ann Watts, 2 ch **Cmte.** Judiciary • Permanent Select on Intelligence
CoS. Alex Evans **LD.** Andrew S. Ginsburg
Sched. Olivia Elkins **PS.** Cait McNamee
Dist. Off. Castro Valley 510.370.3322
R: 231 **T:** 4th 73%
Elected Year: 2012

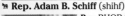

CALIFORNIA

Rep. Mark A. Takano (tah-KAH-no) D-CA-41 p 202.225.2305

Rm. CHOB 420 **Web.** takano.house.gov **f** 202.225.7018
Bio. 12/10/1960 • Riverside, CA • La Sierra High School
(CA), A.B., 1979; Harvard College (MA), A.B., 1983; School
of Education, Univ. of California, Riverside, M.F.A., 2010 •
Methodist • S. **Cmte.** Education & Labor • Veterans' Affairs
CoS. Richard McPike **LD.** Justin Maturo
Sched. Desiree Wroten **PS.** Dayanara Ramirez
Dist. Off. Riverside 951.222.0203

R: 232 **T:** 4th 65%
Elected Year: 2012

Rep. Mike C. Thompson (TOMP-suhn) D-CA-05 p 202.225.3311

Rm. CHOB 406 **Web.** **f** 202.225.4335
mikethompson.house.gov
Bio. 01/24/1951 • St. Helena, CA • State Senator; CA State
Assembly Fellow • Army 1969-73 • California State Univ.,
Chico, B.A., 1982; California State Univ., Chico, M.A., 1996 •
Roman Catholic • M. Janet Thompson, 2 ch ; 3 gr-ch **Cmte.**
Ways & Means
CoS. Melanie Rhinehart Van **LD.** Jennifer Goedke
Tassell
Sched. Ishaan Golding **PS.** Alex MacFarlane
Dist. Off. Napa 707.226.9898 • Santa Rosa 707.542.7182 •
Vallejo 707.645.1888

R: 63 **T:** 11th 79%
Elected Year: 1998

Rep. Norma J. Torres (toe-ress) D-CA-35 p 202.225.6161

Rm. RHOB 2444 **Web.** torres.house.gov **f** 202.225.8671
Bio. 04/04/1965 • Escuintla, Guatemala • National Labor
College (MD), B.A., 2012 • Roman Catholic • M. Louis
Torres, 3 ch **Cmte.** Appropriations • Rules
CoS. James Cho **LD.** Justin Vogt
Sched. Leah Carey **PS.** Veronica Bonilla
Dist. Off. Ontario 909.481.6474

R: 281 **T:** 3rd 69%
Elected Year: 2014

Rep. Juan C. Vargas (VAR-guhs) D-CA-51 p 202.225.8045

Rm. RHOB 2244 **Web.** vargas.house.gov **f** 202.225.2772
Bio. 03/07/1961 • National City, CA • Univ. of San Diego,
B.A., 1983; Harvard Univ. Law School (MA), J.D., 1991
• Roman Catholic • M. Adrienne D'Ascoli, 2 ch **Cmte.**
Financial Services • Foreign Affairs
CoS. Tim Walsh **LD.** Scott Hinkle
Sched. Beth Farvour
Dist. Off. Chula Vista 619.422.5963 • El Centro
760.312.9900

R: 233 **T:** 4th 71%
Elected Year: 2012

Rep. Maxine Waters (WAH-durs) D-CA-43 p 202.225.2201

Rm. RHOB 2221 **Web.** waters.house.gov **f** 202.225.7854
Bio. 08/15/1938 • St. Louis, MO • Head Start Teacher;
Delegate to Democratic National Convention • California
State Univ., Los Angeles, B.A., 1970 • Christian Church •
M. Amb. Sidney Williams, 2 ch; 2 gr ch **Cmte.** Financial
Services
CoS. Twaun Samuel **LD.** Patrick Fergusson
Sched. Symonne Smith **PS.** Rykia Dorsey
Dist. Off. Los Angeles 323.757.8900

R: 20 **T:** 15th 78%
Elected Year: 1990

COLORADO

Governor Jared S. Polis (POLL-lis) p 303.866.2471

136 State Capitol **C:** Denver
Denver, CO 80203-1792 **P:** 5,695,564 (21)
Website colorado.gov **A:** 103,641.75 mi^2 (8th)
Fax 303.866.2003
Term Ends 2023
Lt. Governor
Dianne Primavera, **D**

COLORADO

COLORADO

U.S. Senators
Michael F. Bennet, **D**
Cory S. Gardner, **R**
U.S. Representatives
01 / Diana L. DeGette, **D**
02 / Joseph D. Neguse, **D**
03 / Scott R. Tipton, **R**
04 / Kenneth R. Buck, **R**
05 / Doug L. Lamborn, **R**
06 / Jason Crow, **D**
07 / Ed G. Perlmutter, **D**

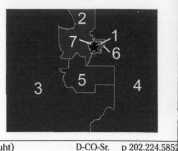

Sen. Michael F. Bennet (BEH-nuht)　　　　D-CO-Sr.　p 202.224.585?

Rm. RSOB 261 **Web.** bennet.senate.gov　**f** 202.228.509?
Bio. 11/28/1964 • New Delhi, India • Schools
Superintendent; Political Aide • Wesleyan Univ. (CT), B.A.,
1987; Yale Univ. Law School (CT), J.D., 1993 • Episcopalian
• M. Susan Daggett Bennet, 3 ch **Cmte.** Agriculture,
Nutrition & Forestry • Finance • Intelligence
CoS. Jonathan Davidson　　**LD.** Brian Appel
Sched. Kristin Mollet　　**PS.** Courtney Gidner
Dist. Off. Alamosa 719.587.0096 • Colorado Springs
719.328.1100 • Denver 303.455.7600 • Durango
970.259.1710 • Fort Collins 970.224.2200 • Grand Junction
970.241.6631 • Pueblo 719.542.7550

R: 41　**T:** 2nd 50%
Elected Year: 2009
Next Election: 2022

Sen. Cory S. Gardner (GARD-nur)　　　　R-CO-Jr.　p 202.224.594?

Rm. RSOB 354 **Web.** gardner.senate.gov　**f** 202.224.652?
Bio. 08/22/1974 • Yuma, CO • Senate Staffer; State
Legislator • Colorado State Univ., B.A., 1997; Univ. of
Colorado School of Law, J.D., 2001 • Lutheran • M. Jamie
Gardner, 2 ch **Cmte.** Commerce, Science & Transportation
• Energy & Natural Resources • Foreign Relations
CoS. Curtis Swager　　**LD.** Curtis Swager
Sched. Amy Barrera　　**PS.** Annalyse Keller
Dist. Off. Colorado Springs 719.632.6706 • Denver
303.391.5777 • Durango 970.259.1231 • Fort Collins
970.484.3502 • Grand Junction 970.245.9553 • Greeley
970.352.5546 • Pueblo 719.543.1324 • Yuma 970.848.3095

R: 72　**T:** 1st 48%
Elected Year: 2014
Next Election: 2020

Rep. Kenneth R. Buck (buck)　　　　R-CO-04　p 202.225.467?

Rm. RHOB 2455 **Web.** buck.house.gov
Bio. 02/16/1959 • Ossining, NY • Princeton Univ. (NJ), A.B.,
1981; Univ. of Wyoming (WY), J.D., 1985 • Wesleyan • M.
Perry Lynn, 2 ch (2 from previous marriage) **Cmte.** Foreign
Affairs • Judiciary
CoS. Ritika Robertson　　**LD.** James Hampson
　　　　　　　　　　　　　PS. Brittany Yanick
Dist. Off. Castle Rock 720.639.9165 • Greeley 970.702.213?

R: 257　**T:** 3rd 61%
Elected Year: 2014

Rep. Jason Crow (kroe)　　　　D-CO-06　p 202.225.788?

Rm. LHOB 1229 **Web.** crow.house.gov
Bio. 03/15/1979 • Beaver Dam, WI • Univ. of Wisconsin
- Madison, B.A., 2002; Univ. of Denver (CO), J.D., 2009 •
Christian - Non-Denominational • M. Deserai Crow, 2 ch
Cmte. Armed Services • Small Business
CoS. Alex Ball　　**LD.** Justin Meuse
Sched. Liz Natonski　　**PS.** Anne Feldman
Dist. Off. Denver 303.295.8000

R: 361　**T:** 1st 54%
Elected Year: 2018

COLORADO

⚑ Rep. Diana L. DeGette (deh-GET)   D-CO-01   p 202.225.4431

Rm. RHOB 2111 **Web.** degette.house.gov   **f** 202.225.5657
Bio. 07/29/1957 • Tachikawa, Japan • Attorney; State
Representative • Colorado College, B.A., 1979; New York
Univ. Law School, J.D., 1982 • Presbyterian • M. Lino
Lipinsky, 2 ch **Cmte.** Energy & Commerce • Natural
Resources
CoS. Lisa B. Cohen   **LD.** Tommy Walker
Sched. Diana Gambrel   **PS.** Ryan Brown
Dist. Off.   Denver 303.844.4988

R: 48   **T:** 12th 74%
Elected Year: 1996

⚑ Rep. Doug L. Lamborn (LAM-born)   R-CO-05   p 202.225.4422

Rm. RHOB 2371 **Web.** lamborn.house.gov   **f** 202.226.2638
Bio. 05/24/1954 • Leavenworth, KS • Attorney • Univ. of
Kansas School of Journalism, B.S., 1978; Univ. of Kansas
School of Law, J.D., 1985 • Christian Church • M. Jeanie
Lamborn, 5 ch **Cmte.** Armed Services • Natural Resources
CoS. Dale Anderson   **LD.** Andrew Braun
Sched. Kate Morgan   **PS.** Savannah Frasier
Dist. Off.   Buena Vista 719.520.0055 • Colorado Springs
719.520.0055

R: 115   **T:** 7th 57%
Elected Year: 2006

⚑ Rep. Joseph D. Neguse (neh-"GOOSE")   D-CO-02   p 202.225.2161

Rm. LHOB 1419 **Web.** neguse.house.gov
Bio. 05/13/1984 • Bakers?eld, CO • Univ. of Colorado,
Boulder, Bach. Deg., 2005; Univ. of Colorado, Boulder, J.D.,
2009 • Christian Church • M. Andrea Neguse, 1 ch **Cmte.**
Judiciary • Natural Resources • Select Committee on the
Climate Crisis
CoS. Lisa Bianco   **LD.** Bo Morris
Sched. Madeline Douglas   **PS.** Sally Tucker
Dist. Off.   Boulder • Fort Collins 970.226.1721

R: 397   **T:** 1st 60%
Elected Year: 2018

⚑ Rep. Ed G. Perlmutter (PERL-muh-ter)   D-CO-07   p 202.225.2645

Rm. LHOB 1226 **Web.** perlmutter.house.gov **f** 202.225.5278
Bio. 05/01/1953 • Denver, CO • Law Firm Director • Univ.
of Colorado, Boulder, B.A., 1975; Univ. of Colorado School
of Law, J.D., 1978 • Protestant - Unspecified Christian • M.
Nancy Perlmutter, 3 ch **Cmte.** Financial Services • Rules •
Science, Space & Technology
CoS. Danielle Radovich   **LD.** Jeffrey O'Neil
Piper (CD)
Sched. Alison Inderfurth   **PS.** Ashley Verville (CD)
Dist. Off.   Lakewood 303.274.7944

R: 119   **T:** 7th 60%
Elected Year: 2006

⚑ Rep. Scott R. Tipton (TIP-tuhn)   R-CO-03   p 202.225.4761

Rm. CHOB 218 **Web.** tipton.house.gov   **f** 202.226.9669
Bio. 11/09/1956 • Espanola, NM • State Legislator • Fort
Lewis College (CO), B.A., 1978 • Anglican • M. Jean Tipton,
2 ch **Cmte.** Financial Services
CoS. Joshua Green   **LD.** Liz Payne
Sched. Agustina Pardal   **PS.** Matthew Atwood
Dist. Off.   Alamosa 719.587.5105 • Durango 970.259.1490 •
Grand Junction 970.241.2499 • Pueblo 719.542.1073

R: 183   **T:** 5th 52%
Elected Year: 2010

CONNECTICUT

⚑ Governor Ned Lamont (LAH-mawnt)   p 860.566.4840

State Capitol, 210 Capitol Ave.   **C:** Hartford
Hartford, CT 06106   **P:** 3,572,665 (29)
Website ct.gov   **A:** 4,842.49 mi² (48th)
Fax 860.524.7395
Term Ends 2023
Lt. Governor
Susan Bysiewicz, **D**

CONNECTICUT

CONNECTICUT

U.S. Senators
Richard Blumenthal, **D**
Chris S. Murphy, **D**
U.S. Representatives
01 / John B. Larson, **D**
02 / Joe Courtney, **D**
03 / Rosa L. DeLauro, **D**
04 / Jim A. Himes, **D**
05 / Jahana Hayes, **D**

🔊 **Sen. Richard Blumenthal** (BLOOM-un-thawl)   D-CT-Sr.   p 202.224.2823

Rm. HSOB 706 **Web.** blumenthal.senate.gov **f** 202.224.9673
Bio. 02/13/1946 • Brooklyn, NY • State Attorney General;
State Legislator • Marine Corps Reserve, 1970-75 • Harvard
College (MA), A.B., 1967; Yale Univ. Law School (CT),
J.D., 1973 • Jewish • M. Cynthia Allison Malkin, 4 ch
Cmte. Aging • Armed Services • Commerce, Science &
Transportation • Judiciary • Veterans' Affairs
CoS. Joel Kelsey   **LD.** Colleen Bell
Sched. Michael Lawson   **PS.** Maria McElwain
Dist. Off. Bridgeport 203.330.0598 • Hartford 860.258.6940

R: 54 **T:** 2nd 63%
Elected Year: 2010
Next Election: 2022

🔊 **Sen. Chris S. Murphy** (MUR-fee)   D-CT-Jr.   p 202.224.4041

Rm. HSOB 136 **Web.** murphy.senate.gov **f** 202.224.9750
Bio. 08/03/1973 • White Plains, NY • State Legislator;
Attorney • Williams College, B.A., 1996; Univ. of
Connecticut School of Law, J.D., 2002 • Protestant -
Unspecified Christian • M. Catherine Holahan Murphy, 2
ch **Cmte.** Appropriations • Foreign Relations • Health,
Education, Labor & Pensions
CoS. Allison Herwitt   **LD.** David Bonine
Sched. Maya Ashwal   **PS.** Laura Maloney
Dist. Off. Hartford 860.549.8463

R: 59 **T:** 2nd 60%
Elected Year: 2012
Next Election: 2024

🔊 **Rep. Joe Courtney** (KORT-nee)   D-CT-02   p 202.225.2076

Rm. RHOB 2332 **Web.** courtney.house.gov **f** 202.225.4977
Bio. 04/06/1953 • West Hartford, CT • Attorney • Tufts Univ.
(MA), B.A., 1975; Univ. of Connecticut School of Law, J.D.,
1978 • Roman Catholic • M. Audrey Courtney, 2 ch **Cmte.**
Armed Services • Education & Labor
CoS. Neil McKiernan   **LD.** Alexa Combelic
Sched. Kathleen Corcoran   **PS.** Patrick Cassidy
Dist. Off. Enfield 860.741.6011 • Norwich 860.886.0139

R: 112 **T:** 7th 62%
Elected Year: 2006

🔊 **Rep. Rosa L. DeLauro** (deh-LOOR-o)   D-CT-03   p 202.225.3661

Rm. RHOB 2413 **Web.** delauro.house.gov **f** 202.225.4890
Bio. 03/02/1943 • New Haven , CT • Executive Director,
Emily's List; Congressional Aide • Marymount College
(NY), B.A., 1964; Columbia Univ. (NY), M.A., 1966 • Roman
Catholic • M. Stanley Greenberg, 3 ch ; 4 gr-ch **Cmte.**
Appropriations • Budget
CoS. Leticia Mederos   **LD.** Liz Albertine
Sched. Ryann Kinney   **PS.** Will Serio
Dist. Off. Derby 203.735.5005 • Naugatuck 203.729.0204 •
New Haven 203.562.3718

R: 18 **T:** 15th 65%
Elected Year: 1990

🔊 **Rep. Jahana Hayes** (hayz)   D-CT-05   p 202.225.4476

Rm. LHOB 1415
Bio. 03/08/1973 • Waterbury, CT • Southern Connecticut
State Univ., B.S., 2005; Univ. of Saint Joseph (CT), M.A., 2012
• Methodist • M. Milford Hayes, 4 ch **Cmte.** Agriculture •
Education & Labor
CoS. Joe Dunn   **LD.** Alex Ginis
Sched. Gianna Judkins   **PS.** Jason Newton
Dist. Off. Waterbury 860.223.8412

R: 380 **T:** 1st 56%
Elected Year: 2018

CONNECTICUT

Rep. Jim A. Himes (hymz)　　　　D-CT-04　　p 202.225.5541

Rm. LHOB 1227 **Web.** himes.house.gov　　**f** 202.225.9629
Bio. 07/05/1966 • Lima, Peru • Financial Executive •
Harvard Univ., B.A., 1988; Oxford Univ. (England), M.Phil,
1990 • Presbyterian • M. Mary Himes, 2 ch **Cmte.** Financial
Services • Permanent Select on Intelligence
CoS. Mark Henson　　　　　　**LD.** Mark Snyder
Sched. Emily Fritcke　　　　　**PS.** Patrick Malone
Dist. Off. Bridgeport 203.333.6600 • Stamford 203.353.9400

R: 132　**T:** 6th 61%
Elected Year: 2008

Rep. John B. Larson (LAR-suhn)　　　D-CT-01　　p 202.225.2265

Rm. LHOB 1501 **Web.** larson.house.gov　　**f** 202.225.1031
Bio. 07/22/1948 • Hartford, CT • State Senator;
Businessman • Central Connecticut State Univ. (CT), B.S.,
1971 • Catholic • M. Leslie Best Larson, 3 ch **Cmte.** Ways &
Means
CoS. Scott Stephanou
Sched. Sarah Gianni　　　　　**PS.** Mary Yatrousis
Dist. Off. Hartford 860.278.8888

R: 59　**T:** 11th 64%
Elected Year: 1998

DELAWARE

Governor John C. Carney Jr. (KAR-nee)　　　　p 302.744.4101

150 Martin Luther King Jr. Blvd.,　**C:** Dover
2nd Floor　　　　　　　　　　　**P:** 967,171 (46)
Dover, DE 19901　　　　　　　　**A:** 1,948.66 mi^2 (50th)
Website delaware.gov
Fax 302.739.2775
Term Ends 2021
Lt. Governor
Bethany Hall-Long, **D**

U.S. Senators
Tom R. Carper, **D**
Christopher A. Coons, **D**
U.S. Representatives
01 / Lisa Blunt Blunt Rochester,
D

Sen. Tom R. Carper (KAR-pur)　　　D-DE-Sr.　　p 202.224.2441

Rm. HSOB 513 **Web.** carper.senate.gov　　**f** 202.228.2190
Bio. 01/23/1947 • Beckley, WV • Governor; U.S.
Representative • Navy 1968-73; Navy Reserve 1973-91 •
Ohio State Univ., B.A., 1968; Univ. of Delaware, Newark,
M.B.A., 1975 • Presbyterian • M. Martha Ann Stacy Carper,
2 ch **Cmte.** Environment & Public Works • Finance •
Homeland Security & Government Affairs
CoS. Emily M. Spain　　　　**LD.** Jan Beukelman
Sched. Diana Naylor　　　　**PS.** Christine E. Brennan
Dist. Off. Dover 302.674.3308 • Georgetown 302.856.7690
• Wilmington 302.573.6291

R: 83　**T:** 1st 60%
Elected Year: 2000
Next Election: 2024

Sen. Christopher A. Coons (koonz)　　D-DE-Jr.　　p 202.224.5042

Rm. RSOB 127-A **Web.** coons.senate.gov　　**f** 202.228.3075
Bio. 09/09/1963 • Greenwich, CT • Amherst College (MA),
B.A., 1985; Yale Univ. Law School (CT), J.D., 1992; Yale
Univ. Divinity School (CT), Mast. Deg., 1992 • Presbyterian
• M. Annie Lingenfelter, 3 ch **Cmte.** Appropriations •
Ethics • Foreign Relations • Judiciary • Small Business &
Entrepreneurship
CoS. Jonathan Stahler　　　　**LD.** Brian Winseck
Sched. Chelsea Moser　　　　**PS.** Sean Coit
Dist. Off. Dover 302.736.5601 • Wilmington 302.573.6345

R: 44　**T:** 2nd 56%
Elected Year: 2010
Next Election: 2020

DELAWARE

🔖 **Rep. Lisa Blunt Blunt Rochester** (RAH-chess-tur) D-DE-01   p 202.225.4165

Rm. LHOB 1519 **Web.**
bluntrochester.house.gov
Bio. 02/10/1962 • Philadelphia, PA • Fairleigh Dickinson
Univ., Bach. Deg., 1985; Univ. of Delaware, M.A., 2003 •
Christian Church • W., 2 ch **Cmte.** Energy & Commerce
CoS. Jacqueline Sanchez
Sched. Kalila Hines   **PS.** Kyle Morse
Dist. Off. Wilmington 302.830.2330

R: 298   **T:** 2nd   65%
Elected Year: 2016

FLORIDA

FLORIDA

🏛 **Governor Ron D. DeSantis** (dee-SAN-tis)   p 850.488.7146

The Capitol   **C:** Tallahassee
400 S. Monroe St.   **P:** 21,299,325 (3)
Tallahassee, FL 32399-0001   **A:** 53,624.55 mi^2 (26th)
Website flgov.com
Fax 850.487.0801
Term Ends 2023
Lt. Governor
Jeanette Nunez, **R**

U.S. Senators
Marco Rubio, **R**
Rick Scott, **R**
U.S. Representatives
01 / Matt Gaetz, **R**
02 / Neal P. Dunn, **R**
03 / Theodore S. Yoho, **R**
04 / John Rutherford, **R**
05 / Alfred J. Lawson, **D**
06 / Michael G. Waltz, **R**
07 / Stephanie Murphy, **D**
08 / Bill Posey, **R**
09 / Darren M. Soto, **D**
10 / Valdez B. Demings, **D**
11 / Daniel A. Webster, **R**
12 / Gus M. Bilirakis, **R**
13 / Charles J. Crist, **D**
14 / Kathy A. Castor, **D**
15 / Ross Spano, **R**
16 / Vern G. Buchanan, **R**
17 / Greg Steube, **R**
18 / Brian Mast, **R**
19 / Francis Rooney, **R**
20 / Alcee L. Hastings, **D**

21 / Lois J. Frankel, **D**
22 / Ted E. Deutch, **D**
23 / Debbie Wasserman Schultz, **D**
24 / Frederica S. Wilson, **D**
25 / Mario Diaz-Balart, **R**
26 / Debbie Mucarsel-Powell, **D**
27 / Donna E. Shalala, **D**

🏛 **Sen. Marco Rubio** (ROO-bee-o)   R-FL-Sr.   p 202.224.304

Rm. RSOB 284 **Web.** rubio.senate.gov   **f** 202.228.0285
Bio. 05/28/1971 • Miami, FL • State Legislator; Spkr., Florida
House of Representatives • Univ. of Florida, B.S., 1993;
Univ. of Miami (FL), J.D., 1996 • Roman Catholic • M.
Jeanette Dousdebes, 4 ch **Cmte.** Aging • Appropriations
• Foreign Relations • Intelligence • Small Business &
Entrepreneurship
CoS. Mike Needham   **LD.** Lauren Reamy
Sched. Bridget Spurlock   **PS.** Nick Iacovella
Dist. Off. Fort Myers • Jacksonville 904.354.4300 •
Miami 305.596.4224 • Orlando 407.254.2573 • Palm
Beach Gardens 561.775.3360 • Pensacola 850.433.2603 •
Tallahassee 850.599.9100 • Tampa 813.853.1099

R: 51   **T:** 2nd   52%
Elected Year: 2010
Next Election: 2022

🏛 **Sen. Rick Scott** (skaht)   R-FL-Jr.   p 202.224.527

Rm. HSOB 716 **Web.** rickscott.senate.gov
Bio. 12/01/1952 • Bloomington, IL • Univ. of Missouri, B.S.,
1975; Southern Methodist Univ. Law School (TX), J.D., 1978
• Christian Church • M. Ann Scott, 2 ch ; 6 gr-ch **Cmte.**
Aging • Armed Services • Budget • Commerce, Science &
Transportation • Homeland Security & Government Affairs
CoS. Jacqueline E. Schutz
Zeckman
Sched. Megan Bailey   **PS.** Chris Hartline
Dist. Off. Tallahassee

R: 100   **T:** 0th   50%
Elected Year: 2018
Next Election: 2024

FLORIDA

🏛 Rep. Gus M. Bilirakis (bih-lih-RAK-uhss) R-FL-12 p 202.225.5755

Rm. RHOB 2227 **Web.** bilirakis.house.gov **f** 202.225.4085
Bio. 02/08/1963 • Gainesville, FL • Attorney; State Legislator • Univ. of Florida, B.S., 1986; Stetson Univ. College of Law (FL), J.D., 1989 • Greek Orthodox • M. Eva Lialios Bilirakis, 4 ch **Cmte.** Energy & Commerce • Veterans' Affairs
CoS. Liz Hittos **LD.** Thomas Power
Dist. Off. New Port Richey 727.232.2921 • Tarpon Springs 727.940.5860 • Wesley Chapel 813.501.4942

R: 107 T: 7th 58%
Elected Year: 2006

🏛 Rep. Vern G. Buchanan (byoo-KA-nuhn) R-FL-16 p 202.225.5015

Rm. RHOB 2427 **Web.** buchanan.house.gov **f** 202.226.0828
Bio. 05/08/1951 • Detroit, MI • Automobile Dealer; Owner, Reinsurance Co. • Michigan Air National Guard 1969-1975 • Cleary Univ. (MI), B.B.A., 1975; Univ. of Detroit (MI), M.B.A., 1986 • Baptist • M. Sandy Harris Buchanan, 2 ch **Cmte.** Ways & Means
CoS. Dave Karvelas **LD.** Sean Brady
Sched. Jaclyn Knight **PS.** Anthony Cruz
Dist. Off. Bradenton 941.747.9081 • Sarasota 941.951.6643

R: 108 T: 7th 55%
Elected Year: 2006

🏛 Rep. Kathy A. Castor (KAS-tur) D-FL-14 p 202.225.3376

Rm. RHOB 2052 **Web.** castor.house.gov **f** 202.225.5652
Bio. 08/20/1966 • Miami, FL • County Commissioner • Emory Univ. - Atlanta (GA), B.A., 1988; Florida State Univ. School of Law, J.D., 1991 • Presbyterian • M. Bill Lewis, 2 ch **Cmte.** Energy & Commerce • Select Committee on the Climate Crisis
CoS. Clay Phillips **LD.** Elizabeth Brown
  PS. Steven Angotti (CD)
Dist. Off. Tampa 813.871.2817

R: 109 T: 7th 100%
Elected Year: 2006

🏛 Rep. Charles J. Crist (Krist) D-FL-13 p 202.225.5961

Rm. CHOB 215 **Web.** crist.house.gov **f** 202.225.9764
Bio. 07/24/1956 • Altoona, PA • 44th Governor of Florida; Attorney General, State of Florida; Deputy Secretary, FL Dept. of Business and Professional Regulation; Candidate, FL State Senate; Candidate, FL State Senate; Member, FL Senate; FL Commissioner of Education • Florida State Univ., B.S., 1978; Cumberland School of Law, Stamford Univ. (AL), J.D., 1981 • Methodist • M. Carole Rome Crist, 2 stepch **Cmte.** Appropriations • Science, Space & Technology
CoS. Austin Durrer **LD.** Christopher Fisher
Sched. Jonathan Pekkala
Dist. Off. St. Petersburg 727.318.6770

R: 304 T: 2nd 58%
Elected Year: 2016

🏛 Rep. Valdez B. Demings (DEH-mingz) D-FL-10 p 202.225.2176

Rm. CHOB 217 **Web.** demings.house.gov **f** 202.226.6559
Bio. 03/12/1957 • Jacksonville, FL • Webster Univ. (MO), M.P.A.; Florida State Univ., B.S., 1979 • African Methodist Episcopal • M. Jerry L. Demings, 3 ch ; 5 gr-ch **Cmte.** Homeland Security • Judiciary • Permanent Select on Intelligence
CoS. Wendy D. Anderson **LD.** Aimee Collins-Mandeville
Sched. Wendy Featherson **PS.** Daniel Gleick
Dist. Off. Orlando 321.388.9808

R: 305 T: 2nd 100%
Elected Year: 2016

🏛 Rep. Ted E. Deutch (doych) D-FL-22 p 202.225.3001

Rm. RHOB 2447 **Web.** teddeutch.house.gov **f** 202.225.5974
Bio. 05/07/1966 • Bethlehem, PA • Univ. of Michigan, B.A., 1988; Univ. of Michigan Law School, J.D., 1990 • Jewish • M. Jill Deutch, 3 ch (twins) **Cmte.** Ethics • Foreign Affairs • Judiciary
CoS. Joshua Rogin **LD.** Joshua Lipman
Sched. Alex Rocha (CD) **PS.** Jason Attermann
Dist. Off. Boca Raton 561.470.5440 • Coral Springs 954.255.8336 • Margate 954.972.6454

R: 147 T: 6th 62%
Elected Year: 2010

FLORIDA

♟ Rep. Mario Diaz-Balart (DEE-az-buh-LART)　　R-FL-25　　p 202.225.4211

Rm. CHOB 404 **Web.** 　　　　　　　　　　　**f** 202.225.8576
mariodiazbalart.house.gov
Bio. 09/25/1961 • Fort Lauderdale, FL • State Legislator;
President, Marketing and PR Firm • Roman Catholic • M. Tia
Diaz-Balart, 1 ch **Cmte.** Appropriations
CoS. Cesar A. Gonzalez　　　**LD.** Chris Sweet
Sched. Elizabeth Dos Santos　**PS.** Katrina V. Bishop
Dist. Off. Doral 305.470.8555 • Naples 239.348.1620

R: 78 **T:** 9th 61%
Elected Year: 2010

♟ Rep. Neal P. Dunn (dun)　　　　　　　R-FL-02　　p 202.225.5235

Rm. CHOB 316 **Web.** dunn.house.gov　　　**f** 202.225.5615
Bio. 02/16/1953 • New Haven, CT • Washington and Lee
Univ. (VA), Bach. Deg.; George Washington Univ. Medical
School (DC), M.D. • Catholic • M. Leah Dunn, 3 ch ; 3 gr-
ch **Cmte.** Agriculture • Science, Space & Technology •
Veterans' Affairs
CoS. Michael Lowry　　　　**LD.** Matt Blackwell
Sched. Marissa Mullen　　**PS.** Shelby Hodgkins
Dist. Off. Panama City 850.785.0812 • Tallahassee
850.891.8610

R: 306 **T:** 2nd 67%
Elected Year: 2016

♞ Rep. Lois J. Frankel (FRANK-uhl)　　　D-FL-21　　p 202.225.9890

Rm. RHOB 2305 **Web.** frankel.house.gov　**f** 202.225.1224
Bio. 05/16/1948 • New York, NY (Manhattan) • Boston
Univ. (MA), B.A., 1970; Georgetown Univ. Law Center (DC),
J.D., 1973 • Jewish • D., 1 ch **Cmte.** Appropriations • Joint
Economic
CoS. Kelsey Moran　　　　**LD.** Ian Wolf
Sched. Kate Regan　　　**PS.** Rachel Huxley-Cohen
Dist. Off. Boca Raton 561.998.9045

R: 207 **T:** 4th 100%
Elected Year: 2012

♟ Rep. Matt Gaetz ("gates")　　　　　　R-FL-01　　p 202.225.4136

Rm. LHOB 1721 **Web.** gaetz.house.gov　　**f** 202.225.3414
Bio. 05/07/1982 • Hollywood, FL • Florida State Univ.,
B.S., 2003; College of William and Mary - Marshall-Wythe
Law School (VA), J.D., 2007 • Baptist • NS. **Cmte.** Armed
Services • Judiciary
CoS. Jillian Lane Wyant　　**LD.** Devin Murphy
Sched. Luke Ball
Dist. Off. Fort Walton Beach 850.479.1183 • Pensacola
850.479.1183

R: 310 **T:** 2nd 67%
Elected Year: 2016

♞ Rep. Alcee L. Hastings (HAY-stingz)　　D-FL-20　　p 202.225.1313

Rm. RHOB 2353 **Web.** 　　　　　　　　**f** 202.225.1171
alceehastings.house.gov
Bio. 09/05/1936 • Altamonte Springs, FL • Attorney; Federal
Judge • Fisk Univ. (TN), B.A., 1958; Florida Agricultural
and Mechanical Univ. College of Law, J.D., 1963 • African
Methodist Episcopal • D., 3 ch **Cmte.** Rules
CoS. Lale M. Morrison　　　**LD.** Tom Carnes
Sched. Edwina Ward (CD)　　**PS.** Evan N. Polisar
Dist. Off. Fort Lauderdale 954.733.2800 • Mangonia Park
561.676.7911

R: 27 **T:** 14th 100%
Elected Year: 1992

♞ Rep. Alfred J. Lawson Jr. (LAW-suhn)　　D-FL-05　　p 202.225.0123

Rm. LHOB 1406 **Web.** lawson.house.gov　**f** 202.225.2256
Bio. 09/23/1948 • Midway, FL • Univ. of Florida, B.S., 1970;
Florida State Univ., M.S., 1973 • Episcopalian • M. Delores
J. Brooks Lawson, 2 ch ; 2 gr-ch **Cmte.** Agriculture •
Financial Services
CoS. Tola R. Thompson　　　**LD.** Margaret Franklin
Sched. Vince Evans　　　**PS.** Stephanie Lambert
Dist. Off. Jacksonville 904.354.1652 • Tallahassee
850.558.9450

R: 321 **T:** 2nd 67%
Elected Year: 2016

Rep. Brian Mast ("mast")　　　　R-FL-18　　p 202.225.3026

Rm. RHOB 2182　**Web.** mast.house.gov　**f** 202.225.8398
Bio. 07/10/1980 • Grand Rapids, MI • Harvard Univ., Bach.
Deg., 2016 • Christian Church • M. Brianna Mast, 3 ch
Cmte. Foreign Affairs • Transportation & Infrastructure
CoS. James Langenderfer　**LD.** Barry Smith
Sched. Jaclyn Neuman　　**PS.** Kyle Von Ende
Dist. Off. North Palm Beach 561.530.7778 • Port St Lucie
772.336.2877 • Stuart 772.403.0900

R: 323　**T:** 2nd　54%
Elected Year: 2016

Rep. Debbie Mucarsel-Powell (moo-kar-SELL　D-FL-26　p 202.225.2778
POU'uhl)

Rm. CHOB 114　**Web.** mucarsel-
powell.house.gov
Bio. 01/18/1971 • Ecuador • Pitzer Univ., B.S., 1992;
Claremont Graduate Univ., Mast. Deg., 1996 • Catholic • M.
Robert Powell, 3 ch　**Cmte.** Judiciary • Transportation &
Infrastructure
CoS. Laura I. Rodriguez　**LD.** Courtney Fogwell
Sched. Laura Forero　　**PS.** Sebastian Silva
Dist. Off. Key West 305.292.4485 • Miami 305.222.0160

R: 396　**T:** 1st　51%
Elected Year: 2018

Rep. Stephanie Murphy (MUR-fee)　　D-FL-07　　p 202.225.4035

Rm. LHOB 1710　**Web.**　　　　**f** 202.226.0821
stephaniemurphy.house.gov
Bio. 09/16/1978 • Ho Chi Minh City, Vietnam • College
of William and Mary (VA), B.A., 2000; Georgetown Univ.
(DC), M.S., 2004 • Christian Church • M. Sean Murphy, 2 ch
Cmte. Ways & Means
CoS. Bradley Neal Howard　**LD.** John Laufer
Sched. Allison Everton　　**PS.** Jonathan Uriarte
Dist. Off. Orlando 888.205.5421 • Sanford 888.205.5421

R: 326　**T:** 2nd　58%
Elected Year: 2016

Rep. Bill Posey (POE-zee)　　　R-FL-08　　p 202.225.3671

Rm. RHOB 2150　**Web.** posey.house.gov　**f** 202.225.3516
Bio. 12/18/1947 • Washington, DC • State Legislator,
Realtor • Brevard Community College (FL), A.A., 1969 •
Methodist • M. Katie Ingram Posey, 2 ch; 3 gr-ch　**Cmte.**
Financial Services • Science, Space & Technology
CoS. Stuart Burns　　**LD.** Valentina J. Valenta
Sched. Molly Vinesett　　**PS.** George Cecala
Dist. Off. Melbourne 321.632.1776

R: 139　**T:** 6th　61%
Elected Year: 2008

Rep. Francis Rooney (ROO-nee)　　R-FL-19　　p 202.225.2536

Rm. CHOB 120　**Web.**　　　　**f** 202.226.3547
francisrooney.house.gov
Bio. 12/04/1953 • Muskogee, OK • Georgetown Univ. (DC),
Bach. Deg., 1975; Georgetown Univ. Law Center (DC), J.D.,
1978 • Roman Catholic • M. Kathleen Rooney, 3 ch ; 2 gr-ch
Cmte. Education & Labor • Foreign Affairs
CoS. Jessica Lynn Carter　**LD.** Corey Schrodt
Sched. Chloe Wick　　**PS.** Chris Berardi
Dist. Off. Cape Coral 239.599.6033 • Naples 239.252.6225

R: 330　**T:** 2nd　62%
Elected Year: 2016

Rep. John Rutherford (RUH-thur-furd)　R-FL-04　p 202.225.2501

Rm. LHOB 1711　**Web.** rutherford.house.gov　**f** 202.225.2504
Bio. 09/02/1952 • Omaha, NE • Florida Junior College,
A.A., 1972; Florida State Univ., B.S., 1974 • Catholic • M.
Patricia Rutherford, 2 ch ; 6 gr-ch　**Cmte.** Appropriations
CoS. Kelly Simpson　　**LD.** Jenifer Bradley
Sched. Carole Anne Spohn　**PS.** Alex Lanfranconi
Dist. Off. Jacksonville 904.831.5205

R: 331　**T:** 2nd　65%
Elected Year: 2016

FLORIDA

Rep. Donna E. Shalala (shuh-LAY-luh) D-FL-27 p 202.225.3931

Rm. LHOB 1320 **Web.** shalala.house.gov
Bio. 02/14/1941 • Cleveland, OH • Western College for Women (OH), B.A., 1962; Syracuse Univ. (NY), Ph.D., 1970 • Catholic • S. **Cmte.** Education & Labor • Rules
CoS. Jessica Killin **LD.** Carla McGarvey
Sched. Nicole Marquez **PS.** Joseph Puente
Dist. Off. Miami 305.668.2855

R: 412 **T:** 1st 52%
Elected Year: 2018

Rep. Darren M. Soto (so-toe) D-FL-09 p 202.225.9889

Rm. LHOB 1507 **Web.** soto.house.gov f 202.225.9742
Bio. 02/25/1978 • Ringwood, NJ • Rutgers Univ. (NJ), B.A., 2000; George Washington Univ. School of Law (DC), J.D., 2004 • Catholic • M. Amanda Soto **Cmte.** Energy & Commerce • Natural Resources
CoS. Christine A. Biron **LD.** Mike Nichola
Sched. Liana Guerra **PS.** Oriana Pina
Dist. Off. Haines City 202.600.0843 • Kissimmee 407.452.1171 • Lake Wales 202.600.0843 • Orlando 202.332.4476 • Winter Haven 202.615.1308

R: 333 **T:** 2nd 58%
Elected Year: 2016

Rep. Ross Spano (SPAN-o) R-FL-15 p 202.225.1252

Rm. CHOB 224 **Web.** spano.house.gov
Bio. 07/16/1966 • Brandon, FL • Univ. of South Florida, B.A., 1994; Florida State Univ. School of Law, J.D., 1998 • Baptist • M. Amie Spano, 4 ch **Cmte.** Small Business • Transportation & Infrastructure
CoS. Jamie Robinette **LD.** Gus Ashton
Sched. Naomi Hilton **PS.** Daniel Bucheli
Dist. Off. Lakeland 863.644.8215

R: 416 **T:** 1st 53%
Elected Year: 2018

Rep. Greg Steube (STOO-bee) R-FL-17 p 202.225.5792

Rm. CHOB 521 **Web.** steube.house.gov
Bio. 05/19/1978 • Bradenton, FL • Univ. of Florida, B.S., 2001; Univ. of Florida Levin College of Law, J.D., 2003 • Methodist • M. Jennifer Mary Retzer, 1 ch **Cmte.** Judiciary • Oversight & Reform • Veterans' Affairs
CoS. Alex Blair **LD.** Reginald B. Darby
Sched. Gabrielle Cirenza **PS.** Rachel Harris
Dist. Off. Lakewood Ranch 941.306.2798

R: 420 **T:** 1st 62%
Elected Year: 2018

Rep. Michael G. Waltz (valts) R-FL-06 p 202.225.2706

Rm. CHOB 216 **Web.** waltz.house.gov
Bio. 01/31/1974 • Boynton Beach, FL • Virginia Military Institute, B.A., 1996 • Christian Church • D., 1 ch **Cmte.** Armed Services • Science, Space & Technology
CoS. Micah T. Ketchel **LD.** Walker B. Barrett
Sched. Deborah Hansen **PS.** Joanna Rodriguez
Dist. Off. Deland 386.279.0707 • Palm Coast 386.302.0442 • Port Orange 386.238.9711

R: 430 **T:** 1st 56%
Elected Year: 2018

Rep. Debbie Wasserman Schultz (WAH-sur-muhn shullts) D-FL-23 p 202.225.7931

Rm. LHOB 1114 **Web.** f 202.226.2052
wassermanschultz.house.gov
Bio. 09/27/1966 • Forest Hills, NY (Queens) • State Legislator; College Administrator • Univ. of Florida, B.A., 1988; Univ. of Florida, M.A., 1990 • Jewish • M. Steve Schultz, 3 ch **Cmte.** Appropriations • Oversight & Reform
CoS. Tracie Pough **LD.** Harry Baumgarten
Sched. Lauren Mylott **PS.** David Damron
Dist. Off. Aventura 305.936.5724 • Sunrise 954.845.1179

R: 104 **T:** 8th 59%
Elected Year: 2004

◪ Rep. Daniel A. Webster (WEB-stur) R-FL-11 p 202.225.1002

Rm. LHOB 1210 **Web.** webster.house.gov **f** 202.226.6559
Bio. 04/27/1949 • Charleston, WV • State Legislator; Spkr.,
House of Representatives • Georgia Institute of Technology,
B.E.E., 1971 • Baptist • M. Sandy Jordan, 6 ch ; 14 gr-ch
Cmte. Natural Resources • Transportation & Infrastructure
CoS. Jaryn Emhof
Sched. Natali Knight
Dist. Off. Brooksville 352.241.9230 • Inverness
352.241.9204 • Leesburg 352.241.9220 • The Villages
352.383.3552

R: 184 **T:** 5th 65%
Elected Year: 2010

◪ Rep. Frederica S. Wilson (WILL-suhn) D-FL-24 p 202.225.4506

Rm. RHOB 2445 **Web.** wilson.house.gov **f** 202.226.0777
Bio. 11/05/1942 • Miami, FL • State Legislator • Miami
Northwestern Senior High School, B.S., 1959; Fisk Univ.
(TN), B.S., 1963; Univ. of Miami (FL), M.Ed., 1972 •
Episcopalian • W., 3 ch ; 5 gr-ch **Cmte.** Education & Labor
• Transportation & Infrastructure
CoS. Chasseny Lewis **LD.** Jean Roseme
Sched. Cheyenne Range **PS.** Joyce Jones
Dist. Off. Hollywood 954.921.3682 • Miami Gardens
305.690.5905 • West Park 954.989.2688

R: 185 **T:** 5th 100%
Elected Year: 2010

◪ Rep. Theodore S. Yoho (YO-ho) R-FL-03 p 202.225.5744

Rm. LHOB 1730 **Web.** yoho.house.gov **f** 202.225.3973
Bio. 04/13/1955 • Minneapolis, MN • Broward Community
College (FL), A.A., 1977; Univ. of Florida, B.S., 1979; Univ. of
Florida Veterinary College, D.V.M., 1983 • Roman Catholic •
M. Carolyn Yoho, 3 ch **Cmte.** Agriculture • Foreign Affairs
CoS. Larry Calhoun **LD.** James Walsh
Sched. Allison Turk **PS.** Brian Kaveney
Dist. Off. Gainesville 352.505.0838 • Ocala 352.390.6413 •
Orange Park 904.276.9626 • Palatka 386.326.7221

R: 241 **T:** 4th 58%
Elected Year: 2012

GEORGIA

◪ Governor Brian Kemp (kemp) p 404.656.1776

200 Washington Street, 111 State
Capitol
Atlanta, GA 30334
Website georgia.gov
Fax 404.657.7332
Term Ends 2023
Lt. Governor
Geoff Duncan, R

C. Atlanta
P: 10,519,475 (8)
A: 57,513.37 mi^2 (21st)

U.S. Senators
Johnny Isakson, R
David A. Perdue, R
U.S. Representatives
01 / Buddy Carter, R
02 / Sanford D. Bishop, D
03 / Drew Ferguson, R
04 / Hank C. Johnson, D
05 / John R. Lewis, D
06 / Lucy McBath, D
07 / Rob Woodall, R
08 / Austin Scott, R
09 / Doug A. Collins, R
10 / Jody B. Hice, R
11 / Barry D. Loudermilk, R
12 / Rick W. Allen, R
13 / David A. Scott, D
14 / Tom Graves, R

GEORGIA

📛 Sen. Johnny Isakson (EYE-zuhk-suhn) R-GA-Sr. p 202.224.3643

Rm. RSOB 131 **Web.** isakson.senate.gov **f** 202.228.0724
Bio. 12/28/1944 • Atlanta, GA • U.S. Representative;
President of Realty Company • Georgia National Guard
1966-72 • Univ. of Georgia, B.B.A., 1966 • Methodist •
M. Diane Davison Isakson, 3 ch ; 9 gr-ch **Cmte.** Ethics •
Finance • Foreign Relations • Health, Education, Labor &
Pensions • Veterans' Affairs
CoS. Joan Kirchner Carr   **LD.** Jay Sulzmann
Sched. Kristine Nichols   **PS.** Amanda Maddox
Dist. Off. Atlanta 770.661.0999

R: 25 **T:** 3rd 55%
Elected Year: 2004
Next Election: 2022

📛 Sen. David A. Perdue Jr. (PUR-doo) R-GA-Jr. p 202.224.3521

Rm. RSOB 455 **Web.** perdue.senate.gov **f** 202.228.1031
Bio. 12/10/1949 • Macon, GA • Georgia Institute of
Technology, B.S., 1972; Georgia Institute of Technology,
Mast. Deg., 1975 • Methodist • M. Bonnie Dunn, 2 ch
Cmte. Agriculture, Nutrition & Forestry • Armed Services •
Banking, Housing & Urban Affairs • Budget
CoS. Derrick Dickey
Sched. Gabriele Forsyth   **PS.** Cherie Paquette
Dist. Off. Atlanta 404.865.0087

R: 77 **T:** 1st 53%
Elected Year: 2014
Next Election: 2020

📛 Rep. Rick W. Allen (A-luhn) R-GA-12 p 202.225.2823

Rm. RHOB 2400 **Web.** allen.house.gov **f** 202.225.3377
Bio. 11/07/1951 • Augusta, GA • Auburn Univ. School of
Architecture and Fine Arts (GA), B.S., 1973 • Methodist • M.
Robin Reeve, 4 ch ; 12 gr-ch **Cmte.** Agriculture • Education
& Labor
CoS. Timothy Baker   **LD.** Katie Hunter
Sched. Heath Wheat   **PS.** Carlton Norwood
Dist. Off. Augusta 706.228.1980 • Dublin 478.272.4030 •
Statesboro 912.243.9452 • Vidalia 912.403.3311

R: 252 **T:** 3rd 60%
Elected Year: 2014

📛 Rep. Sanford D. Bishop Jr. (BIH-shuhp) D-GA-02 p 202.225.3631

Rm. RHOB 2407 **Web.** bishop.house.gov **f** 202.225.2203
Bio. 02/04/1947 • Mobile, AL • Attorney; State Legislator
• Army ROTC 1969-71 • Morehouse College (GA), B.A.,
1968; Emory Univ. Law School (GA), J.D., 1971 • Baptist • M.
Vivian Creighton Bishop, 1 ch ; 1 gr-ch **Cmte.** Appropriations
CoS. Michael Reed   **LD.** Jonathan Halpern
Sched. Lauren Hughes   **PS.** Owen Dodd
Dist. Off. Albany 229.439.8067 • Columbus 706.320.9477 •
Macon 478.803.2631

R: 23 **T:** 14th 60%
Elected Year: 1992

📛 Rep. Buddy Carter (KAR-tur) R-GA-01 p 202.225.5831

Rm. RHOB 2432 **Web.** **f** 202.226.2269
buddycarter.house.gov
Bio. 09/06/1957 • Port Wentworth, GA • Young Harris
College, A.S., 1977; Univ. of Georgia School of Pharmacy
(GA), B.S., 1980 • Methodist • M. Amy Coppage, 3 ch ; 3 gr-
ch **Cmte.** Energy & Commerce • Select Committee on the
Climate Crisis
CoS. Chris Crawford   **LD.** Nick Schemmel
Sched. Brooke Miller   **PS.** Mary Carpenter
Dist. Off. Brunswick 912.265.9010 • Savannah
912.352.0101

R: 258 **T:** 3rd 58%
Elected Year: 2014

R Rep. Doug A. Collins (KAH-luhnz)   R-GA-09   p 202.225.9893

Rm. LHOB 1504 **Web.** dougcollins.house.gov **f** 202.226.1224
Bio. 08/16/1966 • Gainesville, GA • North Hall High School
(GA), B.A.; North Georgia College and State Univ. (Military
College of Georgia) Foundation Inc., B.A., 1988; New
Orleans Baptist Theological Seminary (LA), M.Div., 1996;
John Marshall Univ. Law School (Atlanta), J.D., 2008 •
Baptist • M. Lisa Jordan, 3 ch **Cmte.** Judiciary
CoS. Sally Rose Larson
Sched. Erin Wall   **PS.** Amanda Gonzalez
Dist. Off. Gainesville 770.297.3388

R: 204 **T:** 4th 80%
Elected Year: 2012

R Rep. Drew Ferguson IV (FUR-guh-suhn)   R-GA-03   p 202.225.5901

Rm. LHOB 1032 **Web.** ferguson.house.gov **f** 202.225.2515
Bio. 11/15/1967 • West Point, GA • Univ. of Georgia, Bach.
Deg., 1988; Medical College of Georgia, D.M.D., 1992 •
Catholic • M. Elizabeth Ferguson, 4 ch **Cmte.** Ways &
Means
CoS. Robert Saparow   **LD.** Mary Dee Beal
Sched. Jenna Heard   **PS.** Amy Timmerman
Dist. Off. Newnan 770.683.2033

R: 308 **T:** 2nd 66%
Elected Year: 2016

R Rep. Tom Graves Jr. (grayvz)   R-GA-14   p 202.225.5211

Rm. RHOB 2078 **Web.** tomgraves.house.gov **f** 202.225.8272
Bio. 02/03/1970 • St. Petersburg, FL • Business Owner;
State Legislator • Univ. of Georgia, B.B.A., 1993 • Baptist
• M. Julie Howard Graves, 3 ch **Cmte.** Appropriations •
Select Committee on the Modernization of Congress
CoS. John Donnelly   **LD.** Jason Murphy
Sched. Kristin Fillingim   **PS.** Danielle Stewart
Dist. Off. Dalton 706.226.5320 • Rome 706.290.1776

R: 148 **T:** 6th 77%
Elected Year: 2010

R Rep. Jody B. Hice (hice)   R-GA-10   p 202.225.4101

Rm. CHOB 409 **Web.** hice.house.gov
Bio. 04/22/1960 • Atlanta, GA • Asbury College (KY), B.A.,
1982; Southwestern Baptist Theological Seminary (TX),
M.Div., 1986; Luther Rice Seminary and Univ. (GA), B.A.,
1988 • Southern Baptist • M. Dee Hice, 2 ch ; 4 gr-ch **Cmte.**
Natural Resources • Oversight & Reform
CoS. David Sours   **LD.** Tim Reitz
Sched. Taylor Ford   **PS.** Nadgey Louis-Charles
Dist. Off. Milledgeville 478.457.0007 • Monroe
770.207.1776 • Thomson 770.207.1776

R: 265 **T:** 3rd 63%
Elected Year: 2014

꙾ Rep. Hank C. Johnson Jr. (JAHN-suhn)   D-GA-04   p 202.225.1605

Rm. RHOB 2240 **Web.**   **f** 202.226.0691
hankjohnson.house.gov
Bio. 10/02/1954 • Washington, DC • Judge; Attorney •
Clark College (GA), B.A., 1976; Texas Southern Univ.,
Thurgood Marshall School of Law, J.D., 1979 • Buddhism
• M. Mereda Davis Johnson, 2 ch **Cmte.** Judiciary •
Transportation & Infrastructure
CoS. Arthur D. Sidney   **LD.** Jacqui Kappler
Sched. Alem   **PS.** Andy Phelan (CD)
Tewoldeberhan
Dist. Off. Decatur 770.987.2291

R: 113 **T:** 7th 79%
Elected Year: 2006

꙾ Rep. John R. Lewis (LOO-iss)   D-GA-05   p 202.225.3801

Rm. CHOB 300 **Web.** johnlewis.house.gov **f** 202.225.0351
Bio. 02/21/1940 • Troy, AL • Director, Voter Action Project;
Member, Atlanta City Council; Civil Rights Activist/Leader
• American Baptist Theological Seminary (TN), B.A.,
1961; Fisk Univ. (TN), B.A., 1963 • Protestant - Unspecified
Christian • W., 1 ch **Cmte.** Joint Taxation • Ways & Means
CoS. Michael E. Collins   **LD.** Jamila A. Thompson
Sched. David Bowman   **PS.** Brenda Jones
Dist. Off. Atlanta 404.659.0116

R: 9 **T:** 17th 100%
Elected Year: 1986

GEORGIA

♞ Rep. Barry D. Loudermilk (LOU-dur-milk) R-GA-11 p 202.225.2931

Rm. CHOB 422 **Web.** loudermilk.house.gov **f** 202.225.2944
Bio. 12/22/1963 • Riverdale, GA • Community College of the Air Force (AL), A.A.S., 1987; Wayland Baptist Univ. (TX), B.S., 1992 • Baptist • M. Desiree Loudermilk, 3 ch ; 2 gr-ch
Cmte. Administration • Financial Services
CoS. Robert Adkerson **LD.** Colin Carr
Sched. Ashley Adkerson **PS.** Brandon Cockerham (CD)
Dist. Off. Atlanta 770.429.1776 • Cartersville 770.429.1776 • Woodstock 770.429.1776

R: 271 **T:** 3rd 62%
Elected Year: 2014

♞ Rep. Lucy McBath (mik-BATH) D-GA-06 p 202.225.4501

Rm. LHOB 1513 **Web.** mcbath.house.gov
Bio. 06/01/1960 • Joliet, IL • Virginia State Univ., B.A., 1982 • Christian Church • M. Curtis McBath, 2 ch (2 deceased)
Cmte. Education & Labor • Judiciary
CoS. Joon Suh
Sched. Elizabeth Ahrens **PS.** Jen Fox
Dist. Off. Atlanta

R: 393 **T:** 1st 51%
Elected Year: 2018

♞ Rep. Austin Scott (skaht) R-GA-08 p 202.225.6531

Rm. RHOB 2417 **Web.** austinscott.house.gov **f** 202.225.3013
Bio. 12/10/1969 • Augusta, GA • State Legislator • Univ. of Georgia Terry College of Business, B.B.A., 1993 • Baptist • M. Vivien Scott, 2 ch **Cmte.** Agriculture • Armed Services
CoS. Jason Lawrence **LD.** Michael Tehrani
Sched. Crawford Pierson **PS.** Rachel Ledbetter
Dist. Off. Tifton 229.396.5175 • Warner Robins 478.971.1776

R: 180 **T:** 5th 100%
Elected Year: 2010

♞ Rep. David A. Scott (skaht) D-GA-13 p 202.225.2939

Rm. CHOB 225 **Web.** davidscott.house.gov **f** 202.225.4628
Bio. 06/27/1945 • Aynor, SC • State Legislator • Univ. of Florida, B.A., 1967; Univ. of Pennsylvania Wharton School of Business Aresty Institute, M.B.A., 1969 • Baptist • M. Alfredia Aaron Scott, 2 ch ; 2 gr-ch **Cmte.** Agriculture • Financial Services
CoS. Gary Woodward **LD.** Ashley Smith
Sched. Gerard Henderson
Dist. Off. Jonesboro 770.210.5073 • Smyrna 770.432.5405

R: 86 **T:** 9th 76%
Elected Year: 2002

♞ Rep. Rob Woodall III ("WOOD"-all) R-GA-07 p 202.225.4272

Rm. LHOB 1724 **Web.** woodall.house.gov **f** 202.225.4696
Bio. 02/11/1970 • Athens, GA • Attorney; Congressional Chief of Staff • Marist High School (GA), B.A., 1988; Furman Univ. (SC), B.A., 1992; Univ. of Georgia, J.D., 1998 • Methodist • S. **Cmte.** Budget • Rules • Select Committee on the Modernization of Congress • Transportation & Infrastructure
CoS. Derick Corbett (CD) **LD.** Janet Rossi
Sched. Kelley Kurtz **PS.** Jeff Naft
Dist. Off. Lawrenceville 770.232.3005

R: 187 **T:** 5th 50%
Elected Year: 2010

HAWAII

♞ Governor David Y. Ige (EE-gay) p 808.586.0034

Executive Chambers, State Capitol **C:** Honolulu
Honolulu, HI 96813 **P:** 1,420,491 (41)
Website hawaii.gov **A:** 6,422.81 mi^2 (47th)
Fax 808.586.0006
Term Ends 2022
Lt. Governor
Josh Green, D

U.S. Senators
Brian E. Schatz, **D**
Mazie K. Hirono, **D**
U.S. Representatives
01 / Ed E. Case, **D**
02 / Tulsi Gabbard, **D**

Sen. Mazie K. Hirono (hee-RO-no)　　　　D-HI-Jr.　　p 202.224.6361

Rm. HSOB 713　**Web.** hirono.senate.gov　　**f** 202.224.2126
Bio. 11/03/1947 • Fukushima, Japan • Lawyer • Univ. of
Hawaii, Manoa, B.A., 1970; Georgetown Univ. Law Center
(DC), J.D., 1978 • Buddhism • M. Leighton Kim Oshima,
1 stepch　**Cmte.** Armed Services • Energy & Natural
Resources • Judiciary • Small Business & Entrepreneurship
• Veterans' Affairs
CoS. Coti Haia　　　　　　　**LD.** Jeremy T. Horan
Sched. Blaine Nolan　　　　**PS.** William Dempster
Dist. Off. Honolulu 808.522.8970

R: 60　**T:** 2nd 69%
Elected Year: 2012
Next Election: 2024

Sen. Brian E. Schatz (shahts)　　　　　D-HI-Sr.　　p 202.224.3934

Rm. HSOB 722　**Web.** schatz.senate.gov　　**f** 202.228.1153
Bio. 10/20/1972 • Ann Arbor, MI • Pomona College, B.A.,
1994 • Jewish • M. Linda Kwok Kai Yun, 2 ch　**Cmte.**
Appropriations • Banking, Housing & Urban Affairs •
Commerce, Science & Transportation • Ethics • Indian
Affairs
CoS. Andrew Winer　　　　　**LD.** Arun Revana
Sched. Diane Miyasato-　　　**PS.** Michael Inacay
　　Vizmanos
Dist. Off. Honolulu 808.523.2061

R: 56　**T:** 2nd 70%
Elected Year: 2012
Next Election: 2022

Rep. Ed E. Case (kayss)　　　　　　D-HI-01　　p 202.225.2726

Rm. RHOB 2443
Bio. 09/27/1952 • Hilo, HI • Williams College, B.A., 1975;
Univ. of California Hastings College of Law, J.D., 1981 •
Protestant - Unspecified Christian • M. Audrey Nakamura, 4
ch　**Cmte.** Appropriations • Natural Resources
CoS. Timothy M. Nelson
Sched. Shanise Kaaikala　　**PS.** Nestor R. Garcia (CD)
Dist. Off. Honolulu 808.546.9509

R: 249　**T:** 4th 70%
Elected Year: 2018

Rep. Tulsi Gabbard (GAB-urd)　　　　D-HI-02　　p 202.225.4906

Rm. LHOB 1433　**Web.** gabbard.house.gov　　**f** 202.225.4987
Bio. 04/12/1981 • Leloaloa, AS • Hawaii Pacific Univ., B.S.,
2009 • Hinduism • M. Abraham Williams　**Cmte.** Armed
Services • Financial Services
CoS. Kainoa Penaroza (CD)　**LD.** Adam Schantz
Sched. Amanda Koski　　　**PS.** Lauren McIlvaine
Dist. Off. Honolulu 808.541.1986

R: 208　**T:** 4th 74%
Elected Year: 2012

IDAHO

⚑ Governor Brad Little (LIH-tull)   p 208.334.2100

State Capitol, PO Box 83720
Boise, ID 83720
Website idaho.gov
Fax 208.334.3454
Term Ends 2023
Lt. Governor
Janice McGeachin, **R**

C: Boise
P: 1,754,208 (40)
A: 82,643.20 mi^2 (11th)

U.S. Senators
Mike D. Crapo, **R**
James E. Risch, **R**
U.S. Representatives
01 / Russell M. Fulcher, **R**
02 / Mike K. Simpson, **R**

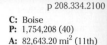

⚑ Sen. Mike D. Crapo (KRAY-poe)   R-ID-Sr.   p 202.224.6142

Rm. DSOB 239 **Web.** crapo.senate.gov   **f** 202.228.1375
Bio. 05/20/1951 • Idaho Falls, ID • U.S. Representative;
Attorney • Brigham Young Univ. (UT), B.A., 1973; Harvard
Univ. Law School (MA), J.D., 1977 • Mormon • M. Susan
Diane Hasleton Crapo, 5 ch ; 8 gr-ch **Cmte.** Banking,
Housing & Urban Affairs • Budget • Finance • Joint Taxation
• Judiciary
CoS. Susan H. Wheeler   **LD.** Scott Riplinger
Sched. Brian Raybon (CD)   **PS.** Robert Sumner
Dist. Off. Boise 208.334.1776 • Coeur D'Alene

R: 15   **T:** 4th 66%   208.664.5490 • Idaho Falls 208.522.9779 • Lewiston
Elected Year: 1998   208.743.1492 • Pocatello 208.236.6775 • Twin Falls
Next Election: 2022   208.734.2515

⚑ Sen. James E. Risch (rish)   R-ID-Jr.   p 202.224.2752

Rm. RSOB 483 **Web.** risch.senate.gov   **f** 202.224.2573
Bio. 05/03/1943 • Milwaukee, WI • Governor of Idaho;
Lt. Governor of Idaho; State Legislator • Univ. of Idaho,
B.S., 1965; Univ. of Idaho, Law School, J.D., 1968 • Roman
Catholic • M. Vicki L. Choborda, 3 ch ; 7 gr-ch **Cmte.**
Energy & Natural Resources • Ethics • Foreign Relations •
Intelligence • Small Business & Entrepreneurship
CoS. John Sandy   **LD.** Charles Adams
Sched. Alexa Green   **PS.** Kaylin Minton
Dist. Off. Boise 208.342.7985 • Coeur d'Alene 208.667.6130
R: 39   **T:** 2nd 65%   • Idaho Falls 208.523.5541 • Lewiston 208.743.0792 •
Elected Year: 2008   Pocatello 208.236.6817 • Twin Falls 208.734.6780
Next Election: 2020

⚑ Rep. Russell M. Fulcher (FUHL-chur)   R-ID-01   p 202.225.661

Rm. LHOB 1520
Bio. 03/09/1962 • Meridian, ID • Boise State Univ.,
B.B.A., 1984; Boise State Univ., M.B.A., 1988 • Protestant
- Unspecified Christian • M. Kara Fulcher, 3 ch **Cmte.**
Education & Labor • Natural Resources
CoS. Cliff Bayer   **LD.** Andrew Neill
Sched. Daniel Tellez   **PS.** Alexah Rogge
Dist. Off. Meridian 208.888.3188

R: 369   **T:** 1st 63%
Elected Year: 2018

⚑ Rep. Mike K. Simpson (SIMP-suhn) R-ID-02 p 202.225.5531

Rm. RHOB 2084 **Web.** simpson.house.gov **f** 202.225.8216
Bio. 09/08/1950 • Burley, ID • Dentist; State Representative; Speaker of State House • Washington Univ. School of Dental Medicine (MO), D.D.S., 1977; Utah State Univ., B.S., 2002 • Mormon • M. Kathy Johnson Simpson **Cmte.** Appropriations
CoS. Lindsay J. Slater **LD.** Sarah Cannon
Sched. Emilee Henshaw **PS.** Nicole Wallace (CD)
Dist. Off. Boise 208.334.1953 • Idaho Falls 208.523.6701 • Twin Falls 208.734.7219

R: 62 **T:** 11th 61%
Elected Year: 1998

ILLINOIS

⚑ Governor J.B. Pritzker (PRIT-skur) p 217.782.0244

207 State House **C:** Springfield
Springfield, IL 62706 **P:** 12,741,080 (6)
Website illinois.gov **A:** 55,518.76 mi^2 (24th)
Fax 217.524.4049
Term Ends 2023

U.S. Senators
Dick Durbin, **D**
Tammy Duckworth, **D**
U.S. Representatives
01 / Bobby L. Rush, **D**
02 / Robin L. Kelly, **D**
03 / Daniel W. Lipinski, **D**
04 / Jesus G. Garcia, **D**
05 / Mike Quigley, **D**
06 / Sean Casten, **D**
07 / Danny K. Davis, **D**
08 / Raja Krishnamoorthi, **D**
09 / Jan D. Schakowsky, **D**
10 / Bradley S. Schneider, **D**
11 / Bill Foster, **D**
12 / Mike Bost, **R**
13 / Rodney L. Davis, **R**
14 / Lauren A. Underwood, **D**
15 / John M. Shimkus, **R**
16 / Adam D. Kinzinger, **R**
17 / Cheri L. Bustos, **D**
18 / Darin M. LaHood, **R**

⚑ Sen. Tammy Duckworth (DUK-wurth) D-IL-Jr. p 202.224.2854

Rm. HSOB 524 **f** 202.228.0618
Bio. 03/12/1968 • Bangkok, Thailand • Veterans Affairs • National Guard • Capella Univ. (MN), Ph.D.; Univ. of Hawaii, B.A., 1989; George Washington Univ. Elliot School of International Affairs (DC), M.A., 1992 • Unspecified/Other • M. Major Bryan Bowlsbey, 2 ch **Cmte.** Armed Services • Commerce, Science & Transportation • Environment & Public Works • Small Business & Entrepreneurship
CoS. Kaitlin Fahey **LD.** Ben Rhodeside
Sched. Kelsey Becker **PS.** Ben Garmisa
Dist. Off. Belleville 618.722.7070 • Carbondale 618.677.7000 • Chicago 312.886.3506 • Rock Island 309.606.7060 • Springfield 217.528.6124

R: 84 **T:** 1st 55%
Elected Year: 2016
Next Election: 2022

⚑ Sen. Dick Durbin (DUR-bin) D-IL-Sr. p 202.224.2152

Rm. HSOB 711 **Web.** durbin.senate.gov **f** 202.228.0400
Bio. 11/21/1944 • East St. Louis, IL • U.S. Representative; Attorney • Georgetown Univ. (DC), B.S., 1966; Georgetown Univ. Law Center (DC), J.D., 1969 • Roman Catholic • M. Loretta Schaefer Durbin, 3 ch (1 deceased); 3 gr-ch **Cmte.** Agriculture, Nutrition & Forestry • Appropriations • Judiciary • Rules & Administration
CoS. Patrick J. Souders **LD.** Corey Tellez
Sched. Claire A. Reuschel **PS.** Emily Hampsten
Dist. Off. Carbondale 618.351.1122 • Chicago 312.353.4952 • Rock Island 309.786.5173 • Springfield 217.492.4062

R: 10 **T:** 4th 54%
Elected Year: 1996
Next Election: 2020

ILLINOIS

Rep. Mike Bost (bahst)
R-IL-12   p 202.225.5661

Rm. LHOB 1440   **Web.** bost.house.gov   **f** 202.225.0285
Bio. 12/30/1960 • Murphysboro, IL • Southern Baptist •
M. Tracy Stanton Bost, 3 ch ; 11 gr-ch   **Cmte.** Agriculture •
Transportation & Infrastructure • Veterans' Affairs
CoS. Matt McCullough   **LD.** Mark Ratto
Sched. Tyler Cianciotti   **PS.** George O'Connor
Dist. Off. Alton 618.622.0766 • Carbondale 618.457.5787
• Granite City 618.622.0766 • Mt. Vernon 618.513.5294 •
O'Fallon 618.622.0766

R: 255   **T:** 3rd   52%
Elected Year: 2014

Rep. Cheri L. Bustos (BOO-stoass)
D-IL-17   p 202.225.5905

Rm. LHOB 1233   **Web.** bustos.house.gov   **f** 202.225.5396
Bio. 10/17/1961 • Springfield, IL • Univ. of Maryland -
College Park, B.A., 1983; Univ. of Illinois - Springfield, M.A.,
1985 • Roman Catholic • M. Gerry Bustos, 3 ch ; 2 gr-ch
Cmte. Agriculture • Appropriations
CoS. Jon S. Pyatt
Sched. Laura Piccioli   **PS.** Sean Higgins
Dist. Off. Peoria 309.966.1813 • Rock Island 309.786.3406
• Rockford 815.968.8011

R: 199   **T:** 4th   62%
Elected Year: 2012

Rep. Sean Casten (KASS-tuhn)
D-IL-06   p 202.225.4561

Rm. CHOB 429   **Web.** casten.house.gov
Bio. 11/23/1971 • Dublin, Ireland • Middlebury College
(VT), B.A., 1993; Dartmouth College, Hanover (NH), M.S.,
1998 • Unspecified/Other • M. Kara Casten, 2 ch   **Cmte.**
Financial Services • Science, Space & Technology • Select
Committee on the Climate Crisis
CoS. Ann Adler   **LD.** Calli Shapiro
Sched. Sameer Chintamani   **PS.** Maddie Carlos
Dist. Off. West Chicago

R: 355   **T:** 1st   54%
Elected Year: 2018

Rep. Danny K. Davis (DAY-vuhs)
D-IL-07   p 202.225.5006

Rm. RHOB 2159   **Web.** davis.house.gov   **f** 202.225.5641
Bio. 09/06/1941 • Parkdale, AR • Cook County
Commissioner; Alderman, Chicago City Council • Arkansas
Agricultural and Mechanical College, B.A., 1961; Chicago
State Univ. (IL), M.A., 1968; Union Institute and Univ., Ph.D.,
1977 • Baptist • M. Vera G. Davis, 2 ch (1 deceased); 4 gr-ch
(1 deceased)   **Cmte.** Ways & Means
CoS. Yul Edwards   **LD.** Jill Hunter-Williams
Sched. Josie Ware (CD)   **PS.** Ira Cohen (CD)
Dist. Off. Chicago 773.533.7520

R: 47   **T:** 12th   88%
Elected Year: 1996

Rep. Rodney L. Davis (DAY-vuhs)
R-IL-13   p 202.225.2371

Rm. LHOB 1740   **Web.**
rodneydavis.house.gov   **f** 202.226.0791
Bio. 01/05/1970 • Des Moines, IA • Millikin Univ. (IL), B.A.,
1992 • Roman Catholic • M. Shannon Davis, 3 ch   **Cmte.**
Administration • Agriculture • Commission Congressional
Mailing Standards • Select Committee on the Modernization
of Congress • Transportation & Infrastructure
CoS. Bret Manley   **LD.** Jimmy Ballard
Sched. Brianna Nagle   **PS.** Ashley Phelps
Dist. Off. Champaign 217.403.4690 • Decatur 217.791.6224
• Maryville 618.205.8660 • Normal 309.252.8834 •
Springfield 217.791.6224 • Taylorville 217.824.5117

R: 206   **T:** 4th   50%
Elected Year: 2012

Rep. Bill Foster (FAHSS-tur)
D-IL-11   p 202.225.3515

Rm. LHOB 2366   **Web.** foster.house.gov   **f** 202.225.9420
Bio. 10/07/1955 • Madison, WI • Physicist • Univ. of
Wisconsin, B.A., 1976; Harvard Univ., Ph.D., 1983 •
Unspecified/Other • M. Aesook Byon, 2 ch   **Cmte.** Financial
Services • Science, Space & Technology
CoS. Scott Shewcraft   **LD.** Samantha R. Warren
Sched. Diana Konate   **PS.** Mary Werden
Dist. Off. Aurora 630.585.7672 • Joliet 815.280.5876

R: 151   **T:** 6th   64%
Elected Year: 2012

⚑ Rep. Jesus G. Garcia (gar-SEE-uh)　　D-IL-04　　p 202.225.8203

Rm. CHOB 530 **Web.** chuygarcia.house.gov
Bio. 04/12/1956 • Durango, Mexico • Univ. of Illinois,
Chicago, B.A., 1999; Univ. of Illinois, Chicago, M.A., 2002 •
Catholic • M. Evelyn Garcia, 3 ch **Cmte.** Financial Services
• Transportation & Infrastructure
CoS. Kari Moe　　　　　　**LD.** Don Andres
　　　　　　　　　　　　PS. Fabiola Rodriguez-
　　　　　　　　　　　　Ciampoli
Dist. Off. Chicago 773.342.0774

R: 370　**T:** 1st 87%
Elected Year: 2018

⚑ Rep. Robin L. Kelly (KEH-lee)　　D-IL-02　　p 202.225.0773

Rm. RHOB 2416 **Web.** robinkelly.house.gov **f** 202.225.4583
Bio. 04/30/1956 • New York, NY • Bradley Univ., B.A., 1977;
Bradley Univ., M.A., 1982; Northern Illinois Univ., Ph.D., 2004
• Christian - Non-Denominational • M. Nathaniel Horn, 2 ch
Cmte. Energy & Commerce • Oversight & Reform
CoS. Brandon Webb　　　**LD.** Zachary Ostro
Sched. Jazmin Alvarez　　**PS.** James Lewis
Dist. Off. Chicago 773.321.2001 • Kankakee 708.679.0078
• Matteson 708.679.0078

R: 242　**T:** 4th 81%
Elected Year: 2013

⚑ Rep. Adam D. Kinzinger (KIN-zing-ur)　　R-IL-16　　p 202.225.3635

Rm. RHOB 2245 **Web.** kinzinger.house.gov **f** 202.225.3521
Bio. 02/27/1978 • Kankakee, IL • Air Force; Air National
Guard • Illinois State Univ., B.A., 2000; Illinois State
Univ., B.A., 2000 • Christian Church • S. **Cmte.** Energy &
Commerce • Foreign Affairs
CoS. Austin Weatherford　　**LD.** Michael Mansour
Sched. Katie Baird　　　　**PS.** Maura Gillespie
Dist. Off. Ottawa 815.431.9271 • Rockford 815.708.8032 •
Watseka 815.432.0580

R: 173　**T:** 5th 59%
Elected Year: 2010

⚑ Rep. Raja Krishnamoorthi (krish-nuh-MOR-thee) D-IL-08　p 202.225.3711

Rm. CHOB 115　　　　　　　　　**f** 202.225.7830
Bio. 07/19/1973 • New Delhi, IN • Princeton Univ. (NJ),
B.A., 1995; Harvard Univ., J.D., 2000 • Hinduism • M.
Priya Krishnamoorthi, 2 ch **Cmte.** Oversight & Reform •
Permanent Select on Intelligence
CoS. Mark Schauerte　　　**LD.** Brian Kaissi
Sched. Amol Shalia　　　　**PS.** Wilson Baldwin
Dist. Off. Schaumburg 847.413.1959

R: 319　**T:** 2nd 66%
Elected Year: 2016

⚑ Rep. Darin M. LaHood (luh-"HOOD")　　R-IL-18　　p 202.225.6201

Rm. LHOB 1424 **Web.** lahood.house.gov **f** 202.225.9249
Bio. 07/05/1968 • Peoria, IL • Loras College, B.A., 1990;
John Marshall Law School, J.D., 1997 • Catholic • M. Kristen
LaHood, 3 ch **Cmte.** Ways & Means
CoS. Steve Pfrang　　　　**LD.** Ashley Antoskiewicz
Sched. Alexis Alavi　　　　**PS.** John Rauber
Dist. Off. Bloomington 309.205.9556 • Jacksonville
217.245.1431 • Peoria 309.671.7027 • Springfield
217.670.1653

R: 287　**T:** 3rd 67%
Elected Year: 2015

⚑ Rep. Daniel W. Lipinski (lih-PIN-skee)　　D-IL-03　　p 202.225.5701

Rm. RHOB 2346 **Web.** lipinski.house.gov **f** 202.225.1012
Bio. 07/15/1966 • Chicago, IL • Professor; Congressional
Aide • Northwestern Univ., B.S., 1988; Stanford Univ. (CA),
M.S., 1989; Duke Univ. (NC), Ph.D., 1998 • Catholic • M. Judy
Berkebile Lipinski **Cmte.** Science, Space & Technology •
Transportation & Infrastructure
CoS. Eric Lausten　　　　**LD.** Sofya Leonova
Sched. Jennifer Lynn Sypolt　**PS.** Phil Davidson (CD)
Dist. Off. Chicago 773.948.6223 • Lockport 815.838.1990 •
Oak Lawn 708.424.0853 • Orland Park 708.403.4379

R: 98　**T:** 8th 73%
Elected Year: 2004

ILLINOIS

⋈ Rep. Mike Quigley (KWIG-lee) D-IL-05 p 202.225.4061
Rm. RHOB 2458 **Web.** quigley.house.gov **f** 202.225.5603
Bio. 10/17/1958 • Indianapolis, IN • Member, Cook County
Board of Commissioners • Roosevelt Univ. (IL), B.A., 1981;
Univ. of Chicago (IL), M.P.P., 1985; Loyola Univ. Law School
(IL), J.D., 1989 • Christian - Non-Denominational • M.
Barbara Quigley, 2 ch **Cmte.** Appropriations • Permanent
Select on Intelligence
CoS. Juan Hinojosa **LD.** Doug Lee
Sched. Isabella Spinozzi
Dist. Off. Chicago 773.267.5926

R: 144 **T:** 6th 77%
Elected Year: 2009

⋈ Rep. Bobby L. Rush (rush) D-IL-01 p 202.225.4372
Rm. RHOB 2188 **Web.** rush.house.gov **f** 202.226.0333
Bio. 11/23/1946 • Albany, GA • Minister; Chicago City
Councilman • Army 1963-68 • Roosevelt Univ. (IL), B.A.,
1973; Univ. of Illinois, Chicago, M.A., 1994; McCormick
Theological Seminary (IL), M.Th., 1998 • Baptist • M.
Carolyn Thomas Rush, 7 ch (1 deceased) **Cmte.** Energy &
Commerce
CoS. Yardly Pollas **LD.** Nishith Pandya
Sched. N. Lenette Myers **PS.** Ryan Johnson
Dist. Off. Chicago 773.779.2400

R: 32 **T:** 14th 74%
Elected Year: 1992

⋈ Rep. Jan D. Schakowsky (shuh-KOU-skee) D-IL-09 p 202.225.2111
Rm. RHOB 2367 **Web.** **f** 202.226.6890
schakowsky.house.gov
Bio. 05/26/1944 • Chicago, IL • Nonprofit Coordinator;
State Legislator • Univ. of Illinois, B.A., 1965 • Jewish • M.
Robert Creamer, 3 ch; 6 gr-ch **Cmte.** Budget • Energy &
Commerce
CoS. Robert N. Marcus **LD.** Sydney Terry
Sched. Kim Muzeroll **PS.** Guy Lee King
Dist. Off. Chicago 773.506.7100 • Evanston 847.328.3409 •
Glenview 847.328.3409

R: 61 **T:** 11th 74%
Elected Year: 1998

⋈ Rep. Bradley S. Schneider (SHNY-dur) D-IL-10 p 202.225.4835
Rm. LHOB 1432 **Web.** schneider.house.gov **f** 202.225.0837
Bio. 08/20/1961 • Denver, CO • Northwestern Univ.,
B.S., 1983; Kellogg Graduate School of Management,
Northwestern Univ. (IL), M.B.A., 1988 • Jewish • M. Julie
Dann, 2 ch **Cmte.** Small Business • Ways & Means
CoS. Casey O'Shea **LD.** Jessica Bernton
Sched. Claire Glezer **PS.** Steven Kirsch
Dist. Off. Lincolnshire 847.383.4870

R: 291 **T:** 3rd 66%
Elected Year: 2016

⋈ Rep. John M. Shimkus (SHIM-kuss) R-IL-15 p 202.225.527
Rm. RHOB 2217 **Web.** shimkus.house.gov **f** 202.225.5880
Bio. 02/21/1958 • Collinsville, IL • Teacher; Madison County
Treasurer • Army 1980-86 ; Army Reserve 1986-pres. •
U.S. Military Academy (NY), B.S., 1990; Southern Illinois
Univ., M.A., 1997 • Lutheran • M. Karen Muth Shimkus, 3 ch
Cmte. Energy & Commerce
CoS. Craig Roberts **LD.** Brian J. Looser
Sched. Molly Harris **PS.** Jordan Haverly
Dist. Off. Danville 217.446.0664 • Effingham 217.347.7947
• Harrisburg 618.252.8271 • Maryville 618.288.7190

R: 54 **T:** 12th 71%
Elected Year: 1996

⋈ Rep. Lauren A. Underwood (UN-dur-"wood") D-IL-14 p 202.225.297
Rm. LHOB 1118 **Web.** underwood.house.gov
Bio. 10/04/1986 • May?eld Heights, OH • Univ. of Michigan,
B.S., 2008; Johns Hopkins Univ., M.S.N., 2009; Johns
Hopkins Univ., M.PH, 2009; Johns Hopkins Univ., M.PH,
2009 • Christian Church • S. **Cmte.** Education & Labor •
Homeland Security • Veterans' Affairs
CoS. Andrea Harris **LD.** Alejandro Renteria
Sched. Ashley Clayton
Dist. Off. St. Charles 630.584.2734

R: 428 **T:** 1st 53%
Elected Year: 2018

INDIANA

Governor Eric Holcomb (HOL-kum)   p 317.232.4567

State House, Room 206   **C:** Indianapolis
Indianapolis, IN 46204   **P:** 6,691,878 (17)
Website in.gov   **A:** 35,826.02 mi^2 (38th)
Fax 317.232.3443
Term Ends 2021
Lt. Governor
Suzanne Crouch, **R**

INDIANA

U.S. Senators
Todd C. Young, **R**
Mike Braun, **R**
U.S. Representatives
01 / Pete J. Visclosky, **D**
02 / Jackie Swihart Walorski, **R**
03 / Jim E. Banks, **R**
04 / Jim Baird, **R**
05 / Susan W. Brooks, **R**
06 / Gregory Pence, **R**
07 / Andre D. Carson, **D**
08 / Larry D. Bucshon, **R**
09 / Trey Hollingsworth, **R**

Sen. Mike Braun ("brown")   R-IN-Jr.   p 202.224.4814

Rm. RSOB B85 **Web.** braun.senate.gov
Bio. 03/24/1954 • Jasper, IN • Wabash College (IN), B.A.,
1976; Harvard Univ., M.B.A., 1978; Jasper, M.B.A., 1978 •
Catholic • M. Braun Braun, 4 ch **Cmte.** Aging • Agriculture,
Nutrition & Forestry • Budget • Environment & Public Works
• Health, Education, Labor & Pensions
CoS. Josh Kelley   **LD.** Katie Bailey
Sched. Jessica Wedgewood **PS.** Jahan Wilcox
Dist. Off.   Evansville 317.822.8240 • Fort Wayne
260.427.2164 • Hammond 219.937.9650 • Indianapolis
317.822.8240 • South Bend 574.288.6302

R: 98 T: 0th 51%
Elected Year: 2018
Next Election: 2024

Sen. Todd C. Young (yung)   R-IN-Sr.   p 202.224.5623

Rm. RSOB 400 **Web.** young.senate.gov
Bio. 08/24/1972 • Lancaster, PA • Attorney • Marine Corps,
1990-2000 • U.S. Naval Academy (MD), B.S., 1995; Univ.
of Chicago's Graduate School of Business, M.B.A., 2000;
Univ. of London's Institute of U.S. Studies, M.A., 2001;
Indiana Univ. Law School, J.D., 2006 • Christian Church
• M. Jennifer B. Young, 4 ch **Cmte.** Commerce, Science
& Transportation • Finance • Foreign Relations • Small
Business & Entrepreneurship
CoS. John Connell   **LD.** Adam Hechavarria
Sched. Lindsay McDonough **PS.** Amy Grappone
Dist. Off.   Evansville 812.288.3999 • Fort Wayne
260.422.7397 • Indianapolis 317.226.6700 • New Albany
812.542.4820

R: 89 T: 1st 52%
Elected Year: 2016
Next Election: 2022

Rep. Jim Baird (baird)   R-IN-04   p 202.225.5037
                                                              f 202.226.0544
Rm. CHOB 532 **Web.** baird.house.gov
Bio. 06/04/1945 • Covington, IN • Purdue Univ. (IN), B.S.,
1967; Purdue Univ. (IN), M.S., 1969; Purdue Univ. (IN),
M.S., 1969; Univ. of Kentucky, Ph.D., 1975 • Methodist • M.
Denise Baird, 3 ch **Cmte.** Agriculture • Science, Space &
Technology
CoS. Ashlee Vinyard   **LD.** Sarah Czufin
Sched. Alyssa Jennings
Dist. Off.   Greencastle 765.653.5321

: 352 T: 1st 64%
Elected Year: 2018

INDIANA

Rep. Jim E. Banks (banks) — R-IN-03 — p 202.225.4436

Rm. LHOB 1713 **Web.** banks.house.gov **f** 202.226.9870
Bio. 07/16/1979 • Columbia City, IN • Indiana Univ.,
Bloomington, Bach. Deg., 2004; Grace College, M.B.A., 2013
• Evangelical • M. Amanda Banks, 3 ch **Cmte.** Armed
Services • Education & Labor • Veterans' Affairs
CoS. David Keller **LD.** Amy Surber
Sched. Nicole Keesling **PS.** T.W. Arrighi
Dist. Off. Fort Wayne 260.702.4750

R: 294 **T:** 2nd 65%
Elected Year: 2016

Rep. Susan W. Brooks ("brooks") — R-IN-05 — p 202.225.2276

Rm. LHOB 2211 **Web.** **f** 202.225.0016
susanwbrooks.house.gov
Bio. 08/25/1960 • Ft. Wayne, IN • Miami Univ. of Ohio, B.A.,
1982; Indiana Univ. Law School, Indianapolis, J.D., 1985 •
Roman Catholic • M. David M. Brooks, 2 ch **Cmte.** Energy
& Commerce • Select Committee on the Modernization of
Congress
CoS. Megan Savage **LD.** Kristina Dunklin
PS. Rebecca Card
Dist. Off. Anderson 765.640.5115 • Carmel 317.848.0201

R: 197 **T:** 4th 57%
Elected Year: 2012

Rep. Larry D. Bucshon (boo-SHAHN) — R-IN-08 — p 202.225.4636

Rm. RHOB 2313 **Web.** bucshon.house.gov **f** 202.225.3284
Bio. 05/31/1962 • Taylorsville, IL • Heart Surgeon • Navy
Reserve, 1989-98 • Univ. of Illinois - Urbana, B.S., 1984; Univ.
of Illinois Medical School - Chicago, M.D., 1988 • Lutheran •
M. Kathryn Bucshon, 4 ch **Cmte.** Energy & Commerce
CoS. Kyle Jackson
Sched. Jessica Graff **PS.** Andrew Hansen
Dist. Off. Evansville 812.465.6484 • Jasper 812.482.4255 •
Terre Haute 812.232.0523 • Vincennes 855.519.1629

R: 155 **T:** 5th 64%
Elected Year: 2010

Rep. Andre D. Carson (KAR-suhn) — D-IN-07 — p 202.225.4011

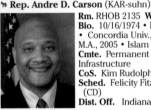

Rm. RHOB 2135 **Web.** carson.house.gov **f** 202.225.5633
Bio. 10/16/1974 • Indianapolis, IN • Marketing Executive
• Concordia Univ., B.S., 2003; Indiana Wesleyan Univ.,
M.A., 2005 • Islam (Muslim) • M. Mariama Carson, 1 ch
Cmte. Permanent Select on Intelligence • Transportation &
Infrastructure
CoS. Kim Rudolph
Sched. Felicity Fitzpatrick **PS.** Copeland Tucker
(CD)
Dist. Off. Indianapolis 317.283.6516

R: 126 **T:** 7th 65%
Elected Year: 2008

Rep. Trey Hollingsworth III (HAH-lingz-wurth) — R-IN-09 — p 202.225.5315

Rm. LHOB 1641 **Web.** **f** 202.226.6866
hollingsworth.house.gov
Bio. 09/12/1983 • Clinton, TN • Univ. of Pennsylvania,
B.S.E., 2004; Georgetown Univ. (DC), M.P.P., 2014 • Christian
Church • M. Kelly Hollingsworth, 1 ch **Cmte.** Financial
Services
CoS. Rebecca Shaw **LD.** Connor Lentz
Sched. Marie Policastro **PS.** Katie Webster
Dist. Off. Franklin 317.851.8710 • Jeffersonville
812.288.3999

R: 315 **T:** 2nd 57%
Elected Year: 2016

Rep. Gregory Pence (pence) — R-IN-06 — p 202.225.302

Rm. CHOB 222 **Web.** pence.house.gov
Bio. 11/04/1956 • Columbus, IN • Loyola Univ. Chicago
(IL), Bach. Deg., 1981; Loyola Univ. Chicago (IL), M.B.A.,
1986 • Catholic • M. Denice Pence, 4 ch ; 5 gr-ch **Cmte.**
Foreign Affairs • Transportation & Infrastructure
CoS. Kyle Robertson **LD.** Hillary Lassiter
Sched. Katherine Hill **PS.** Ted Goodman
Dist. Off. Columbus 812.799.5230

R: 401 **T:** 1st 64%
Elected Year: 2018

Rep. Pete J. Visclosky (vis-KLAWS-kee)   D-IN-01   p 202.225.2461

Rm. RHOB 2328 **Web.** visclosky.house.gov   **f** 202.225.2493
Bio. 08/13/1949 • Gary, IN • Congressional/Committee
Staffer; Attorney • Indiana Univ. Northwest, B.S., 1970; Univ.
of Notre Dame Law School (IN), J.D., 1973; Georgetown
Univ. Law Center (DC), LL.M., 1982 • Roman Catholic • M.
Joanne Royce, 2 ch **Cmte.** Appropriations
CoS. Joe DeVooght   **LD.** Seth Engdahl
Sched. Korry Baack   **PS.** Kevin Spicer
Dist. Off. Merrillville 219.795.1844

R: 7 **T:** 18th 65%
Elected Year: 1984

Rep. Jackie Swihart Walorski (wah-LOR-skee) R-IN-02   p 202.225.3915

Rm. CHOB 419 **Web.** walorski.house.gov   **f** 202.225.6798
Bio. 08/17/1963 • South Bend, IN • Taylor Univ. (IN), B.A.,
1985 • Assembly of God • M. Dean Swihart **Cmte.** Ethics •
Ways & Means
CoS. Mike Dankler   **LD.** Martin Schultz
Sched. Faith Ammen   **PS.** Jack Morrissey
Dist. Off. Mishawaka 574.204.2645 • Rochester
574.223.4373

R: 237 **T:** 4th 55%
Elected Year: 2012

IOWA

Governor Kim Reynolds (REH-nuhldz)   p 515.281.5211

State Capitol   **C:** Des Moines
1007 E. Grand Ave.   **P:** 3,156,145 (32)
Des Moines, IA 50319   **A:** 55,856.99 mi² (23rd)
Website iowa.gov
Fax 515.725.3527
Term Ends 2019
Lt. Governor
Adam Gregg, R

U.S. Senators
Chuck Grassley, R
Joni K. Ernst, R
U.S. Representatives
01 / Abby Finkenauer, D
02 / Dave W. Loebsack, D
03 / Cindy Axne, D
04 / Steve A. King, R

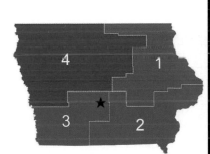

Sen. Joni K. Ernst (urnst)   R-IA-Jr.   p 202.224.3254

Rm. HSOB 730 **Web.** ernst.senate.gov   **f** 202.224.9369
Bio. 07/01/1970 • Red Oak, IA • Iowa State Univ. (IA), B.S.,
1992; Columbus College (IA), M.P.A., 1995 • Lutheran • D.
Gail Ernst, 1 ch ; 2 stepch **Cmte.** Agriculture, Nutrition &
Forestry • Armed Services • Environment & Public Works •
Judiciary • Small Business & Entrepreneurship
CoS. Lisa Smittcamp Goeas **LD.** Jena Baker McNeill
Sched. Josie Beecher   **PS.** Kelsi Daniell
Dist. Off. Cedar Rapids 319.365.4504 • Council Bluffs
712.352.1167 • Davenport 563.322.0677 • Des Moines
515.284.4574 • Sioux City 712.252.1550

: 79 **T:** 1st 52%
Elected Year: 2014
Next Election: 2020

IOWA

⚑ Sen. Chuck Grassley (GRASS-lee) R-IA-Sr. p 202.224.3744

Rm. HSOB 135 **Web.** grassley.senate.gov **f** 202.224.6020
Bio. 09/17/1933 • New Hartford, IA • U.S. Representative; Farmer • Univ. of Northern Iowa, B.A., 1955; Univ. of Northern Iowa, M.A., 1956 • Baptist • M. Barbara Ann Speicher Grassley, 5 ch **Cmte.** Agriculture, Nutrition & Forestry • Budget • Finance • Joint Taxation • Judiciary
CoS. Aaron Cummings **LD.** James Rice
Sched. Jennifer Heins **PS.** Michael Zona
Dist. Off. Cedar Rapids 319.363.6832 • Council Bluffs 712.322.7103 • Davenport 563.322.4331 • Des Moines 515.288.1145 • Sioux City 712.233.1860 • Waterloo 319.232.6657
R: 2 **T:** 7th 60%
Elected Year: 1980
Next Election: 2022

⚑ Rep. Cindy Axne (AKSS-nee) D-IA-03 p 202.225.5476

Rm. CHOB 330 **Web.** axne.house.gov
Bio. 04/20/1965 • Des Moines, IA • Univ. of Iowa, B.A., 1987; Northwestern Univ., M.B.A., 2002 • Catholic • M. John Axne, 2 ch **Cmte.** Agriculture • Financial Services
CoS. Joe Diver **LD.** Denise Fleming
Sched. Amanda Shepherd **PS.** Madeleine Russak
Dist. Off. West Des Moines 515.518.0384
R: 351 **T:** 1st 49%
Elected Year: 2018

⚑ Rep. Abby Finkenauer (FINK-eh-nou-ur) D-IA-01 p 202.225.2911

Rm. CHOB 124
Bio. 12/27/1988 • Dubuque, IA • Drake Univ. (IA), Bach. Deg., 2013 • Catholic • S. **Cmte.** Small Business • Transportation & Infrastructure
CoS. Elizabeth Kerr **LD.** Tyler C. Wilson
Sched. Angela Smith **PS.** Jessica Gail
Dist. Off. Dubuque
R: 367 **T:** 1st 51%
Elected Year: 2018

⚑ Rep. Steve A. King (king) R-IA-04 p 202.225.4426

Rm. RHOB 2210 **Web.** steveking.house.gov **f** 202.225.3193
Bio. 05/28/1949 • Storm Lake, IA • Business Owner; State Senator • Roman Catholic • M. Marilyn King, 3 ch ; 7 gr-ch
CoS. Sarah Stevens **LD.** Suanne Edmiston
Sched. Casaday Loomis **PS.** John Kennedy (CD)
Dist. Off. Ames 515.232.2885 • Fort Dodge 515.573.2738 • Mason City 641.201.1624 • Sioux City 712.224.4692 • Spencer 712.580.7754
R: 80 **T:** 9th 50%
Elected Year: 2002

⚑ Rep. Dave W. Loebsack (LOBE-sak) D-IA-02 p 202.225.657

Rm. LHOB 1211 **Web.** loebsack.house.gov **f** 202.226.075
Bio. 12/23/1952 • Sioux City, IA • Professor • Iowa State Univ. (IA), B.S., 1974; Iowa State Univ. (IA), M.A., 1976; Univ. of California, Ph.D., 1985 • Methodist • M. Teresa Loebsack, 2 ch (2 from previous marriage); 2 stepch ; 3 gr-ch **Cmte.** Energy & Commerce
CoS. Eric Todd Witte **LD.** Scott Stockwell
Sched. Katie Murray
Dist. Off. Davenport 563.323.5988 • Iowa City 319.351.078
R: 116 **T:** 7th 55%
Elected Year: 2006

KANSAS

KANSAS

⚑ Governor Laura Kelly (KEH-lee) p 785.296.323

Kansas State Capitol **C:** Topeka
300 S.W. Tenth Ave., Suite 241-S **P:** 2,911,505 (36)
Topeka, KS 66612 **A:** 81,758.64 mi^2 (13th)
Website kansas.gov
Fax 785.296.7973
Term Ends 2023
Lt. Governor
Lynn Rogers, **D**

U.S. Senators
Pat Roberts, **R**
Jerry Moran, **R**
U.S. Representatives
01 / Roger W. Marshall, **R**
02 / Steve Watkins, **R**
03 / Sharice Davids, **D**
04 / Ron Estes, **R**

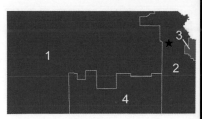

⚑ Sen. Jerry Moran (moor-AHN) R-KS-Jr. p 202.224.6521

f 202.228.6966

Rm. DSOB 521
Bio. 05/29/1954 • Great Bend, KS • State Senator; Attorney • Univ. of Kansas, B.S., 1976; Univ. of Kansas, J.D., 1981 • Methodist • M. Robba Addison Moran, 2 ch **Cmte.** Appropriations • Banking, Housing & Urban Affairs • Commerce, Science & Transportation • Indian Affairs • Veterans' Affairs

CoS. Brennen Britton	**LD.** Thomas Bush
Sched. Emily Whitfield	**PS.** Tom Brandt

Dist. Off. Hays 785.628.6401 • Manhattan 785.539.8973 • Olathe 913.393.0711 • Pittsburg 620.232.2286 • Wichita 316.269.9257

R: 46 **T:** 2nd 62%
Elected Year: 2010
Next Election: 2022

⚑ Sen. Pat Roberts (RAH-burts) R-KS-Sr. p 202.224.4774

Rm. HSOB 109 **Web.** roberts.senate.gov f 202.224.3514
Bio. 04/20/1936 • Topeka, KS • U.S. Representative; Journalist • Marine Corps 1958-62 • Kansas State Univ., B.A., 1958 • Methodist • M. Frankie Fann Roberts, 3 ch ; 5 gr-ch **Cmte.** Agriculture, Nutrition & Forestry • Ethics • Finance • Health, Education, Labor & Pensions • Rules & Administration

CoS. Jackie Cottrell	**LD.** Amber Kirchhoefer
Sched. Jensine Moyer	**PS.** Sarah Little

Dist. Off. Dodge City 620.227.2244 • Overland Park 913.451.9343 • Topeka 785.295.2745 • Wichita 316.263.0416

R: 9 **T:** 4th 53%
Elected Year: 1996
Next Election: 2020

⚑ Rep. Sharice Davids (DAY-vidz) D-KS-03 p 202.225.2865

Rm. LHOB 1541 **Web.** davids.house.gov
Bio. 05/22/1980 • Frankfurt, Germany • Univ. of Missouri, B.A., 2007; Cornell Univ. Law School (NY), J.D., 2010 • Unspecified/Other • S. **Cmte.** Small Business • Transportation & Infrastructure

CoS. Allison Teixeira	**LD.** Brandon Naylor

Dist. Off. Shawnee

R: 363 **T:** 1st 54%
Elected Year: 2018

⚑ Rep. Ron Estes (ESS-tess) R-KS-04 p 202.225.6216

Rm. LHOB 1524 **Web.** estes.house.gov f 202.225.3489
Bio. 07/19/1956 • Topeka, KS • Tennessee Technological Univ., B.S.; Tennessee Technological Univ., M.B.A. • Lutheran • M. Susan Oliver, 3 ch **Cmte.** Ways & Means

CoS. Josh Bell	**LD.** Nicholas O'Boyle
Sched. Brandon Smith	**PS.** Greg Steele

Dist. Off. Wichita 316.262.8992

: 335 **T:** 2nd 59%
Elected Year: 2017

⚑ Rep. Roger W. Marshall (MAR-shull) R-KS-01 p 202.225.2715

Rm. CHOB 312 **Web.** marshall.house.gov
Bio. 08/09/1960 • El Dorado, KS • Butler Community College, A.S., 1980; Kansas State Univ., Bach. Deg., 1982; Univ. of Kansas, M.D., 1987 • Christian Church • M. Laina Marshall, 4 ch ; 1 gr-ch **Cmte.** Agriculture • Science, Space & Technology

CoS. Brent Robertson	**LD.** Michael Brooks
Sched. Madeline Gale	**PS.** Charyssa Parent

Dist. Off. Garden City 620.765.7800 • Salina 785.829.9000

: 322 **T:** 2nd 68%
Elected Year: 2016

KANSAS

⚑ Rep. Steve Watkins (WAHT-kinz) R-KS-02 p 202.225.6601

Rm. LHOB 1205 **Web.** watkins.house.gov
Bio. 09/18/1976 • Lackland Air Force Base, TX •
U.S. Military Academy - West Point (NY), B.S., 1999;
Massachusetts Institute of Technology, M.R.P., 2010; Harvard
Univ., M.P.A., 2017 • Methodist • M. **Cmte.** Education &
Labor • Foreign Affairs • Veterans' Affairs
CoS. Colin C. Brainard   **LD.** Adam York
Sched. Kayla Herron   **PS.** Jim Joice
Dist. Off. Pittsburg 620.231.5966 • Topeka 785.234.5966

R: 431 **T:** 1st 48%
Elected Year: 2018

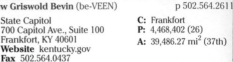

KENTUCKY

⚑ Governor Matthew Griswold Bevin (be-VEEN) p 502.564.2611

State Capitol
700 Capitol Ave., Suite 100
Frankfort, KY 40601
Website kentucky.gov
Fax 502.564.0437
Term Ends 2019
Lt. Governor
Jenean Hampton, R

C: Frankfort
P: 4,468,402 (26)
A: 39,486.27 mi^2 (37th)

U.S. Senators
Mitch McConnell, R
Rand Paul, R
U.S. Representatives
01 / James R. Comer, R
02 / Brett Guthrie, R
03 / John A. Yarmuth, D
04 / Thomas H. Massie, R
05 / Hal D. Rogers, R
06 / Andy Barr, R

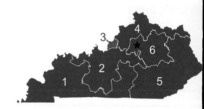

⚑ Sen. Mitch McConnell (mih-KAH-null) R-KY-Sr. p 202.224.254

Rm. RSOB 317 **Web.** mcconnell.senate.gov **f** 202.224.2499
Bio. 02/20/1942 • Tuscumbia, AL • Deputy Assistant
Attorney General (President Ford) • Univ. of Kentucky
Law School, J.D., 1960; Univ. of Louisville (KY), B.A., 1964
• Baptist • M. Elaine Chao, 3 ch from previous marriage
Cmte. Agriculture, Nutrition & Forestry • Appropriations •
Rules & Administration
CoS. Philip Maxson   **LD.** Katelyn Bunning
                           PS. Robert Steurer
Dist. Off. Bowling Green 270.781.1673 • Fort Wright
859.578.0188 • Lexington 859.224.8286 • London
606.864.2026 • Louisville 502.582.6304 • Paducah
270.442.4554

R: 3 **T:** 6th 56%
Elected Year: 1984
Next Election: 2020

⚑ Sen. Rand Paul (pall) R-KY-Jr. p 202.224.434

Rm. RSOB 167 **Web.** paul.senate.gov **f** 202.228.691
Bio. 01/07/1963 • Pittsburgh, PA • Duke Univ. (NC),
M.D., 1988 • Presbyterian • M. Kelley Paul, 3 ch **Cmte.**
Foreign Relations • Health, Education, Labor & Pensions •
Homeland Security & Government Affairs • Small Business
& Entrepreneurship
CoS. William Henderson   **LD.** Brandon Brooker
Sched. Drake Henle   **PS.** Sergio Gor
Dist. Off. Bowling Green 270.782.8303 • Louisville
502.582.5341

R: 53 **T:** 2nd 57%
Elected Year: 2010
Next Election: 2022

⚑ Rep. Andy Barr IV (bar) R-KY-06 p 202.225.470

Rm. RHOB 2430 **Web.** barr.house.gov **f** 202.225.212
Bio. 07/24/1973 • Lexington, KY • Univ. of Virginia,
B.A., 1996; Univ. of Kentucky College of Law, J.D., 2001
• Episcopalian • M. Eleanor Carol Leavell, 2 ch **Cmte.**
Financial Services • Veterans' Affairs
CoS. Mary Rosado
Sched. Gabriela Spence   **PS.** Paige Rusher
Dist. Off. Lexington 859.219.1366

R: 194 **T:** 4th 51%
Elected Year: 2012

⚑ Rep. James R. Comer Jr. (KOAM-ur)   R-KY-01   p 202.225.3115

Rm. LHOB 1037   **f** 202.225.3547
Bio. 08/19/1972 • Carthage, TN • Western Kentucky Univ.,
B.S., 1993 • Baptist • M. Tamera Jo, 3 ch **Cmte.** Agriculture
• Education & Labor • Oversight & Reform
CoS. Caroline Cash   **LD.** James Goldenstein
Sched. Kaity Wolfe   **PS.** Michael Gossum (CD)
Dist. Off. Paducah 270.408.1865 • Tompkinsville
270.487.9509

R: 289   **T:** 3rd 69%
Elected Year: 2016

⚑ Rep. Brett Guthrie (GUH-three)   R-KY-02   p 202.225.3501

Rm. RHOB 2434 **Web.** guthrie.house.gov   **f** 202.226.2019
Bio. 02/18/1964 • Florence, AL • State Legislator • Army
• U.S. Military Academy (NY), B.S., 1987; Yale Univ. (CT),
M.P.A., 1997 • Church of Christ • M. Elizabeth Clemons, 3 ch
Cmte. Education & Labor • Energy & Commerce
CoS. Eric Bergren

                               PS. Lauren Gaydos
Dist. Off. Bowling Green 270.842.9896 • Owensboro
270.842.9896 • Radcliff 270.842.9896

R: 131   **T:** 6th 67%
Elected Year: 2008

⚑ Rep. Thomas H. Massie (MASS-ee)   R-KY-04   p 202.225.3465

Rm. RHOB 2453 **Web.** massie.house.gov   **f** 202.225.0003
Bio. 01/13/1971 • Huntington, WV • Massachusetts
Institute of Technology, B.S., 1993; Massachusetts Institute
of Technology, M.M.E., 1996 • Methodist • M. Rhonda
Massie, 4 ch **Cmte.** Oversight & Reform • Transportation &
Infrastructure
CoS. John Ferland   **LD.** Seana Cranston
Sched. Megan Buckham   **PS.** Laura Lington
Dist. Off. Ashland 606.324.9898 • Crescent Springs
859.426.0080 • LaGrange 502.265.9119

R: 191   **T:** 5th 62%
Elected Year: 2012

⚑ Rep. Hal D. Rogers (RAH-jurz)   R KY 05   p 202.225.4601

Rm. RHOB 2406 **Web.** halrogers.house.gov   **f** 202.225.0940
Bio. 12/31/1937 • Barrier, KY • Commonwealth's
Attorney • Kentucky and North Carolina National Guards
1956-63 • Univ. of Kentucky, Bach. Deg., 1962; Univ. of
Kentucky College of Law, J.D., 1964 • Baptist • M. Cynthia
Doyle Rogers, 3 ch (from a previous marriage) **Cmte.**
Appropriations
CoS. Megan Bell   **LD.** Jakob Johnsen
Sched. Sarah Brown   **PS.** Danielle Smoot (CD)
Dist. Off. Hazard 606.439.0794 • Prestonsburg
606.886.0844 • Somerset 606.679.8346

R: 3   **T:** 20th 79%
Elected Year: 1980

⚑ Rep. John A. Yarmuth (YAR-muhth)   D-KY-03   p 202.225.5401

Rm. CHOB 402 **Web.** yarmuth.house.gov   **f** 202.225.5776
Bio. 11/04/1947 • Louisville, KY • Newspaper Publisher •
Yale Univ. (CT), B.A., 1969 • Jewish • M. Catherine Yarmuth,
1 ch **Cmte.** Budget
CoS. Julie Carr   **LD.** Katy Rowley
Sched. Claire Elliott   **PS.** Christopher Schuler
Dist. Off. Louisville 502.582.5129 • Louisville 502.933.5863

R: 123   **T:** 7th 62%
Elected Year: 2006

LOUISIANA

⚑ Governor John Bel Edwards (EHD-wurdz)   p 225.342.7015

PO Box 94004   **C:** Baton Rouge
Baton Rouge, LA 70804-9004   **P:** 4,659,978 (25)
Website louisiana.gov   **A:** 43,204.04 mi^2 (33rd)
Fax 225.342.7099
Term Ends 2020
Lt. Governor
Billy Nungesser, R

LOUISIANA

U.S. Senators
Bill Cassidy, **R**
John N. Kennedy, **R**
U.S. Representatives
01 / Steve J. Scalise, **R**
02 / Cedric L. Richmond, **D**
03 / Clay Higgins, **R**
04 / Mike Johnson, **R**
05 / Ralph L. Abraham, **R**
06 / Garret N. Graves, **R**

⚑ Sen. Bill Cassidy (KA-sih-dee)　　　R-LA-Sr.　　p 202.224.5824

Rm. HSOB 520　**Web.** cassidy.senate.gov　**f** 202.224.9735
Bio. 09/28/1957 • Highland Park, IL • State Legislator
• Louisiana State Univ., B.S., 1979; Louisiana State
Univ. Medical School, M.D., 1983 • Christian - Non-
Denominational • M. Laura Layden Cassidy, 3 ch **Cmte.**
Energy & Natural Resources • Finance • Health, Education,
Labor & Pensions • Joint Economic • Veterans' Affairs
CoS. James Quinn　　　**LD.** Christopher D. Gillott
Sched. Zoe Aguillard　　**PS.** Matt D. Wolking
Dist. Off. Alexandria 318.448.7176 • Baton Rouge
225.929.7711 • Lafayette 337.261.1400 • Lake Charles
337.277.5398 • Metairie 504.838.0130 • Monroe
318.324.2111 • Shreveport 318.798.3215

R: 71　**T:** 1st 56%
Elected Year: 2014
Next Election: 2020

⚑ Sen. John N. Kennedy (KEH-nuh-dee)　　R-LA-Jr.　　p 202.224.4623

Rm. RSOB 416　**Web.** kennedy.senate.gov　**f** 202.228.0447
Bio. 11/21/1951 • Centreville, MS • Vanderbilt Univ. (TN),
B.A., 1973; Univ. of Virginia School of Law, J.D., 1977; Oxford
Univ. (England), B.CL, 1979 • Methodist • M. Rebecca Stulb
Kennedy, 1 ch **Cmte.** Appropriations • Banking, Housing
& Urban Affairs • Budget • Judiciary • Small Business &
Entrepreneurship
CoS. Preston Robinson　　**LD.** John Steitz
Sched. Kristin Sapperstein　**PS.** Michelle Millhollon
Dist. Off. Baton Rouge 225.926.8033 • Houma •
Lafayette 337.269.5980 • Lake Charles • Mandeville
• Monroe 318.361.1489 • New Orleans 504.581.6190 •
Shreveport 318.670.5192

R: 87　**T:** 1st 61%
Elected Year: 2016
Next Election: 2022

⚑ Rep. Ralph L. Abraham Jr. (AY-bruh-ham)　　R-LA-05　　p 202.225.8490

Rm. CHOB 417　**Web.** abraham.house.gov　**f** 202.225.5639
Bio. 09/16/1954 • Alto, LA • Mangham High School (LA),
D.V.M., 1972; Louisiana State Univ., Bach. Deg., 1978;
Louisiana State Univ. School of Veterinary Medicine, D.V.M.,
1980; Louisiana State Univ. School of Medicine, M.D., 1994
• Baptist • M. Dianne Abraham, 3 ch **Cmte.** Agriculture •
Armed Services
CoS. Luke Letlow　　　**LD.** Ted Verrill
Sched. Emma Herrock　　**PS.** Cole Avery
Dist. Off. Alexandria 318.445.0818 • Monroe 318.322.3500
• St. Francisville 985.516.5858

R: 250　**T:** 3rd 67%
Elected Year: 2014

⚑ Rep. Garret N. Graves (grayvz)　　　R-LA-06　　p 202.225.3901

Rm. RHOB 2402　**Web.**　　　**f** 202.225.7313
garretgraves.house.gov
Bio. 01/31/1972 • Baton Rouge, LA • Roman Catholic
• M. Carissa Graves, 3 ch **Cmte.** Natural Resources •
Select Committee on the Climate Crisis • Transportation &
Infrastructure
CoS. Paul Sawyer　　　**LD.** Maggie Ayrea
Sched. Allison Hagan　　**PS.** Chelbi Johnson (CD)
Dist. Off. Baton Rouge 225.442.1731 • Livingston
225.686.4413 • Thibodaux 985.448.4103

R: 263　**T:** 3rd 70%
Elected Year: 2014

LOUISIANA

🏴 **Rep. Clay Higgins** (HIH-guhnz) R-LA-03 p 202.225.2031

Rm. CHOB 424 **Web.** clayhiggins.house.gov **f** 202.225.5724
Bio. 08/24/1961 • New Orleans, LA • Christian - Non-
Denominational • M. Becca Higgins, 4 ch (1 deceased)
Cmte. Homeland Security • Oversight & Reform
CoS. Kathee Facchiano **LD.** Ward Cormier
Sched. Jordan Lane **PS.** Andrew J. David
Dist. Off. Lafayette 337.703.6105 • Lake Charles
337.656.2833

R: 314 **T:** 2nd 56%
Elected Year: 2016

🏴 **Rep. Mike Johnson** (JAHN-suhn) R-LA-04 p 202.225.2777

Rm. CHOB 418 **Web.** **f** 202.225.8039
mikejohnson.house.gov
Bio. 01/30/1972 • Shreveport, LA • Louisiana State Univ.,
B.S., 1995; Louisiana State Univ. Law School, J.D., 1998 •
Southern Baptist • M. Kelly Lary Johnson, 4 ch **Cmte.**
Judiciary • Natural Resources
CoS. Hayden Haynes **LD.** Brad Morris
Sched. Ruth Ward **PS.** Ainsley Holyfield
Dist. Off. Bossier City 318.840.0309 • Leesville
337.392.3146 • Natchitoches 318.357.5731

R: 317 **T:** 2nd 64%
Elected Year: 2016

🐾 **Rep. Cedric L. Richmond** (RICH-muhnd) D-LA-02 p 202.225.6636

Rm. CHOB 506 **Web.** richmond.house.gov **f** 202.225.1988
Bio. 09/13/1973 • New Orleans, LA • Morehouse College
(GA), B.A., 1995; Tulane Univ. (LA), J.D., 1998 • Baptist •
M. Raquel Greenup, 1 ch **Cmte.** Homeland Security •
Judiciary
CoS. Virgil Miller **LD.** Peter Hunter
PS. Jalina Porter
Dist. Off. Baton Rouge 225.636.5600 • Gretna 504.365.0390
• New Orleans 504.288.3777

R: 177 **T:** 5th 81%
Elected Year: 2010

🏴 **Rep. Steve J. Scalise** (skuh-LEESS) R-LA-01 p 202.225.3015

Rm. RHOB 2049 **Web.** scalise.house.gov **f** 202.226.0386
Bio. 10/06/1965 • New Orleans, LA • State Legislator •
Louisiana State Univ., B.S., 1989; Louisiana State Univ., D.S.,
1989 • Catholic • M. Jennifer Letulle Scalise, 2 ch **Cmte.**
Energy & Commerce
CoS. Megan Bel Miller **LD.** Geoffrey Green
Sched. Ellen Gosnell
Dist. Off. Hammond 985.340.2185 • Houma 985.879.2300
• Mandeville 985.893.9064 • Metairie 504.837.1259

R: 128 **T:** 7th 72%
Elected Year: 2008

MAINE

🏴 **Governor Janet Mills** (millz) p 207.287.3531

One State House Station **C:** Augusta
Augusta, ME 04333-0001 **P:** 1,338,404 (43)
Website maine.gov **A:** 30,842.99 mi^2 (39th)
Fax 207.287.1034
Term Ends 2023

MAINE

MAINE

U.S. Senators
Susan M. Collins, **R**
Angus S. King, **I**
U.S. Representatives
01 / Chellie M. Pingree, **D**
02 / Jared F. Golden, **D**

☙ Sen. Susan M. Collins (KAH-luhnz) R-ME-Sr. p 202.224.2523

Rm. DSOB 413 **Web.** collins.senate.gov **f** 202.224.2693
Bio. 12/07/1952 • Caribou, ME • Association Director; Small
Business Administration Director • St. Lawrence Univ.
(NY), B.A., 1975 • Roman Catholic • M. Thomas Daffron
Cmte. Aging • Appropriations • Health, Education, Labor &
Pensions • Intelligence
CoS. Steve Abbott **LD.** Olivia Kurtz
Sched. Darci Greenacre **PS.** Annie Clark
Dist. Off. Augusta 207.622.8414 • Bangor 207.945.0417 •
Biddeford 207.283.1101 • Caribou 207.493.7873 • Lewiston
207.784.6969 • Portland 207.780.3575

R: 12 **T:** 4th 70%
Elected Year: 1996
Next Election: 2020

☙ Sen. Angus S. King Jr. (king) I-ME-Jr. p 202.224.5344

Caucuses with Democratic Party **f** 202.224.1946
Rm. HSOB 133 **Web.** king.senate.gov
Bio. 03/31/1944 • Alexandria, VA • Governor • Dartmouth
College, A.B., 1966; Univ. of Virginia Law School, J.D., 1969
• Episcopalian • M. Mary J. Herman, 5 ch ; 5 gr-ch **Cmte.**
Armed Services • Energy & Natural Resources • Intelligence
• Rules & Administration
CoS. Kathleen Connery **LD.** Chad Metzler
Dawe
Sched. Claire Bridgeo **PS.** Matthew Felling
Dist. Off. Augusta 207.622.8292 • Bangor 207.945.8000 •
Presque Isle 207.764.5124 • Scarborough 207.883.1588

R: 62 **T:** 2nd 54%
Elected Year: 2012
Next Election: 2024

☙ Rep. Jared F. Golden (GOAL-duhn) D-ME-02 p 202.225.6306

Rm. LHOB 1223 **f** 202.225.2943
Bio. 07/25/1982 • Leed, ME • Bates College (ME), B.A.,
2011 • Unspecified/Other • M. Isobel Golden **Cmte.** Armed
Services • Small Business
CoS. Aisha Woodward **LD.** Eric Kanter
Sched. Gaetan Davis **PS.** Nick Zeller
Dist. Off. Lewiston

R: 372 **T:** 1st 51%
Elected Year: 2018

☙ Rep. Chellie M. Pingree (PING-gree) D-ME-01 p 202.225.611

Rm. RHOB 2162 **Web.** pingree.house.gov **f** 202.225.559
Bio. 04/02/1955 • Minneapolis, MN • State Legislator •
College of the Atlantic (ME), B.A., 1979 • Lutheran • Se.
Donald Sussman, 3 ch (3 from previous marriage); 3 gr-ch
Cmte. Agriculture • Appropriations
CoS. Jesse Connolly (CD) **LD.** Evan Johnston
Sched. Karen Sudbay (CD) **PS.** Victoria Bonney
Dist. Off. Portland 207.774.5019 • Waterville 207.873.5713

R: 138 **T:** 6th 59%
Elected Year: 2008

MARYLAND

MARYLAND

⚑ Governor Larry Hogan (HO-guhn)   p 410.974.3901

100 State Circle
Annapolis, MD 21401
Website maryland.gov
Fax 401.974.3275
Term Ends 2019
Lt. Governor
Boyd Rutherford, **R**

C: Annapolis
P: 6,042,718 (19)
A: 9,707.38 mi^2 (42nd)

U.S. Senators
Ben L. Cardin, **D**
Chris J. Van Hollen, **D**
U.S. Representatives
01 / Andy P. Harris, **R**
02 / Dutch Ruppersberger, **D**
03 / John P. Sarbanes, **D**
04 / Anthony G. Brown, **D**
05 / Steny H. Hoyer, **D**
06 / David Trone, **D**
07 / Elijah E. Cummings, **D**
08 / Jamie B. Raskin, **D**

🕊 Sen. Ben L. Cardin (KAR-din)   D-MD-Sr.   p 202.224.4524

Rm. HSOB 509 **Web.** cardin.senate.gov   **f** 202.224.1651
Bio. 10/05/1943 • Baltimore, MD • U.S. Representative;
Attorney • Univ. of Pittsburgh (PA), B.A., 1964; Univ. of
Maryland School of Law, J.D., 1967; Villa Julie College
(MD), LL.D., 2007 • Jewish • M. Myrna Edelman Cardin,
2 ch (1 deceased); 2 gr-ch **Cmte.** Environment & Public
Works • Finance • Foreign Relations • Small Business &
Entrepreneurship
CoS. Christopher W. Lynch   **LD.** Gray Maxwell
Sched. Lucia Rodriguez   **PS.** Sue Walitsky
Dist. Off. Baltimore 410.962.4436 • Bowie 301.860.0414
• Cumberland 301.777.2957 • Rockville 301.762.2974 •
Salisbury 410.546.4250

R: 27   T: 2nd 65%
Elected Year: 2006
Next Election: 2024

🕊 Sen. Chris J. Van Hollen Jr. (van-HAH-luhn)   D-MD-Jr.   p 202.224.4654

Rm. HSOB 110 **Web.** vanhollen.senate.gov   **f** 202.228.0629
Bio. 01/10/1959 • Karachi, Pakistan • State Senator;
Representative • Swarthmore College (PA), B.A., 1982; John
F. Kennedy School of Government, Harvard Univ., M.PP.,
1985; Georgetown Univ. (DC), J.D., 1990 • Episcopalian • M.
Katherine Wilkens Van Hollen, 3 ch **Cmte.** Appropriations •
Banking, Housing & Urban Affairs • Budget • Environment &
Public Works
CoS. Karen Robb   **LD.** Sarah Schenning
Sched. Liana Pardini   **PS.** Bridgett Frey
Dist. Off. Annapolis 410.263.1325 • Baltimore 667.212.4610
• Cambridge 410.221.2074 • Hagerstown 301.797.2826 •
Largo 301.322.6560 • Rockville 301.545.1500

R: 82   T: 1st 61%
Elected Year: 2016
Next Election: 2022

🕊 Rep. Anthony G. Brown (brown)   D-MD-04   p 202.225.8699

Rm. LHOB 1323 **Web.**
anthonybrown.house.gov
Bio. 11/21/1961 • Huntington, NY • Mbr., Board of
Governors; Council of State Gov't Toll Fellow; Mbr., MD
House of Delegates; MD House Majority Whip • U.S. Army
CPT; U.S. Army Reserves LTC • Harvard College (MA), B.A.,
1984; Harvard Univ. Law School (MA), J.D., 1992 • Roman
Catholic • M. Karmen Bailey Walker Brown, 2 ch; 1 stepch
Cmte. Armed Services • Ethics • Natural Resources •
Transportation & Infrastructure
CoS. Maia Hunt Estes   **LD.** Anna Platt
Sched. Hannah Cooper
Dist. Off. Annapolis 410.266.3249 • Largo 301.458.2600

R: 299   T: 2nd 78%
Elected Year: 2016

🕊 Rep. Elijah E. Cummings (KUH-mingz)   D-MD-07   p 202.225.4741

Rm. RHOB 2163 **Web.** cummings.house.gov   **f** 202.225.3178
Bio. 01/18/1951 • Baltimore, MD • Representative; Attorney
• Howard Univ. (DC), B.S., 1973; Univ. of Maryland School
of Law, J.D., 1976 • Baptist • M. Maya Rockeymoore, 1 ch
(1 from previous marriage) **Cmte.** Oversight & Reform •
Transportation & Infrastructure
CoS. Vernon Simms   **LD.** Yvette Badu-Nimako
Sched. Jean Waskow
Dist. Off. Baltimore 410.685.9199 • Catonsville
410.719.8777 • Ellicott City 410.465.8259

R: 43   T: 13th 76%
Elected Year: 1996

MARYLAND

⚑ Rep. Andy P. Harris (HAIR-iss)　　　R-MD-01　　p 202.225.5311

Rm. RHOB 2334　**Web.** harris.house.gov
Bio. 01/25/1957 • Brooklyn, NY • Johns Hopkins Univ.,
B.S., 1977; Johns Hopkins Univ., M.D., 1980; Johns Hopkins
Univ. Bloomburg School of Hygiene and Public Health (MD),
M.H.S., 1995 • Roman Catholic • M. Nicole Harris, 5 ch ; 6 gr-
ch　**Cmte.** Appropriations
CoS. John C. Dutton　　　　　**LD.** Tim Daniels
Sched. Victoria Cesaro　　　　**PS.** Julia Nista
Dist. Off. Bel Air 410.588.5670 • Chester 410.643.5425 •
Salisbury 443.944.8624

R: 166　**T:** 5th　60%
Elected Year: 2010

⚑ Rep. Steny H. Hoyer (HOY-yur)　　　D-MD-05　　p 202.225.4131

Rm. LHOB 1705　**Web.** hoyer.house.gov　　　**f** 202.225.4300
Bio. 06/14/1939 • New York, NY • Attorney; Member, State
Board of Education • Univ. of Maryland - College Park,
B.S., 1963; Georgetown Univ. Law Center (DC), J.D., 1966 •
Baptist • W., 3 ch ; 3 gr-ch ; 2 great-gr-ch
CoS. Alexis Covey-Brandt　　　**LD.** Jim Notter
Sched. Bridget Brennan　　　　**PS.** Annaliese Davis
Dist. Off. Greenbelt 301.474.0119 • White Plains
301.843.1577

R: 5　**T:** 20th　70%
Elected Year: 1981

⚑ Rep. Jamie B. Raskin (RAS-kin)　　　D-MD-08　　p 202.225.5341

Rm. CHOB 412　**Web.** raskin.house.gov
Bio. 12/13/1962 • Washington, D.C. • Harvard College
(MA), B.A., 1983; Harvard Univ. Law School (MA), J.D.,
1987 • Unspecified/Other • M. Sarah Raskin, 3 ch　**Cmte.**
Administration • Judiciary • Oversight & Reform • Rules
CoS. Julie Tagen
Sched. Candace Johnson　　　**PS.** Lauren Doney
Dist. Off. Rockville 301.354.1000

R: 329　**T:** 2nd　68%
Elected Year: 2016

⚑ Rep. Dutch Ruppersberger III (ROO-purs-bur-gur)　　　D-MD-02　　p 202.225.3061

Rm. RHOB 2206　**Web.**　　　　　　　**f** 202.225.3094
ruppersberger.house.gov
Bio. 01/31/1946 • Baltimore, MD • Member, City Council;
Assistant State Attorney • Univ. of Maryland - College Park,
B.A., 1967; Univ. of Baltimore School of Law (MD), J.D., 1970
• Methodist • M. Kay Murphy Ruppersberger, 2 ch; 3 gr-ch
Cmte. Appropriations
CoS. Tara Oursler　　　　　**LD.** Walter Gonzales
Sched. Elliott Phaup　　　　**PS.** Jaime Lennon (CD)
Dist. Off. Timonium 410.628.2701

R: 83　**T:** 9th　66%
Elected Year: 2002

⚑ Rep. John P. Sarbanes (SAR-baynz)　　　D-MD-03　　p 202.225.4016

Rm. RHOB 2370　**Web.** sarbanes.house.gov　**f** 202.225.9219
Bio. 05/22/1962 • Baltimore, MD • School Superintendent
• Princeton Univ. Woodrow Wilson School of Public and
International Affairs (NJ), B.A., 1984; Harvard Univ., J.D.,
1988 • Greek Orthodox • M. Dina Sarbanes, 3 ch　**Cmte.**
Energy & Commerce • Oversight & Reform
CoS. Dvora Lovinger　　　　**LD.** Raymond O'Mara
Sched. Kelly Moura　　　　　**PS.** Daniel Jacobs
Dist. Off. Annapolis 410.295.1679 • Towson 410.832.8890

R: 120　**T:** 7th　69%
Elected Year: 2006

⚑ Rep. David Trone (troan)　　　D-MD-06　　p 202.225.272

Rm. LHOB 1213　**Web.** trone.house.gov
Bio. 09/21/1955 • Cheverly, MD • Furman Univ. (SC), B.A.,
1977; Univ. of Pennsylvania Wharton School of Business
(PA), M.B.A., 1985 • Lutheran • M. June Trone, 4 ch　**Cmte.**
Education & Labor • Foreign Affairs • Joint Economic
CoS. Andy Flick　　　　**LD.** Christina Tsafoulias
Sched. Jeri Sparling　　　**PS.** Hannah Muldavin
Dist. Off. Gaithersburg 301.926.0300

R: 427　**T:** 1st　59%
Elected Year: 2018

MASSACHUSETTS

Governor Charlie Baker (BAY-kur) p 617.725.4005

Massachusetts State House, Room 280
Boston, MA 02133
Website mass.gov
Fax 617.727.9725
Term Ends 2023
Lt. Governor
Karyn Polito, **R**

C: Boston
P: 6,902,149 (15)
A: 7,800.03 mi² (45th)

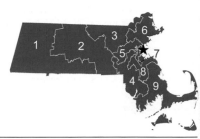

U.S. Senators
Elizabeth A. Warren, **D**
Ed Markey, **D**
U.S. Representatives
01 / Richard E. Neal, **D**
02 / Jim P. McGovern, **D**
03 / Lori Trahan, **D**
04 / Joe P. Kennedy, **D**
05 / Katherine M. Clark, **D**
06 / Seth W. Moulton, **D**
07 / Ayanna Pressley, **D**
08 / Stephen F. Lynch, **D**
09 / Bill R. Keating, **D**

Sen. Ed Markey (MAR-kee) D-MA-Jr. p 202.224.2742

Rm. DSOB 255 **Web.** markey.senate.gov **f** 202.224.8525
Bio. 07/11/1946 • Malden, MA • Representative • Army
Reserves 1968-73 • Boston College (MA), B.A., 1968; Boston
College Law School (MA), J.D., 1972 • Roman Catholic
• M. Susan Blumenthal **Cmte.** Commerce, Science &
Transportation • Environment & Public Works • Foreign
Relations • Small Business & Entrepreneurship
CoS. Paul Tencher **LD.** Morgan Gray
  PS. Giselle Barry
Dist. Off. Boston 617.565.8519 • Fall River 508.677.0523 •
Springfield 413.785.4610

R: 67 **T:** 2nd 62%
Elected Year: 2013
Next Election: 2020

Sen. Elizabeth A. Warren (WAR-ruhn) D-MA-Sr. p 202.224.4543

Rm. HSOB 317 **Web.** warren.senate.gov **f** 202.228.2072
Bio. 06/22/1949 • Oklahoma City, OK • Univ. of Houston
(TX), B.A., 1970; Rutgers Univ. (NJ), J.D., 1976 • Methodist
• M. Bruce H. Mann, 2 ch ; 3 gr-ch **Cmte.** Aging • Armed
Services • Banking, Housing & Urban Affairs • Health,
Education, Labor & Pensions
CoS. Anne Morris Reid **LD.** Beth Pearson
Sched. Emily Ross **PS.** Ashley Woolheater
Dist. Off. Boston 617.565.3170 • Springfield 413.788.2690

R: 65 **T:** 2nd 60%
Elected Year: 2012
Next Election: 2024

Rep. Katherine M. Clark (klark) D-MA-05 p 202.225.2836

Rm. RHOB 2448 **Web.** **f** 202.226.0092
katherineclark.house.gov
Bio. 07/17/1963 • New Haven, CT • Saint Lawrence
Univ., B.A., 1985; Cornell Univ. Law School (NY), J.D., 1989;
Harvard Univ. John F. Kennedy School of Government (MA),
M.P.A., 1997 • Protestant - Unspecified Christian • M. Rodney
Dowell, 3 ch **Cmte.** Appropriations
CoS. Brooke Scannell **LD.** Steve Thornton
Sched. Judah Piepho **PS.** Katheryn Alexander
Dist. Off. Cambridge 617.354.0292 • Framingham
508.319.9757

R: 244 **T:** 4th 76%
Elected Year: 2013

MASSACHUSETTS

⚓ Rep. Bill R. Keating (KEE-ting)　　　D-MA-09　p 202.225.3111

Rm. RHOB 2351 **Web.** keating.house.gov **f** 202.225.5658
Bio. 09/06/1952 • Norwood, MA • Boston College (MA),
B.A., 1974; Boston College (MA), M.B.A., 1982; Suffolk Univ.
School of Law (MA), J.D., 1985 • Roman Catholic • M. Tevis
Keating, 2 ch **Cmte.** Armed Services • Foreign Affairs
CoS. Garrett Donovan **LD.** Gabrielle Gould
Sched. David Oleksak **PS.** Lauren A. McDermott
Dist. Off. Hyannis 508.771.6868 • New Bedford
508.999.6462 • Plymouth 508.746.9000

R: 171 **T:** 5th 59%
Elected Year: 2010

⚓ Rep. Joe P. Kennedy III (KEH-nuh-dee)　　D-MA-04　p 202.225.5931

Rm. CHOB 304 **Web.** kennedy.house.gov **f** 202.225.0182
Bio. 10/04/1980 • Brighton, MA • Stanford Univ. (CA), B.S.,
2003; Harvard Univ. Law School (MA), J.D., 2009 • Roman
Catholic • M. Lauren Birchfield, 2 ch **Cmte.** Energy &
Commerce
CoS. Greg Mecher **LD.** Sarah Curtis
Sched. Nate Matteson **PS.** Dan Black
Dist. Off. Attleboro 508.431.1110 • Newton 617.332.3333

R: 215 **T:** 4th 98%
Elected Year: 2012

⚓ Rep. Stephen F. Lynch (linch)　　　D-MA-08　p 202.225.8273

Rm. RHOB 2109 **Web.** lynch.house.gov **f** 202.225.3984
Bio. 03/31/1955 • Boston, MA • State Legislator •
Wentworth Institute of Technology (MA), B.S., 1988; Boston
College Law School (MA), J.D., 1991; Harvard Univ. John F.
Kennedy School of Government (MA), M.P.A., 1999 • Roman
Catholic • M. Margaret Shaughnessy Lynch, 1 ch **Cmte.**
Financial Services • Oversight & Reform • Transportation &
Infrastructure
CoS. Kevin Ryan **LD.** Bruce Fernandez
Sched. Megan Hollingshead **PS.** Molly Rose Tarpey (CD)
Dist. Off. Boston 617.428.2000 • Brockton 508.586.5555 •
Quincy 617.657.6305

R: 72 **T:** 10th 98%
Elected Year: 2001

⚓ Rep. Jim P. McGovern (mih-GUH-vurn)　　D-MA-02　p 202.225.6101

Rm. CHOB 408 **Web.** mcgovern.house.gov **f** 202.225.5759
Bio. 11/20/1959 • Worcester, MA • Congressional Aide
• American Univ. (DC), B.A., 1981; American Univ. (DC),
M.P.A., 1984 • Roman Catholic • M. Lisa Murray McGovern, 2
ch **Cmte.** Agriculture • Rules
CoS. Jennifer Chandler **LD.** Cindy Buhl
Sched. Daniel Holt **PS.** Matt Bonaccorsi
Dist. Off. Leominster 978.466.3552 • Northampton
413.341.8700 • Worcester 508.831.7356

R: 51 **T:** 12th 67%
Elected Year: 1996

⚓ Rep. Seth W. Moulton (MOAL-tuhn)　　D-MA-06　p 202.225.8020

Rm. LHOB 1127 **Web.** moulton.house.gov **f** 202.225.5915
Bio. 10/24/1978 • Salem, MA • Phillips Academy, (MA),
M.P.A., 1997; Harvard Univ., B.S., 2001; Harvard Business
School (MA), M.B.A., 2011; Harvard Univ. John F. Kennedy
School of Government (MA), M.P.A., 2011 • Christian - Non-
Denominational • M. Liz Boardman, 1 ch **Cmte.** Armed
Services • Budget
CoS. Alexis Prieur **LD.** Julio Lainez
L'Heureux
Sched. Anna Stolitzka **PS.** Tim Biba
Dist. Off. Salem 978.531.1669

R: 274 **T:** 3rd 65%
Elected Year: 2014

⚓ Rep. Richard E. Neal (neel)　　　D-MA-01　p 202.225.5601

Rm. RHOB 2309 **Web.** neal.house.gov **f** 202.225.8112
Bio. 02/14/1949 • Worcester, MA • Mayor (Springfield, MA);
President, Springfield City Council • American International
College (MA), B.A., 1972; Univ. of Hartford Barney School of
Business (CT), M.P.A., 1976 • Roman Catholic • M. Maureen
Conway Neal, 4 ch **Cmte.** Joint Taxation • Ways & Means
CoS. William Tranghese **LD.** Kara Getz
Sched. Elizabeth Quigley
(CD)
Dist. Off. Pittsfield 413.442.0946 • Springfield 413.785.0325

R: 15 **T:** 16th 98%
Elected Year: 1988

⚑ Rep. Ayanna Pressley (PRESS-lee) D-MA-07 p 202.225.5111

Rm. LHOB 1108 **Web.** pressley.house.gov
Bio. 02/03/1974 • Cincinnati, OH • Baptist • M. Conan Harris pressley, 1 stepch **Cmte.** Financial Services • Oversight & Reform
CoS. Sarah Groh **LD.** Aissa Canchola
Sched. Lona B. Watts **PS.** Kalina Francis
Dist. Off. Boston

R: 404 **T:** 1st 98%
Elected Year: 2018

⚑ Rep. Lori Trahan (truh-HAN) D-MA-03 p 202.225.3411

Rm. LHOB 1616 **Web.** trahan.house.gov
Bio. 10/27/1973 • Lowell, MA • Georgetown Univ. (DC), B.S., 1995 • Catholic • M. David Trahan, 2 ch ; 3 stepch
Cmte. Armed Services • Education & Labor
CoS. Alicia Molt-West **LD.** Ron A. Carlton
Sched. Lisa Degou **PS.** Mark McDevitt
Dist. Off. Lawrence • Lowell 978.459.0101

R: 426 **T:** 1st 62%
Elected Year: 2018

MICHIGAN

⚑ Governor Gretchen Whitmer (WHIT-mur) p 517.373.3400

PO Box 30013
Lansing, MI 48909
Website michigan.gov
Fax 517.335.6863
Term Ends 2023
Lt. Governor
Garlin Gilchrist, D

C: Lansing
P: 9,995,915 (10)
A: 56,538.85 mi^2 (22nd)

U.S. Senators
Debbie A. Stabenow, D
Gary C. Peters, D
U.S. Representatives
01 / Jack W. Bergman, R
02 / Bill P. Huizenga, R
03 / Justin Amash, R
04 / John Moolenaar, R
05 / Dan T. Kildee, D
06 / Fred S. Upton, R
07 / Tim L. Walberg, R
08 / Elissa B. Slotkin, D
09 / Andy Levin, D
10 / Paul Mitchell, R
11 / Haley Stevens, D
12 / Debbie Dingell, D
13 / Rashida Tlaib, D
14 / Brenda L. Lawrence, D

⚑ Sen. Gary C. Peters (PEE-turz) D-MI-Jr. p 202.224.6221

Rm. HSOB 724 **Web.** peters.senate.gov **f** 202.224.7387
Bio. 12/01/1958 • Pontiac, MI • State Legislator; Professor • Navy Reserves • Alma College (MI), B.A., 1980; Univ. of Detroit (MI), M.B.A., 1984; Wayne State Univ. Law School (MI), J.D., 1989; Michigan State Univ., M.A., 2007 • Episcopalian • M. Colleen Ochoa, 3 ch **Cmte.** Armed Services • Commerce, Science & Transportation • Homeland Security & Government Affairs • Joint Economic
CoS. Eric Feldman **LD.** Zephranie Buetow
Sched. Angeli Chawla **PS.** Sarah Schakow
Dist. Off. Detroit 313.226.6020 • Grand Rapids 616.233.9150 • Lansing 517.377.1508 • Marquette 906.226.4554 • Rochester 248.608.8040 • Saginaw 989.754.0112 • Traverse City 231.947.7773

R: 70 **T:** 1st 55%
Elected Year: 2014
Next Election: 2020

MICHIGAN

♫ Sen. Debbie A. Stabenow (STAB-uh-nou) D-MI-Sr. p 202.224.4822

Rm. HSOB 731 **Web.** stabenow.senate.gov **f** 202.228.0325
Bio. 04/29/1950 • Gladwin, MI • U.S. Representative; State
Legislator; Social Worker • Michigan State Univ., B.A., 1972;
Michigan State Univ., M.S.W., 1975 • Methodist • D., 2 ch ;
4 gr-ch **Cmte.** Agriculture, Nutrition & Forestry • Budget •
Energy & Natural Resources • Finance • Joint Taxation
CoS. Matt Van Kuiken **LD.** Emily Carwell
Sched. Ellen Rodman (CD) **PS.** Miranda Margowsky
Dist. Off. Detroit 313.961.4330 • East Lansing 517.203.1760
• Flint 810.720.4172 • Grand Rapids 616.975.0052 •
Marquette 906.228.8756 • Traverse City 231.929.1031

R: 17 **T:** 3rd 52%
Elected Year: 2000
Next Election: 2024

♫ Rep. Justin Amash (ah-MAHSH) R-MI-03 p 202.225.3831

Rm. CHOB 106 **Web.** amash.house.gov **f** 202.225.5144
Bio. 04/18/1980 • Grand Rapids, MI • Univ. of Michigan,
B.A., 2002; Univ. of Michigan Law School, J.D., 2005 •
Eastern Orthodox • M. Kara Amash, 3 ch **Cmte.** Oversight
& Reform
CoS. Poppy Nelson **LD.** Carolyn Iodice
Sched. Grace Gumina
Dist. Off. Battle Creek 269.205.3823 • Grand Rapids
616.451.8383

R: 152 **T:** 5th 54%
Elected Year: 2010

♫ Rep. Jack W. Bergman (BAIRG-mahn) R-MI-01 p 202.225.4735

Rm. CHOB 414 **Web.** bergman.house.gov **f** 202.225.4710
Bio. 02/02/1947 • Shakopee, MN • Univ. of West Florida,
M.B.A., 1975 • Lutheran • M. Cindy Bergman, 5 ch ; 8 gr-ch
Cmte. Armed Services • Veterans' Affairs
CoS. Tony Lis
Sched. Amelia Burns **PS.** James Hogge (CD)
Dist. Off. Marquette 906.273.2227 • Traverse City
231.714.4785

R: 296 **T:** 2nd 56%
Elected Year: 2016

♫ Rep. Debbie Dingell (DING-gull) D-MI-12 p 202.225.4071

Rm. CHOB 116 **Web.** **f** 202.226.0371
debbiedingell.house.gov
Bio. 11/23/1953 • Detroit, MI • Georgetown Univ. (DC),
B.S., 1975; Georgetown Univ. (DC), M.S., 1996 • Roman
Catholic • M. Hon. John D. Dingell Jr., 4 ch **Cmte.** Energy &
Commerce • Natural Resources
CoS. Greg Sunstrum **LD.** Kevin Rambosk
Sched. Matthew Dougherty **PS.** Maggie Rousseau
Dist. Off. Dearborn 313.278.2936 • Ypsilanti 734.481.1100

R: 260 **T:** 3rd 68%
Elected Year: 2014

♫ Rep. Bill P. Huizenga (HY-zeng-uh) R-MI-02 p 202.225.4401

Rm. RHOB 2232 **Web.** huizenga.house.gov **f** 202.226.0779
Bio. 01/31/1969 • Zeeland, MI • Calvin College (MI), B.A.,
1991 • Christian Reformed Church • M. Natalie Huizenga, 5
ch **Cmte.** Financial Services
CoS. Jon DeWitte **LD.** Palmer Rafferty
Sched. Emily Zajac **PS.** Brian Patrick
Dist. Off. Grand Haven 616.414.5516 • Grandville
616.570.0917

R: 169 **T:** 5th 55%
Elected Year: 2010

♫ Rep. Dan T. Kildee (KILL-dee) D-MI-05 p 202.225.3611

Rm. CHOB 203 **Web.** dankildee.house.gov **f** 202.225.6393
Bio. 08/11/1958 • Flint, MI • Central Michigan Univ., B.S. •
Roman Catholic • M. Jennifer Kildee, 3 ch ; 2 gr-ch **Cmte.**
Budget • Ways & Means
CoS. Mitchell Rivard **LD.** Troy Nienberg
Sched. Elizabeth Virga **PS.** Robyn Bryan
Dist. Off. Flint 810.238.8627

R: 216 **T:** 4th 60%
Elected Year: 2012

⚑ Rep. Brenda L. Lawrence (LAW-renss)   D-MI-14   p 202.225.5802

Rm. RHOB 2463 **Web.** lawrence.house.gov **f** 202.226.2356
Bio. 10/18/1954 • Detroit, MI • Central Michigan Univ.,
Bach. Deg., 2005 • Christian - Non-Denominational • M.
McArthur Lawrence, 2 ch ; 1 gr-ch **Cmte.** Appropriations •
Oversight & Reform
CoS. Ryan Hedgepeth   **LD.** Varun Krovi
Sched. Eboni Malone   **PS.** Nicole Julius
Dist. Off. Southfield 248.356.2052

R: 269 **T:** 3rd 81%
Elected Year: 2014

⚑ Rep. Andy Levin (LEH-vin)   D-MI-09   p 202.225.4961

Rm. CHOB 228 **Web.** andylevin.house.gov
Bio. 08/10/1960 • Berkley, MI • Williams College, B.A.,
1983; Univ. of Michigan, M.A., 1990; Harvard Univ. Law
School (MA), J.D., 1994 • Jewish • M. Mary Freeman, 4 ch
Cmte. Education & Labor • Foreign Affairs
CoS. Ven Neralla   **LD.** Catherine Rowland
Sched. Taryn Brown   **PS.** Austin Laufersweiler
Dist. Off. Warren 586.498.7122

R: 388 **T:** 1st 60%
Elected Year: 2018

⚑ Rep. Paul Mitchell III (MIH-chull)   R-MI-10   p 202.225.2106

Rm. CHOB 211 **Web.** mitchell.house.gov **f** 202.226.1169
Bio. 05/08/1961 • Boston, MA • Michigan State Univ.,
B.A., 1978 • Protestant - Unspecified Christian • M. Sherry
Mitchell, 6 ch **Cmte.** Armed Services • Transportation &
Infrastructure
CoS. Kyle Kizzier   **LD.** Pat Pelletier
Sched. Molly Harrington   **PS.** Alex Davidson
Dist. Off. Shelby Township 586.997.5010

R: 325 **T:** 2nd 60%
Elected Year: 2016

⚑ Rep. John Moolenaar (MULL-leh-nar)   R-MI-04   p 202.225.3561

Rm. CHOB 117 **Web.** moolenaar.house.gov **f** 202.225.9679
Bio. 05/08/1961 • Midland, MI • Hope College (MI),
B.S., 1983; Harvard Univ., M.P.A., 1989 • Christian - Non-
Denominational • M. Amy Moolenaar, 6 ch **Cmte.**
Appropriations
CoS. Lindsay Ryan   **LD.** Jayson Schimmenti
Sched. Alexa Williams   **PS.** David Russell
Dist. Off. Cadillac 231.942.5070 • Midland 989.631.2552

R: 272 **T:** 3rd 63%
Elected Year: 2014

⚑ Rep. Elissa B. Slotkin (SLAHT-kin)   D-MI-08   p 202.225.4872

Rm. LHOB 1531 **Web.** slotkin.house.gov
Bio. 07/10/1976 • Holly, MI • Columbia Univ. School of
International and Public Affairs, Mast. Deg.; Cornell Univ.
(NY), B.A., 1998 • Jewish • M. Dave Slotkin, 2 stepch **Cmte.**
Armed Services • Homeland Security
CoS. Mela Louise Norman   **LD.** Danielle Most
Sched. Megan Birleson   **PS.** Hannah Lindow
Dist. Off. Lansing 517.993.0510

R: 414 **T:** 1st 51%
Elected Year: 2018

⚑ Rep. Haley Stevens (STEE-vuhnz)   D-MI-11   p 202.225.8171

Rm. CHOB 227 **Web.** stevens.house.gov
Bio. 06/24/1983 • Oakland County, MI • American Univ.
(DC), Bach. Deg., 2005; American Univ. (DC), M.A., 2007 •
Christian Church • S. **Cmte.** Education & Labor • Science,
Space & Technology
CoS. Justin German   **LD.** Sarah Reingold
Sched. John Martin   **PS.** Blake McCarren
Dist. Off. Novi 202.227.7397

R: 421 **T:** 1st 52%
Elected Year: 2018

MICHIGAN

🏛 Rep. Rashida Tlaib (tuh-LEEB) D-MI-13 p 202.225.5126
Rm. LHOB 1628 **Web.** tlaib.house.gov
Bio. 07/24/1976 • Detroit, MI • Wayne State Univ. (MI), B.A., 1998; Western Michigan Univ., J.D., 2004 • Islam (Muslim) • M. Fayez Tlaib, 2 ch **Cmte.** Financial Services • Oversight & Reform
CoS. Ryan Anderson **LD.** Dominique Warren
Sched. Sara Maaiki **PS.** Denzel McCampbell
Dist. Off. River Rouge 313.203.7540

R: 424 **T:** 1st 84%
Elected Year: 2018

🏛 Rep. Fred S. Upton (UP-tuhn) R-MI-06 p 202.225.3761
Rm. RHOB 2183 **Web.** upton.house.gov f 202.225.4986
Bio. 04/23/1953 • St. Joseph, MI • Congressional Staffer • Univ. of Michigan, B.A., 1975 • Congregationalist • M. Amey Rulon-Miller Upton, 2 ch **Cmte.** Energy & Commerce
CoS. Joan Hillebrands **LD.** Mark Ratner
Sched. Suzanne Scruggs **PS.** Josh David Paciorek
Dist. Off. Kalamazoo 269.385.0039 • St. Joseph 269.982.1986

R: 10 **T:** 17th 50%
Elected Year: 1986

🏛 Rep. Tim L. Walberg (WALL-burg) R-MI-07 p 202.225.6276
Rm. RHOB 2266 **Web.** walberg.house.gov f 202.225.6281
Bio. 04/12/1951 • Chicago, IL • Minister; College Administrator • Taylor Univ. (IN), B.S., 1975; Fort Wayne Bible College, B.R.E., 1975; Wheaton College (IL), M.A., 1978 • Protestant - Unspecified Christian • M. Susan Walberg, 3 ch ; 2 gr-ch **Cmte.** Education & Labor • Energy & Commerce
CoS. R.J. Laukitis **LD.** Joanna Brown
Sched. Mary Elizabeth Stringer **PS.** Dan Kotman
Dist. Off. Jackson 517.780.9075

R: 150 **T:** 6th 54%
Elected Year: 2010

MINNESOTA

🏛 Governor Tim J. Walz (wallz) p 651.201.3400
130 State Capitol, 75 Rev. Dr. Martin Luther King Jr. Blvd. St. Paul, MN 55155
Website state.mn.us
Fax 651.797.1850
Term Ends 2023
Lt. Governor Peggy Flanagan, **D**

C: St. Paul
P: 5,611,179 (22)
A: 79,626.59 mi^2 (14th)

U.S. Senators
Amy Klobuchar, **D**
Tina Smith, **D**
U.S. Representatives
01 / James Hagedorn, R
02 / Angela D. Craig, D
03 / Dean Phillips, D
04 / Betty McCollum, D
05 / Ilhan Omar, D
06 / Thomas E. Emmer, R
07 / Collin C. Peterson, D
08 / Peter A. Stauber, R

🏛 Sen. Amy Klobuchar (KLOE-buh-shar)   D-MN-Sr.   p 202.224.3244

Rm. DSOB 425 **Web.** klobuchar.senate.gov   **f** 202.228.2186
Bio. 05/25/1960 • Plymouth, MN • Attorney; Hennepin County Attorney • Yale Univ. (CT), B.A., 1982; Univ. of Chicago (IL), J.D., 1985 • Congregationalist • M. John Bessler, 1 ch **Cmte.** Agriculture, Nutrition & Forestry • Commerce, Science & Transportation • Joint Economic • Judiciary • Rules & Administration
CoS. Rosa Po   **LD.** Elizabeth Farrar
Sched. Blair Mallin   **PS.** Jonathan Beeton
Dist. Off. Minneapolis 612.727.5220 • Moorhead 218.287.2219 • Rochester 507.288.5321 • Virginia 218.741.9690

R: 31 **T:** 2nd 60%
Elected Year: 2006
Next Election: 2024

🏛 Sen. Tina Smith (smith)   D-MN-Jr.   p 202.224.5641

Rm. HSOB 720 **Web.** smith.senate.gov   **f** 202.224.0044
Bio. 03/04/1958 • Alburquerque, NM • Stanford Univ. (CA), B.A.; Dartmouth College Tuck School of Business (NH), M.B.A. • M. Archie Smith, 2 ch **Cmte.** Agriculture, Nutrition & Forestry • Banking, Housing & Urban Affairs • Health, Education, Labor & Pensions • Indian Affairs
CoS. Jeff Lomonaco   **LD.** Gohar Sedighi
Sched. Michael Weiss   **PS.** Molly Morrissey
Dist. Off. Duluth 218.722.2390 • Moorhead 218.284.8721 • Rochester 507.288.2003 • Saint Paul 651.221.1016

R: 57 **T:** 2nd 53%
Elected Year: 2018
Next Election: 2024

🏛 Rep. Angela D. Craig (krayg)   D-MN-02   p 202.225.2271

Rm. LHOB 1523 **Web.** craig.house.gov
Bio. 02/14/1972 • W. Helena, AR • Univ. of Memphis, B.A., 1994 • Lutheran • M. Cheryl Greene, 4 ch **Cmte.** Agriculture • Small Business • Transportation & Infrastructure
CoS. Mara Kunin   **LD.** Will Mitchell
Sched. Savanna Peterson   **PS.** Jen Gates
Dist. Off. St. Paul 901.590.4112

R: 359 **T:** 1st 53%
Elected Year: 2018

🏛 Rep. Thomas E. Emmer Jr. (EH-mur)   R-MN-06   p 202.225.2331

Rm. CHOB 315 **Web.** emmer.house.gov   **f** 202.225.6475
Bio. 03/03/1961 • South Bend, IN • Univ. of Alaska, Fairbanks, B.A., 1984; William Mitchell College of Law (MN), J.D., 1988 • Roman Catholic • M. Jacqueline Samuel Emmer, 7 ch **Cmte.** Financial Services
CoS. Christopher Maneval   **LD.** Landon Zinda
Sched. Alyssa Anderson   **PS.** Abby Rime
Dist. Off. Otsego 763.241.6848

R: 261 **T:** 3rd 61%
Elected Year: 2014

🏛 Rep. James Hagedorn (HAG-uh-dorn)   R-MN-01   p 202.225.2472

Rm. CHOB 325 **Web.** hagedorn.house.gov
Bio. 08/04/1962 • Blue Earth, MN • George Mason Univ., B.A., 1992 • Lutheran • S. **Cmte.** Agriculture • Small Business
CoS. Peter Su
Sched. Karin Mantor   **PS.** Jim Hahn
Dist. Off. Mankato 507.323.6090 • Rochester

R: 378 **T:** 1st 50%
Elected Year: 2018

MINNESOTA

⚑ Rep. Betty McCollum (mih-KAW-lum)   D-MN-04   p 202.225.6631

Rm. RHOB 2256 **Web.** mccollum.house.gov   **f** 202.225.1968
Bio. 07/12/1954 • Minneapolis, MN • Teacher;
Representative • Saint Catherine Univ., B.S., 1986 • Roman
Catholic • D., 2 ch **Cmte.** Appropriations
CoS. Bill Harper (CD)   **LD.** Ben Peterson
Sched. Mia Hartley   **PS.** Amanda Yanchury
Dist. Off. St. Paul 651.224.9191

R: 70   **T:** 10th 66%
Elected Year: 2000

⚑ Rep. Ilhan Omar (O-mar)   D-MN-05   p 202.225.4755

Rm. LHOB 1517 **Web.** ilhanomar.com
Bio. 10/04/1982 • Mogadishu, Somalia • North Dakota State
Univ., B.A., 2011 • Islam (Muslim) • M. Ahmed Hirsi, 3 ch
Cmte. Budget • Education & Labor • Foreign Affairs
CoS. Connor McNutt   **LD.** Kelly Misselwitz
Sched. Tera Proby   **PS.** Jeremy Slevin
Dist. Off. Minneapolis 612.333.1272

R: 399   **T:** 1st 78%
Elected Year: 2018

⚑ Rep. Collin C. Peterson (PEE-tur-suhn)   D-MN-07   p 202.225.2165

Rm. RHOB 2204 **Web.**   **f** 202.225.1593
collinpeterson.house.gov
Bio. 06/29/1944 • Fargo, ND • State Senator; Accountant •
Nationa Guard 1963-69 • Moorhead State Univ. (MN), B.A.,
1966 • Lutheran • S., 3 ch ; 4 gr-ch **Cmte.** Agriculture •
Veterans' Affairs
CoS. Allison Scott (CD)   **LD.** Adam Durand
Sched. Rebekah Solem
Dist. Off. Detroit Lakes 218.847.5056 • Marshall
507.537.2299 • Redwood Falls 507.637.2270 • Thief River
Falls 218.683.5405 • Willmar 320.235.1061

R: 19   **T:** 15th 52%
Elected Year: 1990

⚑ Rep. Dean Phillips (FIH-lips)   D-MN-03   p 202.225.2871

Rm. LHOB 1305 **Web.** phillips.house.gov   **f** 202.225.6351
Bio. 01/20/1969 • St. Paul, MN • Brown Univ. (RI), B.A.,
1991; Univ. of Minnesota, M.B.A., 2000 • Jewish • D., 2 ch
Cmte. Ethics • Financial Services • Foreign Affairs
CoS. Tim Bertocci   **LD.** Imani Augustus
Sched. Sophie Mirviss   **PS.** Samantha Anderson
                                      (CD)
Dist. Off. Bloomington 952.563.4593

R: 402   **T:** 1st 56%
Elected Year: 2018

⚑ Rep. Peter A. Stauber (STAW-bur)   R-MN-08   p 202.225.621

Rm. CHOB 126 **Web.** stauber.house.gov
Bio. 05/10/1966 • Duluth, MN • Lake Superior State Univ.,
B.S., 1988 • Catholic • M. Jodi Stauber, 4 ch **Cmte.** Small
Business • Transportation & Infrastructure
CoS. Desiree Koetzle   **LD.** Jeff Bishop
Sched. Linnea Melbye   **PS.** Kelsey Mix
Dist. Off. Brainerd 218.355.0862 • Cambridge • Chisholm
218.355.0726 • Hermantown 218.481.6396

R: 418   **T:** 1st 51%
Elected Year: 2018

MISSISSIPPI

MISSISSIPPI

⚑ Governor Phil Bryant (BRY-ent)   p 601.359.315

PO Box 139   **C:** Jackson
Jackson, MS 39205   **P:** 2,986,530 (35)
Website mississippi.gov   **A:** 46,923.36 mi^2 (31st)
Fax 601.359.3741
Term Ends 2020
Lt. Governor
Tate Reeves, **R**

MISSISSIPPI

U.S. Senators
Roger F. Wicker, **R**
Cindy Hyde-Smith, **R**
U.S. Representatives
01 / Trent Kelly, **R**
02 / Bennie G. Thompson, **D**
03 / Michael P. Guest, **R**
04 / Steven M. Palazzo, **R**

⚑ Sen. Cindy Hyde-Smith ("hide" smith)   R-MS-Jr.   p 202.224.5054

Rm. HSOB 702 **Web.** hydesmith.senate.gov   **f** 202.224.5321
Bio. Brookhaven, MS • Copiah-Lincoln Community College
(MS), A.A., 1979 • Baptist • M. Michael Smith, 1 ch **Cmte.**
Agriculture, Nutrition & Forestry • Appropriations • Energy &
Natural Resources • Rules & Administration
CoS. Brad White   **LD.** Tim Wolverton
Sched. Alex Calhoon   **PS.** Chris D. Gallegos
Dist. Off. Gulfport 228.867.9710 • Jackson 601.965.4459 •
Oxford 662.236.1018

R: 91   **T:** 1st 42%
Elected Year: 2018
Next Election: 2024

⚑ Sen. Roger F. Wicker (WIH-kur)   R-MS-Sr.   p 202.224.6253

Rm. DSOB 555 **Web.** wicker.senate.gov   **f** 202.228.0378
Bio. 07/05/1951 • Pontotoc, MS • State Senator; Attorney •
Air Force 1976-80 • Univ. of Mississippi, B.A., 1973; Univ. of
Mississippi, J.D., 1975 • Baptist • M. Gayle Long Wicker, 3
ch ; 5 gr-ch **Cmte.** Armed Services • Commerce, Science
& Transportation • Environment & Public Works • Rules &
Administration
CoS. Michelle Barlow   **LD.** Robert Murray
Richardson
Sched. Jen Jett   **PS.** Rick VanMeter
Dist. Off. Gulfport 228.871.7017 • Hernando 662.429.1002
R: 35   **T:** 2nd 59%   • Jackson 601.965.4644 • Tupelo 662.844.5010
Elected Year: 2007
Next Election: 2024

⚑ Rep. Michael P. Guest ("guest")   R-MS-03   p 202.225.5031

Rm. CHOB 230 **Web.** guest.house.gov
Bio. 02/04/1970 • Woodbury, NJ • Mississippi State
Univ., B.A., 1992; Univ. of Mississippi, J.D., 1995 • Baptist
• M. Haley Guest, 2 ch **Cmte.** Ethics • Foreign Affairs •
Homeland Security
CoS. Jordan Downs   **LD.** Elizabeth Joseph
Sched. Debra Boutwell   **PS.** Rob Pillow

R: 376   **T:** 1st 62%
Elected Year: 2018

⚑ Rep. Trent Kelly (KEH-lee)   R-MS-01   p 202.225.4306

Rm. LHOB 1005 **Web.** trentkelly.house.gov   **f** 202.225.3549
Bio. 03/01/1966 • Union, MS • East Central Community
College (MS), A.A., 1986; Univ. of Mississippi Business
School, B.A., 1989; Univ. of Mississippi Law School, J.D.,
1994; Army War College, M.A., 2010 • Methodist • M. Sheila
Kelly Hampton, 3 ch **Cmte.** Agriculture • Armed Services •
Small Business
CoS. Paul Howell   **LD.** Kirby Miller
Sched. Reed Craddock   **PS.** Susan Parker (CD)
Dist. Off. Columbus 662.327.0748 • Corinth 662.687.1525
R: 286   **T:** 3rd 67%   • Eupora 662.258.7240 • Hernando 662.449.3090 • Tupelo
Elected Year: 2015   662.841.8808

MISSISSIPPI

⚑ Rep. Steven M. Palazzo (puh-LAZ-o)   R-MS-04   p 202.225.5772

Rm. RHOB 2349 **Web.** palazzo.house.gov   f 202.225.7074
Bio. 02/21/1970 • Gulfport, MS • Univ. of Southern Mississippi, B.B.A., 1994; Univ. of Southern Mississippi, M.S., 1996 • Roman Catholic • M. Lisa Palazzo, 3 ch **Cmte.** Appropriations
CoS. Hunter Lipscomb
Sched. Leslie Churchwell   **PS.** Colleen Kennedy (CD)
Dist. Off. Gulfport 228.864.7670 • Hattiesburg 601.582.3246 • Pascagoula 228.202.8104

R: 176 **T:** 5th 68%
Elected Year: 2010

⚑ Rep. Bennie G. Thompson (TOMP-suhn)   D-MS-02   p 202.225.5876

Rm. RHOB 2466 **Web.** benniethompson.house.gov   f 202.225.5898
Bio. 01/28/1948 • Bolton, MS • County Supervisor, Hinds Co., MS; Mayor (Bolton, MS) • Tougaloo College, B.A., 1968; Jackson State Univ. (MS), M.S., 1972 • Methodist • M. London Johnson Thompson, 1 ch ; 2 gr-ch **Cmte.** Homeland Security
CoS. Andrea Lee
Sched. Alexis Williams   **PS.** Tyron James
Dist. Off. Bolton 601.866.9003 • Greenville 662.335.9003 • Greenwood 662.455.9003 • Jackson 601.946.9003 • Marks 662.326.9003 • Mound Bayou 662.741.9003

R: 35 **T:** 14th 72%
Elected Year: 1993

MISSOURI

⚑ Governor Michael L. Parson (PAR-suhn)   p 573.751.3222

State Capitol
PO Box 720
Jefferson City, MO 65102-9500
Website mo.gov
Fax 573.526.3291
Term Ends 2021
Lt. Governor
Mike Kehoe, **R**

C: Jefferson City
P: 6,126,452 (18)
A: 68,741.60 mi² (18th)

U.S. Senators
Roy D. Blunt, **R**
Josh Hawley, **R**
U.S. Representatives
01 / Wm. Lacy Clay, **D**
02 / Ann L. Wagner, **R**
03 / Blaine Luetkemeyer, **R**
04 / Vicky Jo Hartzler, **R**
05 / Emanuel Cleaver, **D**
06 / Sam B. Graves, **R**
07 / Billy Long, **R**
08 / Jason T. Smith, **R**

⚑ Sen. Roy D. Blunt (blunt)   R-MO-Sr.   p 202.224.5721

Rm. RSOB 260 **Web.** blunt.senate.gov   f 202.224.8149
Bio. 01/10/1950 • Niangua, MO • Missouri Secretary of State; President of Southwest Baptist University • Southwest Baptist Univ. (MO), B.A., 1970; Southwest Missouri State Univ., M.A., 1972 • Baptist • M. Abigail Blunt, 4 ch ; 6 gr-ch **Cmte.** Appropriations • Commerce, Science & Transportation • Intelligence • Rules & Administration
CoS. Stacy McHatton   **LD.** Dan Burgess McBride
Sched. Richard B. Eddings   **PS.** Katie Boyd
Dist. Off. Cape Girardeau 573.334.7044 • Columbia 573.442.8151 • Kansas City 816.471.7141 • Springfield 417.877.7814 • St. Louis 314.725.4484

R: 45 **T:** 2nd 49%
Elected Year: 2010
Next Election: 2022

⚑ Sen. Josh Hawley (Haw - l ee)   R-MO-Jr.   p 202.224.6154

Rm. DSOB B40A
Bio. 12/31/1979 • Springdale, AR • Stanford Univ. (CA), A.B., 2002; Yale Law School (CT), J.D., 2006 • Evangelical • M. Erin Morrow, 2 ch **Cmte.** Aging • Armed Services • Homeland Security & Government Affairs • Judiciary • Small Business & Entrepreneurship
CoS. Kyle Plotkin   **LD.** Ryan Leavitt
Sched. Ellen James   **PS.** Kelli Ford

R: 99   **T:** 0th 51%
Elected Year: 2018
Next Election: 2024

⚑ Rep. Wm. Lacy Clay Jr. (klay)   D-MO-01   p 202.225.2406

Rm. RHOB 2428 **Web.** lacyclay.house.gov   **f** 202.226.3717
Bio. 07/27/1956 • St. Louis, MO • State Representative • Univ. of Maryland - College Park, B.S., 1983 • Roman Catholic • D., 2 ch **Cmte.** Financial Services • Natural Resources • Oversight & Reform
CoS. Yvette Cravins   **LD.** Erica Powell
Sched. Karyn Long   **PS.** Steven Engelhardt (CD)
Dist. Off. Florissant 314.383.5240 • St. Louis 314.367.1970 • St. Louis 314.669.9393

R: 65   **T:** 10th 80%
Elected Year: 2000

⚑ Rep. Emanuel Cleaver II (KLEE-vur)   D-MO-05   p 202.225.4535

Rm. RHOB 2335 **Web.** cleaver.house.gov   **f** 202.225.4403
Bio. 10/26/1944 • Waxahachie, TX • Pastor; Mayor (Kansas City, MO) • Prairie View Agricultural and Mechanical Univ. (TX), B.S., 1972; St. Paul School of Theology, Kansas City (MO), M.Div., 1974 • Methodist • M. Dianne Cleaver, 4 ch (twins); 3 gr-ch **Cmte.** Financial Services • Homeland Security • Select Committee on the Modernization of Congress
CoS. Jennifer Shapiro   **LD.** Christina Mahoney
Sched. Herline Mathieu   **PS.** Heather Frierson (CD)
Dist. Off. Higginsville 660.584.7373 • Independence 816.833.4545 • Kansas City 816.842.4545

R: 89   **T:** 8th 62%
Elected Year: 2004

⚑ Rep. Sam B. Graves Jr. (grayvz)   R-MO-06   p 202.225.7041

Rm. LHOB 1135 **Web.** graves.house.gov   **f** 202.225.8221
Bio. 11/07/1963 • Tarkio, MO • State Representative • Univ. of Missouri, B.S., 1986 • Baptist • M. Lesley Graves, 3 ch
Cmte. Armed Services • Transportation & Infrastructure
CoS. Tom L. Brown   **LD.** Julie Devine
Sched. Amanda Sollazzo   **PS.** Bryan Nichols
Dist. Off. Hannibal 573.221.3400 • Kansas City 816.792.3976 • St. Joseph 816.749.0800

R: 67   **T:** 10th 65%
Elected Year: 2000

⚑ Rep. Vicky Jo Hartzler (HARTS-lur)   R-MO-04   p 202.225.2876

Rm. RHOB 2235 **Web.** hartzler.house.gov   **f** 202.225.2695
Bio. 10/13/1960 • Harrisonville, MO • High School Teacher; State Representative • Univ. of Missouri, B.S., 1983; Central Missouri State Univ., M.S., 1992 • Evangelical • M. Lowell Hartzler, 3 ch **Cmte.** Agriculture • Armed Services
CoS. Christopher P. Connelly   **LD.** Chrissi Lee
Sched. Jillian Vogl   **PS.** Anna Swick
Dist. Off. Columbia 573.442.9311 • Harrisonville 816.884.3411 • Lebanon 417.532.5582

R: 167   **T:** 5th 65%
Elected Year: 2010

⚑ Rep. Billy Long (long)   R-MO-07   p 202.225.6536

Rm. RHOB 2454 **Web.** long.house.gov   **f** 202.225.5604
Bio. 08/11/1955 • Springfield, MO • Business Owner; Talk Radio Show Host • Presbyterian • M. Barbara Long, 2 ch
Cmte. Energy & Commerce
CoS. Joe Lillis   **LD.** Ben Elleson
Sched. Colton Huthsing   **PS.** Hannah Lynn Smith
Dist. Off. Joplin 417.781.1041 • Springfield 417.889.1800

R: 174   **T:** 5th 66%
Elected Year: 2010

MISSOURI

⚑ Rep. Blaine Luetkemeyer (LOOT-keh-my-ur)   R-MO-03   p 202.225.2956

Rm. RHOB 2230   **Web.**
luetkemeyer.house.gov   **f** 202.225.5712
Bio. 05/07/1952 • Jefferson City, MO • State Representative;
Banker • Lincoln Univ. (MO), B.A., 1974 • Catholic •
M. Jackie Luetkemeyer, 3 ch ; 4 gr-ch   **Cmte.** Financial
Services
CoS. Chad Ramey   **LD.** Hailey Hart
Sched. Ann Vogel   **PS.** Catherine Costakos
Dist. Off. Jefferson City 573.635.7232 • Washington
636.239.2276 • Wentzville 636.327.7055

R: 134   **T:** 6th   65%
Elected Year: 2008

⚑ Rep. Jason T. Smith (smith)   R-MO-08   p 202.225.4404

Rm. RHOB 2418   **Web.** jasonsmith.house.gov   **f** 202.226.0326
Bio. 06/16/1980 • St. Louis, MO • Missouri State Univ., B.S.,
2001; Oklahoma City Univ. Law School (OK), J.D., 2004 •
Assembly of God • NS.   **Cmte.** Budget • Ways & Means
CoS. Mark Roman

PS. Joseph Brown
Dist. Off. Cape Girardeau 573.335.0101 • Farmington
573.756.9755 • Poplar Bluff 573.609.2996 • Rolla
573.364.2455 • West Plains 417.255.1515

R: 243   **T:** 4th   73%
Elected Year: 2013

⚑ Rep. Ann L. Wagner (WAG-nur)   R-MO-02   p 202.225.1621

Rm. RHOB 2350   **Web.** wagner.house.gov   **f** 202.225.2563
Bio. 09/13/1962 • St. Louis, MO • Univ. of Missouri, B.S.,
1984 • Roman Catholic • M. Raymond T. Wagner Jr., 3 ch
Cmte. Financial Services • Foreign Affairs
CoS. Charlie Keller   **LD.** Rachel Wagley
Sched. Emily Ann Smith   **PS.** Arthur Bryant
Dist. Off. Ballwin 636.779.5449

R: 236   **T:** 4th   51%
Elected Year: 2012

MONTANA

⚑ Governor Steve Bullock ("BULL"-luhk)   p 406.444.3111

Montana State Capitol Building   **C:** Helena
PO Box 200801   **P:** 1,062,305 (44)
Helena, MT 59620-0801   **A:** 145,545.78 mi^2 (4th)
Website mt.gov
Fax 406.444.5529
Term Ends 2021
Lt. Governor
Michael Cooney, **D**

U.S. Senators
Jon Tester, **D**
Steve Daines, **R**
U.S. Representatives
01 / Greg Gianforte, **R**

⚑ Sen. Steve Daines (daynz)   R-MT-Jr.   p 202.224.265

Rm. HSOB 320   **Web.** daines.senate.gov   **f** 202.228.123(
Bio. 08/20/1962 • Van Nuys, CA • Montana State Univ.,
Bozeman, B.S., 1984 • Presbyterian • M. Cindy Daines, 4
ch   **Cmte.** Appropriations • Energy & Natural Resources •
Finance • Indian Affairs
CoS. Jason Thielman   **LD.** Darin C. Thacker
Sched. Caitlin Affolter   **PS.** Katie Schoettler
Dist. Off. Billings 406.245.6822 • Bozeman 406.587.3446
• Great Falls 406.453.0148 • Hardin 406.665.4126 •
Helena 406.443.3189 • Kalispell 406.257.3765 • Missoula
406.549.8198 • Sidney 406.482.9010

R: 75   **T:** 1st   58%
Elected Year: 2014
Next Election: 2020

MONTANA

⌗ Sen. Jon Tester (TEHSS-tur)   D-MT-Sr.   p 202.224.2644

Rm. HSOB 311 **Web.** tester.senate.gov   **f** 202.224.8594
Bio. 08/21/1956 • Havre, MT • Farmer • Univ. of Great Falls
(MT), B.S., 1978 • Christian Church • M. Sharla Tester, 2 ch ;
2 gr-ch **Cmte.** Appropriations • Banking, Housing & Urban
Affairs • Commerce, Science & Transportation • Indian
Affairs • Veterans' Affairs
CoS. Dylan Laslovich   **LD.** Justin Folsom
Sched. Trecia McEvoy   **PS.** Sarah Feldman
Dist. Off. Billings 406.252.0550 • Bozeman 406.586.4450
• Butte 406.723.3277 • Great Falls 406.452.9585 •
Helena 406.449.5401 • Kalispell 406.257.3360 • Missoula
406.728.3003

R: 33 **T:** 2nd 50%
Elected Year: 2006
Next Election: 2024

⌗ Rep. Greg Gianforte (JEE-uhn-for-tay)   R-MT-01   p 202.225.3211

Rm. LHOB 1222 **Web.** gianforte.house.gov   **f** 202.225.5687
Bio. 04/17/1961 • San Diego, CA • Stevens Institute of
Technology, B.E., 1983; Stevens Institute of Technology,
M.S., 1983 • Christian - Non-Denominational • M. Susan
Gianforte, 4 ch   **Cmte.** Energy & Commerce
CoS. Christine Heggem   **LD.** Will Carraco
Sched. Maddy Morris   **PS.** Travis Hall
Dist. Off. Billings 406.969.1736 • Great Falls 406.952.1280
• Helena 406.502.1435

R: 336 **T:** 2nd 51%
Elected Year: 2017

NEBRASKA

⌗ Governor Pete Ricketts (RIH-kuhtss)   p 402.471.2244

State Capitol   **C:** Lincoln
PO Box 94848   **P:** 1,929,268 (38)
Lincoln, NE 68509-4848 **A:** 76,824.26 mi^2 (15th)
Website nebraska.gov
Fax 402.471.6031
Term Ends 2023
Lt. Governor
Mike Foley, **R**

U.S. Senators
Deb Fischer, **R**
Ben Sasse, **R**
U.S. Representatives
01 / Jeff L. Fortenberry, **R**
02 / Don J. Bacon, **R**
03 / Adrian M. Smith, **R**

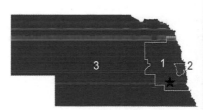

⌗ Sen. Deb Fischer (FIH-shur)   R-NE-Sr.   p 202.224.6551

Rm. RSOB 454 **Web.** fischer.senate.gov   **f** 202.228.1325
Bio. 03/01/1951 • Lincoln, NE • Univ. of Nebraska, Lincoln,
B.S., 1988 • Presbyterian • M. Bruce G. Fischer, 3 ch ; 3
gr-ch **Cmte.** Agriculture, Nutrition & Forestry • Armed
Services • Commerce, Science & Transportation • Rules &
Administration
CoS. Joe Hack   **LD.** Emily Leviner
Sched. Allison Haindfield   **PS.** Brianna Puccini
Dist. Off. Kearney 308.234.2361 • Lincoln 402.441.4600 •
Norfolk 402.200.8816 • Omaha 402.391.3411 • Scottsbluff
308.630.2329

R: 66 **T:** 2nd 58%
Elected Year: 2012
Next Election: 2024

NEBRASKA

🏛 Sen. Ben Sasse (sass)   R-NE-Jr.   p 202.224.4224

Rm. RSOB 136 **Web.** sasse.senate.gov
Bio. 02/22/1972 • Plainview, NE • Yale Univ. (CT), M.A.; Yale Univ. (CT), M.Phil; Harvard Univ., A.B., 1994; Saint John's College (MD), M.A., 1998; Yale Univ. (CT), Ph.D., 2004 • Lutheran • M. Melissa Sasse, 3 ch   **Cmte.** Banking, Housing & Urban Affairs • Intelligence • Joint Economic • Judiciary
CoS. Raymond Sass   **LD.** Patrick Lehman
Sched. Sarah Peer   **PS.** James Wegmann
Dist. Off. Kearney 308.233.3677 • Lincoln 402.476.1400 • Omaha 402.550.8040 • Scottsbluff 308.632.6032

R: 80   **T:** 1st 64%
Elected Year: 2014
Next Election: 2020

🏛 Rep. Don J. Bacon (BAY-kun)   R-NE-02   p 202.225.4155

Rm. LHOB 1024 **Web.** bacon.house.gov
Bio. 08/16/1963 • Momence, IL • Northern Illinois Univ., B.A., 1984; Univ. of Phoenix, Mast. Deg., 1995; National War College (DC), Mast. Deg., 2004; Univ. of Virginia Darden School of Business, Mast. Deg., 2009 • Christian - Non-Denominational • M. Angie Bacon, 4 ch   **Cmte.** Agriculture • Armed Services
CoS. Mark Edward Dreiling   **LD.** Jeff Kratz
Sched. Claire London   **PS.** Aron Wehr
Dist. Off. Omaha 402.938.0300

R: 293   **T:** 2nd 51%
Elected Year: 2016

🏛 Rep. Jeff L. Fortenberry (FOR-tuhn-bair-ee)   R-NE-01   p 202.225.4806

Rm. LHOB 1514 **Web.** fortenberry.house.gov **f** 202.225.5686
Bio. 12/27/1960 • Baton Rouge, LA • Lincoln City Council; Senate Aide • Franciscan Univ. (OH); Louisiana State Univ., B.A., 1982; Georgetown Univ. (DC), M.P.P., 1986; Franciscan Univ. (OH), M.A., 1996 • Roman Catholic • M. Celeste Gregory Fortenberry, 5 ch   **Cmte.** Appropriations
CoS. Reyn Archer   **LD.** Alan Feyerherm
                   PS. James Crotty (CD)
Dist. Off. Fremont 402.727.0888 • Lincoln 402.438.1598 • Norfolk 402.379.2064

R: 93   **T:** 8th 60%
Elected Year: 2004

🏛 Rep. Adrian M. Smith (smith)   R-NE-03   p 202.225.6435

Rm. CHOB 502 **Web.** adriansmith.house.gov **f** 202.225.0207
Bio. 12/19/1970 • Scottsbluff, NE • State Legislator; Realtor • Univ. of Nebraska, Lincoln, B.S., 1993 • Evangelical • M. Andrea Smith, 1 ch   **Cmte.** Ways & Means
CoS. Monica Didiuk   **LD.** Joshua Jackson
Sched. Becca Salter   **PS.** Matthew R. Goulding
Dist. Off. Grand Island 308.384.3900 • Scottsbluff 308.633.6333

R: 121   **T:** 7th 77%
Elected Year: 2006

NEVADA

NEVADA

🏛 Governor Steve Sisolak (Siso-lak)   p 775.684.5670

State Capitol
101 N. Carson St.
Carson City, NV 89701
Website nv.gov
Fax 775.684.5683
Term Ends 2023
Lt. Governor
Kate Marshall, **D**

C: Carson City
P: 3,034,392 (33)
A: 109,781.15 mi^2 (7th)

U.S. Senators
Catherine M. Cortez Masto, **D**
Jacklyn S. Rosen, **D**
U.S. Representatives
01 / Dina Titus, **D**
02 / Mark E. Amodei, **R**
03 / Susie K. Lee, **D**
04 / Steven A. Horsford, **D**

⁺ᵃ **Sen. Catherine M. Cortez Masto** (kor-TEZ-MASS-toe)   D-NV-Sr.   p 202.224.3542

Rm. HSOB 516
Bio. 03/29/1964 • Las Vegas, NV • Univ. of Nevada, Reno, B.S., 1986; Gonzaga Univ. School of Law, J.D., 1990 • Catholic • M. Paul Masto   **Cmte.** Aging • Banking, Housing & Urban Affairs • Energy & Natural Resources • Finance • Indian Affairs • Rules & Administration
CoS. Reynaldo Benitez   **LD.** Joleen Rivera
Sched. Anaisy Tolentino   **PS.** Ryan King
Dist. Off. Las Vegas 702.388.5020 • Reno 775.686.5750

R: 88   **T:** 1st   47%
Elected Year: 2016
Next Election: 2022

⁺ᵃ **Sen. Jacklyn S. Rosen** (RO-zuhn)   D-NV-Jr.   p 202.224.6244

Rm. DSOB G12   **Web.** rosen.senate.gov
Bio. 08/02/1957 • Chicago, IL • Univ. of Minnesota, B.A., 1979 • Jewish • M. Larry Rosen, 1 ch   **Cmte.** Aging • Commerce, Science & Transportation • Health, Education, Labor & Pensions • Homeland Security & Government Affairs • Small Business & Entrepreneurship
CoS. Dara Cohen   **LD.** Grant Dubler
Sched. Nicole Echeto   **PS.** Ilse Zuniga
Dist. Off. Las Vegas 702.388.0205 • Reno 775.337.0110

R: 96   **T:** 0th   50%
Elected Year: 2018
Next Election: 2024

⁺ᵃ **Rep. Mark E. Amodei** (AM uh-day)   R-NV-02   p 202.225.6155

Rm. CHOB 104   **Web.** amodei.house.gov   **f** 202.225.5079
Bio. 06/12/1958 • Carson City, NV • Univ. of Nevada, Reno, B.A., 1980; Univ. of the Pacific McGeorge School of Law (CA), J.D., 1983 • Presbyterian • D., 2 ch   **Cmte.** Appropriations
CoS. Bruce F Miller   **LD.** Molly Lowe
Sched. Jessica Markowitz   **PS.** Logan Ramsey
Dist. Off. Elko 775.777.7705 • Reno 775.686.5760

R: 188   **T:** 5th   58%
Elected Year: 2011

⁺ᵃ **Rep. Steven A. Horsford** (HORSS-furd)   D-NV-04   p 202.225.9894

Rm. LHOB 1330   **Web.** horsford.house.gov
Bio. 04/29/1973 • Las Vegas, NV • NV State Senator • Univ. of Nevada, Reno, B.A., 2014 • Baptist • M. Dr. Sonya Horsford, 3 ch   **Cmte.** Budget • Natural Resources • Ways & Means
CoS. Jason Rodriguez   **LD.** Josie Villanueva
Sched. Oscar Dunham   **PS.** Robyn Patterson
Dist. Off. North Las Vegas 702.963.9360

R: 348   **T:** 2nd   52%
Elected Year: 2018

NEVADA

⚐ Rep. Susie K. Lee (lee)   D-NV-03   p 202.225.3252

Rm. CHOB 522 **Web.** susielee.house.gov
Bio. 11/07/1966 • Canton, OH • Carnegie Mellon Univ., B.S.,
1989; Carnegie Mellon Univ., M.P.A., 1990 • Catholic • M.
Dan Lee, 2 ch **Cmte.** Education & Labor • Veterans' Affairs
CoS. Brandon Cox   **LD.** Sam Morgante
Sched. Sreyashe Dhar   **PS.** Renzo Olivari
Dist. Off. Las Vegas 702.963.9336

R: 387 **T:** 1st 52%
Elected Year: 2018

⚐ Rep. Dina Titus (TY-tuhs)   D-NV-01   p 202.225.5965

Rm. RHOB 2464 **Web.** titus.house.gov   **f** 202.225.3119
Bio. 05/23/1950 • Thomasville, GA • State Legislator;
Professor • College of William and Mary (VA), A.B., 1970;
Univ. of Georgia, M.A., 1973; Florida State Univ., Ph.D., 1976
• Greek Orthodox • M. Thomas Clayton Wright **Cmte.**
Foreign Affairs • Homeland Security • Transportation &
Infrastructure
CoS. Jay Gertsema   **LD.** Ben Rosenbaum
Sched. Colleen Hearin   **PS.** Kevin Gerson
Dist. Off. Las Vegas 702.220.9823

R: 193 **T:** 5th 66%
Elected Year: 2012

NEW HAMPSHIRE

NEW HAMPSHIRE

▣ Governor Chris Sununu (suh-NOO-noo)   p 603.271.2121

State House   **C:** Concord
107 N. Main St.   **P:** 1,356,458 (42)
Concord, NH 03301   **A:** 8,952.55 mi^2 (44th)
Website nh.gov
Fax 603.271.7640
Term Ends 2021

U.S. Senators
Jeanne Shaheen, **D**
Maggie Hassan, **D**
U.S. Representatives
01 / Christopher C. Pappas, **D**
02 / Ann McLane Kuster, **D**

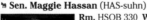

⚐ Sen. Maggie Hassan (HAS-suhn)   D-NH-Jr.   p 202.224.332

Rm. HSOB 330 **Web.** hassan.senate.gov   **f** 202.228.058
Bio. 02/27/1958 • Boston, MA • Brown Univ. (RI), A.B.,
1980; Northeastern Univ. Law School (MA), J.D., 1985 •
United Church of Christ • M. Thomas Hassan, 2 ch **Cmte.**
Finance • Health, Education, Labor & Pensions • Homeland
Security & Government Affairs • Joint Economic
CoS. Marc P. Goldberg   **LD.** Dave Christie
Sched. Catherine E. George **PS.** Aaron Jacobs
Dist. Off. Berlin 603.752.6190 • Concord 603.622.2204
• Manchester 603.622.2204 • Nashua 603.880.3314 •
Portsmouth 603.433.4445

R: 85 **T:** 1st 48%
Elected Year: 2016
Next Election: 2022

⬆ Sen. Jeanne Shaheen (shuh-HEEN)　　　D-NH-Sr.　　p 202.224.2841

Rm. HSOB 506 **Web.** shaheen.senate.gov　　**f** 202.228.3194
Bio. 01/28/1947 • St. Charles, MO • Governor, NH; State
Legislator; Teacher • Shippensburg Univ. (PA), B.A., 1969;
Univ. of Mississippi, M.S., 1973 • Protestant - Unspecified
Christian • M. William Shaheen, 3 ch ; 7 gr-ch **Cmte.**
Appropriations • Armed Services • Ethics • Foreign
Relations • Small Business & Entrepreneurship
CoS. Chad Kreikemeier　　　　**LD.** Robert Diznoff
Sched. Meaghan D'Arcy　　　　**PS.** Ryan Nickel
Dist. Off. Berlin 603.752.6300 • Claremont 603.542.4872
• Dover 603.750.3004 • Keene 603.358.6604 • Manchester
603.647.7500 • Nashua 603.883.0196

R: 37 **T:** 2nd 52%
Elected Year: 2008
Next Election: 2020

⬆ Rep. Ann McLane Kuster (mih-KLAIN KUH-stur)　D-NH-02　p 202.225.5206

Rm. CHOB 320 **Web.** kuster.house.gov　　**f** 202.225.2946
Bio. 09/05/1956 • Concord, NH • Dartmouth College,
A.B., 1978; Georgetown Univ. Law Center (DC), J.D., 1984 •
Christian Church • M. Brad Kuster, 2 ch **Cmte.** Energy &
Commerce
CoS. Abby Curran Horrell　　　**LD.** Travis Krogman
Sched. Maria Ewing　　　　　**PS.** Nick Brown
Dist. Off. Concord 603.226.1002 • Littleton 603.444.7700 •
Nashua 603.595.2006

R: 218 **T:** 4th 56%
Elected Year: 2012

⬆ Rep. Christopher C. Pappas (PAP-puhss)　　D-NH-01　p 202.225.5456

Rm. CHOB 323 **Web.** pappas.house.gov
Bio. 06/04/1980 • Manchester, NH • Harvard College (MA),
B.A., 2002 • Greek Orthodox • S. **Cmte.** Transportation &
Infrastructure • Veterans' Affairs
CoS. Matt Lee　　　　　　**LD.** Steven Carlson
Sched. Elizabeth Kulig　　　**PS.** Wyatt Ronan (CD)
Dist. Off. Dover 603.285.4300

R: 400 **T:** 1st 54%
Elected Year: 2018

NEW JERSEY

⬆ Governor Phil Murphy (MUR-fee)　　　　　　p 609.292.6000

The State House　　　　　**C:** Trenton
PO Box 001　　　　　　　**P:** 8,908,520 (11)
Trenton, NJ 08625　　　　**A:** 7,354.08 mi^2 (46th)
Website nj.gov
Fax 609.292.3454
Term Ends 2022
Lt. Governor
Sheila Oliver, **D**

U.S. Senators
Bob Menendez, **D**
Cory A. Booker, **D**
U.S. Representatives
1 / Donald W. Norcross, **D**
2 / Jeff Van Drew, **D**
3 / Andrew Kim, **D**
4 / Chris H. Smith, **R**
5 / Josh S. Gottheimer, **D**
6 / Frank J. Pallone, **D**
7 / Tom Malinowski, **D**
8 / Albio Sires, **D**
9 / Bill J. Pascrell, **D**
10 / Donald M. Payne, **D**
11 / Mikie Sherrill, **D**
12 / Bonnie Watson Coleman, **D**

NEW JERSEY

⅋ Sen. Cory A. Booker ("BOOK"-ur) D-NJ-Jr. p 202.224.3224

Rm. HSOB 717 **Web.** booker.senate.gov **f** 202.224.8378
Bio. 04/27/1969 • Washington, DC • Stanford Univ. (CA),
B.A., 1991; Stanford Univ. (CA), M.A., 1992; Yale Law School
(CT), J.D., 1997 • Baptist • S. **Cmte.** Environment & Public
Works • Foreign Relations • Judiciary • Small Business &
Entrepreneurship
CoS. Tricia Russell **LD.** Veronica Duron
Sched. Jane Wiesenberg **PS.** Kristin Lynch
Dist. Off. Camden 856.338.8922 • Newark 973.639.8700

R: 68 **T:** 2nd 56%
Elected Year: 2013
Next Election: 2020

⅋ Sen. Bob Menendez (meh-NEN-dehz) D-NJ-Sr. p 202.224.4744

Rm. HSOB 528 **Web.** menendez.senate.gov **f** 202.228.2197
Bio. 01/01/1954 • New York, NY • State Senator; Mayor of
Union City • St. Peter's College (NJ), B.A., 1976; Rutgers
Univ. Law School (NJ), J.D., 1979 • Roman Catholic • D., 2
ch **Cmte.** Banking, Housing & Urban Affairs • Finance •
Foreign Relations
CoS. Fred Turner
Sched. Maria Almeida (CD) **PS.** Patricia Enright
Dist. Off. Barrington 856.757.5353 • Newark 973.645.3030

R: 26 **T:** 3rd 54%
Elected Year: 2006
Next Election: 2024

⅋ Rep. Josh S. Gottheimer (GAHT-hy-mur) D-NJ-05 p 202.225.4465

Rm. CHOB 213 **Web.** gottheimer.house.gov **f** 202.225.9048
Bio. 03/08/1975 • Livingston, NJ • Univ. of Pennsylvania,
B.A., 1997; Harvard Law School (MA), J.D., 2004 • Jewish
• M. Marla Brooke Tusk Gottheimer, 2 ch **Cmte.** Financial
Services
CoS. Ashley Lantz **LD.** Hannah Berner
Sched. Jenna Christiansen **PS.** Matt Fried
Dist. Off. Glen Rock 201.389.1100 • Hackensack
973.814.4076 • Newton 973.940.1117 • Ringwood
973.814.4076 • Vernon Township 973.814.4076 •
Washington 973.814.4076

R: 313 **T:** 2nd 56%
Elected Year: 2016

⅋ Rep. Andrew Kim (kim) D-NJ-03 p 202.225.4765

Rm. LHOB 1516 **Web.** kim.house.gov
Bio. 07/12/1982 • Boston, MA • Univ. of Chicago (IL),
B.A., 2004; Univ. of Oxford (UK), B.A., 2004; Oxford Univ.
(England), M.Phil, 2007 • Presbyterian • M. Kammy Kim, 2
ch **Cmte.** Armed Services • Small Business
CoS. Amy M. Pfeiffer **LD.** Yujin Lee
Sched. Cecily Scott Scott **PS.** Anthony DeAngelo
Martin
Dist. Off. Marlton

R: 386 **T:** 1st 50%
Elected Year: 2018

⅋ Rep. Tom Malinowski (ma-lih-NOU-skee) D-NJ-07 p 202.225.5361

Rm. CHOB 426 **Web.** malinowski.house.gov
Bio. 09/15/1965 • Slupsk, Poland • Unspecified/Other
• D., 1 ch **Cmte.** Foreign Affairs • Transportation &
Infrastructure
CoS. Colston Reid **LD.** Eliza Ramirez
Sched. D'Andre Carter **PS.** Amanda Osborne
Dist. Off. Somerville 908.547.3307

R: 391 **T:** 1st 52%
Elected Year: 2018

⭐ Rep. Donald W. Norcross (NOR-krawss)　　D-NJ-01　p 202.225.6501

Rm. RHOB 2437 **Web.** norcross.house.gov　**f** 202.225.6583
Bio. 12/13/1958 • Camden, NJ • Camden County College
(NJ), A.S., 1979; Pennsauken High School (NJ), A.S., 1979 •
Lutheran • M. Andrea Doran, 3 ch; 2 gr-ch **Cmte.** Armed
Services • Education & Labor
CoS. Michael Maitland　　　**LD.** Ryan Ehly
Sched. Lara Weinstein　　　**PS.** Allyson Kehoe
Dist. Off. Cherry Hill 856.427.7000

R: 247　T: 4th 64%
Elected Year: 2014

⭐ Rep. Frank J. Pallone Jr. (puh-LOAN)　　D-NJ-06　p 202.225.4671

Rm. RHOB 2107 **Web.** pallone.house.gov　**f** 202.225.9665
Bio. 10/30/1951 • Long Branch, NJ • State Senator;
Member, City Council • Middlebury College (VT), B.A.,
1973; Tufts Univ. Fletcher School of Law and Diplomacy
(MA), M.A., 1974; Rutgers Univ. Law School (NJ), J.D., 1978 •
Roman Catholic • M. Sarah Hospodor Pallone, 3 ch **Cmte.**
Energy & Commerce
CoS. Liam Fitzsimmons　　　**LD.** Roberto Sada
Sched. Alexander Gristina　　　**PS.** Anton Becker
Dist. Off. Long Branch 732.571.1140 • New Brunswick
732.249.8892

R: 12　T: 17th 64%
Elected Year: 1988

⭐ Rep. Bill J. Pascrell Jr. (PASS-krell)　　D-NJ-09　p 202.225.5751

Rm. RHOB 2409 **Web.** pascrell.house.gov　**f** 202.225.5782
Bio. 01/25/1937 • Paterson, NJ • Attorney • Army 1961-62;
Army Reserves 1962-67 • Fordham Univ. (NY), B.S., 1959;
Fordham Univ. (NY), M.A., 1961 • Roman Catholic • M. Elsie
Marie Botto Pascrell, 3 ch ; 3 gr-ch **Cmte.** Ways & Means
CoS. Benjamin Rich　　　**LD.** Elaina Houser
Sched. Christopher Hadad　　　**PS.** Mark Greenbaum
Dist. Off. Englewood 201.935.2248 • Lyndhurst
201.935.2248 • Passaic 973.472.4510 • Paterson
973.523.5152

R: 52　T: 12th 70%
Elected Year: 1996

⭐ Rep. Donald M. Payne Jr. (pain)　　D-NJ-10　p 202.225.3436

Rm. CHOB 103 **Web.** payne.house.gov　**f** 202.225.4160
Bio. 12/17/1958 • Newark, NJ • Baptist • M. Bea Payne, 3
ch (triplets) **Cmte.** Homeland Security • Transportation &
Infrastructure
CoS. LaVerne Alexander
Sched. Shannon Casey　　　**PS.** R. Kyle Alagood
Dist. Off. Hillside 862.229.2994 • Jersey City 201.369.0392
• Newark 973.645.3213

R: 192　T: 5th 88%
Elected Year: 2012

⭐ Rep. Mikie Sherrill (SHAIR-uhl)　　D-NJ-11　p 202.225.5034

Rm. LHOB 1208 **Web.** sherrill.house.gov
Bio. 01/19/1972 • Alexandria, VA • U.S. Naval Academy
(MD), B.S., 1994; London School of Economics and Political
Science, Mast. Deg., 2003; Georgetown Univ. (DC), J.D.,
2007 • Catholic • M. Jason Hedberg, 4 ch **Cmte.** Armed
Services • Science, Space & Technology
CoS. Ethan Saxon　　　**LD.** Tom Stewart
Sched. Julie Jochem　　　**PS.** Jackie Burns
Dist. Off. Parsippany 973.526.5668

: 413　T: 1st 57%
elected Year: 2018

⭐ Rep. Albio Sires (SEER-ehz)　　D-NJ-08　p 202.225.7919

Rm. RHOB 2268 **Web.** sires.house.gov　**f** 202.226.0792
Bio. 01/26/1951 • Bejucal, Cuba • State Legislator;
Insurance Executive • Middlebury College (VT), M.A., 1985;
Saint Peter's College (NJ), M.A., 1985 • Roman Catholic • M.
Adrienne Sires, 1 stepch **Cmte.** Budget • Foreign Affairs •
Transportation & Infrastructure
CoS. Gene Martorony　　　**LD.** Clare Plassche
Sched. Judi Wolford　　　**PS.** Erica Daughtrey (CD)
Dist. Off. Elizabeth 908.820.0692 • Jersey City 201.309.0301
• West New York 201.558.0800

: 106　T: 8th 78%
elected Year: 2006

🏛 Rep. Chris H. Smith (smith) R-NJ-04 p 202.225.3765

Rm. RHOB 2373 **Web.** chrissmith.house.gov **f** 202.225.7768
Bio. 03/04/1953 • Rahway, NJ • State Legislator; Wholesaler
• Trenton State College (NJ), B.A., 1975 • Roman Catholic •
M. Marie Hahn Smith, 4 ch **Cmte.** Foreign Affairs
CoS. Mary Noonan **LD.** Kelsey Griswold
Sched. Angela Ryan **PS.** Matt Hadro
Dist. Off. Freehold 732.780.3035 • Hamilton 609.585.7878
• Plumsted 609.585.7878

R: 4 **T:** 20th 55%
Elected Year: 1980

🏛 Rep. Jeff Van Drew (droo) D-NJ-02 p 202.225.6572

Rm. CHOB 331 **Web.** vandrew.house.gov
Bio. 02/23/1953 • New York, NY • Rutgers Univ. (NJ),
B.S., 1975; Fairleigh Dickinson Univ., D.D.S., 1979; Veterans
Administration New Jersey Healthcare; Lyons and East
Orange Veterans Hospitals, D.D.S., 1979 • Catholic • M.
Ricarda Drew, 2 ch **Cmte.** Agriculture • Natural Resources
CoS. Allison Murphy **LD.** Javier Gamboa
Sched. Justin Mark O'Leary **PS.** MacKenzie Lucas
Dist. Off. Mays Landing 609.625.5008

R: 429 **T:** 1st 53%
Elected Year: 2018

🏛 Rep. Bonnie Watson Coleman (WAHT-suhn D-NJ-12 p 202.225.5801
KOAL-muhn)

Rm. RHOB 2442 **Web.** **f** 202.225.6025
watsoncoleman.house.gov
Bio. 02/06/1945 • Camden, NJ • Thomas Edison State
College (NJ), B.A., 1985 • Baptist • M. William E. Coleman
Jr., 1 ch ; 2 stepch ; 3 gr-ch **Cmte.** Appropriations •
Homeland Security
CoS. James Gee **LD.** Kevin Block
Sched. Jaimee Gilmartin **PS.** Courtney Cochran
(CD)
Dist. Off. Ewing 609.883.0026

R: 283 **T:** 3rd 69%
Elected Year: 2014

NEW MEXICO

🏛 Governor Michelle Lujan Grisham (LOO-hahn GRIH- p 505.476.2200
shuhm)

State Capitol **C:** Santa Fe
490 Old Sante Fe Trail, Room 400 **P:** 2,095,428 (37)
Santa Fe, NM 87501 **A:** 121,298.19 mi^2 (5th)
Website newmexico.gov
Fax 505.476.2226
Term Ends 2023
Lt. Governor
Howie Morales, **D**

U.S. Senators
Tom S. Udall, **D**
Martin T. Heinrich, **D**
U.S. Representatives
01 / Debra A. Haaland, **D**
02 / Xochitl Liana I. Torres-
Small, **D**
03 / Ben Ray Lujan, **D**

NEW MEXICO

᛫ Sen. Martin T. Heinrich (HYN-rihk)   D-NM-Jr.   p 202.224.5521

Rm. HSOB 303   **Web.** heinrich.senate.gov   **f** 202.228.2841
Bio. 10/17/1971 • Fallon, NV • Businessman • Univ. of Missouri, B.S., 1995 • Lutheran • M. Julie Heinrich, 2 ch
Cmte. Armed Services • Energy & Natural Resources • Intelligence • Joint Economic
CoS. Joe Britton   **LD.** Virgilio Barrera
Sched. Caitlin Terry   **PS.** Whitney Potter
Dist. Off. Albuquerque 505.346.6601 • Farmington 505.325.5030 • Las Cruces 575.523.6561 • Roswell 575.622.7113 • Santa Fe 505.988.6647

R: 61   **T:** 2nd   54%
Elected Year: 2012
Next Election: 2024

᛫ Sen. Tom S. Udall (YOO-dahl)   D-NM-Sr.   p 202.224.6621

Rm. HSOB 531   **Web.** tomudall.senate.gov   **f** 202.228.3261
Bio. 05/18/1948 • Tucson, AZ • NM Attorney General; Attorney • Prescott College (AZ), B.A., 1970; Cambridge Univ. (England), LL.B., 1975; Univ. of New Mexico Law School, J.D., 1977 • Mormon • M. Jill Cooper Udall, 1 ch   **Cmte.** Appropriations • Commerce, Science & Transportation • Foreign Relations • Indian Affairs • Rules & Administration
CoS. Bianca Ortiz-Wertheim   **LD.** Andrew Wallace
Sched. Devon Wohl   **PS.** Ned Adriance
Dist. Off. Albuquerque 505.346.6791 • Carlsbad 575.234.0366 • Las Cruces 575.526.5475 • Portales 575.356.6811 • Santa Fe 505.988.6511

R: 36   **T:** 2nd   56%
Elected Year: 2008
Next Election: 2020

᛫ Rep. Debra A. Haaland (HAH-lund)   D-NM-01   p 202.225.6316

Rm. LHOB 1237   **Web.** haaland.house.gov
Bio. 12/02/1960 • Winslow, AZ • Univ. of New Mexico, B.A., 1994; Univ. of New Mexico Law School, J.D., 2006 • Catholic • S., 1 ch   **Cmte.** Natural Resources
CoS. Jennifer Van der Heide   **LD.** Eric Werwa
Sched. Christopher Garcia   **PS.** Felicia Salazar
Dist. Off. Albuquerque 505.346.6781

R: 377   **T:** 1st   59%
Elected Year: 2018

᛫ Rep. Ben Ray Lujan Jr. (LOO-hahn)   D-NM-03   p 202.225.6190

Rm. RHOB 2323   **Web.** lujan.house.gov   **f** 202.226.1528
Bio. 06/07/1972 • Santa Fe, NM • Chairman, New Mexico Public Regulation Commission • New Mexico Highlands Univ., B.A., 2007 • Roman Catholic • S.   **Cmte.** Energy & Commerce • Select Committee on the Climate Crisis
CoS. Angela Ramirez   **LD.** Kimberly Espinosa
Sched. Matthew Hoeck   **PS.** Lauren Dart
Dist. Off. Farmington 505.324.1005 • Gallup 505.863.0582 • Las Vegas 505.454.3038 • Rio Rancho 505.994.0499 • Santa Fe 505.984.8950 • Tucumcari 575.461.3020

R: 135   **T:** 6th   63%
Elected Year: 2008

᛫ Rep. Xochitl Liana I. Torres-Small ()   D-NM-02   p 202.225.2365

Rm. CHOB 430   **Web.** torressmall.house.gov
Bio. 11/15/1984 • Portland, OR • Georgetown Univ. (DC), Bach. Deg., 2007; Univ. of New Mexico Law School, J.D., 2015 • Lutheran • M. Nathan Small   **Cmte.** Armed Services • Homeland Security
CoS. Rene Munoz   **LD.** Brooke Stuedell
Sched. Edna Tapia   **PS.** Brian Sowyrda
Dist. Off. Las Cruces

R: 425   **T:** 1st   51%
Elected Year: 2018

NEW YORK

NEW YORK

🏛 **Governor Andrew Mark Cuomo** (KWO-moe)   p 518.474.8390

State Capitol
Executive Chambers
Albany, NY 12224
Website ny.gov
Fax 518.474.1513
Term Ends 2022
Lt. Governor
Kathy Hochul, **D**

C: Albany
P: 19,542,209 (4)
A: 47,126.45 mi^2 (30th)

U.S. Senators
Charles E. Schumer, **D**
Kirsten E. Gillibrand, **D**
U.S. Representatives
01 / Lee M. Zeldin, **R**
02 / Pete T. King, **R**
03 / Thomas R. Suozzi, **D**
04 / Kathleen M. Rice, **D**
05 / Gregory W. Meeks, **D**
06 / Grace Meng, **D**
07 / Nydia M. Velazquez, **D**
08 / Hakeem S. Jeffries, **D**
09 / Yvette D. Clarke, **D**
10 / Jerry L. Nadler, **D**
11 / Max N. Rose, **D**
12 / Carolyn B. Maloney, **D**
13 / Adriano Espaillat, **D**
14 / Alexandria Ocasio-Cortez, **D**
15 / Jose E. Serrano, **D**
16 / Eliot L. Engel, **D**
17 / Nita M. Lowey, **D**
18 / Sean P. Maloney, **D**
19 / Antonio Delgado, **D**
20 / Paul D. Tonko, **D**
21 / Elise M. Stefanik, **R**
22 / Anthony J. Brindisi, **D**
23 / Tom W. Reed, **R**
24 / John M. Katko, **R**
25 / Joseph D. Morelle, **D**
26 / Brian M. Higgins, **D**
27 / Chris C. Collins, **R**

🏛 **Sen. Kirsten E. Gillibrand** (JIH-luh-brand)   D-NY-Jr.   p 202.224.445

Rm. RSOB 478 **Web.** gillibrand.senate.gov   **f** 202.228.028
Bio. 12/09/1966 • Albany, NY • Attorney • Dartmouth
College, B.A., 1988; Univ. of California, Los Angeles, J.D.,
1991 • Roman Catholic • M. Jonathan Gillibrand, 2 ch
Cmte. Aging • Agriculture, Nutrition & Forestry • Armed
Services • Environment & Public Works
CoS. Joi Chaney   **LD.** Brooke Jamison
Sched. Angelica Annino   **PS.** Whitney Brennan
Dist. Off. Albany 518.431.0120 • Buffalo 716.854.9725
• Lowville 315.376.6118 • Melville 631.249.2825 • New
York 212.688.6262 • Rochester 585.263.6250 • Syracuse
315.448.0470 • Yonkers 845.875.4585

R: 42 **T:** 2nd 67%
Elected Year: 2009
Next Election: 2024

🏛 **Sen. Charles E. Schumer** (SHOO-mur)   D-NY-Sr.   p 202.224.654

Rm. HSOB 322 **Web.** schumer.senate.gov   **f** 202.228.302
Bio. 11/23/1950 • Brooklyn, NY • U.S. Representative;
Attorney • Harvard Univ., B.A., 1971; Harvard Univ., J.D.,
1974 • Jewish • M. Iris Weinshall, 2 ch ; 1 gr-ch **Cmte.**
Rules & Administration
CoS. Michael Lynch   **LD.** Meghan Taira
Sched. Michelle Mittler   **PS.** Allison Biasotti
Dist. Off. Albany 518.431.4070 • Binghamton 607.772.679
• Buffalo 716.846.4111 • Melville 631.753.0978 • New
York 212.486.4430 • Peekskill 914.734.1532 • Rochester
585.263.5866 • Syracuse 315.423.5471

R: 14 **T:** 4th 71%
Elected Year: 1998
Next Election: 2022

Rep. Anthony J. Brindisi (brin-DIH-see)   D-NY-22   p 202.225.3665
Rm. CHOB 329 **Web.** brindisi.house.gov
Bio. 11/22/1978 • Utica, NY • Siena College (NY), B.S.,
2000; Albany Law School, J.D., 2004 • Catholic • M. Erica
McGovern, 2 ch **Cmte.** Agriculture • Veterans' Affairs
CoS. Ellen Foster   **LD.** Robert Dougherty
Sched. Caroline Ehlich   **PS.** Macey Matthews
Dist. Off. Utica 315.765.0463

R: 353 **T:** 1st 51%
Elected Year: 2018

Rep. Yvette D. Clarke (klark)   D-NY-09   p 202.225.6231
Rm. RHOB 2058 **Web.** clarke.house.gov   **f** 202.226.0112
Bio. 11/21/1964 • Brooklyn, NY • State Representative
• African Methodist Episcopal • S. **Cmte.** Energy &
Commerce • Homeland Security
CoS. Charlyn Stanberry   **LD.** David Dorfman
Sched. Tria Stallings   **PS.** Christine Bennett
Dist. Off. Brooklyn 718.287.1142

R: 110 **T:** 7th 89%
Elected Year: 2006

Rep. Chris C. Collins (KAH-luhnz)   R-NY-27   p 202.225.5265
Rm. RHOB 2243 **Web.** chriscollins.house.gov **f** 202.225.5910
Bio. 05/20/1950 • Schenectady, NY • North Carolina State
Univ., B.S., 1972; Univ. of Alabama, Birmingham, M.B.A.,
1975 • Roman Catholic • M. Mary Sue Collins, 3 ch ; 4 gr-ch
CoS. Michael Hook
Sched. Megan Paulsen
Dist. Off. Geneseo 585.519.4002 • Williamsville
716.634.2324

R: 203 **T:** 4th 49%
Elected Year: 2012

Rep. Antonio Delgado (del-GAH-"doc")   D-NY-19   p 202.225.5614
Rm. LHOB 1007 **Web.** delgado.house.gov
Bio. 01/28/1977 • Schenectady, NY • Colgate Univ., B.A.,
1999; Oxford Univ. (England), M.A., 2001, Harvard Univ.
Law School (MA), J.D., 2005 • Unspecified/Other • M.
Lacey Delgado, 2 ch **Cmte.** Agriculture • Small Business •
Transportation & Infrastructure
CoS. John Bivona
Sched. Julia Carnes   **PS.** Laura Epstein
Dist. Off. Rhinebeck 845.235.6081

R: 365 **T:** 1st 51%
Elected Year: 2018

Rep. Eliot L. Engel (ENG-gull)   D-NY-16   p 202.225.2464
Rm. RHOB 2426 **Web.** engel.house.gov   **f** 202.225.5513
Bio. 02/18/1947 • Bronx, NY • State Legislator • Hunter-
Lehman College (NY), B.A., 1969; City Univ. of New York -
Herbert H. Lehman College, M.S., 1973; New York Univ. Law
School, J.D., 1987 • Jewish • M. Patricia Ennis Engel, 3 ch
Cmte. Energy & Commerce • Foreign Affairs
CoS. William F. Weitz (CD)   **LD.** Brian Skretny
Sched. Darlene Murray   **PS.** Bryant Daniels (CD)
Dist. Off. Bronx 718.320.2314 • Bronx 718.796.9700 •
Mount Vernon 914.699.4100

: 13 **T:** 16th 99%
lected Year: 1988

Rep. Adriano Espaillat (eh-spy-YAHT)   D-NY-13   p 202.225.4365
Rm. LHOB 1630 **Web.** espaillat.house.gov   **f** 202.226.9731
Bio. 09/27/1954 • Santiago, Dominican Republic • Univ.
of New York Queens College (NY), B.S., 1978 • Roman
Catholic • M. Marthera Madera Espaillat, 2 ch **Cmte.**
Foreign Affairs • Small Business • Transportation &
Infrastructure
CoS. Aneiry Batista   **LD.** Todd Sloves
Sched. Raphael Dominguez   **PS.** Candace Person
Dist. Off. Bronx 718.450.8241 • New York 212.663.3900

: 307 **T:** 2nd 94%
ected Year: 2016

NEW YORK

ꙮ Rep. Brian M. Higgins (HIH-guhnz) D-NY-26 p 202.225.3306
Rm. RHOB 2459 **Web.** higgins.house.gov **f** 202.226.0347
Bio. 10/06/1959 • Buffalo, NY • Member, State Assembly; Member, City Council • Buffalo State College (NY), B.S., 1984; Buffalo State College (NY), M.A., 1985; Harvard Univ. John F. Kennedy School of Government (MA), M.A., 1996 • Catholic • M. Mary Jane Hannon, 2 ch **Cmte.** Budget • Ways & Means
CoS. Matthew J. Fery   **LD.** Kayla L. Williams
Sched. Cooper Ehrendreich   **PS.** Theresa Kennedy (CD)
Dist. Off. Buffalo 716.852.3501 • Niagara Falls 716.282.1274
R: 97 **T:** 8th 73%
Elected Year: 2004

ꙮ Rep. Hakeem S. Jeffries (JEHF-reez) D-NY-08 p 202.225.5936
Rm. RHOB 2433 **Web.** jeffries.house.gov **f** 202.225.1018
Bio. 08/04/1970 • Brooklyn, NY • State Univ. of New York, Binghamton, B.A., 1992; Georgetown Univ. (DC), M.P.P., 1994; New York Univ. Law School, J.D., 1997 • Baptist • M. Kennisandra Jeffries, 2 ch **Cmte.** Budget • Judiciary
CoS. Tasia Jackson   **LD.** Zoe Oreck
Sched. Lauren Milnes   **PS.** Michael Hardaway
Dist. Off. Brooklyn 718.237.2211 • Brooklyn 718.373.0033
R: 213 **T:** 4th 94%
Elected Year: 2012

ꙮ Rep. John M. Katko (KAT-ko) R-NY-24 p 202.225.3701
Rm. RHOB 2457 **Web.** katko.house.gov **f** 202.225.4042
Bio. 11/09/1962 • Syracuse, NY • Niagara Univ., B.A., 1984; Syracuse Univ. - College of Law (NY), J.D., 1988 • Roman Catholic • M. Robin Katko, 3 ch **Cmte.** Homeland Security • Transportation & Infrastructure
CoS. Zach Howell   **LD.** Jennifer Wood
Sched. Emily Bazydlo   **PS.** Erin O'Connor (CD)
Dist. Off. Auburn 315.253.4068 • Lyons 315.253.4068 • Oswego 315.423.5657 • Syracuse 315.423.5657
R: 268 **T:** 3rd 53%
Elected Year: 2014

ꙮ Rep. Pete T. King (king) R-NY-02 p 202.225.7896
Rm. CHOB 302 **Web.** peteking.house.gov **f** 202.226.2279
Bio. 04/05/1944 • New York, NY • Nassau County Comptroller; Hempstead Town Council Member • Army Reserve National Guard 1968-73 • St. Francis College (NY), B.A., 1965; Univ. of Notre Dame Law School (IN), J.D., 1968 • Roman Catholic • M. Rosemary Wiedel King, 2 ch ; 2 gr-ch
Cmte. Financial Services • Homeland Security
CoS. Kevin C. Fogarty   **LD.** Deena Tauster
Dist. Off. Massapequa Park 516.541.4225
R: 29 **T:** 14th 53%
Elected Year: 1992

ꙮ Rep. Nita M. Lowey (LOE-ee) D-NY-17 p 202.225.650
Rm. RHOB 2365 **Web.** lowey.house.gov **f** 202.225.054
Bio. 07/05/1937 • Bronx, NY • Assistant Secretary of State for NY • Mount Holyoke College (MA), B.S., 1959 • Jewish • M. Stephen Lowey, 3 ch ; 8 gr-ch **Cmte.** Appropriations
CoS. Elizabeth Stanley   **LD.** Dana Acton
Sched. Kathlyn Connolly (CD)   **PS.** Katelynn Thorpe
Dist. Off. New City 845.639.3485 • White Plains 914.428.1707
R: 14 **T:** 16th 88%
Elected Year: 1988

ꙮ Rep. Carolyn B. Maloney (muh-LOAN-ee) D-NY-12 p 202.225.794
Rm. RHOB 2308 **Web.** maloney.house.gov **f** 202.225.470
Bio. 02/19/1946 • Greensboro, NC • NYC Board of Education; NYC Council Member • Greensboro College (NC), Bach. Deg., 1968 • Presbyterian • W., 2 ch **Cmte.** Financial Services • Joint Economic • Oversight & Reform
CoS. Michael Iger   **LD.** Christina Parisi
Sched. Rebecca Tulloch   **PS.** Jennifer Bell
Dist. Off. Astoria 718.932.1804 • Brooklyn 718.349.5972 • New York 212.860.0606
R: 30 **T:** 14th 86%
Elected Year: 1992

➤ Rep. Sean P. Maloney (muh-LO-nee) — D-NY-18 — p 202.225.5441

Rm. RHOB 2331 **Web.** f 202.225.3289
seanmaloney.house.gov
Bio. 07/30/1966 • Sherbrooke, Canada • Univ. of Virginia,
B.A., 1988; Univ. of Virginia School of Law, J.D., 1992 •
Roman Catholic • M. Randy Florke, 3 ch **Cmte.** Agriculture
• Permanent Select on Intelligence • Transportation &
Infrastructure
CoS. Timothy Persico **LD.** Molly Carey
Sched. Kevin Golden **PS.** Ian Lee
Dist. Off. Newburgh 845.561.1259

R: 221 T: 4th 56%
Elected Year: 2012

➤ Rep. Gregory W. Meeks (meeks) — D-NY-05 — p 202.225.3461

Rm. RHOB 2310 **Web.** meeks.house.gov f 202.226.4169
Bio. 09/25/1953 • Harlem, NY • Assistant District Attorney;
State Legislator • Adelphi Univ. (NY), B.A., 1975; Howard
Univ. Law School (DC), J.D., 1978 • African Methodist
Episcopal • M. Simone-Marie Meeks, 3 ch **Cmte.** Financial
Services • Foreign Affairs
CoS. Sophia Lafargue **LD.** Ernie Jolly
Sched. Reginald Belon **PS.** Andrei D. Vasilescu
Dist. Off. Arverne 347.230.4032 • Jamaica 718.725.6000

R: 56 T: 12th 99%
Elected Year: 1998

➤ Rep. Grace Meng (mehng) — D-NY-06 — p 202.225.2601

Rm. RHOB 2209 **Web.** meng.house.gov f 202.225.1589
Bio. 10/01/1975 • Queens, NY • Univ. of Michigan, B.A.,
1997; Yeshiva Univ. Benjamin N. Cardozo School of Law
(NY), J.D., 2002 • Christian Church • M. Wayne Kye, 2 ch
Cmte. Appropriations • Ethics
CoS. Justin Oswald **LD.** Helen Beaudreau
Sched. Brenda Connolly **PS.** Jordan Goldes (CD)
Dist. Off. Flushing 718.358.6364 • Forest Hills 718.358.6364

R: 223 T: 4th 91%
Elected Year: 2012

➤ Rep. Joseph D. Morelle (mor-REH-lee) — D-NY-25 — p 202.225.3615

Rm. LHOB 1317 **Web.** morelle.house.gov f 202.225.7822
Bio. 04/29/1957 • Utica, NY • State Univ. of New York at
Geneseo, B.A., 1986 • Roman Catholic • M. Mary Beth
Morelle, 3 ch (1 deceased) **Cmte.** Budget • Education &
Labor • Rules
CoS. Nick Weatherbee **LD.** Abbie M. Sorrendino
Sched. Daniel Lemire **PS.** Sean Hart (CD)
Dist. Off. Rochester 585.232.4850

R: 345 T: 2nd 59%
Elected Year: 2018

➤ Rep. Jerry L. Nadler (NAD-lur) — D-NY-10 — p 202.225.5635

Rm. RHOB 2132 **Web.** nadler.house.gov f 202.225.6923
Bio. 06/13/1947 • Brooklyn, NY • State Representative; NY
State Legislative Staffer • Columbia Univ. (NY), Bach. Deg.,
1969; Fordham Univ. School of Law (NY), J.D., 1978 • Jewish
• M. Joyce L. Miller, 1 ch **Cmte.** Judiciary
CoS. John Doty **LD.** Melissa Connolly
Sched. Brigid Campbell **PS.** Daniel Schwarz
Dist. Off. Brooklyn 718.373.3198 • New York 212.367.7350

R: 21 T: 15th 82%
Elected Year: 1992

➤ Rep. Alexandria Ocasio-Cortez (o-kah-SEE-o KOR-tehz) — D-NY-14 — p 202.225.3965

Rm. CHOB 229 **Web.** ocasio-
cortez.house.gov
Bio. 10/13/1989 • Bronx, NY • Boston Univ. (MA), B.A.,
2011 • Catholic • S. **Cmte.** Financial Services • Oversight &
Reform
CoS. Saikat Chakrabarti **LD.** Ariel Eckblad
Sched. Daniel Bonthius **PS.** Corbin Trent
Dist. Off. Jackson Heights

R: 398 T: 1st 78%
Elected Year: 2018

NEW YORK

▥ Rep. Tom W. Reed II (reed)   R-NY-23   p 202.225.3161

Rm. RHOB 2263 **Web.** reed.house.gov   **f** 202.226.6599
Bio. 11/18/1971 • Joliet, IL • Attorney • Alfred Univ. (NY), Bach. Deg., 1993; Ohio Northern Univ. College of Law, J.D., 1996 • Roman Catholic • M. Jean Reed, 2 ch **Cmte.** Ways & Means
CoS. Drew Wayne   **LD.** Elise Tollefson
Sched. Johannah Murphy   **PS.** Will Reinert
Dist. Off. Corning 607.654.7566 • Geneva 315.759.5229 • Jamestown 716.708.6369 • Olean 716.379.8434

R: 149   **T:** 6th 54%
Elected Year: 2010

⚘ Rep. Kathleen M. Rice ("rice")   D-NY-04   p 202.225.5516

Rm. RHOB 2435 **Web.**   **f** 202.225.5758
kathleenrice.house.gov
Bio. 02/15/1965 • New York City, NY • Catholic Univ. of America (DC), B.A., 1987; Touro Law Center, J.D., 1991 • Roman Catholic • S. **Cmte.** Homeland Security • Veterans' Affairs
CoS. Nell Reilly   **LD.** Liz Amster
Sched. Landy Wade   **PS.** Michael Aciman
Dist. Off. Garden City 516.739.3008

R: 278   **T:** 3rd 61%
Elected Year: 2014

⚘ Rep. Max N. Rose (roaz)   D-NY-11   p 202.225.3371

Rm. LHOB 1529 **Web.** maxrose.house.gov
Bio. 11/28/1986 • Brooklyn, NY • Wesleyan Univ. (CT), B.A. 2008; London School of Economics (England), M.S., 2009 • Jewish • M. Leigh Byrne **Cmte.** Homeland Security • Veterans' Affairs
CoS. Anne Sokolov   **LD.** Erin Meegan
Sched. Lily Wacker   **PS.** Jonas Edwards-Jenks
Dist. Off. Staten Island 718.667.3313

R: 408   **T:** 1st 53%
Elected Year: 2018

⚘ Rep. Jose E. Serrano (seh-RAH-noe)   D-NY-15   p 202.225.436

Rm. RHOB 2354 **Web.** serrano.house.gov   **f** 202.225.600
Bio. 10/24/1943 • Mayaguez, PR • State Representative; N.Y City School District Employee • Army Medical Corps 1964-66 • Roman Catholic • D., 5 ch **Cmte.** Appropriations
CoS. Matthew Alpert   **LD.** Angel Nigaglioni
Sched. Alexis Philbrick   **PS.** Paola Amador
Dist. Off. Bronx 718.620.0084

R: 16   **T:** 16th 96%
Elected Year: 1990

▥ Rep. Elise M. Stefanik (steh-FAH-nik)   R-NY-21   p 202.225.461

Rm. CHOB 318 **Web.** stefanik.house.gov   **f** 202.226.062
Bio. 07/02/1984 • Albany, NY • Harvard Univ., A.B., 2006 • Roman Catholic • M. Matthew Manda **Cmte.** Armed Services • Education & Labor • Permanent Select on Intelligence
CoS. Anthony Pileggi   **LD.** Julia Angelotti
Sched. Emily Cosci   **PS.** Madison Anderson
Dist. Off. Glens Falls 518.743.0964 • Plattsburgh 518.561.2324 • Watertown 315.782.3150

R: 280   **T:** 3rd 56%
Elected Year: 2014

⚘ Rep. Thomas R. Suozzi (SWAH-zee)   D-NY-03   p 202.225.333

Rm. CHOB 214 **Web.** suozzi.house.gov   **f** 202.225.466
Bio. 08/31/1962 • Glen Cove, NY • Boston College (MA), B.S., 1984; Fordham Univ. School of Law (NY), J.D., 1989 • Roman Catholic • M. Helene Suozzi, 3 ch **Cmte.** Ways & Means
CoS. Michael Florio   **LD.** Diane Shust
Sched. Danielle Hupper   **PS.** Conor Walsh
Dist. Off. Huntington 631.923.4100 • Little Neck 718.631.0400

R: 334   **T:** 2nd 59%
Elected Year: 2016

NEW YORK

🔹 Rep. Paul D. Tonko (TAHN-ko)   D-NY-20   p 202.225.5076
Rm. RHOB 2369 **Web.** tonko.house.gov   **f** 202.225.5077
Bio. 06/18/1949 • Amsterdam, NY • Engineer • Clarkson Univ. (NY), B.S., 1971 • Roman Catholic • S. **Cmte.** Energy & Commerce • Natural Resources • Science, Space & Technology
CoS. Clinton Britt   **LD.** Jeff Morgan
Sched. Diana Bennett (CD)   **PS.** Matt Sonneborn
Dist. Off. Albany 518.465.0700 • Amsterdam 518.843.3400 • Schenectady 518.374.4547

R: 143   **T:** 6th 67%
Elected Year: 2008

🔹 Rep. Nydia M. Velazquez (veh-LAS-kez)   D-NY-07   p 202.225.2361
Rm. RHOB 2302 **Web.** velazquez.house.gov   **f** 202.226.0327
Bio. 03/28/1953 • Yabucoa, PR • Director, Dept. of Puerto Rican Community Affairs; Congressional Staffer • Univ. of Puerto Rico (Rio Piedras), B.A., 1974; New York Univ., M.A., 1976 • Roman Catholic • M. Paul Bader   **Cmte.** Financial Services • Natural Resources
CoS. Adam Minehardt   **LD.** Justin Pelletier
Sched. Richard Ryan Bruno   **PS.** Alex Haurek
Dist. Off. Brooklyn 718.222.5819 • Brooklyn 718.599.3658 • New York 212.619.2606

R: 34   **T:** 14th 93%
Elected Year: 1992

🔹 Rep. Lee M. Zeldin (ZEL-duhn)   R-NY-01   p 202.225.3826
Rm. RHOB 2441 **Web.** zeldin.house.gov
Bio. 01/30/1980 • East Meadow, NY • State Univ. of New York - Albany, B.A., 2001; Albany Law School, J.D., 2003 • Jewish • M. Diana Zeldin, 2 ch (twins)   **Cmte.** Financial Services • Foreign Affairs
CoS. Eric Amidon   **LD.** Kevin Dowling
Sched. Andrea Grace   **PS.** Katie Vincentz
Dist. Off. Patchogue 631.289.1097

R: 285   **T:** 3rd 52%
Elected Year: 2014

NORTH CAROLINA

🔹 Governor Roy Cooper (KOO-pur)   p 919.814.2000
Office of the Governor, 20301 Mail C: Raleigh
Service Center   **P:** 10,383,620 (9)
Raleigh, NC 27699-0301   **A:** 48,617.96 mi^2 (29th)
Website nc.gov
Fax 919.733.2120
Term Ends 2021
Lt. Governor
Dan Forest, **R**

U.S. Senators
Richard M. Burr, **R**
Thom R. Tillis, **R**
U.S. Representatives
01 / G.K. Butterfield, **D**
02 / George E.B. Holding, **R**
03 / Vacant
04 / David E. Price, **D**
05 / Virginia A. Foxx, **R**
06 / Mark Walker, **R**
07 / David C. Rouzer, **R**   10 / Patrick T. McHenry, **R**
08 / Richard L. Hudson, **R**   11 / Mark R. Meadows, **R**
09 / Vacant   12 / Alma S. Adams, **D**
   13 / Ted P. Budd, **R**

NORTH CAROLINA

STATE/LEGISLATOR PROFILES

NORTH CAROLINA

⚑ Sen. Richard M. Burr (bur)   R-NC-Sr.   p 202.224.3154
Rm. RSOB 217 **Web.** burr.senate.gov   **f** 202.228.2981
Bio. 11/30/1955 • Charlottesville, VA • U.S. Representative; Businessman • Wake Forest Univ. (NC), B.A., 1978 • Methodist • M. Brooke Fauth Burr, 2 ch **Cmte.** Aging • Finance • Health, Education, Labor & Pensions • Intelligence
CoS. Natasha Hickman   **LD.** Chris Toppings
Sched. Michael Sorensen   **PS.** Caitlin A. Carroll
Dist. Off. Asheville 828.350.2437 • Rocky Mount 252.977.9522 • Wilmington 910.251.1058 • Winston-Salem 336.631.5125

R: 23   **T:** 3rd 51%
Elected Year: 2004
Next Election: 2022

⚑ Sen. Thom R. Tillis (TIH-liss)   R-NC-Jr.   p 202.224.6342
Rm. DSOB 185 **Web.** tillis.senate.gov   **f** 202.228.2563
Bio. 08/30/1960 • Jacksonville, FL • Univ. of Maryland Univ. College, B.S., 1996 • Catholic • M. Susan Tillis, 2 ch **Cmte.** Armed Services • Banking, Housing & Urban Affairs • Judiciary • Veterans' Affairs
CoS. Ted Lehman   **LD.** Courtney Temple
Sched. Angela Schulze   **PS.** Daniel Keylin
Dist. Off. Charlotte 704.509.9087 • Greenville 252.329.0371 • Hendersonville 828.693.8750 • High Point 336.885.0685 • Raleigh 919.856.4630

R: 78   **T:** 1st 49%
Elected Year: 2014
Next Election: 2020

⚑ Rep. Alma S. Adams (AD-uhmz)   D-NC-12   p 202.225.1510

Rm. RHOB 2436 **Web.** adams.house.gov   **f** 202.225.1512
Bio. 05/27/1946 • High Point, NC • North Carolina Agricultural and Technical State Univ., M.S., 1972; Ohio State Univ., Ph.D., 1981 • Baptist • D., 2 ch; 4 gr-ch **Cmte.** Agriculture • Education & Labor • Financial Services
CoS. Rhonda Foxx   **LD.** John Christie
Sched. Sandra Brown
Dist. Off. Charlotte 704.344.9950

R: 246   **T:** 4th 73%
Elected Year: 2014

⚑ Rep. Ted P. Budd ("bud")   R-NC-13   p 202.225.4531

Rm. CHOB 118 **Web.** budd.house.gov
Bio. 10/21/1971 • Winston-Salem, NC • Appalachian State Univ. (NC), B.S., 1994; Dallas Theological Seminary (TX), M.Th., 1998; Wake Forest Univ. (NC), M.B.A., 2007 • Christian - Non-Denominational • M. Amy Kate, 3 ch **Cmte.** Financial Services
CoS. Andrew Bell   **LD.** Alex Vargo
Sched. Elizabeth Dews   **PS.** Chase Jennings
Dist. Off. Advance 336.998.1313 • High Point 336.858.5013

R: 300   **T:** 2nd 52%
Elected Year: 2016

⚑ Rep. G.K. Butterfield Jr. (BUT-ur-"field")   D-NC-01   p 202.225.310

Rm. RHOB 2080 **Web.** butterfield.house.gov **f** 202.225.335
Bio. 04/27/1947 • Wilson, NC • North Carolina Supreme Court Judge; Attorney • Army 1968-70 • North Carolina Central Univ., B.A., 1971; North Carolina Central Univ. School of Law, J.D., 1974 • Baptist • D., 3 ch ; 3 gr-ch **Cmte.** Administration • Energy & Commerce
CoS. Kendra Brown   **LD.** Dennis Sills
Sched. Lindsey Bowen   **PS.** Meaghan Lynch
Dist. Off. Durham 919.908.0164 • Wilson 252.237.9816

R: 88   **T:** 9th 70%
Elected Year: 2004

℞ Rep. Virginia A. Foxx (fahks)   R-NC-05   p 202.225.2071

Rm. RHOB 2462 **Web.** foxx.house.gov   **f** 202.225.2995
Bio. 06/29/1943 • Bronx, NY • Business Owner; Board of
Education • Univ. of North Carolina Chapel Hill (UNC),
Bach. Deg., 1968; Univ. of North Carolina Chapel Hill (UNC),
M.A., 1972; Univ. of North Carolina, Greensboro, Ed.D.,
1985 • Roman Catholic • M. Thomas A. Foxx, 1 ch ; 2 gr-ch
Cmte. Education & Labor • Oversight & Reform
CoS. Cyrus Artz
Sched. Jordan Pic   **PS.** Sara Werner
Dist. Off. Boone 828.265.0240 • Clemmons 336.778.0211

R: 94   **T:** 8th 57%
Elected Year: 2004

℞ Rep. George E.B. Holding (HOAL-ding)   R-NC-02   p 202.225.3032

Rm. LHOB 1110 **Web.** holding.house.gov   **f** 202.225.0181
Bio. 04/17/1968 • Raleigh, NC • Wake Forest Univ. (NC),
B.A., 1991; Wake Forest Univ. (NC), J.D., 1996 • Baptist •
M. Lucy E. Herriott, 4 ch   **Cmte.** Budget • Ethics • Ways &
Means
CoS. Tucker Knott   **LD.** Curtis Rhyne
Sched. Katie Smith   **PS.** William Glenn (CD)
Dist. Off. Raleigh 919.782.4400

R: 210   **T:** 4th 51%
Elected Year: 2012

℞ Rep. Richard L. Hudson Jr. (HUD-suhn)   R-NC-08   p 202.225.3715

Rm. RHOB 2112 **Web.** hudson.house.gov   **f** 202.225.4036
Bio. 11/04/1971 • Franklin, VA • Univ. of North Carolina,
Charlotte, B.A., 1996 • Methodist • M. Renee Hudson, 1 ch
Cmte. Energy & Commerce
CoS. Chris Carter   **LD.** Preston Bell
Sched. Kristine Bieniek   **PS.** Tatum Gibson
Dist. Off. Concord 704.786.1612 • Fayetteville 910.997.2070
• Pinehurst 910.246.5374

R: 211   **T:** 4th 55%
Elected Year: 2012

℞ Rep. Patrick T. McHenry (mik-HEN-ree)   R-NC-10   p 202.225.2576

Rm. RHOB 2004 **Web.** mchenry.house.gov   **f** 202.225.0316
Bio. 10/22/1975 • Charlotte, NC • Realtor; Campaign Aide •
Belmont Abbey College (NC), B.A., 2000 • Roman Catholic
• M. Giulia Cangiano McHenry, 2 ch   **Cmte.** Financial
Services
CoS. Jeff Butler   **LD.** Doug Nation
Sched. Grace Tricomi   **PS.** Taylor Theodossiou
Dist. Off. Black Mountain 828.669.0600 • Gastonia
704.833.0096 • Hickory 828.327.6100

R: 101   **T:** 8th 59%
Elected Year: 2004

℞ Rep. Mark R. Meadows (MEH-"doze")   R-NC-11   p 202.225.6401

Rm. LHOB 2160 **Web.** meadows.house.gov   **f** 202.226.6422
Bio. 07/28/1959 • Verdun, French Republic • Univ. of
South Florida, B.A., 1981 • Christian Church • M. Debbie
Meadows, 2 ch ; 1 gr-ch   **Cmte.** Oversight & Reform •
Transportation & Infrastructure
CoS. Paul Fitzpatrick   **LD.** Chad Yelinski
Sched. Mallory Rascher   **PS.** Ben Williamson
Dist. Off. Hendersonville 828.693.5660 • Lenoir
828.426.8701 • Spruce Pine 828.765.0573 • Waynesville
828.452.6022

R: 222   **T:** 4th 59%
Elected Year: 2012

℞ Rep. David E. Price (price)   D-NC-04   p 202.225.1784

Rm. RHOB 2108 **Web.** price.house.gov   **f** 202.225.2014
Bio. 08/17/1940 • Erwin, TN • Professor of Political Sciences
& Policy Sciences • The Univ. of North Carolina System,
B.A., 1961; Yale Univ. (CT), B.D., 1964; Yale Univ. (CT), Ph.D.,
1969 • Baptist • M. Lisa Kanwit Price, 2 ch ; 2 gr-ch   **Cmte.**
Appropriations • Budget
CoS. Justin Wein   **LD.** Sean Maxwell
Sched. Janssen White   **PS.** Gloria Nlewedim
Dist. Off. Chapel Hill 919.967.7924 • Raleigh 919.859.5999

R: 17   **T:** 16th 72%
Elected Year: 1996

NORTH CAROLINA

★ Rep. David C. Rouzer (ROU-zur)   R-NC-07   p 202.225.2731

Rm. RHOB 2439 **Web.** rouzer.house.gov   **f** 202.225.5773
Bio. 02/16/1972 • Landstuhl, Germany • North Carolina
State Univ., B.A., 1994; North Carolina State Univ., B.S., 1994
• Southern Baptist • S. **Cmte.** Agriculture • Transportation
& Infrastructure
CoS. Melissa Murphy   **LD.** Jason Cooke
Sched. Kelley Billy   **PS.** Danielle R. Smotkin
Dist. Off. Bolivia 910.253.6111 • Four Oaks 919.938.3040 •
Wilmington 910.395.0202

R: 279   **T:** 3rd 56%
Elected Year: 2014

★ Rep. Mark Walker (WALL-kur)   R-NC-06   p 202.225.3065

Rm. LHOB 1725 **Web.** walker.house.gov   **f** 202.225.8611
Bio. 05/20/1969 • Dothan, AL • Piedmont International
Univ. (NC), B.A., 1999 • Baptist • M. Kelly Walker, 3 ch
Cmte. Administration • Education & Labor • Homeland
Security
CoS. Scott Luginbill   **LD.** Ryan Walker
Sched. Emily Cambon   **PS.** Jack Minor
Dist. Off. Asheboro 336.626.3060 • Graham 336.229.0159
• Greensboro 336.333.5005

R: 282   **T:** 3rd 57%
Elected Year: 2014

NORTH DAKOTA

★ Governor Doug Burgum (BUR-guhm)   p 701.328.2200

600 E. Boulevard Ave.   **C:** Bismarck
Bismarck, ND 58505-0001   **P:** 760,077 (48)
Website nd.gov   **A:** 69,000.67 mi^2 (17th)
Fax 701.328.2205
Term Ends 2020
Lt. Governor
Brent Sanford, **R**

U.S. Senators
John H. Hoeven, **R**
Kevin J. Cramer, **R**
U.S. Representatives
01 / Kelly M. Armstrong, **R**

★ Sen. Kevin J. Cramer (KRAY-mur)   R-ND-Jr.   p 202.224.2043

Rm. DSOB B40-C **Web.** cramer.senate.gov
Bio. 01/21/1961 • Rolette, ND • Concordia College (MN),
B.A., 1983; Univ. of Mary (ND), M.A., 2003 • Evangelical • M.
Kris Neumann, 5 ch (1 deceased); 5 gr-ch **Cmte.** Armed
Services • Banking, Housing & Urban Affairs • Budget •
Environment & Public Works • Veterans' Affairs
CoS. Mark Gruman
Sched. Bridget Hobbs   **PS.** Jake Wilkins
Dist. Off. Fargo 701.232.5094 • Minot 701.837.6141

R: 94   **T:** 0th 55%
Elected Year: 2018
Next Election: 2024

Sen. John H. Hoeven III (HO-vuhn)   R-ND-Sr.   p 202.224.2551

Rm. RSOB 338 **Web.** hoeven.senate.gov   **f** 202.224.7999
Bio. 03/13/1957 • Bismarck, ND • Former Chair, Gov.'s Ethanol Coalition; Chair, Midwestern Governors Assn.; Chair, District 47 North Dakota Republican Party; Chair, Interstate Oil and Gas Compact Commission • Dartmouth College, Hanover (NH), B.A., 1979; Northwestern Univ. Kellogg School Management (IL), M.B.A., 1981 • Roman Catholic • M. Mikey Hoeven, 2 ch ; 3 gr-ch **Cmte.** Agriculture, Nutrition & Forestry • Appropriations • Energy & Natural Resources • Indian Affairs

CoS. Cassie Bladow   **LD.** Daniel Auger
Sched. Sydney Fitzpatrick   **PS.** Kami Capener
Dist. Off. Bismarck 701.250.4618 • Fargo 701.239.5389 • Grand Forks 701.746.8972 • Minot 701.838.1361

R: 50   T: 2nd 79%
Elected Year: 2010
Next Election: 2022

Rep. Kelly M. Armstrong (ARM-strong)   R-ND-01   p 202.225.2611

Rm. LHOB 1004 **Web.** armstrong.house.gov
Bio. 10/08/1976 • Dickinson, ND • Univ. of North Dakota, B.A., 2000; Univ. of North Dakota, B.A., 2000; Univ. of North Dakota School of Law, J.D., 2003 • Lutheran • M. Kjersti Armstrong, 2 ch **Cmte.** Judiciary • Oversight & Reform • Select Committee on the Climate Crisis

CoS. Rosalyn A. Leighton   **LD.** Casey Fitzpatrick
Sched. Elly Peterson   **PS.** Brandon VerVelde
Dist. Off. Bismarck 701.660.5412

R: 350   T: 1st 60%
Elected Year: 2018

OHIO

Governor Mike DeWine (duh-WINE)   p 614.466.3555

Riffe Center
77 S. High St., 30th Floor
Columbus, OH 43215
Website ohio.gov
Fax 614.466.9354
Term Ends 2023
Lt. Governor
Jon A. Husted, R

C: Columbus
P: 11,689,442 (7)
A: 40,860.79 mi² (35th)

U.S. Senators
Sherrod C. Brown, D
Rob J. Portman, R

U.S. Representatives
01 / Steve Chabot, R
02 / Brad R. Wenstrup, R
03 / Joyce B. Beatty, D
04 / Jim D. Jordan, R
05 / Robert E. Latta, R
06 / Bill Johnson, R
07 / Bob B. Gibbs, R
08 / Warren Davidson, R
09 / Marcy C. Kaptur, D
10 / Michael R. Turner, R
11 / Marcia L. Fudge, D
12 / Troy Balderson, R
13 / Tim J. Ryan, D
14 / Dave P. Joyce, R
15 / Steve E. Stivers, R
16 / Anthony E. Gonzalez, R

Sen. Sherrod C. Brown ("brown")   D-OH-Sr.   p 202.224.2315

Rm. HSOB 503 **Web.** brown.senate.gov   **f** 202.228.6321
Bio. 11/09/1952 • Mansfield, OH • Professor; Representative • Yale Univ. (CT), B.A., 1974; Ohio State Univ., M.A., 1979; Ohio State Univ., M.P.A., 1981 • Lutheran • M. Connie Schultz, 2 ch ; 2 stepch ; 6 gr-ch **Cmte.** Agriculture, Nutrition & Forestry • Banking, Housing & Urban Affairs • Finance • Veterans' Affairs

CoS. Sarah Benzing   **LD.** Jeremy Hekhuis
Sched. John Patterson (CD)   **PS.** Jennifer Donohue
Dist. Off. Cincinnati 513.684.1021 • Cleveland 216.522.7272 • Columbus 614.469.2083 • Lorain 440.242.4100

R: 29   T: 2nd 53%
Elected Year: 2006
Next Election: 2024

OHIO

⚑ Sen. Rob J. Portman (PORT-muhn) R-OH-Jr. p 202.224.3353

Rm. RSOB 448 **Web.** portman.senate.gov **f** 202.224.9075
Bio. 12/19/1955 • Cincinnati, OH • Dartmouth College,
B.A., 1979; Univ. of Michigan Law School, J.D., 1984 •
Methodist • M. Jane Portman, 3 ch **Cmte.** Finance •
Foreign Relations • Homeland Security & Government
Affairs • Joint Economic
CoS. Mark Isakowitz   **LD.** Pam Thiessen
                          PS. Kevin Smith
Dist. Off. Cincinnati 513.684.3265 • Cleveland
216.522.7095 • Columbus 614.469.6774 • Toledo
419.259.3895

R: 47 **T:** 2nd 58%
Elected Year: 2010
Next Election: 2022

⚑ Rep. Troy Balderson (ball-dur-sun) R-OH-12 p 202.225.5355

Rm. LHOB 1221 **Web.** balderson.house.gov **f** 202.226.4523
Bio. 01/16/1962 • Zanesville, OH • Christian Church • M.
Angie Albright, 1 ch **Cmte.** Science, Space & Technology •
Small Business • Transportation & Infrastructure
CoS. Teri Geiger   **LD.** Brittany Madni
Sched. Kim Waskowsky   **PS.** Erin Collins
Dist. Off. Worthington 614.523.2555

R: 343 **T:** 2nd 51%
Elected Year: 2018

⚑ Rep. Joyce B. Beatty (BAY-dee) D-OH-03 p 202.225.4324

Rm. RHOB 2303 **Web.** beatty.house.gov **f** 202.225.1984
Bio. 03/12/1950 • Dayton, OH • Central State Univ. (OH),
B.A., 1972; Wright State Univ. (OH), M.S., 1974 • Baptist • M.
Justice Otto Beatty Jr., 2 stepch ; 2 gr-ch **Cmte.** Financial
Services • Joint Economic
CoS. Kimberly Ross   **LD.** Nicholas Semanko
                        PS. Dominic J. Manecke
Dist. Off. Columbus 614.220.0003

R: 195 **T:** 4th 74%
Elected Year: 2012

⚑ Rep. Steve Chabot (SHA-buht) R-OH-01 p 202.225.2216

Rm. RHOB 2408 **Web.** chabot.house.gov **f** 202.225.3012
Bio. 01/22/1953 • Cincinnati, OH • College of William and
Mary (VA), B.A., 1975; Northern Kentucky Univ. Salmon P.
Chase College of Law (KY), J.D., 1978 • Roman Catholic •
M. Donna Chabot, 2 ch ; 1 gr-ch **Cmte.** Foreign Affairs •
Judiciary • Small Business
CoS. Stacy Barton   **LD.** Jonathan Lowe
Sched. Lisa Feldman   **PS.** Brian Griffith (CD)
Dist. Off. Cincinnati 513.684.2723 • Lebanon 513.421.8704

R: 58 **T:** 12th 51%
Elected Year: 2010

⚑ Rep. Warren Davidson (DAY-vid-suhn) R-OH-08 p 202.225.6205

Rm. LHOB 1107 **Web.** davidson.house.gov **f** 202.225.0704
Bio. 03/01/1970 • Troy, OH • Univ. of Notre Dame (IN),
M.B.A.; U.S. Military Academy - West Point (NY), B.A., 1995
• Unspecified/Other • M. Lisa Davidson, 2 ch **Cmte.**
Financial Services
CoS. Douglas Branch   **LD.** Matthew Silver
Sched. Molly O'Connell   **PS.** Matthew Henderson
Dist. Off. Springfield 937.322.1120 • Troy 937.339.1524 •
West Chester 513.779.5400

R: 288 **T:** 3rd 67%
Elected Year: 2016

⚑ Rep. Marcia L. Fudge (fuhj) D-OH-11 p 202.225.7032

Rm. RHOB 2344 **Web.** fudge.house.gov **f** 202.225.1339
Bio. 10/29/1952 • Cleveland, OH • Mayor (Warrensville
Heights); Congressional Staffer; Attorney • Ohio State Univ.
B.S., 1975; Cleveland State Univ. Marshall College of Law
(OH), J.D., 1983 • Baptist • S. **Cmte.** Administration •
Agriculture • Education & Labor
CoS. Veleter Mazyck
                        PS. Bernadine Stallings
Dist. Off. Akron 330.835.4758 • Warrensville Heights
216.522.4900

R: 129 **T:** 7th 82%
Elected Year: 2008

OHIO

♜ Rep. Bob B. Gibbs (gibz) — R-OH-07 — p 202.225.6265

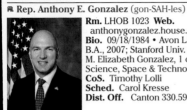

Rm. RHOB 2446 **Web.** gibbs.house.gov **f** 202.225.3394
Bio. 06/14/1954 • Peru, IN • Ohio State Univ. Agricultural
Technical Institute, A.A.S., 1974 • Methodist • M. Jody
Gibbs, 3 ch **Cmte.** Oversight & Reform • Transportation &
Infrastructure
CoS. Hillary Gross   **LD.** Alex Briggs
Sched. Rachael Van
Mersbergen
Dist. Off. Ashland 419.207.0650 • Canton 330.737.1631

R: 163 **T:** 5th 59%
Elected Year: 2010

♜ Rep. Anthony E. Gonzalez (gon-SAH-les) — R-OH-16 — p 202.225.3876

Rm. LHOB 1023 **Web.**
anthonygonzalez.house.gov
Bio. 09/18/1984 • Avon Lake, OH • Ohio State Univ.,
B.A., 2007; Stanford Univ. (CA), M.B.A., 2014 • Catholic •
M. Elizabeth Gonzalez, 1 ch **Cmte.** Financial Services •
Science, Space & Technology
CoS. Timothy Lolli   **LD.** Stephen Hostelley
Sched. Carol Kresse   **PS.** Emily Carlin
Dist. Off. Canton 330.599.7037 • Strongsville 440.783.3696

R: 373 **T:** 1st 57%
Elected Year: 2018

♜ Rep. Bill Johnson (JAHN-suhn) — R-OH-06 — p 202.225.5705

Rm. RHOB 2336 **Web.** billjohnson.house.gov **f** 202.225.5907
Bio. 11/10/1954 • Roseboro, NC • Troy Univ. (AL), B.S.,
1979; Georgia Institute of Technology, M.S., 1984 • Protestant
- Unspecified Christian • M. LeeAnn Johnson, 4 ch ; 6 gr-ch
Cmte. Budget • Energy & Commerce
CoS. Mike Smullen   **LD.** David Rardin
Sched. Katherine Gwyn   **PS.** Natalie Kretzschmar
Dist. Off. Cambridge 740.432.2366 • Ironton 740.534.9431
• Marietta 740.376.0868 • Salem 330.337.6951

R: 170 **T:** 5th 69%
Elected Year: 2010

♜ Rep. Jim D. Jordan (JOR-duhn) — R-OH-04 — p 202.225.2676

Rm. RHOB 2056 **Web.** jordan.house.gov **f** 202.226.0577
Bio. 02/17/1964 • Urbana, OH • State Representative •
Univ. of Wisconsin, B.S., 1986; Ohio State Univ., M.A., 1991,
Capital Univ. (OH), J.D., 2001 • Evangelical • M. Polly Jordan,
4 ch ; 2 gr-ch **Cmte.** Judiciary • Oversight & Reform
CoS. Kevin Christopher   **LD.** Jared Dilley
Eichinger
Sched. Emma Summers   **PS.** Ian Fury
Dist. Off. Bucyrus 419.663.1426 • Lima 419.999.6455 •
Norwalk 419.663.1426

R: 114 **T:** 7th 65%
Elected Year: 2006

♜ Rep. Dave P. Joyce (joyss) — R-OH-14 — p 202.225.5731

Rm. LHOB 1124 **Web.** joyce.house.gov **f** 202.225.3307
Bio. 03/17/1957 • Cleveland, OH • Univ. of Dayton (OH),
B.S., 1979; Univ. of Dayton (OH), J.D., 1982 • Roman
Catholic • M. Kelly Joyce, 3 ch **Cmte.** Appropriations
CoS. Anna Alburger   **LD.** Kendall Kalagher
Sched. Emma Vaughn   **PS.** Katherine Sears
Dist. Off. Mentor 440.352.3939 • Twinsburg 330.357.4139

R: 214 **T:** 4th 55%
Elected Year: 2012

♜ Rep. Marcy C. Kaptur (KAP-tur) — D-OH-09 — p 202.225.4146

Rm. RHOB 2186 **Web.** kaptur.house.gov **f** 202.225.7711
Bio. 06/17/1946 • Toledo, OH • Domestic Policy Staffer,
President Jimmy Carter; Urban Planner • Univ. of
Wisconsin, B.A., 1968; Univ. of Michigan, M.A., 1974 •
Catholic • S. **Cmte.** Appropriations
                                LD. Jenny Perrino
Sched. Courtney Hruska   **PS.** Griffin Anderson
Dist. Off. Cleveland 216.767.5933 • Lorain 440.288.1500 •
Toledo 419.259.7500

: 6 **T:** 19th 68%
Elected Year: 1982

OHIO

☗ Rep. Robert E. Latta (LAT-uh)   R-OH-05   p 202.225.6405

Rm. RHOB 2467 **Web.** latta.house.gov   **f** 202.225.1985
Bio. 04/18/1956 • Bluffton, OH • State Legislator; Attorney •
Bowling Green State Univ. (OH), B.A., 1978; Univ. of Toledo
College of Law (OH), J.D., 1981 • Roman Catholic • M.
Marcia Sloan Latta, 2 ch **Cmte.** Commission Congressional
Mailing Standards • Energy & Commerce
CoS. Allison H. Witt-Poulios   **LD.** Madeline Vey
Sched. Erin Cassidy   **PS.** Drew Griffin
Dist. Off. Bowling Green 419.354.8700 • Defiance
419.782.1996 • Findlay 419.422.7791

R: 124   **T:** 7th 62%
Elected Year: 2006

☗ Rep. Tim J. Ryan (RY-uhn)   D-OH-13   p 202.225.5261

Rm. LHOB 1126 **Web.** timryan.house.gov   **f** 202.225.3719
Bio. 07/16/1973 • Niles, OH • State Senator • Bowling
Green State Univ. (OH), B.A., 1995; Franklin Pierce College
Law Center (NH), J.D., 2000 • Catholic • M. Andrea Zetts, 1
ch ; 2 stepch **Cmte.** Appropriations
CoS. Ron Grimes   **LD.** Ryan Keating
Sched. Erin Isenberg   **PS.** Michael Zetts
Dist. Off. Akron 330.630.7311 • Warren 330.373.0074 •
Youngstown 330.740.0193

R: 84   **T:** 9th 61%
Elected Year: 2002

☗ Rep. Steve E. Stivers (STY-vurz)   R-OH-15   p 202.225.2015

Rm. RHOB 2234 **Web.** stivers.house.gov   **f** 202.225.3529
Bio. 03/24/1965 • Cincinnati, OH • Ohio State Univ., B.A.,
1989; Ohio State Univ., M.B.A., 1996; U.S. Army War College
(PA), M.A., 2012 • Methodist • M. Karen Stivers, 2 ch **Cmte.**
Financial Services
CoS. Courtney D.   **LD.** Nick Bush
   Whetstone (CD)
Sched. Sara Donlon   **PS.** AnnMarie Graham
Dist. Off. Hilliard 614.771.4968 • Lancaster 740.654.2654 •
Wilmington 937.283.7049

R: 182   **T:** 5th 58%
Elected Year: 2010

☗ Rep. Michael R. Turner (TUR-nur)   R-OH-10   p 202.225.6465

Rm. RHOB 2082 **Web.** turner.house.gov   **f** 202.225.6754
Bio. 01/11/1960 • Dayton, OH • Corporate Counsel; Mayor
(Dayton, OH) • Ohio Northern Univ., B.A., 1982; Case
Western Reserve Univ. School of Law (OH), J.D., 1985; Univ.
of Dayton (OH), M.B.A., 1992 • Presbyterian • D. Majida
Mourad, 2 ch (2 from previous marriage) **Cmte.** Armed
Services • Permanent Select on Intelligence
CoS. Adam Howard   **LD.** Jeffrey Wilson
Sched. Kate Pictkiewicz   **PS.** Morgan Rako
Dist. Off. Dayton 937.225.2843

R: 87   **T:** 9th 56%
Elected Year: 2002

☗ Rep. Brad R. Wenstrup (WEN-strup)   R-OH-02   p 202.225.3164

Rm. RHOB 2419 **Web.** wenstrup.house.gov   **f** 202.225.1992
Bio. 06/17/1958 • Cincinnati, OH • St. Xavier High School
(OH), B.S., 1976; Univ. of Cincinnati, B.A., 1980; Rosalind
Franklin Univ. (IL), B.S., 1985 • Roman Catholic • M. Monica
Klein, 1 ch **Cmte.** Permanent Select on Intelligence • Ways
& Means
CoS. Derek Harley   **LD.** Greg Brooks
Sched. Abbie Sumbrum   **PS.** Ann Tumolo
Dist. Off. Cincinnati 513.474.7777 • Peebles 513.605.1380

R: 239   **T:** 4th 58%
Elected Year: 2012

OKLAHOMA

⚑ Governor Kevin Stitt (stit)   p 405.521.2342

State Capitol Building
2300 N. Lincoln Blvd., Room 212
Oklahoma City, OK 73105
Website ok.gov
Fax 405.521.3353
Term Ends 2023
Lt. Governor
Matt Pinnell, **R**

C: Oklahoma City
P: 3,943,079 (28)
A: 68,594.88 mi^2 (19th)

U.S. Senators
James M. Inhofe, **R**
James P. Lankford, **R**
U.S. Representatives
01 / Kevin R. Hern, **R**
02 / Markwayne Mullin, **R**
03 / Frank D. Lucas, **R**
04 / Tom J. Cole, **R**
05 / Kendra Horn, **D**

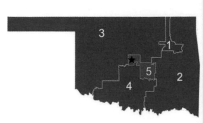

⚑ Sen. James M. Inhofe (IN-hahf)   R-OK-Sr.   p 202.224.4721

Rm. RSOB 205 **Web.** inhofe.senate.gov   **f** 202.228.0380
Bio. 11/17/1934 • Des Moines, IA • U.S. Representative;
Insurance Executive • Army 1954-56 • Univ. of Tulsa (LK),
B.A., 1973 • Presbyterian • M. Kay Kirkpatrick Inhofe, 4 ch (1
deceased); 16 gr-ch **Cmte.** Armed Services • Environment
& Public Works • Small Business & Entrepreneurship
CoS. Luke Holland   **LD.** Andrew Forbes
Sched. Wendi Price   **PS.** Leacy Burke
Dist. Off. Enid 580.234.5105 • McAlester 918.426.0933 •
Oklahoma City 405.208.8841 • Tulsa 918.748.5111

R: 7 **T:** 5th 68%
Elected Year: 1994
Next Election: 2020

⚑ Sen. James P. Lankford (LANK-furd)   R-OK-Jr.   p 202.224.5754

Rm. HSOB 316 **Web.** lankford.senate.gov
Bio. 03/04/1968 • Dallas, TX • Univ. of Texas, B.S.,
1990; Southwestern Theological Baptist Seminary
(TX), M.Div., 1994 • Baptist • M. Cindy Lankford, 2 ch
Cmte. Appropriations • Finance • Homeland Security &
Government Affairs • Indian Affairs
CoS. Michelle Altman   **LD.** Sarah Seitz
Sched. Kristen Adams (CD)   **PS.** Aly Deley
Dist. Off. Oklahoma City 405.231.4941 • Tulsa
918.581.7651

R: 73 **T:** 1st 68%
Elected Year: 2014
Next Election: 2022

⚑ Rep. Tom J. Cole (koal)   R-OK-04   p 202.225.6165

Rm. RHOB 2207 **Web.** cole.house.gov   **f** 202.225.3512
Bio. 04/28/1949 • Shreveport, LA • Chief of Staff,
Republican National Committee; Secretary of State •
Grinnell College (IA), B.A., 1971; Institute for Historical
Research - London (England), B.A., 1972; Yale Univ.
(CT), M.A., 1974; Univ. of Oklahoma (OK), Ph.D., 1984 •
Methodist • M. Ellen Elizabeth Decker Cole, 1 ch **Cmte.**
Appropriations • Rules
CoS. Josh Grogis
Sched. Charlotte Mitchell   **PS.** Sarah A. Corley
(CD)
Dist. Off. Ada 580.436.5375 • Lawton 580.357.2131 •
Norman 405.329.6500

R: 77 **T:** 9th 63%
Elected Year: 2002

OKLAHOMA

♟ Rep. Kevin R. Hern (hurn) — R-OK-01 — p 202.225.2211

Rm. LHOB 1019 **Web.** hern.house.gov   **f** 202.225.9187
Bio. 12/04/1961 • Belton, MO • Univ. of Arkansas-Little Rock, B.S., 1986; Univ. of Arkansas-Little Rock, M.B.A., 1999 • Evangelical • M. Tammy Hern, 3 ch   **Cmte.** Budget • Natural Resources • Small Business
CoS. Cameron Foster   **LD.** Jeff Billman
Sched. Courtney Ballenger   **PS.** Miranda Dabney
Dist. Off. Tulsa 918.935.3222

R: 344   **T:** 2nd 59%
Elected Year: 2018

♞ Rep. Kendra Horn (horn) — D-OK-05 — p 202.225.2132

Rm. CHOB 415 **Web.** horn.house.gov
Bio. 06/09/1976 • Chickasha, OK • Univ. of Tulsa (LK), B.A., 1998; Southern Methodist Univ. Law School (TX), J.D., 2001 • Methodist • D.   **Cmte.** Armed Services • Science, Space & Technology
CoS. Brady King   **LD.** Rayshon Payton
Sched. Kyle Dunn   **PS.** Catherine Sweeney
Dist. Off. Oklahoma City 405.602.3074

R: 382   **T:** 1st 51%
Elected Year: 2018

♟ Rep. Frank D. Lucas (LOO-kuhss) — R-OK-03 — p 202.225.5565

Rm. RHOB 2405 **Web.** lucas.house.gov   **f** 202.225.8696
Bio. 01/06/1960 • Cheyenne, OK • State Representative; Farmer/Rancher • Oklahoma State Univ., B.S., 1982 • Baptist • M. Lynda Bradshaw Lucas, 3 ch ; 2 gr-ch   **Cmte.** Financial Services • Science, Space & Technology
CoS. Stacey Glasscock   **LD.** Nicole Scott
Sched. Meg Wagner   **PS.** Patrick Bond
Dist. Off. Yukon 405.373.1958

R: 36   **T:** 14th 74%
Elected Year: 1994

♟ Rep. Markwayne Mullin (MUHL-luhn) — R-OK-02 — p 202.225.2701

Rm. RHOB 2421 **Web.** mullin.house.gov   **f** 202.225.3038
Bio. 07/26/1977 • Tulsa, OK • Stillwell High School (OK), Assc. Deg.; Oklahoma State Univ. Institute of Technology, Assc. Deg., 2010 • Pentecostal • M. Christie Mullin, 5 ch (twins)   **Cmte.** Energy & Commerce
CoS. Kayla Priehs   **LD.** Taylor Hittle
Sched. Madison Thames   **PS.** Amy Lawrence
Dist. Off. Claremore 918.283.6262 • McAlester 918.423.5951 • Muskogee 918.687.2533

R: 224   **T:** 4th 65%
Elected Year: 2012

OREGON

OREGON

♞ Governor Katherine Brown ("brown") — p 503.378.458?

160 State Capitol
900 Court St. NE, Rm. 160
Salem, OR 97301-4047
Website oregon.gov
Fax 503.378.8970
Term Ends 2019

C: Salem
P: 4,190,713 (27)
A: 95,988.05 mi^2 (10th)

U.S. Senators
Ron Wyden, **D**
Jeff A. Merkley, **D**
U.S. Representatives
01 / Suzanne M. Bonamici, **D**
02 / Greg P. Walden, **R**
03 / Earl Blumenauer, **D**
04 / Pete A. DeFazio, **D**
05 / Kurt Schrader, **D**

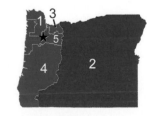

⚑ Sen. Jeff A. Merkley (MURK-lee)

D-OR-Jr.   p 202.224.3753

Rm. HSOB 313 **Web.** merkley.senate.gov   **f** 202.228.3997
Bio. 10/24/1956 • Myrtle Creek, OR • State Legislator •
Stanford Univ. (CA), B.A., 1979; Princeton Univ. Woodrow
Wilson School of Public and International Affairs (NJ),
M.P.P., 1982 • Lutheran • M. Mary Sorteberg, 2 ch **Cmte.**
Appropriations • Budget • Environment & Public Works •
Foreign Relations
CoS. Michael Zamore   **LD.** Laura Updegrove
Sched. Carly Vandegrift   **PS.** Raymond Zaccaro
Dist. Off. Bend 541.318.1298 • Eugene 541.465.6750 •
Medford 541.608.9102 • Pendleton 541.278.1129 • Portland
503.326.3386 • Salem 503.362.8102

R: 40   **T:** 2nd 56%
Elected Year: 2008
Next Election: 2020

⚑ Sen. Ron Wyden (WY-duhn)

D-OR-Sr.   p 202.224.5244

Rm. DSOB 221 **Web.** wyden.senate.gov   **f** 202.228.2717
Bio. 05/03/1949 • Wichita, KS • Senior Citizen Advocacy
Group State Director; Professor, Gerontology • Univ. of
California, B.A., 1969; Stanford Univ. (CA), B.A., 1971; Univ.
of Oregon Law School, J.D., 1974 • Jewish • M. Nancy Bass
Wyden, 5 ch (2 from previous marriage) **Cmte.** Budget •
Energy & Natural Resources • Finance • Intelligence • Joint
Taxation
CoS. Jeffrey Michels   **LD.** Isaiah Akin
Sched. Montana Judd   **PS.** Keith Chu
Dist. Off. Bend 541.330.9142 • Eugene 541.431.0229 • La
Grande 541.962.7691 • Medford 541.858.5122 • Portland
503.326.7525 • Salem 503.589.4555

R: 8   **T:** 4th 57%
Elected Year: 1996
Next Election: 2022

⚑ Rep. Earl Blumenauer (BLOO-meh-nou-ur)

D-OR-03   p 202.225.4811

Rm. LHOB 1111 **Web.**   **f** 202.225.8941
blumenauer.house.gov
Bio. 08/16/1948 • Portland, OR • Attorney • Lewis & Clark
College (OR), B.A., 1970; Northwestern Law School, Lewis
and Clark College (OR), J.D., 1976 • Unspecified/Other •
M. Margaret Kirkpatrick Blumenauer, 2 ch **Cmte.** Ways &
Means
CoS. David Skillman   **LD.** Laura Still Thrift
Sched. Kyle King   **PS.** Anna Nguyen
Dist. Off. Portland 503.231.2300

R: 44   **T:** 13th 73%
Elected Year: 1996

⚑ Rep. Suzanne M. Bonamici (baw-nuh-MEE-chee)

D-OR-01   p 202.225.0855

Rm. RHOB 2231 **Web.** bonamici.house.gov   **f** 202.225.9497
Bio. 10/14/1954 • Detroit, MI • State Legislator; Attorney •
Lane Community College (OR), A.A., 1978; Univ. of Oregon,
B.A., 1980; Univ. of Oregon, B.A., 1980; Univ. of Oregon
Law School, J.D., 1983 • Episcopalian • M. Michael H.
Simon, 2 ch **Cmte.** Education & Labor • Science, Space &
Technology • Select Committee on the Climate Crisis
CoS. Rachael Bornstein
Sched. Ethan Rank   **PS.** Natalie Crofts
Dist. Off. Beaverton 503.469.6010

R: 189   **T:** 5th 64%
Elected Year: 2012

⚑ Rep. Pete A. DeFazio (deh-FAH-zee-o)

D-OR-04   p 202.225.6416

Rm. RHOB 2134 **Web.** defazio.house.gov   **f** 202.226.3493
Bio. 05/27/1947 • Needham, MA • Congressional Aide;
Chair Lane County Commission • Air Force 1967-71 •
Tufts Univ. (MA), B.A., 1969; Univ. of Oregon, M.S., 1977 •
Roman Catholic • M. Myrnie Daut **Cmte.** Transportation &
Infrastructure
CoS. Kristie M. Greco   **LD.** Kris M. Pratt
Johnson
Sched. Matt Leasure   **PS.** Beth Schoenbach
Dist. Off. Coos Bay 541.269.2609 • Eugene 541.465.6732 •
Roseburg 541.440.3523

R: 8   **T:** 17th 56%
Elected Year: 1986

OREGON

ᐅ Rep. Kurt Schrader (SHRAY-dur) D-OR-05 p 202.225.5711

Rm. RHOB 2431 **Web.** schrader.house.gov f 202.225.5699
Bio. 10/19/1951 • Bridgeport, CT • State Legislator;
Veterinarian • Cornell Univ. (NY), B.A., 1973; Univ. of Illinois,
B.A., 1975; Univ. of Illinois College of Veterinary Medicine
(IL), D.V.M., 1977 • Episcopalian • D., 5 ch **Cmte.** Energy &
Commerce
CoS. Paul Gage   **LD.** Chris Huckleberry
Sched. Larkin Parker   **PS.** Carlee Griffeth
Dist. Off. Oregon City 503.557.1324 • Salem 503.588.9100

R: 141 **T:** 6th 55%
Elected Year: 2008

ᐅ Rep. Greg P. Walden (WALL-duhn) R-OR-02 p 202.225.6730

Rm. RHOB 2185 **Web.** walden.house.gov f 202.225.5774
Bio. 01/10/1957 • The Dalles, OR • State Legislator •
Univ. of Oregon, B.S., 1981 • Episcopalian • M. Mylene Ann
Simons Walden, 1 ch **Cmte.** Energy & Commerce
CoS. Lorissa Bounds   **LD.** Riley Bushue
Sched. Jenny Forrest   **PS.** Justin Discigil
Dist. Off. Bend 541.389.4408 • La Grande 541.624.2400 •
Medford 541.776.4646

R: 64 **T:** 11th 56%
Elected Year: 1998

PENNSYLVANIA

ᐅ Governor Thomas W. Wolf (wulf) p 717.787.2500

Main Capitol Building, Rm. 225   **C:** Harrisburg
Harrisburg, PA 17120   **P:** 12,807,060 (5)
Website pa.gov   **A:** 44,742.66 mi^2 (32nd)
Fax 717.772.8284
Term Ends 2023
Lt. Governor
Michael J. Stack, **D**

U.S. Senators
Bob Casey, **D**
Pat J. Toomey, **R**
U.S. Representatives
01 / Brian K. Fitzpatrick, **R**
02 / Brendan F. Boyle, **D**
03 / Dwight Evans, **D**
04 / Madeleine Dean, **D**
05 / Mary Gay Scanlon, **D**
06 / Chrissy Jampoler Houlahan,
D
07 / Susan Ellis Wild, **D**
08 / Matthew A. Cartwright, **D**
09 / Daniel P. Meuser, **R**

10 / Scott Perry, **R**   14 / Guy L. Reschenthaler, **R**
11 / Lloyd K. Smucker, **R**   15 / Glenn W. Thompson, **R**
12 / Vacant   16 / Mike Kelly, **R**
13 / John Joyce, **R**   17 / Conor Lamb, **D**
                                       18 / Mike F. Doyle, **D**

ᐅ Sen. Bob Casey Jr. (KAY-see) D-PA-Sr. p 202.224.632

Rm. RSOB 393 **Web.** casey.senate.gov f 202.228.060
Bio. 04/13/1960 • Scranton, PA • Teacher; Attorney •
College of The Holy Cross (MA), B.A., 1982; Catholic Univ.
of America (DC), J.D., 1988 • Roman Catholic • M. Terese
Foppiano Casey, 4 ch **Cmte.** Aging • Agriculture, Nutrition
Forestry • Finance • Health, Education, Labor & Pensions
CoS. Kristen E. Gentile   **LD.** Derek J. Miller
Sched. Jessica Butherus   **PS.** John J. Rizzo
Dist. Off. Allentown 610.782.9470 • Bellefonte
814.357.0314 • Erie 814.874.5080 • Harrisburg 717.231.7540
• Philadelphia 215.405.9660 • Pittsburgh 412.803.7370 •
Scranton 570.941.0930

R: 30 **T:** 2nd 56%
Elected Year: 2006
Next Election: 2024

Sen. Pat J. Toomey (TOO-mee)   R-PA-Jr.   p 202.224.4254

Rm. RSOB 248   **Web.** toomey.senate.gov   **f** 202.228.0284
Bio. 11/17/1961 • Providence, RI • Harvard Univ., B.A., 1984
• Roman Catholic • M. Kris Toomey, 3 ch   **Cmte.** Banking,
Housing & Urban Affairs • Budget • Finance
CoS. Daniel Brandt   **LD.** Brad Grantz
Sched. Danielle Quercia   **PS.** Bill Jaffee
Dist. Off. Allentown 610.434.1444 • Erie 814.453.3010
• Harrisburg 717.782.3951 • Johnstown 814.266.5970 •
Philadelphia 215.241.1090 • Pittsburgh 412.803.3501 •
Wilkes-Barre 570.820.4088

R: 49   **T:** 2nd   49%
Elected Year: 2010
Next Election: 2022

Rep. Brendan F. Boyle (BOY-uhl)   D-PA-02   p 202.225.6111

Rm. LHOB 1133   **Web.** boyle.house.gov   **f** 202.226.0611
Bio. 02/06/1977 • Philadelphia, PA • Univ. of Notre Dame
(IN), B.A., 1999; Harvard Univ. John F. Kennedy School
of Government (MA), M.P.P., 2005 • Roman Catholic • M.
Jennifer Morgan, 1 ch   **Cmte.** Budget • Ways & Means
CoS. John W. McCarthy   **LD.** Helena Mastrogianis
Sched. Daniel Maher   **PS.** Sean Tobin
Dist. Off. Philadelphia 267.519.2252

R: 256   **T:** 3rd   79%
Elected Year: 2014

Rep. Matthew A. Cartwright (KART-rite)   D-PA-08   p 202.225.5546

Rm. LHOB 1034   **Web.** cartwright.house.gov   **f** 202.226.0996
Bio. 05/01/1961 • Erie, PA • Hamilton College (NY), A.B.,
1983; Univ. of Pennsylvania, J.D., 1986 • Roman Catholic •
M. Marion Munley, 2 ch   **Cmte.** Appropriations • Natural
Resources
CoS. R. Hunter Ridgway   **LD.** Stephen Coffey
Sched. Evie Kirschke-Schwartz   **PS.** Melvin Felix

R: 201   **T:** 4th   55%
Elected Year: 2012

Rep. Madeleine Dean (deen)   D-PA-04   p 202.225.4731

Rm. CHOB 129   **Web.** mad4pa.com
Bio. 06/06/1959 • Glenside, PA • Widener Univ. School of
Law - Delaware, J.D., 1984 • Christian Church • M. Patrick J.
Cunnane, 3 ch; 1 gr-ch   **Cmte.** Financial Services • Judiciary
CoS. Koh T. Chiba   **LD.** Colleen Carlos
Sched. Yodit Tewelde   **PS.** Tim Mack
Dist. Off. Jenkintown 215.886.4444

R: 364   **T:** 1st   100%
Elected Year: 2018

Rep. Mike F. Doyle Jr. (DOY-ull)   D-PA-18   p 202.225.2135

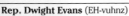

Rm. CHOB 306   **Web.** doyle.house.gov   **f** 202.225.3084
Bio. 08/05/1953 • Swissvale, PA • Insurance Agency Co-
owner; Congressional Aide • Pennsylvania State Univ., B.S.,
1975 • Roman Catholic • M. Susan Erlandson Doyle, 4 ch
Cmte. Energy & Commerce
CoS. David G. Lucas   **LD.** Philip Murphy
Sched. Ellen Young   **PS.** Natalie Young

R: 38   **T:** 13th   100%
Elected Year: 1994

Rep. Dwight Evans (EH-vuhnz)   D-PA-03   p 202.225.4001

Rm. LHOB 1105   **Web.** evans.house.gov   **f** 202.225.5392
Bio. 05/16/1954 • Philadelphia, PA • Community College of
Philadelphia, A.A., 1973; La Salle College (PA), B.A., 1975 •
Baptist • S.   **Cmte.** Small Business • Ways & Means
CoS. Kimberly Turner (CD)
Sched. Randy Love (CD)   **PS.** Ben Turner

R: 290   **T:** 3rd   93%
Elected Year: 2016

PENNSYLVANIA

Rep. Brian K. Fitzpatrick (fits-PAT-rik)   R-PA-01   p 202.225.4276

Rm. LHOB 1722 **Web.** f 202.225.9511
brianfitzpatrick.house.gov
Bio. 12/17/1973 • Levittown, PA • LaSalle Univ., Bach. Deg., 1996; Pennsylvania State Univ., M.B.A., 2001; Pennsylvania State Univ. School of Law, J.D., 2001 • Roman Catholic • S.
Cmte. Foreign Affairs • Transportation & Infrastructure
CoS. Andrew Renteria   **LD.** Joseph Knowles
Sched. Emily Boyer   **PS.** Christopher Auray

R: 309   **T:** 2nd 51%
Elected Year: 2016

Rep. Chrissy Jampoler Houlahan (HOO-luh-han) D-PA-06   p 202.225.4315

Rm. LHOB 1218 **Web.** houlahan.house.gov
Bio. 06/05/1967 • Patuxent River, Md • Stanford Univ. (CA), B.S., 1989; Massachusetts Institute of Technology, M.S., 1994 • Unspecified/Other • M. Bart Houlahan, 2 ch **Cmte.** Armed Services • Foreign Affairs • Small Business
CoS. Michelle Dorothy   **LD.** Caitlin Frazer
Sched. Vanessa Feldman   **PS.** Connor Lounsbury
Dist. Off. Reading 610.295.0815

R: 383   **T:** 1st 59%
Elected Year: 2018

Rep. John Joyce (joyss)   R-PA-13   p 202.225.243

Rm. LHOB 1337 **Web.** johnjoyce.house.gov
Bio. 02/08/1957 • Altoona, PA • Pennsylvania State Univ., Bach. Deg., 1979; Temple Univ. (PA), M.D., 1983 • Catholic • M. Alice Joyce, 3 ch **Cmte.** Homeland Security • Small Business
CoS. Jeremy R. Shoemaker   **LD.** Matt Tucker
                                   PS. Andrew Romeo
Dist. Off. Altoona 814.656.6081 • Chambersburg 717.753.6344

R: 385   **T:** 1st 71%
Elected Year: 2018

Rep. Mike Kelly Jr. (KEH-lee)   R-PA-16   p 202.225.540

Rm. LHOB 1707 **Web.** kelly.house.gov   f 202.225.310
Bio. 05/10/1948 • Pittsburgh, PA • Univ. of Notre Dame (IN) B.A., 1970 • Roman Catholic • M. Victoria Kelly, 4 ch ; 10 gr-ch **Cmte.** Ways & Means
CoS. Matthew Stroia   **LD.** Lori Prater
Sched. Marci Mustello (CD)   **PS.** Andrew Eisenberger

R: 172   **T:** 5th 52%
Elected Year: 2010

Rep. Conor Lamb (lam)   D-PA-17   p 202.225.230

Rm. RHOB 1224 **Web.** lamb.house.gov   f 202.225.184
Bio. 06/27/1984 • Washington, DC • Univ. of Pennsylvania, B.A., 2006; Univ. of Pennsylvania Law School, J.D., 2009 • Catholic • NS. **Cmte.** Science, Space & Technology • Veterans' Affairs
CoS. Craig Kwiecinski   **LD.** Chris Bowman
                                     PS. Reenie Kuhlman

R: 340   **T:** 2nd 56%
Elected Year: 2018

Rep. Daniel P. Meuser (MYOO-zur)   R-PA-09   p 202.225.65

Rm. CHOB 326 **Web.** meuser.house.gov
Bio. 02/10/1954 • Babylon, NY • Cornell Univ. (NY), B.A., 1986; Cornell Univ. (NY), B.A., 1986 • Catholic • M. Shelley Van Acker, 3 ch **Cmte.** Budget • Education & Labor • Veterans' Affairs
CoS. Dante Cutrona   **LD.** Patrick Rooney
Sched. Hali Gruber   **PS.** John Elizandro
Dist. Off. Palmyra • Pottsville 570.871.6370

R: 394   **T:** 1st 60%
Elected Year: 2018

Rep. Scott Perry (PAIR-ree) R-PA-10 p 202.225.5836
Rm. LHOB 1207 **Web.** perry.house.gov **f** 202.226.1000
Bio. 05/27/1962 • San Diego, CA • U.S. Army War College
(PA), M.S.; Pennsylvania State Univ., B.S., 1991 • Church of
the United Brethren in Christ • M. Christy Perry, 2 ch **Cmte.**
Foreign Affairs • Transportation & Infrastructure
CoS. Lauren Muglia **LD.** Jared Culver
Sched. Carol Wiest (CD) **PS.** Brandy Brown
Dist. Off. Harrisburg 717.603.4980

R: 225 T: 4th 51%
Elected Year: 2012

Rep. Guy L. Reschenthaler (REH-shen-thaw- R-PA-14 p 202.225.2065
lur)
Rm. CHOB 531 **Web.**
reschenthaler.house.gov
Bio. 04/07/1983 • Pittsburgh, PA • Pennsylvania State Univ.,
B.A., 2004; Duquesne Univ., J.D., 2007 • Christian Church •
S. **Cmte.** Foreign Affairs • Judiciary
CoS. Aaron R. Bonnaure **LD.** Emily Ackerman
Sched. Alana Lomis **PS.** Elizabeth Argall
Dist. Off. Greensburg 724.219.4200 • Washington
724.206.4800

R: 405 T: 1st 58%
Elected Year: 2018

Rep. Mary Gay Scanlon (scan-lin) D-PA-05 p 202.225.2011
Rm. LHOB 1535 **Web.** scanlon.house.gov **f** 202.226.0280
Bio. 08/30/1959 • Syracuse, NY • Colgate Univ., B.A., 1980;
Univ. of Pennsylvania Law School, J.D., 1984 • Catholic •
M. Mark Scanlon, 3 ch **Cmte.** Judiciary • Rules • Select
Committee on the Modernization of Congress
CoS. Roddy Flynn **LD.** Armita Pedramrazi
Sched. Mary Kate Clement **PS.** Gabby Richards
Dist. Off. Springfield 610.690.7323

R: 346 T: 2nd 63%
Elected Year: 2018

Rep. Lloyd K. Smucker (SMUH-kur) R-PA-11 p 202.225.2411
Rm. CHOB 127 **Web.** smucker.house.gov **f** 202.225.2013
Bio. 01/23/1964 • Lancaster, PA • Lutheran • M. Cynthia
Smucker, 3 ch **Cmte.** Education & Labor • Transportation &
Infrastructure
CoS. Greg V. Facchiano **LD.** Andrew Robreno
Sched. Liz Butler **PS.** Allison Nielsen
Dist. Off. Hanover 717.969.6132 • Red Lion 717.969.6133

: 332 T: 2nd 59%
elected Year: 2016

Rep. Glenn W. Thompson Jr. (TOMP-suhn) R-PA-15 p 202.225.5121
Rm. CHOB 124 **Web.** thompson.house.gov **f** 202.225.5796
Bio. 07/27/1959 • Bellefonte, PA • School Board Member;
Health Care Executive • Pennsylvania State Univ., B.S., 1981;
Temple Univ. (PA), M.Ed., 1998 • Protestant - Unspecified
Christian • M. Penny Thompson, 3 ch **Cmte.** Agriculture •
Education & Labor
CoS. Matthew Brennan **LD.** John Busovsky
Sched. Alissa Stechschulte **PS.** Renee Gamela

142 T: 6th 68%
ected Year: 2008

Rep. Susan Ellis Wild ("wild") D-PA-07 p 202.225.6411
Rm. LHOB 1607 **Web.** wild.house.gov
Bio. 06/07/1957 • Wiesbaden, Germany • American Univ.
(DC), B.A., 1978; George Washington Univ. (DC), J.D., 1982
• Jewish • D., 2 ch **Cmte.** Education & Labor • Ethics •
Foreign Affairs
CoS. Jed Ober **LD.** Dorcas Adekunle
Sched. Rebekah Kirkwood **PS.** Zoe Wilson-Meyer
Dist. Off. Allentown 484.781.6000 • Easton 610.333.1170

347 T: 2nd 54%
ected Year: 2018

RHODE ISLAND

RHODE ISLAND

🔊 **Governor Gina Raimondo** (ruh-MON-doh)   p 401.222.2371

82 Smith St.
Providence, RI 02903
Website ri.gov
Fax 401.222.2012
Term Ends 2023
Lt. Governor
Daniel Mckee, **D**

C: Providence
P: 1,057,315 (45)
A: 1,033.98 mi^2 (51st)

U.S. Senators
Jack F. Reed, **D**
Sheldon Whitehouse, **D**
U.S. Representatives
01 / David N. Cicilline, **D**
02 / Jim R. Langevin, **D**

🔊 **Sen. Jack F. Reed** (reed)   D-RI-Sr.   p 202.224.4642

Rm. HSOB 728 **Web.** reed.senate.gov   f 202.224.4680
Bio. 11/12/1949 • Cranston, RI • Attorney; Professor at West
Point • Army 1967-79 • U.S. Military Academy (NY), B.S.,
1971; Harvard Univ. John F. Kennedy School of Government
(MA), M.P.P., 1973; Harvard Univ. School of Law (MA), J.D.,
1982 • Roman Catholic • M. Julia Hart Reed, 1 ch **Cmte.**
Appropriations • Armed Services • Banking, Housing &
Urban Affairs
CoS. Neil Campbell   **LD.** Elyse Wasch
Sched. Rosanne Haroian   **PS.** Chip Unruh
Dist. Off. Cranston 401.943.3100 • Providence
401.528.5200

R: 11 **T:** 4th 71%
Elected Year: 1996
Next Election: 2020

🔊 **Sen. Sheldon Whitehouse** (WHITE-house)   D-RI-Jr.   p 202.224.292

Rm. HSOB 530 **Web.** whitehouse.senate.gov f 202.228.636
Bio. 10/20/1955 • New York City, NY • Attorney • Yale Univ.
(CT), B.Arch., 1978; Univ. of Virginia Law School, J.D., 1982 •
Episcopalian • M. Sandra Thornton Whitehouse, 2 ch **Cmte**
Budget • Environment & Public Works • Finance • Judiciary
CoS. Samuel Goodstein   **LD.** Josh Karetny
Sched. Leah Seigle   **PS.** Caleb Gibson
Dist. Off. Providence 401.453.5294

R: 32 **T:** 2nd 61%
Elected Year: 2006
Next Election: 2024

🔊 **Rep. David N. Cicilline** (sih-sih-LEE-nee)   D-RI-01   p 202.225.491

Rm. RHOB 2233 **Web.** cicilline.house.gov   f 202.225.329
Bio. 07/15/1961 • Providence, RI • Narragansett High
School, J.D.; Brown Univ. (RI), B.A., 1983; Georgetown Univ
Law Center (DC), J.D., 1986 • Jewish • S. **Cmte.** Foreign
Affairs • Judiciary
CoS. Peter Karafotas
Sched. Francis Grubar   **PS.** Richard Luchette
Dist. Off. Pawtucket 401.729.5600

R: 156 **T:** 5th 67%
Elected Year: 2010

🔊 **Rep. Jim R. Langevin** (LAN-jeh-vin)   D-RI-02   p 202.225.27

Rm. RHOB 2077 **Web.** langevin.house.gov   f 202.225.59
Bio. 04/22/1964 • Providence, RI • RI Secretary of State;
State Representative • Rhode Island College, B.A., 1990;
Harvard Univ. John F. Kennedy School of Government (MA
M.P.A., 1994 • Roman Catholic • S. **Cmte.** Armed Services
• Homeland Security
CoS. Todd L. Adams   **LD.** Nick JM Leiserson
Sched. Katie Albert (CD)   **PS.** Stuart Malec (CD)
Dist. Off. Warwick 401.732.9400

R: 68 **T:** 10th 64%
Elected Year: 2000

SOUTH CAROLINA

⚑ Governor Henry McMaster (mik-MASS-tur)   p 803.734.2100

Office of the Governor
1205 Pendleton St.
Columbia, SC 29201
Website sc.gov
Fax 803.734.5167
Term Ends 2023
Governor
Henry McMaster, **R**

C: Columbia
P: 5,084,127 (23)
A: 30,060.74 mi^2 (40th)

U.S. Senators
Lindsey Graham, **R**
Tim E. Scott, **R**
U.S. Representatives
01 / Joe K. Cunningham, **D**
02 / Joe Wilson, **R**
03 / Jeff D. Duncan, **R**
04 / William R. Timmons, **R**
05 / Ralph W. Norman, **R**
06 / James E. Clyburn, **D**
07 / Tom Rice, **R**

⚑ Sen. Lindsey Graham (gram)   R-SC-Sr.   p 202.224.5972

Rm. RSOB 290 **Web.** lgraham.senate.gov   **f** 202.224.3808
Bio. 07/09/1955 • Central, SC • U.S. Representative •
Air Force Judge Advocate General Corps 1982-88; South
Carolina Air National Guard 1989-95, Air Force Reserve
1995-present • Univ. of South Carolina, B.S., 1977; Univ. of
South Carolina, M.P.A., 1978; Univ. of South Carolina School
of Law, J.D., 1981 • Baptist • S. **Cmte.** Appropriations •
Budget • Foreign Relations • Judiciary
CoS. Richard S. Perry   **LD.** Matt Rimkunas
Sched. Edward Mercer (CD) **PS.** Alice James
Dist. Off. Columbia 803.933.0112 • Florence 843.669.1505
• Greenville 864.250.1417 • Mt. Pleasant 843.849.3887 •
Pendleton 864.646.4090 • Rock Hill 803.366.2828

R: 21 **T:** 3rd 54%
Elected Year: 2002
Next Election: 2020

⚑ Sen. Tim E. Scott (skaht)   R-SC-Jr.   p 202.224.6121

Rm. HSOB 104 **Web.** scott.senate.gov   **f** 202.228.5143
Bio. 09/19/1965 • North Charleston, SC • Charleston
Southern Univ. (SC), B.S., 1988 • Evangelical • S. **Cmte.**
Aging • Banking, Housing & Urban Affairs • Finance •
Health, Education, Labor & Pensions • Small Business &
Entrepreneurship
CoS. Jennifer DeCasper   **LD.** Chuck Cogar
Sched. Brie Kelly   **PS.** Sean Smith
Dist. Off. Columbia 803.771.6112 • Greenville
864.233.5366 • North Charleston 843.727.4525

: 16 **T:** 3rd 61%
Elected Year: 2013
Next Election: 2022

⚑ Rep. James E. Clyburn (KLY-burn)   D-SC-06   p 202.225.3315

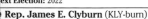

Rm. CHOB 200 **Web.** clyburn.house.gov   **f** 202.225.2313
Bio. 07/21/1940 • Sumter, SC • SC Human Affairs
Commissioner; Gubernatorial Assistant • South Carolina
State Univ., B.S., 1962; Univ. of South Carolina School of Law,
B.S., 1974 • African Methodist Episcopal • M. Emily England
Clyburn, 3 ch ; 4 gr-ch
CoS. Yelberton R. Watkins   **LD.** Willie Lyles
Sched. Lindy Birch Kelly   **PS.** Hope Derrick
Dist. Off. Columbia 803.799.1100 • Kingstree 843.355.1211
• Santee 803.854.4700

: 25 **T:** 14th 70%
ected Year: 1992

SOUTH CAROLINA

‣ Rep. Joe K. Cunningham (KUH-ning-ham) D-SC-01 p 202.225.3176

Rm. CHOB 423 **Web.** cunningham.house.gov
Bio. 05/26/1982 • Kuttawa, KY • Florida Atlantic Univ., B.S., 2005; Northern Kentucky Univ., J.D., 2014 • Christian Church • M. Amanda Cunningham, 1 ch **Cmte.** Natural Resources • Veterans' Affairs
CoS. Lane Lofton   **LD.** RaShawn Mitchell
Sched. Jesse Mayer   **PS.** Rebecca Drago
Dist. Off. Johns Island

R: 362 **T:** 1st 51%
Elected Year: 2018

▥ Rep. Jeff D. Duncan (DUN-kuhn) R-SC-03 p 202.225.5301

Rm. RHOB 2229 **Web.** jeffduncan.house.gov **f** 202.225.3216
Bio. 01/07/1966 • Greenville, SC • Clemson Univ. (SC), B.A., 1988 • Baptist • M. Melody Duncan, 3 ch **Cmte.** Energy & Commerce
CoS. Allen Klump   **LD.** Joshua Gross
Sched. Thomas McAllister   **PS.** Addie Patterson
Dist. Off. Anderson 864.224.7401 • Clinton 864.681.1028

R: 160 **T:** 5th 68%
Elected Year: 2010

▥ Rep. Ralph W. Norman Jr. (NOR-muhn) R-SC-05 p 202.225.550

Rm. CHOB 319 **Web.** norman.house.gov **f** 202.225.0464
Bio. 06/20/1953 • York County, SC • Rock Hill High School, B.S., 1971; Presbyterian College (SC), B.S., 1975 • Presbyterian • M. Elaine Rice, 4 ch ; 16 gr-ch **Cmte.** Budget • Oversight & Reform • Science, Space & Technology
CoS. Mark Piland   **LD.** Jake Hilkin
Sched. Amber Peoples   **PS.** Austin Livingston
Dist. Off. Rock Hill 803.327.1114

R: 338 **T:** 2nd 57%
Elected Year: 2017

▥ Rep. Tom Rice Jr. ("rice") R-SC-07 p 202.225.989

Rm. CHOB 512 **Web.** rice.house.gov **f** 202.225.969
Bio. 08/04/1957 • Charleston, SC • Univ. of South Carolina, B.S., 1979; Univ. of South Carolina, Mast. Deg., 1982; Univ. of South Carolina School of Law, J.D., 1982 • Episcopalian • M. Wrenzie Rice, 3 ch **Cmte.** Ways & Means
CoS. Jennifer Watson   **LD.** Walker Truluck
Sched. McKayla Dunn   **PS.** Sophica Seid
Dist. Off. Florence 843.679.9781 • Myrtle Beach 843.445.6459

R: 228 **T:** 4th 60%
Elected Year: 2012

▥ Rep. William R. Timmons IV (TIH-muhnz) R-SC-04 p 202.225.603

Rm. CHOB 313 **Web.** timmons.house.gov
Bio. 04/30/1984 • Greenville, SC • George Washington Univ. (DC), B.A., 2006; Univ. of South Carolina, Mast. Deg., 2009; Univ. of South Carolina, J.D., 2010 • Church of Christ • S. **Cmte.** Budget • Education & Labor • Select Committee on the Modernization of Congress
CoS. Moutray McLaren   **LD.** Hilary Ranieri
Sched. Olivia Widenhouse   **PS.** Joshua Goodwin
Dist. Off. Greenville 864.241.0175 • Spartanburg 864.583.3264

R: 423 **T:** 1st 60%
Elected Year: 2018

▥ Rep. Joe Wilson (WILL-suhn) R-SC-02 p 202.225.24

Rm. LHOB 1436 **Web.** joewilson.house.gov **f** 202.225.24
Bio. 07/31/1947 • Charleston, SC • State Senator; Attorney; Founding Partner; Judge, Springdale • Army Reserve 1972-75; SC Army National Guard 1975-03 • Washington an Lee Univ. (VA), B.A., 1969; Univ. of South Carolina, J.D., 197 • Presbyterian • M. Roxanne Dusenbury McCrory Wilson, 4 ch ; 7 gr-ch **Cmte.** Armed Services • Foreign Affairs
CoS. Jonathan Day   **LD.** Oren Adaki
Sched. Stephanie Pendarvis   **PS.** Stami Williams
Dist. Off. Aiken 803.642.6416 • West Columbia 803.939.0041

R: 73 **T:** 10th 56%
Elected Year: 2001

SOUTH DAKOTA

⚑ Governor Kristi Lynn Noem (noam)　　　　　p 605.773.3212

State Capitol
500 E. Capitol Ave.
Pierre, SD 57501-5070
Website sd.gov
Fax 605.773.4711
Term Ends 2023
Lt. Governor
Larry Rhoden, R

C: Pierre
P: 882,235 (47)
A: 75,811.13 mi^2 (16th)

U.S. Senators
John Thune, R
Mike Rounds, R
U.S. Representatives
01 / Dusty Johnson, R

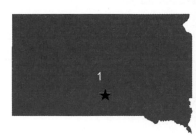

1

★

⚑ Sen. Mike Rounds (rounz)　　　　R-SD-Jr.　　p 202.224.5842

Rm. HSOB 502 **Web.** rounds.senate.gov　　**f** 202.224.7482
Bio. 10/24/1954 • Huron, SD • Majority Leader, SD Senate;
Mbr., SD Senate • South Dakota State Univ., B.S., 1977 •
Roman Catholic • M. Jean Vedvei Rounds, 4 ch ; 6 gr-ch
Cmte. Armed Services • Banking, Housing & Urban Affairs
• Environment & Public Works • Veterans' Affairs
CoS. Mark Johnston　　　　**LD.** Gregg Rickman
Sched. Jordan Fashimpaur　　**PS.** Natalie Krings
Dist. Off. Aberdeen 605.225.0366 • Pierre 605.224.1450 •
Rapid City 605.343.5035 • Sioux Falls 605.336.0486

R: 76　T: 1st 50%
Elected Year: 2014
Next Election: 2020

⚑ Sen. John Thune (thoon)　　　　R-SD-Sr.　　p 202.224.2321

Rm. DSOB 511 **Web.** thune.senate.gov　　**f** 202.228.5429
Bio. 01/07/1961 • Pierre, SD • U.S. Representative;
Congressional Aide • Biola Univ., B.B.A., 1983; Univ. of
South Dakota, M.B.A., 1984 • Evangelical • M. Kimberley
Joe Weems Thune, 2 ch ; 2 gr-ch **Cmte.** Agriculture,
Nutrition & Forestry • Commerce, Science & Transportation
• Finance
CoS. Ryan Nelson　　　　**LD.** Jessica McBride
Sched. Johanna Scheich　　**PS.** Ryan Wrasse
Dist. Off. Aberdeen 605.225.8823 • Rapid City
605.348.7551 • Sioux Falls 605.334.9596

: 24　T: 3rd 72%
Elected Year: 2004
Next Election: 2022

Rep. Dusty Johnson (JAHN-suhn)　　　R-SD-01　　p 202.225.2801

Rm. LHOB 1508 **Web.**
dustyjohnson.house.gov
Bio. 09/30/1976 • Pierre, SD • Univ. of South Dakota, B.A.,
1999; Univ. of Kansas, M.P.A., 2002 • Christian Church • M.
Jacquelyn Johnson, 3 ch **Cmte.** Agriculture • Education &
Labor
CoS. Andrew Christianson　　**LD.** Darren Hedlund
Sched. Carly Reedholm　　**PS.** Jazmine Kemp
Dist. Off. Aberdeen 605.937.8522 • Rapid City　•Sioux
Falls

: 384　T: 1st 60%
Elected Year: 2018

TENNESSEE

Governor Bill Lee (lee)   p 615.741.2001

Tennessee State Capitol, 1st Floor **C:** Nashville
Nashville, TN 37243   **P:** 6,770,010 (16)
Website tennessee.gov   **A:** 41,234.92 mi² (34th)
Fax 615.532.9711
Term Ends 2023
Lt. Governor
Rand McNally, **R**

U.S. Senators
Lamar Alexander, **R**
Marsha Blackburn, **R**
U.S. Representatives
01 / Phil Roe, **R**
02 / Tim Burchett, **R**
03 / Chuck J. Fleischmann, **R**
04 / Scott E. DesJarlais, **R**
05 / Jim H.S. Cooper, **D**
06 / John W. Rose, **R**
07 / Mark E. Green, **R**
08 / David F. Kustoff, **R**
09 / Steve I. Cohen, **D**

Sen. Lamar Alexander (a-leks-AN-dur)   R-TN-Sr.   p 202.224.4944

Rm. DSOB 455   **f** 202.228.3398
Bio. 07/03/1940 • Maryville, TN • Chairman of Education-
Related Company; Secretary U.S. Department of Education
• Vanderbilt Univ. (TN), B.A., 1962; New York Univ. Law
School, J.D., 1965 • Presbyterian • M. Leslee Buhler Buhler,
4 ch ; 6 gr-ch **Cmte.** Appropriations • Energy & Natural
Resources • Health, Education, Labor & Pensions • Rules &
Administration
CoS. David Cleary   **LD.** Lindsay Garcia
                                            PS. Ashton Davies
Dist. Off. Blountville 423.325.6240 • Chattanooga

R: 22   T: 3rd 62%   423.752.5337 • Jackson 731.664.0289 • Knoxville
Elected Year: 2002   865.545.4253 • Memphis 901.544.4224 • Nashville
Next Election: 2020   615.736.5129

Sen. Marsha Blackburn (BLAK-burn)   R-TN-Jr.   p 202.224.334

Rm. DSOB 357 **Web.** blackburn.senate.gov   **f** 202.228.056
Bio. 06/06/1952 • Laurel, MS • Small Business Owner; State
Senator • Mississippi State Univ., B.S., 1973 • Presbyterian •
M. Chuck Blackburn, 2 ch ; 2 gr-ch **Cmte.** Armed Services
• Commerce, Science & Transportation • Judiciary •
Veterans' Affairs
CoS. Charles A. Flint   **LD.** Sean Farrell
                                            PS. Kathryn McQuade
Dist. Off. Chattanooga 423.541.2939 • Jackson
731.660.3971 • Jonesborough 423.753.4009 • Knoxville
R: 92   T: 0th 55%   865.540.3781 • Memphis 901.527.9199
Elected Year: 2018
Next Election: 2024

Rep. Tim Burchett (BUR-chuht)   R-TN-02   p 202.225.543

Rm. LHOB 1122 **Web.** burchett.house.gov
Bio. 08/25/1964 • Knoxville, TN • Univ. of Tennessee, B.S.,
1988 • Presbyterian • M. Kelly Burchett, 1 ch   **Cmte.** Budge
• Foreign Affairs • Small Business
CoS. Michael Grider   **LD.** Zachary Dooley
Sched. Denise Lambert   **PS.** Jennifer Linginfelter
Dist. Off. Knoxville 865.207.4936

R: 354   T: 1st 66%
Elected Year: 2018

✎ Rep. Steve I. Cohen (KO-uhn)   D-TN-09   p 202.225.3265
Rm. RHOB 2104 **Web.** cohen.house.gov   **f** 202.225.5663
Bio. 05/24/1949 • Memphis, TN • Attorney; State
Representative • Vanderbilt Univ. (TN), B.A., 1971; Memphis
State Univ. - Cecil C. Humphreys School of Law (TN), J.D.,
1973 • Jewish • S., 1 ch **Cmte.** Judiciary • Science, Space
& Technology • Transportation & Infrastructure
CoS. Marilyn Dillihay   **LD.** Matthew Weisman
Sched. Alex Lipow   **PS.** Bart Sullivan
Dist. Off. Memphis 901.544.4131

R: 111 **T:** 7th 80%
Elected Year: 2006

✎ Rep. Jim H.S. Cooper (KOO-pur)   D-TN-05   p 202.225.4311
Rm. LHOB 1536 **Web.** cooper.house.gov   **f** 202.226.1035
Bio. 06/19/1954 • Nashville, TN • Investment banker;
Attorney • Univ. of North Carolina at Chapel Hill, B.A., 1975;
Oxford Univ. (England), M.A., 1977; Harvard Univ. Law
School (MA), J.D., 1980 • Episcopalian • M. Martha Hays
Cooper, 3 ch **Cmte.** Armed Services • Budget • Oversight &
Reform
CoS. Lisa Quigley
Sched. Brandi Jackson   **PS.** Cara Ince (CD)
Dist. Off. Nashville 615.736.5295

R: 22 **T:** 15th 68%
Elected Year: 2002

🐎 Rep. Scott E. DesJarlais (deh-zhar-LAY)   R-TN-04   p 202.225.6831
Rm. RHOB 2301 **Web.** desjarlais.house.gov   **f** 202.226.5172
Bio. 02/21/1964 • Des Moines, IA • Univ. of South Dakota,
B.S., 1987; Univ. of South Dakota School of Medicine, M.D.,
1991 • Episcopalian • M. Amy DesJarlais, 4 ch (1 from
previous marriage) **Cmte.** Agriculture • Armed Services
CoS. Richard Vaughn   **LD.** Richard Wilkins
Sched. MeKenna Carman   **PS.** Brendan Thomas
Dist. Off. Cleveland 423.472.7500 • Columbia 931.381.9920
• Murfreesboro 615.896.1986 • Winchester 931.962.3180

R: 158 **T:** 5th 63%
Elected Year: 2010

🐎 Rep. Chuck J. Fleischmann (FLYSH-muhn)   R-TN-03   p 202.225.3271
Rm. RHOB 2410 **Web.**
fleischmann.house.gov   **f** 202.225.3494
Bio. 10/11/1962 • New York, NY • Univ. of Illinois, B.A.,
1983; Univ. of Tennessee College of Law, Knoxville, J.D.,
1986 • Roman Catholic • M. Brenda Fleischmann, 3 ch
Cmte. Appropriations
CoS. James Hill Hippe   **LD.** Daniel Tidwell
                                 PS. Kasey Lovett
Dist. Off. Athens 423.745.4671 • Chattanooga 423.756.2342
• Oak Ridge 865.576.1976

R: 161 **T:** 5th 64%
Elected Year: 2010

🐎 Rep. Mark E. Green (green)   R-TN-07   p 202.225.2811
Rm. CHOB 533
Bio. 11/08/1964 • Jacksonville, FL • U.S. Military Academy
- West Point (NY), B.S., 1986; Univ. of Southern California,
Mast. Deg., 1987; Wright State Univ. (OH), M.D., 1999 •
Christian Church • M. Camilla Joy Guenther, 2 ch **Cmte.**
Homeland Security • Oversight & Reform
CoS. Stephen Siao   **LD.** Jay Kronzer
Sched. Jerrica Proferes   **PS.** Mitchell Hailstone
Dist. Off. Ashland City

R: 375 **T:** 1st 67%
Elected Year: 2018

🐎 Rep. David F. Kustoff (KUS-tawf)   R-TN-08   p 202.225.4714
Rm. CHOB 523   **f** 202.225.1765
Bio. 10/08/1966 • Memphis, TN • Univ. of Memphis, B.B.A.,
1989; Univ. of Memphis School of Law, J.D., 1992 • Jewish •
M. Roberta Kustoff, 2 ch **Cmte.** Financial Services
CoS. Tyler Threadgill   **LD.** Andrew Hogin
Sched. Anderson
Okoniewski
Dist. Off. Dyersburg 731.412.1037 • Jackson 731.423.4848
• Memphis 901.682.4422

R: 320 **T:** 2nd 68%
Elected Year: 2016

TENNESSEE

⚑ Rep. Phil Roe (roe) R-TN-01 p 202.225.6356
Rm. CHOB 102 **Web.** roe.house.gov **f** 202.225.5714
Bio. 07/21/1945 • Clarksville, TN • Mayor (Johnston City, TN); Obstetrician • Army Medical Corps • Austin Peay State Univ. (TN), B.S., 1967; Univ. of Tennessee, Memphis, M.D., 1973 • Methodist • M. Pam Roe, 3 ch (3 from previous marriage); 2 gr-ch **Cmte.** Education & Labor • Veterans' Affairs
CoS. Matthew Meyer **LD.** Aaron Bill
Sched. Courtney Eubanks **PS.** Whitley Alexander
Dist. Off. Kingsport 423.247.8161 • Morristown 423.254.1400
R: 140 **T:** 6th 77%
Elected Year: 2008

⚑ Rep. John W. Rose (roaz) R-TN-06 p 202.225.4231
Rm. LHOB 1232 **Web.** johnrose.house.gov
Bio. 02/23/1965 • Cookeville, TN • Tennessee Tech Univ., B.S., 1988; Purdue Univ. (IN), M.S., 1990; Vanderbilt Univ. (TN), J.D., 1993 • Christian Church • M. Chelsea Rose, 1 ch
Cmte. Financial Services
CoS. Van Hilleary **LD.** Alexandra Igleheart
Sched. Braden Stover **PS.** Rachel Lee
Dist. Off. Cookeville 931.854.9430 • Gallatin 615.206.8204

R: 407 **T:** 1st 70%
Elected Year: 2018

TEXAS

⚑ Governor Greg Abbott (A-buht) p 512.463.2000
PO Box 12428 **C:** Austin
Austin, TX 78711-2428 **P:** 28,701,845 (2)
Website texas.gov **A:** 261,231.59 mi^2 (2nd)
Fax 512.463.5571
Term Ends 2021
Lt. Governor
Dan Patrick, R

U.S. Senators
John Cornyn, R
Ted Cruz, R
U.S. Representatives
01 / Louie B. Gohmert, R
02 / Daniel Crenshaw, R
03 / Van Taylor, R
04 / John L. Ratcliffe, R
05 / Lance Gooden, R
06 / Ronald J. Wright, R
07 / Elizabeth Pannill Fletcher, D
08 / Kevin P. Brady, R
09 / Al Green, D
10 / Michael T. McCaul, R
11 / Mike Conaway, R
12 / Kay N. Granger, R
13 / Mac Thornberry, R
14 / Randy Weber, R
15 / Vicente Gonzalez, D
16 / Veronica Escobar, D
17 / Bill H. Flores, R
18 / Sheila Jackson Lee, D
19 / Jodey Cook Arrington, R
20 / Joaquin Castro, D
21 / Chip Roy, R
22 / Pete G. Olson, R
23 / Will Hurd, R
24 / Kenny E. Marchant, R
25 / Roger Williams, R
26 / Michael C. Burgess, R
27 / Michael J. Cloud, R

28 / Henry R. Cuellar, D
29 / Sylvia R. Garcia, D
30 / Eddie Bernice Johnson, D
31 / John R. Carter, R
32 / Colin Allred, D
33 / Marc A. Veasey, D
34 / Filemon B. Vela, D
35 / Lloyd A. Doggett, D
36 / Brian Babin, R

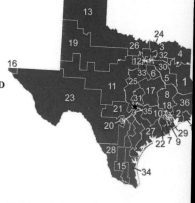

Sen. John Cornyn III (KOR-nuhn) R-TX-Sr. p 202.224.2934

Rm. HSOB 517 **Web.** cornyn.senate.gov **f** 202.228.2856
Bio. 02/02/1952 • Houston, TX • State Attorney General;
State Supreme Court Judge • Trinity Univ. (TX), B.A., 1973;
St. Mary's School of Law (TX), J.D., 1977; Univ. of Virginia,
LL.M., 1995 • Church of Christ • M. Sandra Hansen Cornyn,
2 ch **Cmte.** Finance • Intelligence • Judiciary
CoS. Beth Jafari **LD.** Stephen A. Tausend
Sched. Paige Kerr **PS.** Drew Brandewie
Dist. Off. Austin 512.469.6034 • Dallas 972.239.1310
• Harlingen 956.423.0162 • Houston 713.572.3337 •
Lubbock 806.472.7533 • San Antonio 210.224.7485 • Tyler
903.593.0902

R: 19 **T:** 3rd 62%
Elected Year: 2002
Next Election: 2020

Sen. Ted Cruz (krooz) R-TX-Jr. p 202.224.5922

Rm. RSOB 404 **Web.** cruz.senate.gov **f** 202.228.0755
Bio. 12/22/1970 • Calgary, Alberta, Canada • Princeton
Univ. (NJ), A.B., 1992; Harvard Law School (MA), J.D.,
1995 • Southern Baptist • M. Heidi Nelson, 2 ch **Cmte.**
Commerce, Science & Transportation • Foreign Relations •
Joint Economic • Judiciary • Rules & Administration
CoS. Prerak Shah **LD.** Sean McLean
Sched. Amy Herod **PS.** Maria Jeffrey
Dist. Off. Austin 512.916.5834 • Dallas 214.599.8749
• Houston 713.718.3057 • McAllen 956.686.7339 • San
Antonio 210.340.2885 • Tyler 903.593.5130

R: 64 **T:** 2nd 51%
Elected Year: 2012
Next Election: 2024

Rep. Colin Allred (ALL-red) D-TX-32 p 202.225.2231

Rm. CHOB 328 **Web.** allred.house.gov
Bio. 04/15/1983 • Dallas, TX • Hillcrest High School (TX),
B.A., 2005; Baylor Univ. (TX), B.A., 2005; Univ. of California,
Berkeley, J.D., 2014 • M. Allred Alexandra **Cmte.** Foreign
Affairs • Transportation & Infrastructure • Veterans' Affairs
CoS. Paige Hutchinson **LD.** Janelle McClure
Sched. Mina Pulitzer **PS.** Joshua Stewart
Dist. Off. Dallas 469.573.3916

R: 349 **T:** 1st 52%
Elected Year: 2018

Rep. Jodey Cook Arrington (AIR-ring-ten) R-TX-19 p 202.225.4005

Rm. LHOB 1029 **Web.** arrington.house.gov **f** 202.225.9615
Bio. 03/09/1972 • Kansas City, MO • Texas Tech Univ., B.A.,
1994; Texas Tech Univ., M.P.A., 1997 • Presbyterian • M.
Anne Arrington, 3 ch **Cmte.** Ways & Means
CoS. Chelsea Brown
Sched. Marisa Burleson **PS.** Alex Attebery
Dist. Off. Abilene 325.675.9779 • Lubbock 806.763.1611

: 292 **T:** 2nd 75%
Elected Year: 2016

Rep. Brian Babin (BA-bin) R-TX-36 p 202.225.1555

Rm. RHOB 2236 **Web.** babin.house.gov **f** 202.226.0396
Bio. 03/23/1948 • Port Arthur, TX • Lamur Univ. (TX), B.S.,
1973; Univ. of Texas-Houston, D.D.S., 1976 • Southern Baptist
• M. Roxanne Babin, 5 ch ; 13 gr-ch **Cmte.** Science, Space
& Technology • Transportation & Infrastructure
CoS. Benjamin H. Couhig **LD.** Steve Janushkowsky
Sched. Beth Barber **PS.** Bradley Jaye
Dist. Off. Deer Park 832.780.0966 • Orange 409.883.8075 •
Woodville 409.331.8066

: 253 **T:** 3rd 73%
ected Year: 2014

TEXAS

■ Rep. Kevin P. Brady (BRAY-dee) R-TX-08 p 202.225.4901

Rm. LHOB 1011 **Web.** kevinbrady.house.gov **f** 202.225.5524
Bio. 04/11/1955 • Vermillion, SD • State Representative;
Chamber of Commerce Executive • Univ. of South Dakota,
B.S., 1990 • Roman Catholic • M. Cathy Brady, 2 ch **Cmte.**
Joint Taxation • Ways & Means
CoS. David W. Davis
Sched. Laura Cureton **PS.** Shana Teehan
Dist. Off. Conroe 936.441.5700 • Huntsville 936.439.9532

R: 46 T: 12th 73%
Elected Year: 1996

■ Rep. Michael C. Burgess (BUR-juhs) R-TX-26 p 202.225.7772

Rm. RHOB 2161 **Web.** burgess.house.gov **f** 202.225.2919
Bio. 12/23/1950 • Rochester, MN • Obstetrician • North
Texas State Univ., Dallas, B.S., 1972; North Texas State Univ.,
M.S., 1976; Univ. of Texas-Houston, M.D., 1977; Univ. of Texas
at Dallas, M.S., 2000 • Anglican • M. Laura Burgess, 3 ch ; 2
gr-ch **Cmte.** Energy & Commerce • Rules
CoS. James A. Decker **LD.** Rachel Huggins
PS. Emma Thomson
Dist. Off. Lake Dallas 940.497.5031

R: 75 T: 9th 59%
Elected Year: 2002

■ Rep. John R. Carter (KAR-tur) R-TX-31 p 202.225.3864

Rm. RHOB 2110 **Web.** carter.house.gov **f** 202.225.5886
Bio. 11/06/1941 • Houston, TX • Williamson County District
Judge; Attorney • Texas Technical Univ., B.A., 1964; Univ. of
Texas School of Law, J.D., 1969 • Lutheran • M. Erika Carter,
4 ch; 6 gr-ch **Cmte.** Appropriations
CoS. Jonas Miller **LD.** Grady Bourn
PS. Emily Dowdwell
Dist. Off. Round Rock 512.246.1600 • Temple 254.933.1392

R: 76 T: 9th 51%
Elected Year: 2002

⚑ Rep. Joaquin Castro (KAS-tro) D-TX-20 p 202.225.3236

Rm. RHOB 2241 **Web.** castro.house.gov **f** 202.225.1915
Bio. 09/16/1974 • San Antonio, TX • Stanford Univ. (CA),
A.B., 1996; Harvard Univ. Law School (MA), J.D., 2000 •
Roman Catholic • M. Anna Flores, 2 ch **Cmte.** Education &
Labor • Foreign Affairs • Permanent Select on Intelligence
CoS. Danny Meza **LD.** Ben Thomas
Sched. Danielle Moon **PS.** Jamie Geller
Dist. Off. San Antonio 210.348.8216

R: 202 T: 4th 81%
Elected Year: 2012

■ Rep. Michael J. Cloud ("cloud") R-TX-27 p 202.225.774

Rm. RHOB 1314 **Web.** cloud.house.gov **f** 202.226.113
Bio. 05/13/1975 • Baton Rouge, LA • Oral Roberts Univ.,
Bach. Deg. • M. Rosel Cloud, 3 ch **Cmte.** Oversight &
Reform • Science, Space & Technology
CoS. Adam Magary **LD.** Hugh Fike
Sched. Emily Helms **PS.** Brian Cruickshanks (CD
Dist. Off. Corpus Christi 361.884.2222 • Victoria
361.894.6446

R: 342 T: 2nd 60%
Elected Year: 2018

■ Rep. Mike Conaway (KAH-nuh-way) R-TX-11 p 202.225.360

Rm. RHOB 2469 **Web.** conaway.house.gov **f** 202.225.178
Bio. 06/11/1948 • Borger, TX • CPA; Bank Superintendent/
CFO • Army 1970-72 • Texas A & M Univ., Commerce,
B.B.A., 1970 • Baptist • M. Suzanne Conaway, 4 ch ; 7 gr-ch
Cmte. Agriculture • Armed Services • Permanent Select on
Intelligence
CoS. Mark R. Williams **LD.** Matthew Russell
Sched. Maggie Mullins **PS.** Emily Hytha
Dist. Off. Brownwood 325.646.1950 • Granbury
682.936.2577 • Llano 325.247.2826 • Midland 432.687.2390
• Odessa 432.331.9667 • San Angelo 325.659.4010

R: 90 T: 8th 80%
Elected Year: 2004

Rep. Daniel Crenshaw (KREN-shaw) R-TX-02 p 202.225.6565

Rm. CHOB 413
Bio. 03/14/1984 • Aberdeen, Scotland • Tufts Univ. (MA),
B.A., 2006; Taubman Center for State & Local Government –
Harvard Kennedy School, M.P.A., 2017 • Methodist • M. Tara
Crenshaw **Cmte.** Budget • Homeland Security
CoS. Eliza Baker **LD.** Matt Hodge
Sched. Danny Walden **PS.** Kerry Rom

R: 360 **T:** 1st 53%
Elected Year: 2018

Rep. Henry R. Cuellar (KWAY-ar) D-TX-28 p 202.225.1640

Rm. RHOB 2372 **Web.** cuellar.house.gov **f** 202.225.1641
Bio. 09/19/1955 • Laredo, TX • State Representative; United
States Customs Broker • Laredo Community College (TX),
A.A., 1976; Georgetown Univ. (DC), B.S., 1978; Univ. of Texas
School of Law, J.D., 1981; Texas A and M International Univ.,
M.B.A., 1982; Univ. of Texas, Ph.D., 1998 • Roman Catholic •
M. Imelda Rios Cuellar, 2 ch **Cmte.** Appropriations
CoS. Catherine Edmonson **LD.** Zack Linick
Sched. Madeline Abadie **PS.** Olya Voytovich
Dist. Off. Laredo 956.725.0639 • Mission 956.424.3942 •
Rio Grande City 956.487.5603 • San Antonio 210.271.2851

R: 92 **T:** 8th 84%
Elected Year: 2004

Rep. Lloyd A. Doggett II (DAWG-eht) D-TX-35 p 202.225.4865

Rm. RHOB 2307 **Web.** doggett.house.gov **f** 202.225.3073
Bio. 10/06/1946 • Austin, TX • State Supreme Court Justice;
Professor • Univ. of Texas, B.B.A., 1967; Univ. of Texas Law
School, J.D., 1970 • Methodist • M. Libby Belk Doggett, 2 ch ;
4 gr-ch **Cmte.** Joint Taxation • Ways & Means
CoS. Michael Mucchetti
Sched. Christina Nunez **PS.** Kate Stotesbery
Dist. Off. Austin 512.916.5921 • San Antonio 210.704.1080

R: 37 **T:** 13th 71%
Elected Year: 1994

Rep. Veronica Escobar (ess-ko-BAR) D-TX-16 p 202.225.4831

Rm. LHOB 1505 **Web.** escobar.house.gov
Bio. 09/15/1969 • El Paso, TX • Univ. of Texas, El Paso, B.A.,
1991; New York Univ., M.A., 1993 • Catholic • M. Michael
Pleters, 2 ch **Cmte.** Armed Services • Judiciary
CoS. Eduardo Lerma **LD.** Jacqueline Sanchez
Sched. Jessica Andino **PS.** Elizabeth Lopez-
Sandoval
Dist. Off. El Paso 915.760.0192

R: 366 **T:** 1st 69%
Elected Year: 2018

Rep. Elizabeth Pannill Fletcher (FLEH-chur) D-TX-07 p 202.225.2571

Rm. LHOB 1429 **Web.** fletcher.house.gov
Bio. 02/13/1975 • Houston, TX • Kenyon College (OH),
B.A., 1997 • Methodist • M. Scott Fletcher PE, 2 stepch
Cmte. Science, Space & Technology • Transportation &
Infrastructure
CoS. Sarah Kaplan **LD.** Ben Jackson
Feinmann
Sched. Olivia Cox **PS.** Alaina Berner
Dist. Off. Houston 281.645.9388

R: 368 **T:** 1st 53%
Elected Year: 2018

Rep. Bill H. Flores (FLOOR-ehz) R-TX-17 p 202.225.6105

Rm. RHOB 2228 **Web.** flores.house.gov **f** 202.225.0350
Bio. 02/25/1954 • Warren Air Force Base, Cheyenne, WY
• Texas A and M Univ., B.B.A., 1976; Houston Baptist Univ.
(TX), M.B.A., 1985 • Baptist • M. Gina Flores, 2 ch ; 2 gr-ch
Cmte. Budget • Energy & Commerce
CoS. Jon Oehmen **LD.** Eric Gustafson
Sched. Jessica Harrison **PS.** Andre Castro
Dist. Off. Austin 512.373.3378 • Bryan 979.703.4037 •
Waco 254.732.0748

R: 162 **T:** 5th 57%
Elected Year: 2010

TEXAS

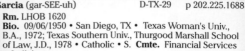

🕊 Rep. Sylvia R. Garcia (gar-SEE-uh)   D-TX-29   p 202.225.1688

Rm. LHOB 1620
Bio. 09/06/1950 • San Diego, TX • Texas Woman's Univ.,
B.A., 1972; Texas Southern Univ., Thurgood Marshall School
of Law, J.D., 1978 • Catholic • S. **Cmte.** Financial Services
• Judiciary
CoS. John Chapa   **LD.** Pat Bond
Gorczynski
Sched. Ariel Garayar
Dist. Off. Houston 832.869.7529

R: 371   T: 1st 75%
Elected Year: 2018

🏛 Rep. Louie B. Gohmert Jr. (GO-murt)   R-TX-01   p 202.225.3035

Rm. RHOB 2267 **Web.** gohmert.house.gov   **f** 202.226.1230
Bio. 08/18/1953 • Pittsburg, TX • Chief Justice for the 12th
Circuit Court of Appeals; Attorney • Texas Agricultural and
Mechanical Univ., B.A., 1975; Baylor Univ. School of Law
(TX), J.D., 1977 • Baptist • M. Kathy Gohmert, 3 ch **Cmte.**
Judiciary • Natural Resources
CoS. Connie Hair   **LD.** Caralee Conklin
Sched. Chelsea Cohen   **PS.** Kimberly Willingham
Dist. Off. Longview 903.236.8597 • Lufkin 936.632.3180 •
Marshall 903.938.8386 • Nacogdoches 936.715.9514 • Tyler
903.561.6349

R: 95   T: 8th 72%
Elected Year: 2004

🕊 Rep. Vicente Gonzalez (gon-SAH-les)   D-TX-15   p 202.225.2531

Rm. CHOB 113 **Web.** gonzalez.house.gov   **f** 202.225.5688
Bio. 09/04/1967 • Corpus Christi, TX • Embry-Riddle
Aeronautical Univ., B.A., 1992; Texas Wesleyan School of
Law (formerly Texas Wesleyan School of Law), J.D., 1996
• Catholic • M. Lorena Saenz **Cmte.** Financial Services •
Foreign Affairs
CoS. Jose Borjon   **LD.** Louise Colbath Bentsen
Sched. Paulina Carrillo   **PS.** Aaron Morales
Dist. Off. Benavides 888.217.0261 • Falfurrias 361.209.3027
• McAllen 888.217.0261 • San Diego 888.217.0261 • Seguin
830.358.0497

R: 312   T: 2nd 60%
Elected Year: 2016

🏛 Rep. Lance Gooden (GOOD-un)   R-TX-05   p 202.225.3484

Rm. CHOB 425
Bio. 12/01/1982 • Terrell, TX • Univ. of Texas, B.A., 2004
• Church of Christ • M. Alexa Calligas **Cmte.** Financial
Services
CoS. Aaron Harris   **LD.** Ryan Ethington
Sched. MacKenzie Morales   **PS.** Will Martin
Dist. Off. Mesquite 903.386.0289

R: 374   T: 1st 62%
Elected Year: 2018

🏛 Rep. Kay N. Granger (GRAIN-jur)   R-TX-12   p 202.225.5071

Rm. LHOB 1026 **Web.** kaygranger.house.gov **f** 202.225.5683
Bio. 01/18/1943 • Greenville, TX • Insurance Agent;
Business Owner; Mayor (Ft. Worth, TX) • Texas Wesleyan
Univ., B.S., 1965 • Methodist • D., 3 ch; 5 gr-ch **Cmte.**
Appropriations
CoS. Spencer Freebairn   **LD.** Suzi Plasencia
Sched. Brenan Tjelmeland   **PS.** Kate Kelly
Dist. Off. Fort Worth 817.338.0909

R: 49   T: 12th 64%
Elected Year: 1996

🕊 Rep. Al Green (green)   D-TX-09   p 202.225.7508

Rm. RHOB 2347 **Web.** algreen.house.gov   **f** 202.225.2947
Bio. 09/01/1947 • New Orleans, LA • Attorney • Tuskegee
Univ. (AL), Bach. Deg.; Texas Southern Univ., Thurgood
Marshall School of Law, J.D., 1973 • Baptist • NS. **Cmte.**
Financial Services • Homeland Security
CoS. Amena Ross
Sched. Martina Morgan   **PS.** Kwentoria Williams (CD
Dist. Off. Houston 713.383.9234

R: 96   T: 8th 89%
Elected Year: 2004

♜ Rep. Will Hurd (hurd)   R-TX-23   p 202.225.4511

Rm. CHOB 317 **Web.** hurd.house.gov   f 202.225.2237
Bio. 08/19/1977 • San Antonio, TX • Texas A&M Univ.,
College Station, B.S., 2000 • Christian - Non-Denominational
• S. **Cmte.** Appropriations • Permanent Select on
Intelligence
CoS. John Byers   **LD.** Austin Agrella
Sched. Nancy Williamson   **PS.** Callie Strock
Dist. Off. Del Rio 830.422.2040 • Eagle Pass 210.921.3130
• Fort Stockton 210.245.1961 • San Antonio 210.921.3130 •
Socorro 915.235.6421

R: 267 **T:** 3rd 49%
Elected Year: 2014

♞ Rep. Sheila Jackson Lee (JAK-suhn-lee)   D-TX-18   p 202.225.3816

Rm. RHOB 2079 **Web.** jacksonlee.house.gov f 202.225.3317
Bio. 01/12/1950 • Jamaica, NY • Judge; Attorney • Yale
Univ. (CT), B.A., 1972; Univ. of Virginia Law School, J.D.,
1975 • Seventh-Day Adventist • M. Elwyn C. Lee, 2 ch ; 2 gr-
ch **Cmte.** Budget • Homeland Security • Judiciary
CoS. Glenn Rushing   **LD.** Lillie Coney
Sched. Martha Hernandez   **PS.** Robin Chand
(CD)
Dist. Off. Houston 713.227.7740 • Houston 713.655.0050 •
Houston 713.691.4882 • Houston 713.861.4070

R: 39 **T:** 13th 75%
Elected Year: 1994

♞ Rep. Eddie Bernice Johnson (JAHN-suhn)   D-TX-30   p 202.225.8885

Rm. RHOB 2306 **Web.** ebjohnson.house.gov   f 202.226.1477
Bio. 12/03/1935 • Waco, TX • Nurse; State Legislator
• St. Mary's College at the Univ. of Notre Dame (IN),
M.P.A., 1955; Texas Christian Univ., B.S., 1967; Southern
Methodist Univ. (TX), M.P.A., 1976 • Baptist • D., 1 ch; 3 gr-
ch **Cmte.** Science, Space & Technology • Transportation &
Infrastructure
CoS. Murat Gokcigdem
                              PS. Sameer Assanie (CD)
Dist. Off. Dallas 214.922.8885

R: 28 **T:** 14th 91%
Elected Year: 1992

♜ Rep. Kenny E. Marchant (MAR-chuhnt)   R-TX-24   p 202.225.6605

Rm. RHOB 2304 **Web.** marchant.house.gov   f 202.225.0074
Bio. 02/23/1951 • Bonham, TX • Member Carrollton City
Council; Mayor, Carrollton • Southern Nazarene Univ. (OK),
B.A., 1974 • Nazarene • M. Donna Walker Marchant, 4 ch ; 4
gr-ch **Cmte.** Ethics • Ways & Means
CoS. Brian Thomas   **LD.** John Deoudes
Sched. Lindsay Hurley   **PS.** Luke Bunting
Dist. Off. Irving 972.556.0162

R: 99 **T:** 8th 51%
Elected Year: 2004

♜ Rep. Michael T. McCaul (mih-KALL)   R-TX-10   p 202.225.2401

Rm. RHOB 2001 **Web.** mccaul.house.gov   f 202.225.5955
Bio. 01/14/1962 • Dallas, TX • Attorney; Federal prosecutor
• Trinity Univ. (TX), B.A., 1984 • Catholic • M. Linda
McCaul, 5 ch (triplets) **Cmte.** Foreign Affairs • Homeland
Security
CoS. Johnna L. Carlson   **LD.** Thomas Hester
Sched. Kelly Cotner   **PS.** Amanda Smith
Dist. Off. Austin 512.473.2357 • Brenham 979.830.8497 •
Katy 281.398.1247 • Tornball 281.255.8372

R: 100 **T:** 8th 51%
Elected Year: 2004

♜ Rep. Pete G. Olson (OLL-suhn)   R-TX-22   p 202.225.5951

Rm. RHOB 2133 **Web.** olson.house.gov   f 202.225.5241
Bio. 12/09/1962 • Fort Lewis, WA • Congressional Staffer
• Navy; Navy Reserves • Rice Univ. (TX), B.A., 1985; Univ.
of Texas Law School, J.D., 1988 • Methodist • M. Nancy
Olson, 2 ch **Cmte.** Energy & Commerce • Science, Space
& Technology
CoS. Melissa Kelly   **LD.** Richard England
Sched. Keeley Tenney   **PS.** Cate Cullen
Dist. Off. Pearland 281.485.4855 • Sugar Land
281.494.2690

R: 137 **T:** 6th 51%
Elected Year: 2008

TEXAS

🏛 Rep. John L. Ratcliffe (RAT-klif)   R-TX-04   p 202.225.6673

Rm. CHOB 223 **Web.** ratcliffe.house.gov   **f** 202.225.3332
Bio. 10/20/1965 • Chicago, IL • Univ. of Notre Dame (IN), B.A., 1987; Southern Methodist Univ. Law School (TX), J.D., 1989 • Roman Catholic • M. Michele Ratcliffe, 2 ch
CoS. Dustin Carmack   **LD.** Davis Pace
Sched. Crystal Johnson   **PS.** Rachel Stephens
Dist. Off. Rockwall 972.771.0100 • Sherman 903.813.5270 • Texarkana 903.823.3173

R: 277 **T:** 3rd 76%
Elected Year: 2014

🏛 Rep. Chip Roy (roy)   R-TX-21   p 202.225.4236

Rm. LHOB 1319 **Web.** roy.house.gov   **f** 202.225.8628
Bio. 08/07/1972 • Bethesda, MD • Univ. of Virginia, B.S., 1994; Univ. of Virginia, M.S., 1995; Univ. of Texas, J.D., 2003 • Baptist • M. Carrah Roy, 2 ch **Cmte.** Budget • Oversight & Reform • Veterans' Affairs
CoS. Wade Miller   **LD.** Maggie Harrell
Sched. Courtney Butler   **PS.** Robert Donachie
Dist. Off. San Antonio 210.821.5024

R: 410 **T:** 1st 50%
Elected Year: 2018

🏛 Rep. Van Taylor (TAY-lur)   R-TX-03   p 202.225.4201

Rm. LHOB 1404 **Web.** vantaylor.house.gov
Bio. 08/01/1972 • Dallas, TX • Harvard College (MA), A.B., 1995; St. Pauls High School, A.B., 1995; Harvard Business School (MA), M.B.A., 2001 • Episcopalian • M. Anne Taylor, 3 ch **Cmte.** Education & Labor • Homeland Security
CoS. Lonnie Dietz   **LD.** Jett E. Thompson
Sched. Hunter Anne Stoner   **PS.** Anna Vetter
Dist. Off. Plano 972.202.4150

R: 422 **T:** 1st 54%
Elected Year: 2018

🏛 Rep. Mac Thornberry (THORN-bair-ee)   R-TX-13   p 202.225.3706

Rm. RHOB 2208 **Web.** thornberry.house.gov **f** 202.225.3486
Bio. 07/15/1958 • Clarendon, TX • U.S. Deputy Assistant Secretary of State for Legislative Affairs; Attorney • Texas Tech Univ., B.A., 1980; Univ. of Texas Law School, J.D., 1983 • Presbyterian • M. Sally Adams Thornberry, 2 ch **Cmte.** Armed Services
CoS. Josh Martin   **LD.** Michael Seeds
Sched. Jessica Sunday   **PS.** Jordan Hunter
Dist. Off. Amarillo 806.371.8844 • Wichita Falls 940.692.1700

R: 42 **T:** 13th 82%
Elected Year: 1994

🏛 Rep. Marc A. Veasey (VEE-zee)   D-TX-33   p 202.225.9897

Rm. RHOB 2348 **Web.** veasey.house.gov   **f** 202.225.9702
Bio. 01/03/1971 • Tarrant County, TX • Texas Wesleyan Univ., B.S., 1995 • Christian Church • M. Tonya Veasey, 1 ch
Cmte. Energy & Commerce • Small Business
CoS. Askia M. Suruma   **LD.** Nicole Varner
Sched. Jane Phipps   **PS.** Anna Pacilio
Dist. Off. Dallas 214.741.1387 • Fort Worth 817.920.9086

R: 234 **T:** 4th 76%
Elected Year: 2012

🏛 Rep. Filemon B. Vela (VEH-lah)   D-TX-34   p 202.225.990?

Rm. CHOB 307 **Web.** vela.house.gov   **f** 202.225.9770
Bio. 02/13/1963 • Harlingen, TX • Georgetown Univ. (DC), B.A., 1985; Univ. of Texas, Ausitn, J.D., 1987 • Roman Catholic • M. Rose Vela **Cmte.** Agriculture • Armed Services
CoS. Perry Brody   **LD.** Julie Merberg
Sched. Liza Lynch   **PS.** Mickeala Carter
Dist. Off. Alice 361.230.9776 • Brownsville 956.544.8352 • San Benito 956.276.4497 • Weslaco 956.520.8273

R: 235 **T:** 4th 60%
Elected Year: 2012

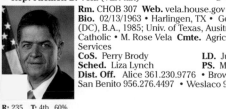

Rep. Randy Weber (WEH-bur)   R-TX-14   p 202.225.2831

Rm. CHOB 107   **Web.** weber.house.gov   **f** 202.225.0271
Bio. 07/02/1953 • Pearland, TX • Univ. of Houston, Clear Lake (TX), B.S., 1977 • Baptist • M. Brenda Weber, 3 ch ; 7 gr-ch   **Cmte.** Science, Space & Technology • Transportation & Infrastructure
CoS. Chara McMichael   **LD.** William Christian
Sched. Kelly Vidor   **PS.** Emma Polefko
Dist. Off. Beaumont 409.835.0108 • Lake Jackson 979.285.0231 • League City 281.316.0231

R: 238   **T:** 4th 59%
Elected Year: 2012

Rep. Roger Williams (WILL-yuhmz)   R-TX-25   p 202.225.9896

Rm. LHOB 1708   **Web.** williams.house.gov   **f** 202.225.9692
Bio. 09/13/1949 • Evanston, IL • Texas Christian Univ., B.S., 1972 • Disciples of Christ • M. Patty Williams, 2 ch   **Cmte.** Financial Services
CoS. John Etue   **LD.** Patrick Arlantico
Sched. Cat Curry   **PS.** Hanna Allred
Dist. Off. Austin 512.473.8910 • Cleburne 817.774.2575

R: 240   **T:** 4th 54%
Elected Year: 2012

Rep. Ronald J. Wright ("right")   R-TX-06   p 202.225.2002

Rm. CHOB 428   **Web.** wright.house.gov
Bio. 04/08/1953 • Jacksonville, TX • Roman Catholic • M. Susan Mazanti, 3 ch ; 9 gr-ch   **Cmte.** Education & Labor • Foreign Affairs
CoS. Ryan Thompson   **LD.** Blair Rotert
Sched. Caroline Waller   **PS.** Micah Cavanaugh
Dist. Off. Arlington • Ennis

R: 433   **T:** 1st 53%
Elected Year: 2018

UTAH

Governor Gary R. Herbert (HUR-burt)   p 801.538.1000

Utah State Capitol Complex
350 North State St., Suite 200
Salt Lake City, UT 84114-2220
Website utah.gov
Fax 801.538.1133
Term Ends 2021
Lt. Governor
Spencer J. Cox, R

C: Salt Lake City
P: 3,161,105 (31)
A: 82,169.46 mi^2 (12th)

U.S. Senators
Mike Lee, R
Mitt Romney, R
U.S. Representatives
01 / Rob W. Bishop, R
02 / Chris D. Stewart, R
03 / John R. Curtis, R
04 / Ben McAdams, D

Sen. Mike Lee (lee)   R-UT-Sr.   p 202.224.5444

Rm. RSOB 361-A   **Web.** lee.senate.gov   **f** 202.228.1168
Bio. 06/04/1971 • Mesa, AZ • Brigham Young Univ. (UT), B.A., 1994; Brigham Young Univ. (UT), J.D., 1997 • Mormon • M. Sharon Lee, 3 ch   **Cmte.** Commerce, Science & Transportation • Energy & Natural Resources • Joint Economic • Judiciary
CoS. Allyson Bell   **LD.** Christy Woodruff
Sched. Kate Cannon   **PS.** Conn Carroll
Dist. Off. Ogden 801.392.9633 • Salt Lake City 801.524.5933 • St. George 435.628.5514

R: 55   **T:** 2nd 68%
Elected Year: 2010
Next Election: 2022

UTAH

℞ Sen. Mitt Romney (RAHM-nee)   R-UT-Jr.   p 202.224.5251

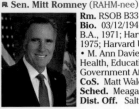

Rm. RSOB B33 **Web.** romney.senate.gov
Bio. 03/12/1947 • Detroit, MI • Brigham Young Univ. (UT), B.A., 1971; Harvard Univ. School of Business (MA), M.B.A., 1975; Harvard Univ. Law School (MA), J.D., 1975 • Mormon • M. Ann Davies, 5 ch; 16 gr-ch **Cmte.** Foreign Relations • Health, Education, Labor & Pensions • Homeland Security & Government Affairs • Small Business & Entrepreneurship
CoS. Matt Waldrip
Sched. Meagan Shepherd   **PS.** Liz Johnson
Dist. Off. Salt Lake City 801.524.4380

R: 97   **T:** 0th   63%
Elected Year: 2018
Next Election: 2024

℞ Rep. Rob W. Bishop (BIH-shuhp)   R-UT-01   p 202.225.0453

Rm. CHOB 123 **Web.** robbishop.house.gov   **f** 202.225.5857
Bio. 07/13/1951 • Kaysville, UT • State Legislator • Univ. of Utah, B.A., 1974 • Mormon • M. Jeralynn Hansen Bishop, 5 ch; 7 gr-ch **Cmte.** Armed Services • Natural Resources
CoS. Devin Wiser   **LD.** Adam Stewart
Sched. Barbara Andrade   **PS.** Lee Lonsberry
Dist. Off. Ogden 801.625.0107 • Vernal 435.781.5302

R: 74   **T:** 9th   62%
Elected Year: 2002

℞ Rep. John R. Curtis (KUR-tiss)   R-UT-03   p 202.225.7751

Rm. CHOB 125 **Web.** curtis.house.gov   **f** 202.225.5629
Bio. 05/10/1960 • Salt Lake City, UT • Skyline High School, B.S., 1978; Brigham Young Univ. (UT), B.S., 1985 • Mormon • M. Sue Snarr, 6 ch ; 5 gr-ch **Cmte.** Foreign Affairs • Natural Resources
CoS. Corey Norman   **LD.** Jake Bornstein
Sched. Stephanie Heinrich   **PS.** Ally Riding
Dist. Off. Provo 801.922.5400

R: 339   **T:** 2nd   68%
Elected Year: 2017

℞ Rep. Ben McAdams (mik-AD-uhms)   D-UT-04   p 202.225.3011

Rm. CHOB 130 **Web.** mcadams.house.gov
Bio. 12/05/1974 • Salt Lake City, UT • Univ. of Utah, B.A., 2000; Columbia Univ. Law School (NY), J.D., 2003 • Mormon • M. Julie Mcadams, 4 ch **Cmte.** Financial Services • Science, Space & Technology
CoS. Nichole Dunn   **LD.** Eric May
Sched. Stephanie Withers   **PS.** Alyson Heyrend
Dist. Off. West Jordan 801.999.9801

R: 392   **T:** 1st   50%
Elected Year: 2018

℞ Rep. Chris D. Stewart (STOO-urt)   R-UT-02   p 202.225.9730

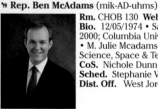

Rm. RHOB 2242 **Web.** stewart.house.gov   **f** 202.225.5629
Bio. 07/15/1960 • Logan, UT • Utah State Univ., B.S., 1984 • Mormon • M. Evie Stewart, 6 ch **Cmte.** Appropriations • Budget • Permanent Select on Intelligence
CoS. Christopher Harmer   **LD.** Clay White
Sched. Mark Coffield   **PS.** Madison Schupe
Dist. Off. Salt Lake City 801.364.5550 • St. George 435.627.1500

R: 230   **T:** 4th   56%
Elected Year: 2012

STATE/LEGISLATOR PROFILES

VERMONT

VERMONT

🏛 **Governor Phil Scott** (skaht)　　　　p 802.828.3333

109 State Street Pavilion
Montpelier, VT 05609-0101
Website vermont.gov
Fax 802.828.3339
Term Ends 2021

C: Montpelier
P: 626,299 (51)
A: 9,216.64 mi^2 (43rd)

U.S. Senators
Patrick J. Leahy, **D**
Bernie Sanders, **I**
U.S. Representatives
01 / Peter F. Welch, **D**

🏛 **Sen. Patrick J. Leahy** (LAY-hee)　　　D-VT-Sr.　p 202.224.4242

Rm. RSOB 437 **Web.** leahy.senate.gov　　f 202.224.3479
Bio. 03/31/1940 • Montpelier, VT • Attorney; Prosecutor
• St. Michael's College (VT), B.A., 1961; Georgetown
Univ. Law Center (DC), J.D., 1964 • Roman Catholic • M.
Marcelle Pomerleau Leahy, 3 ch ; 5 gr-ch **Cmte.** Agriculture,
Nutrition & Forestry • Appropriations • Judiciary • Rules &
Administration
CoS. J.P. Dowd　　　　　**LD.** Erica Chabot
Sched. Kevin McDonald　　**PS.** David Carle
Dist. Off. Burlington 802.863.2525 • Montpelier
802.229.0569

R: 1　**T:** 8th 60%
Elected Year: 1974
Next Election: 2022

🏛 **Sen. Bernie Sanders** (SAN-durz)　　　I-VT-Jr.　p 202.224.5141

Caucuses with Democratic Party　　　　f 202.228.0776
Rm. DSOB 332 **Web.** sanders.senate.gov
Bio. 09/08/1941 • Brooklyn, NY • U.S. Representative
• Univ. of Chicago (IL), B.A., 1964 • Jewish • M. Jane
O'Meara Driscoll, 1 ch ; 3 stepch **Cmte.** Budget • Energy &
Natural Resources • Environment & Public Works • Health,
Education, Labor & Pensions • Veterans' Affairs
CoS. Caryn Compton
Sched. Jacob Gillison　　　**PS.** Josh Miller-Lewis
Dist. Off. Burlington 802.862.0697 • St. Johnsbury
800.339.9834

R: 28　**T:** 2nd 64%
Elected Year: 2006
Next Election: 2024

🏛 **Rep. Peter F. Welch** (welch)　　　　D-VT-01　p 202.225.4115

Rm. RHOB 2187 **Web.** welch.house.gov　　f 202.225.6790
Bio. 05/02/1947 • Springfield, MA • Attorney • College
of The Holy Cross (MA), B.A., 1969; Univ. of California,
Berkeley, J.D., 1973 • Roman Catholic • M. Margaret
Cheney, 5 ch ; 3 stepch **Cmte.** Energy & Commerce •
Oversight & Reform • Permanent Select on Intelligence
CoS. Robert Rogan　　　**LD.** Patrick Satalin
Sched. Patrick Etka　　　**PS.** Kate Hamilton
Dist. Off. Burlington 802.652.2450

: 122　**T:** 7th 68%
Elected Year: 2006

VIRGINIA

VIRGINIA

🏛 **Governor Ralph S. Northam** (north-UM)　　　p 804.786.2211

P.O. Box 1475
Richmond, VA 23218
Website virginia.gov
Fax 804.371.6351
Term Ends 2021
Lt. Governor
Justin Fairfax, **D**

C: Richmond
P: 8,517,685 (12)
A: 39,490.13 mi^2 (36th)

VIRGINIA

U.S. Senators
Mark R. Warner, **D**
Tim M. Kaine, **D**
U.S. Representatives
01 / Rob J. Wittman, **R**
02 / Elaine G. Luria, **D**
03 / Bobby C. Scott, **D**
04 / A. Donald McEachin, **D**
05 / Denver L. Riggleman, **R**
06 / Benjamin L. Cline, **R**
07 / Abigail D. Spanberger, **D**
08 / Don S. Beyer, **D**
09 / Morgan M. Griffith, **R**
10 / Jennifer T. Wexton, **D**   11 / Gerry E. Connolly, **D**

⋈ Sen. Tim M. Kaine (kain)   D-VA-Jr.   p 202.224.4024

Rm. RSOB 231 **Web.** kaine.senate.gov   **f** 202.228.6363
Bio. 02/26/1958 • St. Paul, MN • Mayor, City of Richmond;
Mbr., Richmond City Council; Lt. Governor & President of
the Senate, VA; Governor, Commonwealth of Virginia •
Univ. of Missouri, A.B., 1979; Harvard Law School (MA), J.D.,
1983 • Roman Catholic • M. Anne Bright Holton, 3 ch **Cmte.**
Armed Services • Budget • Foreign Relations • Health,
Education, Labor & Pensions
CoS. Mike Henry   **LD.** Mary Naylor
Sched. Kate McCarroll   **PS.** Sarah Peck
Dist. Off. Abingdon 276.525.4790 • Danville 434.792.0976
• Manassas 703.361.3192 • Richmond 804.771.2221 •
Roanoke 540.682.5693 • Virginia Beach 757.518.1674

R: 63 **T:** 2nd 57%
Elected Year: 2012
Next Election: 2024

⋈ Sen. Mark R. Warner (WAR-nur)   D-VA-Sr.   p 202.224.2023

Rm. HSOB 703 **Web.** warner.senate.gov   **f** 202.224.6920
Bio. 12/15/1954 • Indianapolis, IN • Governor of Virginia
• George Washington Univ. (DC), B.A., 1977; Harvard Univ.
Law School (MA), J.D., 1980 • Presbyterian • M. Lisa Collis,
3 ch **Cmte.** Banking, Housing & Urban Affairs • Budget •
Finance • Intelligence • Rules & Administration
CoS. Mike Harney   **LD.** Elizabeth Falcone
Sched. Malcolm Fouhy   **PS.** Rachel Cohen
Dist. Off. Abingdon 276.628.8158 • Norfolk 757.441.3079 •
Richmond 804.775.2314 • Roanoke 540.857.2676 • Vienna
703.442.0670

R: 38 **T:** 2nd 49%
Elected Year: 2008
Next Election: 2020

⋈ Rep. Don S. Beyer Jr. (BY-ur)   D-VA-08   p 202.225.4376

Rm. LHOB 1119 **Web.** beyer.house.gov   **f** 202.225.0017
Bio. 06/20/1950 • Trieste, Italy • Williams College, B.A.,
1972 • Episcopalian • M. Megan Carroll, 4 ch ; 2 gr-ch
Cmte. Joint Economic • Science, Space & Technology •
Ways & Means
CoS. Ann O'Hanlon   **LD.** Zachary Cafritz
Sched. Sophia Rubio   **PS.** Aaron Fritschner
Dist. Off. Arlington 703.658.5403

R: 254 **T:** 3rd 76%
Elected Year: 2014

⋈ Rep. Benjamin L. Cline (kline)   R-VA-06   p 202.225.543

Rm. LHOB 1009
Bio. 02/29/1972 • Stillwater, OK • Lexington High School,
B.A.; Bates College (ME), B.A., 1994; Univ. of Richmond
(VA), J.D., 2007 • Roman Catholic • M. Elizabeth Rocovich,
ch **Cmte.** Education & Labor • Judiciary
CoS. Matt M. Miller   **LD.** Nicole Manley
Sched. Beth Kaczmarek   **PS.** Ryan Saylor
Dist. Off. Lexington 540.463.3828

R: 357 **T:** 1st 60%
Elected Year: 2018

VIRGINIA

🏛 Rep. Gerry E. Connolly (KAH-nuh-lee) D-VA-11 p 202.225.1492

Rm. RHOB 2238 Web. connolly.house.gov f 202.225.3071
Bio. 03/30/1950 • Boston, MA • Transportation
Commissioner; US Senate Committee Staffer • Maryknoll
College (IL), B.A., 1971; Harvard Univ., M.P.A., 1979 • Roman
Catholic • M. Cathy Connolly, 1 ch Cmte. Foreign Affairs •
Oversight & Reform
CoS. James Walkinshaw LD. Collin Davenport
Sched. Lauren Covington PS. Jamie Smith
Dist. Off. Annandale 703.256.3071 • Woodbridge
571.408.4407

R: 130 T: 6th 71%
Elected Year: 2008

🏛 Rep. Morgan M. Griffith (GRIH-fith) R-VA-09 p 202.225.3861

Rm. RHOB 2202 Web. f 202.225.0076
morgangriffith.house.gov
Bio. 03/15/1958 • Philadelphia, PA • Emory and Henry
College (VA), B.A., 1980; Washington and Lee Univ. School
of Law (VA), J.D., 1983 • Episcopalian • M. Hilary Davis, 3
ch Cmte. Energy & Commerce • Select Committee on the
Climate Crisis
CoS. Kelly Lungren LD. Kristin Seum
McCollum
Sched. Emily Zavrel PS. Kevin Baird
Dist. Off. Abingdon 276.525.1405 • Big Stone Gap
276.525.1405 • Christiansburg 540.381.5671

R: 165 T: 5th 65%
Elected Year: 2010

🏛 Rep. Elaine G. Luria (LUR-ree-uh) D-VA-02 p 202.225.4215

Rm. CHOB 534 Web. luria.house.gov
Bio. 08/15/1975 • Birmingham, AL • U.S. Naval Academy
(MD), B.S., 1997; Old Dominion Univ. (VA), M.E.M., 2004 •
Jewish • M. Bob Blondin, 1 ch ; 2 stepch Cmte. Armed
Services • Veterans' Affairs
CoS. Kathryn Sorenson LD. Tyrone Bratton
Sched. Katharine Fegley PS. Chris Carroll
Dist. Off. Virginia Beach 757.364.7650

R: 390 T: 1st 51%
Elected Year: 2018

🏛 Rep. A. Donald McEachin (muh-KEE-chuhn) D-VA-04 p 202.225.6365

Rm. CHOB 314 Web. mceachin.house.gov f 202.226.1170
Bio. 10/10/1961 • Nuremberg • American Univ. (DC), B.S.,
1982; Univ. of Virginia Law School, J.D., 1986; Virginia Union
Univ. Samuel DeWitt Proctor School of Theology, M.Div.,
2008 • Baptist • M. Colette Wallace McEachin, 3 ch Cmte.
Commission Congressional Mailing Standards • Energy &
Commerce • Natural Resources • Select Committee on the
Climate Crisis
CoS. Keenan Austin Reed LD. Corey Solow
Sched. Jediah Jones
Dist. Off. Richmond 804.486.1840 • Suffolk 757.942.6050

R: 324 T: 2nd 63%
Elected Year: 2016

🏛 Rep. Denver L. Riggleman III (RIG-gull-muhn) R-VA-05 p 202.225.4711

Rm. LHOB 1022 Web. riggleman.house.gov
Bio. 03/17/1970 • Manassas, VA • Jackson High School
(MI), A.A.S., 1988; Burlington County College, A.A., 1996;
Community College of the Air Force (AL), A.A.S., 1996; Univ.
of Virginia, Bach. Deg., 1998; Villanova Univ., Mast. Deg.,
2007 • Christian Church • M. Christine Riggleman, 3 ch
Cmte. Financial Services
CoS. Dave Natonski LD. Borden Hoskins
Sched. Haley Brady PS. Joe Chelak
Dist. Off. Charlottesville 434.973.9631 • Danville
434.791.2596

R: 406 T: 1st 53%
Elected Year: 2018

🏛 Rep. Bobby C. Scott (skaht) D-VA-03 p 202.225.8351

Rm. LHOB 1201 Web. bobbyscott.house.gov f 202.225.8354
Bio. 04/30/1947 • Washington , DC • State Legislator • Army
Reserve 1970-74; Massachusetts National Guard 1974-76 •
Harvard Univ., B.A., 1969; Boston College Law School (MA),
J.D., 1973 • Episcopalian • D. Cmte. Budget • Education &
Labor
CoS. David Dailey
Sched. Randi Petty PS. Austin Barbera
Dist. Off. Newport News 757.380.1000

R: 33 T: 14th 91%
Elected Year: 1992

VIRGINIA

🔊 Rep. Abigail D. Spanberger (SPAN-bur-gur) D-VA-07 p 202.225.2815

Rm. LHOB 1239 **Web.** spanberger.house.gov
Bio. 08/07/1979 • Red Bank, NJ • Univ. of Virginia, B.A., 2001 • Christian Church • M. Adam Spanberger, 3 ch **Cmte.** Agriculture • Foreign Affairs
CoS. Roscoe Jones **LD.** Maryam Janani
Sched. Emma Carl **PS.** Connor Joseph
Dist. Off. Glen Allen 202.225.2815 • Spotsylvania

R: 415 **T:** 1st 50%
Elected Year: 2018

🔊 Rep. Jennifer T. Wexton (WEHK-stuhn) D-VA-10 p 202.225.5136

Rm. LHOB 1217 **Web.** wexton.house.gov **f** 202.225.0437
Bio. 05/27/1968 • Washington, DC • Univ. of Maryland, Baltimore (UMB), B.A., 1991; College of William and Mary - Marshall-Wythe Law School (VA), J.D., 1995 • Unspecified/ Other • M. Andrew Wexton, 2 ch **Cmte.** Financial Services • Science, Space & Technology
CoS. Abby M. Carter **LD.** Mike Lucier
Sched. Meaghan Johnson **PS.** Amir Avin
Dist. Off. Sterling 703.687.7122

R: 432 **T:** 1st 56%
Elected Year: 2018

▣ Rep. Rob J. Wittman (WIT-muhn) R-VA-01 p 202.225.4261

Rm. RHOB 2055 **Web.** wittman.house.gov **f** 202.225.4382
Bio. 02/03/1959 • Washington, DC • Mayor (Montrose Town, VA); State Legislator • Virginia Polytechnic Institute, B.S., 1981; Univ. of North Carolina in Chapel Hill, M.PH, 1990; Virginia Commonwealth Univ., Ph.D., 2002 • Episcopalian • M. Kathryn Jane Sisson Wittman, 2 ch ; 4 gr-ch **Cmte.** Armed Services • Natural Resources
CoS. Carolyn King **LD.** Brent Robinson
Sched. Jordan Wilson **PS.** Kathleen Gayle
Dist. Off. Mechanicsville 804.730.6595 • Stafford 540.659.2734 • Tappahannock 804.443.0668

R: 125 **T:** 7th 55%
Elected Year: 2007

WASHINGTON

WASHINGTON

🔊 Governor Jay Inslee (INZ-lee) p 360.902.4111

PO Box 40002
Olympia, WA 98404-0002
Website wa.gov
Fax 360.753.4110
Term Ends 2021
Lt. Governor
Cyrus Habib, **D**

C: Olympia
P: 7,535,591 (13)
A: 66,455.49 mi^2 (20th)

U.S. Senators
Patty Murray, **D**
Maria Cantwell, **D**
U.S. Representatives
01 / Suzan K. DelBene, **D**
02 / Rick R. Larsen, **D**
03 / Jaime L. Herrera Beutler, R
04 / Dan M. Newhouse, R
05 / Cathy A. McMorris Rodgers, R
06 / Derek Kilmer, **D**
07 / Pramila Jayapal, **D**
08 / Kim Schrier, **D**
09 / Adam Smith, **D**
10 / Denny Heck, **D**

WASHINGTON

Sen. Maria Cantwell (KANT-wel) D-WA-Jr. p 202.224.3441

Rm. HSOB 511 **Web.** cantwell.senate.gov **f** 202.228.0514
Bio. 10/13/1958 • Indianapolis, IN • Representative •
Miami Univ. of Ohio, B.A., 1980 • Roman Catholic • S.
Cmte. Commerce, Science & Transportation • Energy
& Natural Resources • Finance • Indian Affairs • Small
Business & Entrepreneurship
CoS. Travis Lumpkin
Sched. Sheila M. Dwyer **PS.** Reid Walker
Dist. Off. Everett 425.303.0114 • Richland 509.946.8106
• Seattle 206.220.6400 • Spokane 509.353.2507 • Tacoma
253.572.2281 • Vancouver 360.696.7838

R: 18 **T:** 3rd 58%
Elected Year: 2000
Next Election: 2024

Sen. Patty Murray (MUR-ree) D-WA-Sr. p 202.224.2621

Rm. RSOB 154 **Web.** murray.senate.gov **f** 202.224.0238
Bio. 10/11/1950 • Bothell, WA • State Senator; Teacher •
Washington State Univ., B.A., 1972 • Roman Catholic • M.
Robert Randall Murray, 2 ch **Cmte.** Appropriations • Budget
• Health, Education, Labor & Pensions • Veterans' Affairs
CoS. Mike Spahn
Sched. Meghan Mahoney **PS.** Eli Zupnick
Dist. Off. Everett 425.259.6515 • Seattle 206.553.5545 •
Spokane 509.624.9515 • Tacoma 253.572.3636 • Vancouver
360.696.7797 • Yakima 509.453.7462

R: 6 **T:** 5th 59%
Elected Year: 1992
Next Election: 2022

Rep. Suzan K. DelBene (del-BEH-nay) D-WA-01 p 202.225.6311

Rm. RHOB 2330 **Web.** delbene.house.gov **f** 202.226.1606
Bio. 02/17/1962 • Selma, AL • Reed College (OR), B.A.,
1983; Univ. of Washington, M.B.A., 1990 • Episcopalian •
M. Kurt Delbene, 2 ch **Cmte.** Select Committee on the
Modernization of Congress • Ways & Means
CoS. Aaron Schmidt **LD.** Kyle Hill
Sched. Mary Kate McTague **PS.** Louis Wasson
Dist. Off. Bothell 425.485.0085 • Mount Vernon
360.416.7879

R: 190 **T:** 5th 59%
Elected Year: 2012

Rep. Denny Heck (heck) D-WA-10 p 202.225.9740

Rm. RHOB 2452 **Web.** dennyheck.house.gov
Bio. 07/29/1952 • Vancouver, WA • Evergreen State College
(WA), B.A., 1973 • Lutheran • M. Paula Heck, 2 ch ; 1 gr-ch
Cmte. Financial Services • Joint Economic • Permanent
Select on Intelligence
CoS. Jami Burgess **LD.** Brendan Woodbury
Sched. Lauren Meininger
Dist. Off. Lacey 360.459.8514 • Lakewood 253.533.8332

R: 209 **T:** 4th 62%
Elected Year: 2012

Rep. Jaime L. Herrera Beutler (heh-RAIR-uh R-WA-03 p 202.225.3536
BUT-lur)

Rm. RHOB 2352 **Web.** **f** 202.225.3478
herrerabeutler.house.gov
Bio. 11/03/1978 • Glendale, CA • Bellevue Community
College (WA), A.A., 2003; Univ. of Washington, B.A., 2004
• Christian Church • M. Daniel Beutler, 2 ch **Cmte.**
Appropriations
CoS. Jordan Evich
Sched. Rachel **PS.** Angeline Riesterer
Nepomuceno
Dist. Off. Chehalis 360.695.6292 • Vancouver 360.695.6292

R: 168 **T:** 5th 53%
Elected Year: 2010

WASHINGTON

⤷ Rep. Pramila Jayapal (JIE-ah-pall)   D-WA-07   p 202.225.3106

Rm. LHOB 1510   **f** 202.225.6197
Bio. 09/21/1965 • Chennai, India • Georgetown Univ. (DC), A.B., 1986; Northwestern Univ., M.B.A., 1990 • Hinduism • M. Steve Williamson, 1 ch ; 1 stepch   **Cmte.** Budget • Education & Labor • Judiciary
CoS. Gautam Raghavan   **LD.** Lindsay Owens
Sched. Emily Cummins   **PS.** Vedant Patel
Dist. Off. Seattle 206.674.0040

R: 316   **T:** 2nd   84%
Elected Year: 2016

⤷ Rep. Derek Kilmer (KILL-mur)   D-WA-06   p 202.225.5916

Rm. LHOB 1410   **Web.** kilmer.house.gov   **f** 202.226.3575
Bio. 01/01/1974 • Port Angeles, WA • Princeton Univ. (NJ), A.B., 1996; Univ. of Oxford (UK), Ph.D., 2003 • Methodist • M. Jennifer Kilmer, 2 ch   **Cmte.** Appropriations • Select Committee on the Modernization of Congress
CoS. Rachel Kelly   **LD.** Katie Allen
Sched. Keanu Rivera   **PS.** Natasha Dembrowski
Dist. Off. Bremerton 360.373.9725 • Port Angeles 360.797.3623 • Tacoma 253.272.3515

R: 217   **T:** 4th   64%
Elected Year: 2012

⤷ Rep. Rick R. Larsen (LAR-suhn)   D-WA-02   p 202.225.2605

Rm. RHOB 2113   **Web.** larsen.house.gov   **f** 202.225.4420
Bio. 06/15/1965 • Arlington, WA • Economic Development official; Member, Snohomish County Council • Pacific Lutheran Univ. (WA), B.A., 1987; Univ. of Minnesota, M.P.A., 1990 • Methodist • M. Tiia Karlen Larsen, 2 ch   **Cmte.** Armed Services • Transportation & Infrastructure
CoS. Kimberly Johnston   **LD.** Terra Sabag
Sched. Lauren Gros   **PS.** Amanda Munger
Dist. Off. Bellingham 360.733.4500 • Everett 425.252.3188

R: 69   **T:** 10th   71%
Elected Year: 2000

⤷ Rep. Cathy A. McMorris Rodgers (mik-MOR-iss   R-WA-05   p 202.225.2006
RAH-jurz)

Rm. LHOB 1035   **Web.** mcmorris.house.gov   **f** 202.225.3392
Bio. 05/22/1969 • Salem, OR • State Legislator • Pensacola Christian College (FL), B.A., 1990; Univ. of Washington, M.B.A., 2002 • Evangelical • M. Brian Rodgers, 3 ch   **Cmte.** Energy & Commerce
CoS. Nate Hodson   **LD.** Michael Taggart
Sched. Emily King   **PS.** Jared Powell
Dist. Off. Colville 509.684.3481 • Spokane 509.353.2374 • Walla Walla 509.529.9358

R: 103   **T:** 8th   55%
Elected Year: 2004

⤷ Rep. Dan M. Newhouse (NOO-hous)   R-WA-04   p 202.225.5816

Rm. LHOB 1414   **Web.** newhouse.house.gov   **f** 202.225.3251
Bio. 07/10/1955 • Sunnyside, WA • Washington State Univ. B.S., 1977 • Presbyterian • W. Carol Newhouse, 2 ch   **Cmte.** Appropriations • Select Committee on the Modernization of Congress
CoS. Carrie Meadows   **LD.** Sean V. O'Brien
                               PS. William Boyington
Dist. Off. Richland 509.713.7374 • Twisp 509.433.7760 • Yakima 509.452.3243

R: 275   **T:** 3rd   63%
Elected Year: 2014

⤷ Rep. Kim Schrier (SHRY-uhr)   D-WA-08   p 202.225.7761

Rm. LHOB 1123   **Web.** schrier.house.gov
Bio. 08/23/1968 • Los Angeles, CA • Univ. of California, Berkeley, B.A., 1991; Univ. of California, M.D., 1997 • Jewish • M. David Gowing, 1 ch   **Cmte.** Agriculture • Education & Labor
CoS. Erin O'Quinn   **LD.** Alex Payne
Sched. Shanley Miller   **PS.** Elizabeth Carlson
Dist. Off. Issaquah 425.657.1001

R: 411   **T:** 1st   52%
Elected Year: 2018

⚲ Rep. Adam Smith (smith) D-WA-09 p 202.225.8901

Rm. RHOB 2264 **Web.** adamsmith.house.gov
Bio. 06/15/1965 • Washington, DC • Attorney • Fordham
Univ. (NY), B.A., 1987; Univ. of Washington, J.D., 1990 •
Christian Church • M. Sara Bickle-Eldridge Smith, 2 ch
Cmte. Armed Services
CoS. Shana Chandler   **LD.** Jonathan Pawlow
Sched. Salem Mariam   **PS.** Rebecca Bryant
Dist. Off. Renton 425.793.5180

R: 55 **T:** 12th 68%
Elected Year: 1996

WEST VIRGINIA

⚲ Governor Jim Justice (JUHS-tiss) p 304.558.2000

State Capitol   **C:** Charleston
1900 Kanawha Blvd., East **P:** 1,805,832 (39)
Charleston, WV 25305   **A:** 24,038.32 mi^2 (41st)
Website wv.gov
Fax 304.342.7025
Term Ends 2021
Lt. Governor
Mitch Carmichael, **R**

U.S. Senators
Joe Manchin, **D**
Shelley Moore Capito, **R**
U.S. Representatives
01 / David B. McKinley, **R**
02 / Alex X. Mooney, **R**
03 / Carol D. Miller, **R**

⚲ Sen. Shelley Moore Capito (KA-plh-toe) R-WV-Jr. p 202.224.6472

Rm. RSOB 172 **Web.** capito.senate.gov f 202.224.7665
Bio. 11/26/1953 • Glen Dale, WV • State Legislator •
Duke Univ. (NC), B.S., 1975; Univ. of Virginia, M.Ed., 1976
• Presbyterian • M. Dr. Charles Lewis Capito, 3 ch ; 4
gr-ch **Cmte.** Appropriations • Commerce, Science &
Transportation • Environment & Public Works • Rules &
Administration
CoS. Joel Brubaker   **LD.** Adam Tomlinson
Sched. Lauren A. Russell   **PS.** Tyler Hernandez
Dist. Off. Beckley 304.347.5372 • Charleston 304.347.5372
• Martinsburg 304.262.9285 • Morgantown 304.292.2310

: 69 **T:** 1st 62%
Elected Year: 2014
Next Election: 2020

⚲ Sen. Joe Manchin III (MAN-shin) D-WV-Sr. p 202.224.3954

Rm. HSOB 306 **Web.** manchin.senate.gov f 202.228.0002
Bio. 08/24/1947 • Farmington, WV • Candidate, Governor
of West Virginia; President, Marion County Rescue Squad;
Secretary of State, West Virginia; Mbr., WV House of
Delegates; Mbr., WV Senate; Mbr., Marion County Airport
Authority • West Virginia Univ., B.S., 1970 • Catholic •
M. Gayle Conelly, 3 ch ; 8 gr-ch **Cmte.** Appropriations •
Armed Services • Energy & Natural Resources • Veterans'
Affairs
CoS. Patrick Hayes   **LD.** Wes Kungel
Sched. Bryer Davis   **PS.** Jon Kott
Dist. Off. Charleston 304.342.5855 • Fairmont 304.368.0567
• Martinsburg 304.264.4626

: 43 **T:** 2nd 50%
Elected Year: 2010
Next Election: 2024

WEST VIRGINIA

🏛 **Rep. David B. McKinley** (mih-KIN-lee)   R-WV-01   p 202.225.4172

Rm. RHOB 2239 **Web.** mckinley.house.gov   **f** 202.225.7564
Bio. 03/28/1947 • Wheeling, WV • Purdue Univ. (IN), B.S.,
1969 • Episcopalian • M. Mary McKinley, 4 ch ; 6 gr-ch
Cmte. Energy & Commerce
CoS. Mike Hamilton   **LD.** Christopher Buki
Sched. Kaitlin Brown   **PS.** Amanda Hyman
Dist. Off. Morgantown 304.284.8506 • Parkersburg
304.422.5972 • Wheeling 304.232.3801

R: 175 **T:** 5th 65%
Elected Year: 2010

🏛 **Rep. Carol D. Miller** (MIH-lur)   R-WV-03   p 202.225.3452

Rm. LHOB 1605 **Web.** miller.house.gov
Bio. 11/04/1950 • Columbus, OH • Columbia College,
B.S., 1972 • Baptist • M. Matt Miller, 2 ch **Cmte.** Oversight
& Reform • Select Committee on the Climate Crisis •
Transportation & Infrastructure
CoS. Matthew Donnellan   **LD.** Lauren Billman
Sched. Emily Kinner   **PS.** Samantha Cantrell
Dist. Off. Beckley 304.250.6177 • Bluefield • Huntington
304.522.2201

R: 395 **T:** 1st 56%
Elected Year: 2018

🏛 **Rep. Alex X. Mooney** (MOON-ee)   R-WV-02   p 202.225.2711

Rm. RHOB 2440 **Web.** mooney.house.gov   **f** 202.225.7856
Bio. 06/07/1971 • Washington, DC • Dartmouth College,
A.B., 1993 • Roman Catholic • M. Grace Gonzalez, 3 ch
Cmte. Financial Services
CoS. Michael J. Hough   **LD.** Scott Rausch
Sched. Katie Beaumont   **PS.** Ted Dacey
Dist. Off. Charleston 304.925.5964 • Martinsburg
304.264.8810

R: 273 **T:** 3rd 54%
Elected Year: 2014

WISCONSIN

WISCONSIN

🏛 **Governor Tony Evers** (EV-urz)   p 608.266.1212

115 E. Capitol   **C:** Madison
Madison, WI 53702   **P:** 5,813,568 (20)
Website wisconsin.gov   **A:** 54,157.76 mi^2 (25th)
Fax 608.267.8983
Term Ends 2023
Lt. Governor
Mandela Barnes, **D**

U.S. Senators
Ron H. Johnson, R
Tammy Baldwin, **D**
U.S. Representatives
01 / Bryan G. Steil, R
02 / Mark Pocan, **D**
03 / Ron J. Kind, **D**
04 / Gwen S. Moore, **D**
05 / Jim Sensenbrenner, R
06 / Glenn S. Grothman, R
07 / Sean P. Duffy, R
08 / Michael J. Gallagher, R

ᵖ Sen. Tammy Baldwin (BALLD-win) D-WI-Jr. p 202.224.5653

Rm. HSOB 709 **Web.** baldwin.senate.gov **f** 202.224.9787
Bio. 02/11/1962 • Madison, WI • City Council Member;
Member, State Assembly • Smith College (MA), A.B., 1984;
Univ. of Wisconsin Law School, J.D., 1989 • Unspecified/
Other • S. **Cmte.** Appropriations • Commerce, Science &
Transportation • Health, Education, Labor & Pensions
CoS. Bill Murat **LD.** Dan M. McCarthy
Sched. Carolyn D. Walser **PS.** John W. Kraus
Dist. Off. Ashland 715.450.3754 • Eau Claire 715.832.8424
• Green Bay 920.498.2668 • La Crosse 608.796.0045 •
Madison 608.264.5338 • Milwaukee 414.297.4451 • Wausau
715.261.2611

R: 58 T: 2nd 55%
Elected Year: 2012
Next Election: 2024

ᴿ Sen. Ron H. Johnson (JAHN-suhn) R-WI-Sr. p 202.224.5323

Rm. HSOB 328 **Web.** ronjohnson.senate.gov **f** 202.228.6965
Bio. 04/08/1955 • Mankato, MN • Univ. of Minnesota, B.S.,
1977 • Lutheran • M. Jane Johnson, 3 ch ; 2 gr-ch **Cmte.**
Budget • Commerce, Science & Transportation • Foreign
Relations • Homeland Security & Government Affairs
CoS. Tony Blando **LD.** Sean Riley
Sched. Chloe Pickle **PS.** Ben Voelkel
Dist. Off. Madison 608.240.9629 • Milwaukee 414.276.7282
• Oshkosh 920.230.7250

R: 52 T: 2nd 50%
Elected Year: 2010
Next Election: 2022

ᴿ Rep. Sean P. Duffy (DUH-fee) R-WI-07 p 202.225.3365

Rm. RHOB 1714 **Web.** duffy.house.gov
Bio. 10/03/1971 • Hayward, WI • St. Mary's Univ. (MN),
B.A., 1994; William Mitchell College of Law (MN), J.D., 1999
• Roman Catholic • M. Rachel Campos-Duffy, 8 ch **Cmte.**
Financial Services
CoS. Pete Meachum **LD.** Ryan McCormack
Sched. Eleanor Traynham **PS.** Mark Bednar
Dist. Off. Hayward 715.392.3984 • Hudson 715.808.8160 •
Wausau 715.298.9344

R: 159 T: 5th 60%
Elected Year: 2010

ᴿ Rep. Michael J. Gallagher (GA-luh-gur) R-WI-08 p 202.225.5665

Rm. LHOB 1230 **Web.** gallagher.house.gov **f** 202.225.5729
Bio. 03/03/1984 • Green Day, WI • Princeton Univ.
Woodrow Wilson School of Public and International Affairs
(NJ), B.A., 2006; National Intelligence Univ. (DC), M.S., 2010;
Georgetown Univ. (DC), M.A., 2012; Georgetown Univ. (DC),
M.A., 2013; Georgetown Univ. (DC), Ph.D., 2015 • Catholic •
S. **Cmte.** Armed Services • Transportation & Infrastructure
CoS. Taylor Andreae **LD.** Charles Morrison
Sched. Betsy Goodman **PS.** Madison Wiberg
(CD)
Dist. Off. De Pere 920.301.4500

: 311 T: 2nd 64%
lected Year: 2016

ᴿ Rep. Glenn S. Grothman ("GROWTH"-muhn) R-WI-06 p 202.225.2476

Rm. LHOB 1427 **Web.** grothman.house.gov **f** 202.225.2356
Bio. 07/03/1955 • Milwaukee, WI • Univ. of Wisconsin -
Madison, B.B.A., 1977; Univ. of Wisconsin Law School, J.D.,
1983 • Lutheran • S. Growth Muhn **Cmte.** Education &
Labor • Oversight & Reform
CoS. Rachel VerVelde **LD.** Ryan Croft
  PS. Patrick Konrath
Dist. Off. Fond du Lac 920.907.0624

264 T: 3rd 56%
ected Year: 2014

WISCONSIN

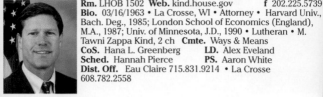

♫ Rep. Ron J. Kind (kind) D-WI-03 p 202.225.5506
Rm. LHOB 1502 **Web.** kind.house.gov **f** 202.225.5739
Bio. 03/16/1963 • La Crosse, WI • Attorney • Harvard Univ.,
Bach. Deg., 1985; London School of Economics (England),
M.A., 1987; Univ. of Minnesota, J.D., 1990 • Lutheran • M.
Tawni Zappa Kind, 2 ch **Cmte.** Ways & Means
CoS. Hana L. Greenberg **LD.** Alex Eveland
Sched. Hannah Pierce **PS.** Aaron White
Dist. Off. Eau Claire 715.831.9214 • La Crosse
608.782.2558

R: 50 **T:** 12th 60%
Elected Year: 1996

♫ Rep. Gwen S. Moore (mor) D-WI-04 p 202.225.4572
Rm. RHOB 2252 **Web.** **f** 202.225.8135
gwenmoore.house.gov
Bio. 04/18/1951 • Racine, WI • State Senator; Member,
State Assembly • Marquette Univ. (WI), B.A., 1978 • Baptist
• S., 3 ch ; 3 gr-ch **Cmte.** Ways & Means
CoS. Sean Gard **LD.** Christopher Goldson
Sched. Robert Montgomery
Dist. Off. Milwaukee 414.297.1140

R: 102 **T:** 8th 76%
Elected Year: 2004

♫ Rep. Mark Pocan (po-KAN) D-WI-02 p 202.225.2906
Rm. LHOB 1421 **Web.** pocan.house.gov **f** 202.225.6942
Bio. 08/14/1964 • Kenosha, WI • Univ. of Wisconsin
- Madison, B.A., 1986 • Unspecified/Other • M. Philip
Frank **Cmte.** Appropriations • Select Committee on the
Modernization of Congress
CoS. Glenn Wavrunek **LD.** David Bagby
Sched. Kelly McCone **PS.** Ron Boehmer
Dist. Off. Beloit 608.365.8001 • Madison 608.258.9800

R: 227 **T:** 4th 97%
Elected Year: 2012

♠ Rep. Jim Sensenbrenner Jr. (SEHN-sehn-
brehn-ur) R-WI-05 p 202.225.510
Rm. RHOB 2449 **Web.** **f** 202.225.319
sensenbrenner.house.gov
Bio. 06/14/1943 • Chicago, IL • State Legislator • Stanford
Univ. (CA), B.A., 1965; Univ. of Wisconsin Law School, J.D.,
1968 • Roman Catholic • M. Cheryl Warren Sensenbrenner,
2 ch ; 1 gr-ch **Cmte.** Foreign Affairs • Judiciary
CoS. Matthew Bisenius **LD.** Amy Bos
Sched. Nathan Cobb **PS.** Christopher Krepich
Dist. Off. Brookfield 262.784.1111

R: 2 **T:** 21st 62%
Elected Year: 1978

♠ Rep. Bryan G. Steil ("style") R-WI-01 p 202.225.303
Rm. LHOB 1408 **Web.** steil.house.gov
Bio. 03/03/1981 • Janesville, WI • Georgetown Univ. (DC),
B.S., 2003; Univ. of Wisconsin, J.D., 2007 • Catholic • S.
Cmte. Financial Services
CoS. Ryan Carney **LD.** David Goldfarb
Sched. Matthew Brown **PS.** Sally Fox
Dist. Off. Janesville 608.752.4050

R: 419 **T:** 1st 55%
Elected Year: 2018

WYOMING

Governor Mark Gordon (GOR-duhn)   p 307.777.7434

State Capitol   **C:** Cheyenne
200 W. 24th St.   **P:** 577,737 (52)
Cheyenne, WY 82002-0010   **A:** 97,093.07 mi^2 (9th)
Website wyoming.gov
Fax 307.632.3909
Term Ends 2023

U.S. Senators
Mike B. Enzi, **R**
John A. Barrasso, **R**
U.S. Representatives
01 / Liz L. Cheney, **R**

1

Sen. John A. Barrasso (bah-RAH-so)   R-WY-Jr.   p 202.224.6441

Rm. DSOB 307 **Web.** barrasso.senate.gov   **f** 202.224.1724
Bio. 07/21/1952 • Reading, PA • State Legislator;
Orthopedic Surgeon • Georgetown Univ. (DC), B.S.,
1974; Georgetown Univ. School of Medicine (DC), M.D.,
1978 • Presbyterian • M. Bobbi Brown, 3 ch (2 from
previous marriage) **Cmte.** Energy & Natural Resources •
Environment & Public Works • Foreign Relations • Indian
Affairs
CoS. Dan Kunsman   **LD.** Bryn Stewart
Sched. Kathi Wise   **PS.** Bronwyn E. Lance
Dist. Off. Casper 307.261.6413 • Cheyenne 307.772.2451
• Riverton 307.856.6642 • Rock Springs 307.362.5012 •
Sheridan 307.672.6456

: 34   T: 2nd 67%
lected Year: 2007
ext Election: 2024

Sen. Mike B. Enzi (EHN-zee)   R-WY-Sr.   p 202.224.3424

Rm. RSOB 379-A **Web.** enzi.senate.gov   **f** 202.228.0359
Bio. 02/01/1944 • Bremerton, WA • State Senator; State
Representative • Air National Guard 1967-73 • George
Washington Univ. (DC), B.B.A., 1966; Univ. of Denver (CO),
M.B.A., 1968 • Presbyterian • M. Diana Buckley Enzi, 3 ch ; 4
gr-ch **Cmte.** Budget • Finance • Health, Education, Labor
& Pensions • Homeland Security & Government Affairs •
Joint Taxation
CoS. Coy R. Knobel   **LD.** Doug Dziak
Sched. Alana Hyman   **PS.** Max D'Onofrio
Dist. Off. Casper 307.261.6572 • Cheyenne 307.772.2477
• Cody 307.527.9444 • Gillette 307.682.6268 • Jackson
307.739.9507

: 13   T: 4th 72%
ected Year: 1996
ext Election: 2020

Rep. Liz L. Cheney (CHAY-nee)   R-WY-01   p 202.225.2311

Rm. CHOB 416 **Web.** cheney.house.gov   **f** 202.225.3057
Bio. 07/28/1966 • Madison, WI • Colorado College, B.A.,
1988; Univ. of Chicago Law School, J.D., 1996 • Methodist
• M. Philip Perry, 5 ch **Cmte.** Armed Services • Natural
Resources
CoS. Kara Ahern
Sched. Katelyn Seago   **PS.** Maddy Weast
Dist. Off. Casper 307.261.6595 • Cheyenne 307.772.2595 •
Gillette 307.414.1677 • Riverton 307.463.0482

302   T: 2nd 64%
ected Year: 2016

AMERICAN SAMOA

Governor Lolo Letalu Matalasi Moliga (mo-LEE-gah)   p 684.633.4116

Executive Office Building, Third Floor, Utulei
Pago Pago, AS 96799
Website americansamoa.gov
Fax 684.633.2269
Term Ends 2021
Lt. Governor
Lemanu Peleti Mauga, I

C: Pago Pago
P: 55,689 (55)
A: 76.45 mi^2 (55th)

Delegate

⚑ Del. Aumua Amata Coleman Radewagen   R-AS-01   p 202.225.8577
(RAD-eh-wag-uhn)

Rm. LHOB 1339 **Web.** radewagen.house.gov **f** 202.225.8757
Bio. 12/29/1947 • Pago Pago, American Samoa • Univ. of Guam, B.S., 1975 • Roman Catholic • M. Fred Radewagen, 3 ch; 1 gr-ch **Cmte.** Natural Resources • Small Business • Veterans' Affairs
CoS. Leafaina Yahn   **LD.** Richard Stanton
Sched. Nancy Dehlinger   **PS.** Joel Hannahs
Dist. Off. Fagatogo 684.633.3601

R: 0   **T:** 1st 83%
Elected Year: 2014

DISTRICT OF COLUMBIA

➴ Mayor Muriel Bowser (BOU-zur)   p 202.727.2643

Executive Office of the Mayor
1350 Pennsylvania Avenue NW, Suite 316
Washington, DC 20004
Website dc.gov
Fax 202.727.0505
Term Ends 2023

C: Washington
P: 702,455 (50)
A: 61.00 mi^2 (56th)

Delegate

➴ Del. Eleanor Holmes Norton (NOR-tuhn)   D-DC-01   p 202.225.8050

Rm. RHOB 2136 **Web.** norton.house.gov   **f** 202.225.3002
Bio. 06/13/1937 • Washington, DC • Professor; Employment Commission Chair • Antioch College (OH), B.A., 1960; Yale Univ. (CT), M.A., 1963; Yale Univ. Law School (CT), J.D., 1964 • Episcopalian • D., 2 ch **Cmte.** Oversight & Reform • Transportation & Infrastructure
CoS. Raven Reeder   **LD.** Bradley Truding
Sched. Try Onaghise-
Coburn
Dist. Off. Washington 202.408.9041 • Washington
202.678.8900

R: 0   **T:** 1st 87%
Elected Year: 1990

GUAM

➴ Governor Lou Leon Guerrero (guh-RAIR-o)   p 671.472.8931

Richard J. Bordallo Governor's Complex
Adelup, GU 96910
Website guam.gov
Fax 671.477.4826
Term Ends 2023
Lt. Governor
Josh Tenorio, **D**

C: Hagatna
P: 164,229 (53)
A: 209.65 mi^2 (52nd)

Delegate

⋈ Rep. Michael F.Q. San Nicolas (san nee-ko-LAH) D-GU-01   p 202.225.1188

Rm. LHOB 1632 **Web.** sannicolas.house.gov
Bio. 01/30/1981 • Talofofo, Guam • Univ. of Guam, B.A.,
2004 • M. Kathryn Santos Ko, 2 ch **Cmte.** Financial
Services • Natural Resources
Sched. T'Nelta Mori
Dist. Off. Hagatna

R: 0   **T:** 1st 55%
Elected Year: 2018

MARIANA ISLANDS

⋈ Governor Ralph Torres (toe-ress)   p 670.664.2280

Juan Atalig Memorial Building   **C:** Saipan
Isla Dr., Capitol Hill, Caller Box   **P:** 52,263 (56)
10007   **A:** 182.24 mi^2 (53rd)
Saipan, MP 96950
Website gov.mp
Fax 670.664.2211
Term Ends 2019
Lt. Governor
Arnold Palacios, **R**

Delegate

⋈ Del. Gregorio K.C. Sablan (sah-BLAHN) D-MP-01   p 202.225.2646

Rm. RHOB 2411 **Web.** sablan.house.gov   **f** 202.226.4249
Bio. 01/19/1955 • Saipan, MP • Public Administrator •
Army • Roman Catholic • M. Andrea C. Sablan, 6 ch **Cmte.**
Education & Labor • Natural Resources • Veterans' Affairs
CoS. Robert Schwalbach   **LD.** Seth Maiman
Sched. Agnes Cornibert
Dist. Off. Rota 670.532.2647 • Saipan 670.323.2647 •
Tinian 670.433.2647

R: 0   **T:** 1st 64%
Elected Year: 2008

PUERTO RICO

Governor Ricardo Rossello ("rose"-AY-o)   p 787.721.7000

PO Box 9023431   **C:** San Juan
San Juan, PR 00902-0082   **P:** 3,195,153 (30)
Website pr.gov   **A:** 3,423.95 mi^2 (49th)
Fax 787.729.5072
Term Ends 2021

Delegate

⋈ Del. Jenniffer A. Gonzalez-Colon (gon-SAH-les R-PR-01   p 202.225.2615
ko-LOAN)

Rm. LHOB 1609 **Web.** gonzalez-   **f** 202.225.2154
colon.house.gov
Bio. 08/05/1976 • San Juan, PR • Univ. of Puerto Rico,
Bach. Deg., Inter-American Univ. of Puerto Rico, J.D.;
Inter-American Univ. of Puerto Rico, LL.M. • Unspecified/
Other • S. **Cmte.** Natural Resources • Transportation &
Infrastructure
CoS. Gabriella Boffelli   **LD.** Ross Dietrich
                                   PS. Natasha Marquez
Dist. Off. San Juan 787.723.6333

R: 0   **T:** 1st 49%
Elected Year: 2016

VIRGIN ISLANDS

VIRGIN ISLANDS

🐦 **Governor Albert Bryan** (BRY-uhn)   p 340.774.0001

Government House
21-22 Kongens Gade, Charlotte
Amalie
St. Thomas, VI 00802
Website vi.gov
Fax 340.774.1361
Term Ends 2023
Lt. Governor
Tregenza Roach, **D**

C: Charlotte Amalie
P: 104,901 (54)
A: 134.36 mi^2 (54th)

Delegate

🐦 **Del. Stacey E. Plaskett** (PLAS-ket)   D-VI-01   p 202.225.1790

Rm. RHOB 2404 **Web.** plaskett.house.gov   **f** 202.225.5517
Bio. 05/13/1964 • New York, NY • Georgetown Univ.
Foreign Service School (DC), B.S., 1984; American Univ.,
Washington College of Law, J.D., 1994 • Lutheran • M.
Jeremy Buckney Small, 5 ch **Cmte.** Agriculture • Oversight
& Reform • Transportation & Infrastructure
CoS. Erik Prince   **LD.** Angeline Jabbar
Sched. Lewis H. Myers   **PS.** Michael J. McQuerry
Dist. Off. Frederiksted 340.778.5900 • St. Thomas
340.774.4408

R: 0   **T:** 1st 100%
Elected Year: 2014

INDEX OF COMMITTEES AND SUBCOMMITTEES

Below is an alphabetical listing of all committees and subcommittees by name.
Bold type indicates committee, non-bold type indicates subcommittee. Entries
are grouped by Senate, Joint and House.

SENATE

SENATE COMMITTEES

Committee rosters are listed in order of ranking membership with the Chairman and Ranking Member indicated with "C" and "RM" respectively. The chairman and ranking member of each committee usually have membership status on all subcommittees of which they are not members. This is referred to as ex officio membership. These memberships are subject to the rules of the individual committees.

AGRICULTURE, NUTRITION & FORESTRY

Room: RSOB 328A
Website: www.agriculture.senate.gov
Phone: 202.224.2035
Ratio: 11 Republicans/9 Democrats
Subcommittees: 5

Majority:		Minority:	
C: Pat Roberts, KS	HSOB 109	RM: Debbie Stabenow, MI	HSOB 731
Mitch McConnell, KY	RSOB 317	Patrick Leahy, VT	RSOB 437
John Boozman, AR	HSOB 141	Sherrod Brown, OH	HSOB 503
John Hoeven, ND	RSOB 338	Amy Klobuchar, MN	DSOB 425
Joni Ernst, IA	HSOB 730	Michael Bennet, CO	RSOB 261
Cindy Hyde-Smith, MS	HSOB 702	Kirsten Gillibrand, NY	RSOB 478
Mike Braun, IN	RSOB B85	Bob Casey, PA	RSOB 393
David Perdue, GA	RSOB 455	Tina Smith, MN	HSOB 720
Chuck Grassley, IA	HSOB 135	Dick Durbin, IL	HSOB 711
John Thune, SD	DSOB 511		
Deb Fischer, NE	RSOB 454		

Majority CoS: James Glueck Jr.   **Minority CoS:** Joseph Shultz

――――――――――― Subcommittees ―――――――――――

COMMODITIES, RISK MANAGEMENT & TRADE
Room:

Majority:		Minority:	
C: John Boozman, AR	HSOB 141	RM: Sherrod Brown, OH	HSOB 503
Mitch McConnell, KY	RSOB 317	Michael Bennet, CO	RSOB 261
John Hoeven, ND	RSOB 338	Kirsten Gillibrand, NY	RSOB 478
Cindy Hyde-Smith, MS	HSOB 702	Tina Smith, MN	HSOB 720
David Perdue, GA	RSOB 455	Dick Durbin, IL	HSOB 711
Chuck Grassley, IA	HSOB 135	Debbie Stabenow, MI	HSOB 731
Pat Roberts, KS	HSOB 109		

CONSERVATION, FORESTRY & NATURAL RESOURCES
Room:

Majority:		Minority:	
C: Mike Braun, IN	RSOB B85	RM: Michael Bennet, CO	RSOB 261
John Boozman, AR	HSOB 141	Patrick Leahy, VT	RSOB 437
Cindy Hyde-Smith, MS	HSOB 702	Amy Klobuchar, MN	DSOB 425
David Perdue, GA	RSOB 455	Bob Casey, PA	RSOB 393
Chuck Grassley, IA	HSOB 135	Dick Durbin, IL	HSOB 711
John Thune, SD	DSOB 511	Debbie Stabenow, MI	HSOB 731
Pat Roberts, KS	HSOB 109		

LIVESTOCK, MARKETING & AGRICULTURE SECURITY
Room:

Majority:		Minority:	
C: Cindy Hyde-Smith, MS	HSOB 702	RM: Kirsten Gillibrand, NY	RSOB 478
Joni Ernst, IA	HSOB 730		
Mike Braun, IN	RSOB B85	Patrick Leahy, VT	RSOB 437
David Perdue, GA	RSOB 455	Amy Klobuchar, MN	DSOB 425
Chuck Grassley, IA	HSOB 135	Bob Casey, PA	RSOB 393
Deb Fischer, NE	RSOB 454	Tina Smith, MN	HSOB 720
Pat Roberts, KS	HSOB 109	Debbie Stabenow, MI	HSOB 731

NUTRITION, AGRICULTURAL RESEARCH & SPECIALTY CROPS
Room:

Majority:		Minority:	
C: Deb Fischer, NE	RSOB 454	RM: Bob Casey, PA	RSOB 393
Mitch McConnell, KY	RSOB 317	Patrick Leahy, VT	RSOB 437
John Boozman, AR	HSOB 141	Sherrod Brown, OH	HSOB 503
John Hoeven, ND	RSOB 338	Amy Klobuchar, MN	DSOB 425
Joni Ernst, IA	HSOB 730	Kirsten Gillibrand, NY	RSOB 478
John Thune, SD	DSOB 511	Debbie Stabenow, MI	HSOB 731
Pat Roberts, KS	HSOB 109		

RURAL DEVELOPMENT & ENERGY
Room:

Majority:		Minority:	

C: Joni Ernst, IA	HSOB 730	**RM: Tina Smith, MN**	HSOB 720
Mitch McConnell, KY	RSOB 317	Sherrod Brown, OH	HSOB 503
John Hoeven, ND	RSOB 338	Amy Klobuchar, MN	DSOB 425
Mike Braun, IN	RSOB B85	Michael Bennet, CO	RSOB 261
John Thune, SD	DSOB 511	Dick Durbin, IL	HSOB 711
Deb Fischer, NE	RSOB 454	Debbie Stabenow, MI	HSOB 731
Pat Roberts, KS	HSOB 109		

APPROPRIATIONS

Room: The Capitol S-128
Website: www.appropriations.senate.gov
Phone: 202.224.7257
Ratio: 16 Republicans/15 Democrats
Subcommittees: 12

Majority:		Minority:	
C: Richard Shelby, AL	RSOB 304	**RM: Patrick Leahy, VT**	RSOB 437
Mitch McConnell, KY	RSOB 317	Patty Murray, WA	RSOB 154
Lamar Alexander, TN	DSOB 455	Dianne Feinstein, CA	HSOB 331
Susan Collins, ME	DSOB 413	Dick Durbin, IL	HSOB 711
Lisa Murkowski, AK	HSOB 522	Jack Reed, RI	HSOB 728
Lindsey Graham, SC	RSOB 290	Jon Tester, MT	HSOB 311
Roy Blunt, MO	RSOB 260	Tom Udall, NM	HSOB 531
Jerry Moran, KS	DSOB 521	Jeanne Shaheen, NH	HSOB 506
John Hoeven, ND	RSOB 338	Jeff Merkley, OR	HSOB 313
John Boozman, AR	HSOB 141	Christopher Coons, DE	RSOB 127 A
Shelley Capito, WV	RSOB 172	Brian Schatz, HI	HSOB 722
John Kennedy, LA	RSOB 416	Tammy Baldwin, WI	HSOB 709
Cindy Hyde-Smith, MS	HSOB 702	Chris Murphy, CT	HSOB 136
Steve Daines, MT	HSOB 320	Joe Manchin, WV	HSOB 306
Marco Rubio, FL	RSOB 284	Chris Van Hollen, MD	HSOB 110
James Lankford, OK	HSOB 316		

Majority CoS: Shannon Hines   **Minority CoS:** Charles E. Kieffer

─────────────── Subcommittees ───────────────

AGRICULTURE, RURAL DEVELOPMENT, FDA & RELATED AGENCIES
Room: DSOB 129
Phone: 202.224.7257

Majority:		Minority:	
C: John Hoeven, ND	RSOB 338	**RM: Jeff Merkley, OR**	HSOB 31?
Mitch McConnell, KY	RSOB 317	Dianne Feinstein, CA	HSOB 33?
Susan Collins, ME	DSOB 413	Jon Tester, MT	HSOB 31
Roy Blunt, MO	RSOB 260	Tom Udall, NM	HSOB 53
Jerry Moran, KS	DSOB 521	Patrick Leahy, VT	RSOB 43
Cindy Hyde-Smith, MS	HSOB 702	Tammy Baldwin, WI	HSOB 70?
John Kennedy, LA	RSOB 416		
Richard Shelby, AL	RSOB 304		

COMMERCE, JUSTICE, SCIENCE & RELATED AGENCIES
Room: DSOB 142
Phone: 202.224.7277

Majority:		Minority:	
C: Jerry Moran, KS	DSOB 521	**RM: Jeanne Shaheen, NH**	HSOB 5(
Lamar Alexander, TN	DSOB 455	Patrick Leahy, VT	RSOB 43
Lisa Murkowski, AK	HSOB 522	Dianne Feinstein, CA	HSOB 33
Susan Collins, ME	DSOB 413	Jack Reed, RI	HSOB 72
Lindsey Graham, SC	RSOB 290	Christopher Coons, DE	RSOB 127-
John Boozman, AR	HSOB 141	Brian Schatz, HI	HSOB 72
Shelley Capito, WV	RSOB 172	Joe Manchin, WV	HSOB 3(
John Kennedy, LA	RSOB 416	Chris Van Hollen, MD	HSOB 1?
Marco Rubio, FL	RSOB 284		
Richard Shelby, AL	RSOB 304		

DEPARTMENT OF DEFENSE
Room: DSOB 122
Phone: 202.224.7255

Majority:		Minority:	
C: Richard Shelby, AL	RSOB 304	**RM: Dick Durbin, IL**	HSOB 7
Mitch McConnell, KY	RSOB 317	Patrick Leahy, VT	RSOB 4
Lamar Alexander, TN	DSOB 455	Dianne Feinstein, CA	HSOB 3.
Susan Collins, ME	DSOB 413	Patty Murray, WA	RSOB 1
Lisa Murkowski, AK	HSOB 522	Jack Reed, RI	HSOB 7
Lindsey Graham, SC	RSOB 290	Jon Tester, MT	HSOB 3
Roy Blunt, MO	RSOB 260	Tom Udall, NM	HSOB 5
Jerry Moran, KS	DSOB 521	Brian Schatz, HI	HSOB 7
John Hoeven, ND	RSOB 338	Tammy Baldwin, WI	HSOB 7
John Boozman, AR	HSOB 141		

DEPARTMENT OF HOMELAND SECURITY
Room: DSOB 131
Phone: 202.224.8244

Majority:		Minority:	
C: Shelley Capito, WV	RSOB 172	RM: Jon Tester, MT	HSOB 311
Richard Shelby, AL	RSOB 304	Jeanne Shaheen, NH	HSOB 506
Lisa Murkowski, AK	HSOB 522	Patrick Leahy, VT	RSOB 437
John Hoeven, ND	RSOB 338	Patty Murray, WA	RSOB 154
John Kennedy, LA	RSOB 416	Tammy Baldwin, WI	HSOB 709
Cindy Hyde-Smith, MS	HSOB 702	Joe Manchin, WV	HSOB 306
James Lankford, OK	HSOB 316		

DEPARTMENT OF THE INTERIOR, ENVIRONMENT & RELATED AGENCIES
Room: DSOB 131
Phone: 202.224.7233

Majority:		Minority:	
C: Lisa Murkowski, AK	HSOB 522	RM: Tom Udall, NM	HSOB 531
Lamar Alexander, TN	DSOB 455	Dianne Feinstein, CA	HSOB 331
Roy Blunt, MO	RSOB 260	Patrick Leahy, VT	RSOB 437
Mitch McConnell, KY	RSOB 317	Jack Reed, RI	HSOB 728
Shelley Capito, WV	RSOB 172	Jon Tester, MT	HSOB 311
Cindy Hyde-Smith, MS	HSOB 702	Jeff Merkley, OR	HSOB 313
Steve Daines, MT	HSOB 320	Chris Van Hollen, MD	HSOB 110
Marco Rubio, FL	RSOB 284		
Richard Shelby, AL	RSOB 304		

DOL, HHS & EDUCATION & RELATED AGENCIES
Room: DSOB 136
Phone: 202.224.7230

Majority:		Minority:	
C: Roy Blunt, MO	RSOB 260	RM: Patty Murray, WA	RSOB 154
Richard Shelby, AL	RSOB 304	Dick Durbin, IL	HSOB 711
Lamar Alexander, TN	DSOB 455	Jack Reed, RI	HSOB 728
Lindsey Graham, SC	RSOB 290	Jeanne Shaheen, NH	HSOB 506
Jerry Moran, KS	DSOB 521	Jeff Merkley, OR	HSOB 313
Shelley Capito, WV	RSOB 172	Brian Schatz, HI	HSOB 722
John Kennedy, LA	RSOB 416	Tammy Baldwin, WI	HSOB 709
Cindy Hyde-Smith, MS	HSOB 702	Chris Murphy, CT	HSOB 136
Marco Rubio, FL	RSOB 284	Joe Manchin, WV	HSOB 306
James Lankford, OK	HSOB 316	Patrick Leahy, VT	RSOB 437

ENERGY & WATER DEVELOPMENT
Room: DSOB 142
Phone: 202.224.7257

Majority:		Minority:	
C: Lamar Alexander, TN	DSOB 455	RM: Dianne Feinstein, CA	HSOB 331
Mitch McConnell, KY	RSOB 317	Patty Murray, WA	RSOB 154
Richard Shelby, AL	RSOB 304	Jon Tester, MT	HSOB 311
Susan Collins, ME	DSOB 413	Dick Durbin, IL	HSOB 711
Lisa Murkowski, AK	HSOB 522	Tom Udall, NM	HSOB 531
Lindsey Graham, SC	RSOB 290	Jeanne Shaheen, NH	HSOB 506
John Hoeven, ND	RSOB 338	Christopher Coons, DE	RSOB 127-A
John Kennedy, LA	RSOB 416	Patrick Leahy, VT	RSOB 437
Cindy Hyde-Smith, MS	HSOB 702		

FINANCIAL SERVICES & GENERAL GOVERNMENT
Room: DSOB 133
Phone: 202.224.2104

Majority:		Minority:	
C: John Kennedy, LA	RSOB 416	RM: Christopher Coons, DE	RSOB 127-A
Jerry Moran, KS	DSOB 521		
John Boozman, AR	HSOB 141	Dick Durbin, IL	HSOB 711
Steve Daines, MT	HSOB 320	Joe Manchin, WV	HSOB 306
James Lankford, OK	HSOB 316	Chris Van Hollen, MD	HSOB 110
Richard Shelby, AL	RSOB 304	Patrick Leahy, VT	RSOB 437

LEGISLATIVE BRANCH
Room: The Capitol S-128
Phone: 202.224.9722

Majority:		Minority:	
C: Cindy Hyde-Smith, MS	HSOB 702	RM: Chris Murphy, CT	HSOB 136
Richard Shelby, AL	RSOB 304	Chris Van Hollen, MD	HSOB 110
James Lankford, OK	HSOB 316	Patrick Leahy, VT	RSOB 437

MILITARY CONSTRUCTION & VETERAN AFFAIRS & RELATED AGENCIES
Room: DSOB 125
Phone: 202.224.5245

Majority:		Minority:	
C: John Boozman, AR	HSOB 141	RM: Brian Schatz, HI	HSOB 722
Mitch McConnell, KY	RSOB 317	Jon Tester, MT	HSOB 311
Lisa Murkowski, AK	HSOB 522	Patty Murray, WA	RSOB 154
John Hoeven, ND	RSOB 338	Jack Reed, RI	HSOB 728
Susan Collins, ME	DSOB 413	Tom Udall, NM	HSOB 531
Shelley Capito, WV	RSOB 172	Tammy Baldwin, WI	HSOB 709
Marco Rubio, FL	RSOB 284	Chris Murphy, CT	HSOB 136
Steve Daines, MT	HSOB 320	Patrick Leahy, VT	RSOB 437
Richard Shelby, AL	RSOB 304		

STATE, FOREIGN OPERATIONS & RELATED PROGRAMS
Room: DSOB 127
Phone: 202.224.4424

Majority:		Minority:	
C: Lindsey Graham, SC	RSOB 290	RM: Patrick Leahy, VT	RSOB 437
Mitch McConnell, KY	RSOB 317	Dick Durbin, IL	HSOB 711
Roy Blunt, MO	RSOB 260	Jeanne Shaheen, NH	HSOB 506
John Boozman, AR	HSOB 141	Christopher Coons, DE	RSOB 127-A
Jerry Moran, KS	DSOB 521	Jeff Merkley, OR	HSOB 313
Marco Rubio, FL	RSOB 284	Chris Murphy, CT	HSOB 136
James Lankford, OK	HSOB 316	Chris Van Hollen, MD	HSOB 110
Steve Daines, MT	HSOB 320		
Richard Shelby, AL	RSOB 304		

TRANSPORTATION, HUD & RELATED AGENCIES
Room: DSOB 184
Phone: 202.224.5310

Majority:		Minority:	
C: Susan Collins, ME	DSOB 413	RM: Jack Reed, RI	HSOB 728
Richard Shelby, AL	RSOB 304	Patty Murray, WA	RSOB 154
Lamar Alexander, TN	DSOB 455	Dick Durbin, IL	HSOB 711
Roy Blunt, MO	RSOB 260	Dianne Feinstein, CA	HSOB 331
John Boozman, AR	HSOB 141	Christopher Coons, DE	RSOB 127-A
Shelley Capito, WV	RSOB 172	Brian Schatz, HI	HSOB 722
Lindsey Graham, SC	RSOB 290	Chris Murphy, CT	HSOB 136
John Hoeven, ND	RSOB 338	Joe Manchin, WV	HSOB 306
Steve Daines, MT	HSOB 320	Patrick Leahy, VT	RSOB 437

ARMED SERVICES
Room: RSOB 228
Website: www.armed-services.senate.gov
Phone: 202.224.3871
Ratio: 14 Republicans/13 Democrats
Subcommittees: 7

Majority:		Minority:	
C: James Inhofe, OK	RSOB 205	RM: Jack Reed, RI	HSOB 72
Roger Wicker, MS	DSOB 555	Jeanne Shaheen, NH	HSOB 50
Deb Fischer, NE	RSOB 454	Kirsten Gillibrand, NY	RSOB 47
Tom Cotton, AR	RSOB 124	Richard Blumenthal, CT	HSOB 70
Mike Rounds, SD	HSOB 502	Mazie Hirono, HI	HSOB 71
Joni Ernst, IA	HSOB 730	Tim Kaine, VA	RSOB 23
Thom Tillis, NC	DSOB 185	Angus King, ME	HSOB 13
Dan Sullivan, AK	HSOB 302	Martin Heinrich, NM	HSOB 30
David Perdue, GA	RSOB 455	Elizabeth Warren, MA	HSOB 3
Kevin Cramer, ND	DSOB B40 C	Gary Peters, MI	HSOB 72
Martha McSally, AZ	DSOB B40D	Joe Manchin, WV	HSOB 30
Rick Scott, FL	HSOB 716	Tammy Duckworth, IL	HSOB 52
Marsha Blackburn, TN	DSOB 357	Doug Jones, AL	RSOB 32
Josh Hawley, MO	DSOB B40A		

Majority CoS: John Bonsell   **Minority CoS:** Hon. Elizabeth L. King
———————————— Subcommittees ————————————

AIRLAND
Room: RSOB 228
Phone: 202.224.3871

Majority:		Minority:	
C: Tom Cotton, AR	RSOB 124	RM: Angus King, ME	HSOB 1
Roger Wicker, MS	DSOB 555	Richard Blumenthal, CT	HSOB 7
Thom Tillis, NC	DSOB 185	Elizabeth Warren, MA	HSOB 3
Dan Sullivan, AK	HSOB 302	Gary Peters, MI	HSOB 7
Kevin Cramer, ND	DSOB B40-C	Tammy Duckworth, IL	HSOB 5
Martha McSally, AZ	DSOB B40D	Doug Jones, AL	RSOB 3

Rick Scott, FL	HSOB 716		

CYBERSECURITY
Room: RSOB 228
Phone: 202.224.3871

Majority:		Minority:	
C: Mike Rounds, SD	HSOB 502	RM: Joe Manchin, WV	HSOB 306
Roger Wicker, MS	DSOB 555	Kirsten Gillibrand, NY	RSOB 478
David Perdue, GA	RSOB 455	Richard Blumenthal, CT	HSOB 706
Rick Scott, FL	HSOB 716	Martin Heinrich, NM	HSOB 303
Marsha Blackburn, TN	DSOB 357		

EMERGING THREATS & CAPABILITIES
Room: RSOB 228
Phone: 202.224.3871

Majority:		Minority:	
C: Joni Ernst, IA	HSOB 730	RM: Gary Peters, MI	HSOB 724
Deb Fischer, NE	RSOB 454	Jeanne Shaheen, NH	HSOB 506
Kevin Cramer, ND	DSOB B40-C	Martin Heinrich, NM	HSOB 303
Marsha Blackburn, TN	DSOB 357	Mazie Hirono, HI	HSOB 713
Josh Hawley, MO	DSOB B40A		

PERSONNEL
Room:

Majority:		Minority:	
C: Thom Tillis, NC	DSOB 185	RM: Kirsten Gillibrand, NY	RSOB 478
Mike Rounds, SD	HSOB 502		
Martha McSally, AZ	DSOB B40D	Elizabeth Warren, MA	HSOB 317
Rick Scott, FL	HSOB 716	Tammy Duckworth, IL	HSOB 524

READINESS & MANAGEMENT SUPPORT
Room:

Majority:		Minority:	
C: Dan Sullivan, AK	HSOB 302	RM: Tim Kaine, VA	RSOB 231
Deb Fischer, NE	RSOB 454	Jeanne Shaheen, NH	HSOB 506
Joni Ernst, IA	HSOB 730	Mazie Hirono, HI	HSOB 713
David Perdue, GA	RSOB 455	Tammy Duckworth, IL	HSOB 524
Martha McSally, AZ	DSOB B40D	Doug Jones, AL	RSOB 326
Marsha Blackburn, TN	DSOB 357		

SEAPOWER
Room: RSOB 228
Phone: 202.224.3871

Majority:		Minority:	
C: David Perdue, GA	RSOB 455	RM: Mazie Hirono, HI	HSOB 713
Roger Wicker, MS	DSOB 555	Jeanne Shaheen, NH	HSOB 506
Tom Cotton, AR	RSOB 124	Richard Blumenthal, CT	HSOB 706
Joni Ernst, IA	HSOB 730	Tim Kaine, VA	RSOB 231
Thom Tillis, NC	DSOB 185	Angus King, ME	HSOB 133
Josh Hawley, MO	DSOB B40A		

STRATEGIC FORCES
Room: RSOB 228
Phone: 202.224.3871

Majority:		Minority:	
C: Deb Fischer, NE	RSOB 454	RM: Martin Heinrich, NM	HSOB 303
Tom Cotton, AR	RSOB 124	Angus King, ME	HSOB 133
Mike Rounds, SD	HSOB 502	Elizabeth Warren, MA	HSOB 317
Dan Sullivan, AK	HSOB 302	Joe Manchin, WV	HSOB 306
Kevin Cramer, ND	DSOB B40-C	Doug Jones, AL	RSOB 326
Josh Hawley, MO	DSOB B40A		

BANKING, HOUSING & URBAN AFFAIRS
Room: DSOB 534
Website: www.banking.senate.gov
Phone: 202.224.7391
Ratio: 13 Republicans/12 Democrats
Subcommittees: 5

Majority:		Minority:	
C: Mike Crapo, ID	DSOB 239	RM: Sherrod Brown, OH	HSOB 503
Richard Shelby, AL	RSOB 304	Jack Reed, RI	HSOB 728
Pat Toomey, PA	RSOB 248	Bob Menendez, NJ	HSOB 528
Tim Scott, SC	HSOB 104	Jon Tester, MT	HSOB 311
Ben Sasse, NE	RSOB 136	Mark Warner, VA	HSOB 703
Tom Cotton, AR	RSOB 124	Elizabeth Warren, MA	HSOB 317
Mike Rounds, SD	HSOB 502	Brian Schatz, HI	HSOB 722
David Perdue, GA	RSOB 455	Chris Van Hollen, MD	HSOB 110
Thom Tillis, NC	DSOB 185		

John Kennedy, LA	RSOB 416	Catherine Cortez Masto,	HSOB 516
Martha McSally, AZ	DSOB B40D	NV	
Jerry Moran, KS	DSOB 521	Doug Jones, AL	RSOB 326
Kevin Cramer, ND	DSOB B40 C	Tina Smith, MN	HSOB 720
		Kyrsten Sinema, AZ	HSOB 825B C

Majority CoS: Gregg Richard   **Minority CoS:** Laura Swanson

──────────── Subcommittees ────────────

ECONOMIC POLICY
Room: DSOB 124
Phone: 202.224.2353

Majority:		Minority:	
C: Tom Cotton, AR	RSOB 124	**RM: Catherine Cortez**	HSOB 516
Kevin Cramer, ND	DSOB B40-C	**Masto, NV**	
Ben Sasse, NE	RSOB 136	Bob Menendez, NJ	HSOB 528
David Perdue, GA	RSOB 455	Doug Jones, AL	RSOB 326
Thom Tillis, NC	DSOB 185	Tina Smith, MN	HSOB 720
John Kennedy, LA	RSOB 416	Kyrsten Sinema, AZ	HSOB 825B-C
Mike Crapo, ID	DSOB 239	Sherrod Brown, OH	HSOB 503

FINANCIAL INSTITUTIONS & CONSUMER PROTECTION
Room: HSOB 104
Phone: 202.224.6121

Majority:		Minority:	
C: Tim Scott, SC	HSOB 104	**RM: Elizabeth Warren, MA**	HSOB 317
Mike Rounds, SD	HSOB 502	Jack Reed, RI	HSOB 728
Thom Tillis, NC	DSOB 185	Jon Tester, MT	HSOB 31
John Kennedy, LA	RSOB 416	Mark Warner, VA	HSOB 703
Jerry Moran, KS	DSOB 521	Brian Schatz, HI	HSOB 722
Kevin Cramer, ND	DSOB B40-C	Chris Van Hollen, MD	HSOB 11
Richard Shelby, AL	RSOB 304	Catherine Cortez Masto,	HSOB 516
Pat Toomey, PA	RSOB 248	NV	
Ben Sasse, NE	RSOB 136	Doug Jones, AL	RSOB 326
Mike Crapo, ID	DSOB 239	Sherrod Brown, OH	HSOB 503

HOUSING, TRANSPORTATION & COMMUNITY DEVELOPMENT
Room: RSOB 455
Phone: 202.224.3521

Majority:		Minority:	
C: David Perdue, GA	RSOB 455	**RM: Bob Menendez, NJ**	HSOB 52
Richard Shelby, AL	RSOB 304	Jack Reed, RI	HSOB 72
Tom Cotton, AR	RSOB 124	Elizabeth Warren, MA	HSOB 31
Mike Rounds, SD	HSOB 502	Catherine Cortez Masto,	HSOB 51
Martha McSally, AZ	DSOB B40D	NV	
Jerry Moran, KS	DSOB 521	Doug Jones, AL	RSOB 32
Kevin Cramer, ND	DSOB B40-C	Tina Smith, MN	HSOB 72
Mike Crapo, ID	DSOB 239	Sherrod Brown, OH	HSOB 50

NATIONAL SECURITY & INTERNATIONAL TRADE & FINANCE
Room:

Majority:		Minority:	
C: Ben Sasse, NE	RSOB 136	**RM: Mark Warner, VA**	HSOB 70
Martha McSally, AZ	DSOB B40D	Brian Schatz, HI	HSOB 72
Jerry Moran, KS	DSOB 521	Chris Van Hollen, MD	HSOB 11
Pat Toomey, PA	RSOB 248	Kyrsten Sinema, AZ	HSOB 825B-
Tim Scott, SC	HSOB 104	Sherrod Brown, OH	HSOB 50
Mike Crapo, ID	DSOB 239		

SECURITIES, INSURANCE & INVESTMENT
Room: RSOB 248
Phone: 202.224.4254

Majority:		Minority:	
C: Pat Toomey, PA	RSOB 248	**RM: Chris Van Hollen, MD**	HSOB 1
Richard Shelby, AL	RSOB 304	Jack Reed, RI	HSOB 7
Martha McSally, AZ	DSOB B40D	Bob Menendez, NJ	HSOB 5
Tim Scott, SC	HSOB 104	Jon Tester, MT	HSOB 3
Tom Cotton, AR	RSOB 124	Mark Warner, VA	HSOB 7
Mike Rounds, SD	HSOB 502	Elizabeth Warren, MA	HSOB 3
David Perdue, GA	RSOB 455	Tina Smith, MN	HSOB 7
Thom Tillis, NC	DSOB 185	Kyrsten Sinema, AZ	HSOB 825B
John Kennedy, LA	RSOB 416	Sherrod Brown, OH	HSOB 5
Mike Crapo, ID	DSOB 239		

BUDGET

Room: DSOB 624
Website: www.budget.senate.gov
Phone: 202.224.0642
Ratio: 11 Republicans/10 Democrats
Subcommittees: 0

Majority:		Minority:	
C: Mike Enzi, WY	RSOB 379 A	RM: Bernie Sanders, VT	DSOB 332
Chuck Grassley, IA	HSOB 135	Patty Murray, WA	RSOB 154
Mike Crapo, ID	DSOB 239	Ron Wyden, OR	DSOB 221
Lindsey Graham, SC	RSOB 290	Debbie Stabenow, MI	HSOB 731
Pat Toomey, PA	RSOB 248	Sheldon Whitehouse, RI	HSOB 530
Ron Johnson, WI	HSOB 328	Mark Warner, VA	HSOB 703
David Perdue, GA	RSOB 455	Jeff Merkley, OR	HSOB 313
Mike Braun, IN	RSOB B85	Tim Kaine, VA	RSOB 231
Rick Scott, FL	HSOB 716	Chris Van Hollen, MD	HSOB 110
John Kennedy, LA	RSOB 416	Kamala Harris, CA	HSOB 112
Kevin Cramer, ND	DSOB B40 C		

Majority CoS: Betsy McDonnell   **Minority CoS:** Warren Scott Gunnels

COMMERCE, SCIENCE & TRANSPORTATION

Room: DSOB 512
Website: www.commerce.senate.gov
Phone: 202.224.1251
Ratio: 14 Republicans/12 Democrats
Subcommittees: 6

Majority:		Minority:	
C: Roger Wicker, MS	DSOB 555	RM: Maria Cantwell, WA	HSOB 511
John Thune, SD	DSOB 511	Amy Klobuchar, MN	DSOB 425
Roy Blunt, MO	RSOB 260	Richard Blumenthal, CT	HSOB 706
Ted Cruz, TX	RSOB 404	Brian Schatz, HI	HSOB 722
Deb Fischer, NE	RSOB 454	Ed Markey, MA	DSOB 255
Jerry Moran, KS	DSOB 521	Tom Udall, NM	HSOB 531
Dan Sullivan, AK	HSOB 302	Gary Peters, MI	HSOB 724
Cory Gardner, CO	RSOB 354	Tammy Baldwin, WI	HSOB 709
Marsha Blackburn, TN	DSOB 357	Tammy Duckworth, IL	HSOB 524
Shelley Capito, WV	RSOB 172	Jon Tester, MT	HSOB 311
Mike Lee, UT	RSOB 361 A	Kyrsten Sinema, AZ	HSOB 825B C
Ron Johnson, WI	HSOB 328	Jacklyn Rosen, NV	DSOB G12
Todd Young, IN	RSOB 400		
Rick Scott, FL	HSOB 716		

Majority CoS: John Keast   **Minority CoS:** Kim E. Lipsky
Majority Sched: Theresa Eugene

---------- Subcommittees ----------

COMMUNICATIONS, TECHNOLOGY, INNOVATION & THE INTERNET
Room: DSOB 512
Phone: 202.224.1251

Majority:		Minority:	
C: John Thune, SD	DSOB 511	RM: Brian Schatz, HI	HSOB 722
Marsha Blackburn, TN	DSOB 357	Tammy Baldwin, WI	HSOB 709
Roy Blunt, MO	RSOB 260	Richard Blumenthal, CT	HSOB 706
Shelley Capito, WV	RSOB 172	Tammy Duckworth, IL	HSOB 524
Ted Cruz, TX	RSOB 404	Amy Klobuchar, MN	DSOB 425
Deb Fischer, NE	RSOB 454	Ed Markey, MA	DSOB 255
Cory Gardner, CO	RSOB 354	Gary Peters, MI	HSOB 724
Ron Johnson, WI	HSOB 328	Jacklyn Rosen, NV	DSOB G12
Mike Lee, UT	RSOB 361-A	Kyrsten Sinema, AZ	HSOB 825B-C
Jerry Moran, KS	DSOB 521	Jon Tester, MT	HSOB 311
Rick Scott, FL	HSOB 716	Tom Udall, NM	HSOB 531
Dan Sullivan, AK	HSOB 302	Maria Cantwell, WA	HSOB 511
Todd Young, IN	RSOB 400		
Roger Wicker, MS	DSOB 555		

SUBCOMMITTEE MANUFACTURING, TRADE & CONSUMER PROTECTION
Room: DSOB 512
Phone: 202.224.1251

Majority:		Minority:	
C: Jerry Moran, KS	DSOB 521	RM: Richard Blumenthal, CT	HSOB 706
Roy Blunt, MO	RSOB 260		
Shelley Capito, WV	RSOB 172	Tammy Baldwin, WI	HSOB 709
Deb Fischer, NE	RSOB 454	Amy Klobuchar, MN	DSOB 425
Ron Johnson, WI	HSOB 328	Ed Markey, MA	DSOB 255
Mike Lee, UT	RSOB 361-A	Jacklyn Rosen, NV	DSOB G12
Dan Sullivan, AK	HSOB 302	Brian Schatz, HI	HSOB 722

SENATE COMMITTEES

John Thune, SD	DSOB 511	Kyrsten Sinema, AZ	HSOB 825B-C
Todd Young, IN	RSOB 400	Tom Udall, NM	HSOB 531
Roger Wicker, MS	DSOB 555	Maria Cantwell, WA	HSOB 511

SUBCOMMITTEE ON AVIATION & SPACE
Room: DSOB 512
Phone: 202.224.1251

Majority:		Minority:	
C: Ted Cruz, TX	RSOB 404	RM: Kyrsten Sinema, AZ	HSOB 825B-C
Marsha Blackburn, TN	DSOB 357	Tammy Duckworth, IL	HSOB 524
Roy Blunt, MO	RSOB 260	Gary Peters, MI	HSOB 724
Shelley Capito, WV	RSOB 172	Jacklyn Rosen, NV	DSOB G12
Cory Gardner, CO	RSOB 354	Brian Schatz, HI	HSOB 722
Mike Lee, UT	RSOB 361-A	Jon Tester, MT	HSOB 311
Jerry Moran, KS	DSOB 521	Tom Udall, NM	HSOB 531
John Thune, SD	DSOB 511	Maria Cantwell, WA	HSOB 511
Roger Wicker, MS	DSOB 555		

SUBCOMMITTEE ON SCIENCE, OCEANS, FISHERIES & WEATHER
Room: DSOB 512
Phone: 202.224.1251

Majority:		Minority:	
C: Cory Gardner, CO	RSOB 354	RM: Tammy Baldwin, WI	HSOB 709
Ted Cruz, TX	RSOB 404	Richard Blumenthal, CT	HSOB 706
Ron Johnson, WI	HSOB 328	Gary Peters, MI	HSOB 724
Rick Scott, FL	HSOB 716	Brian Schatz, HI	HSOB 722
Dan Sullivan, AK	HSOB 302	Maria Cantwell, WA	HSOB 511
Roger Wicker, MS	DSOB 555		

SUBCOMMITTEE ON SECURITY
Room: DSOB 512
Phone: 202.224.1251

Majority:		Minority:	
C: Dan Sullivan, AK	HSOB 302	RM: Ed Markey, MA	DSOB 255
Marsha Blackburn, TN	DSOB 357	Richard Blumenthal, CT	HSOB 706
Roy Blunt, MO	RSOB 260	Tammy Duckworth, IL	HSOB 524
Ted Cruz, TX	RSOB 404	Amy Klobuchar, MN	DSOB 42
Deb Fischer, NE	RSOB 454	Jacklyn Rosen, NV	DSOB G1
Ron Johnson, WI	HSOB 328	Brian Schatz, HI	HSOB 72
Mike Lee, UT	RSOB 361-A	Kyrsten Sinema, AZ	HSOB 825B-C
Rick Scott, FL	HSOB 716	Tom Udall, NM	HSOB 53
Todd Young, IN	RSOB 400	Maria Cantwell, WA	HSOB 51
Roger Wicker, MS	DSOB 555		

SUBCOMMITTEE ON TRANSPORTATION & SAFETY
Room: DSOB 512
Phone: 202.224.1251

Majority:		Minority:	
C: Deb Fischer, NE	RSOB 454	RM: Tammy Duckworth, IL	HSOB 52
Roy Blunt, MO	RSOB 260		
Shelley Capito, WV	RSOB 172	Tammy Baldwin, WI	HSOB 70
Cory Gardner, CO	RSOB 354	Richard Blumenthal, CT	HSOB 70
Jerry Moran, KS	DSOB 521	Amy Klobuchar, MN	DSOB 42
Rick Scott, FL	HSOB 716	Ed Markey, MA	DSOB 25
John Thune, SD	DSOB 511	Gary Peters, MI	HSOB 72
Todd Young, IN	RSOB 400	Kyrsten Sinema, AZ	HSOB 825B
Roger Wicker, MS	DSOB 555	Maria Cantwell, WA	HSOB 5

ENERGY & NATURAL RESOURCES

Room: DSOB 304
Website: www.energy.senate.gov
Phone: 202.224.4971
Ratio: 11 Republicans/9 Democrats
Subcommittees: 8

Majority:		Minority:	
C: Lisa Murkowski, AK	HSOB 522	RM: Joe Manchin, WV	HSOB 3
John Barrasso, WY	DSOB 307	Maria Cantwell, WA	HSOB 5
James Risch, ID	RSOB 483	Ron Wyden, OR	DSOB 2
Mike Lee, UT	RSOB 361 A	Bernie Sanders, VT	DSOB 3
Steve Daines, MT	HSOB 320	Debbie Stabenow, MI	HSOB 7
Bill Cassidy, LA	HSOB 520	Martin Heinrich, NM	HSOB 3
Cory Gardner, CO	RSOB 354	Mazie Hirono, HI	HSOB 7
Cindy Hyde-Smith, MS	HSOB 702	Angus King, ME	HSOB 1
Martha McSally, AZ	DSOB B40D	Catherine Cortez Masto, NV	HSOB 5
Lamar Alexander, TN	DSOB 455		
John Hoeven, ND	RSOB 338		

Majority CoS: Brian Patrick Hughes   **Minority CoS:** Sarah Venuto

———————————— Subcommittees ————————————

ENERGY
Room: DSOB 304
Phone: 202.224.4971

Majority:		Minority:	
Martin Heinrich, NM	HSOB 303	Bill Cassidy, LA	HSOB 520
Debbie Stabenow, MI	HSOB 731	James Risch, ID	RSOB 483
Mazie Hirono, HI	HSOB 713	Mike Lee, UT	RSOB 361-A
Bernie Sanders, VT	DSOB 332	Steve Daines, MT	HSOB 320
Ron Wyden, OR	DSOB 221	Cory Gardner, CO	RSOB 354
Maria Cantwell, WA	HSOB 511	Cindy Hyde-Smith, MS	HSOB 702
Angus King, ME	HSOB 133	Martha McSally, AZ	DSOB B40D
Catherine Cortez Masto, NV	HSOB 516	Lamar Alexander, TN	DSOB 455
		John Hoeven, ND	RSOB 338

ENERGY
Room:

Majority:		Minority:	
C: Bill Cassidy, LA	HSOB 520	RM: Martin Heinrich, NM	HSOB 303
James Risch, ID	RSOB 483	Ron Wyden, OR	DSOB 221
Mike Lee, UT	RSOB 361-A	Maria Cantwell, WA	HSOB 511
Steve Daines, MT	HSOB 320	Bernie Sanders, VT	DSOB 332
Cory Gardner, CO	RSOB 354	Debbie Stabenow, MI	HSOB 731
Cindy Hyde-Smith, MS	HSOB 702	Mazie Hirono, HI	HSOB 713
Martha McSally, AZ	DSOB B40D	Angus King, ME	HSOB 133
Lamar Alexander, TN	DSOB 455	Catherine Cortez Masto, NV	HSOB 516
John Hoeven, ND	RSOB 338	Joe Manchin, WV	HSOB 306
Lisa Murkowski, AK	HSOB 522		

NATIONAL PARKS
Room:

Majority:		Minority:	
C: Steve Daines, MT	HSOB 320	RM: Angus King, ME	HSOB 133
John Barrasso, WY	DSOB 307	Bernie Sanders, VT	DSOB 332
Mike Lee, UT	RSOB 361-A	Debbie Stabenow, MI	HSOB 731
Cory Gardner, CO	RSOB 354	Martin Heinrich, NM	HSOB 303
Cindy Hyde-Smith, MS	HSOB 702	Mazie Hirono, HI	HSOB 713
Lamar Alexander, TN	DSOB 455	Joe Manchin, WV	HSOB 306
John Hoeven, ND	RSOB 338		
Lisa Murkowski, AK	HSOB 522		

NATIONAL PARKS
Room: DSOB 304
Phone: 202.224.4971

Majority:		Minority:	
Angus King, ME	HSOB 133	Steve Daines, MT	HSOB 320
Debbie Stabenow, MI	HSOB 731	John Barrasso, WY	DSOB 307
Mazie Hirono, HI	HSOB 713	Lamar Alexander, TN	DSOB 455
Bernie Sanders, VT	DSOB 332	John Hoeven, ND	RSOB 338
Martin Heinrich, NM	HSOB 303	Cory Gardner, CO	RSOB 354
		Mike Lee, UT	RSOB 361-A
		Cindy Hyde-Smith, MS	HSOB 702

PUBLIC LANDS, FORESTS & MINING
Room:

Majority:		Minority:	
C: Mike Lee, UT	RSOB 361-A	RM: Ron Wyden, OR	DSOB 221
John Barrasso, WY	DSOB 307	Maria Cantwell, WA	HSOB 511
James Risch, ID	RSOB 483	Debbie Stabenow, MI	HSOB 731
Steve Daines, MT	HSOB 320	Martin Heinrich, NM	HSOB 303
Bill Cassidy, LA	HSOB 520	Mazie Hirono, HI	HSOB 713
Cory Gardner, CO	RSOB 354	Angus King, ME	HSOB 133
Cindy Hyde-Smith, MS	HSOB 702	Catherine Cortez Masto, NV	HSOB 516
Martha McSally, AZ	DSOB B40D		
John Hoeven, ND	RSOB 338	Joe Manchin, WV	HSOB 306
Lisa Murkowski, AK	HSOB 522		

PUBLIC LANDS, FORESTS, AND MINING
Room: DSOB 304
Phone: 202.224.4971

Majority:		Minority:	
Ron Wyden, OR	DSOB 221	Mike Lee, UT	RSOB 361-A
Debbie Stabenow, MI	HSOB 731	John Barrasso, WY	DSOB 307
Mazie Hirono, HI	HSOB 713	James Risch, ID	RSOB 483
Martin Heinrich, NM	HSOB 303	Bill Cassidy, LA	HSOB 520
Maria Cantwell, WA	HSOB 511	John Hoeven, ND	RSOB 338
Angus King, ME	HSOB 133	Cory Gardner, CO	RSOB 354
		Steve Daines, MT	HSOB 320

Catherine Cortez Masto, NV	HSOB 516	Martha McSally, AZ	DSOB B40D
		Cindy Hyde-Smith, MS	HSOB 702

WATER & POWER
Room:

Majority:		Minority:	
C: Martha McSally, AZ	DSOB B40D	**RM: Catherine Cortez Masto, NV**	HSOB 516
John Barrasso, WY	DSOB 307		
James Risch, ID	RSOB 483	Ron Wyden, OR	DSOB 221
Bill Cassidy, LA	HSOB 520	Maria Cantwell, WA	HSOB 511
Cory Gardner, CO	RSOB 354	Bernie Sanders, VT	DSOB 332
Lamar Alexander, TN	DSOB 455	Joe Manchin, WV	HSOB 306
Lisa Murkowski, AK	HSOB 522		

WATER AND POWER
Room: DSOB 304
Phone: 202.224.4971

Majority:		Minority:	
Catherine Cortez Masto, NV	HSOB 516	Martha McSally, AZ	DSOB B40D
		John Barrasso, WY	DSOB 307
Bernie Sanders, VT	DSOB 332	James Risch, ID	RSOB 483
Ron Wyden, OR	DSOB 221	Lamar Alexander, TN	DSOB 455
Maria Cantwell, WA	HSOB 511	Bill Cassidy, LA	HSOB 520
		Cory Gardner, CO	RSOB 354

ENVIRONMENT & PUBLIC WORKS

Room: DSOB 410
Website: www.epw.senate.gov
Phone: 202.224.6176
Ratio: 11 Republicans/10 Democrats
Subcommittees: 4

Majority:		Minority:	
C: John Barrasso, WY	DSOB 307	**RM: Tom Carper, DE**	HSOB 51
James Inhofe, OK	RSOB 205	Ben Cardin, MD	HSOB 50
Shelley Capito, WV	RSOB 172	Bernie Sanders, VT	DSOB 33
Kevin Cramer, ND	DSOB B40 C	Sheldon Whitehouse, RI	HSOB 53
Mike Braun, IN	RSOB B85	Jeff Merkley, OR	HSOB 31
Mike Rounds, SD	HSOB 502	Kirsten Gillibrand, NY	RSOB 47
Dan Sullivan, AK	HSOB 302	Cory Booker, NJ	HSOB 71
John Boozman, AR	HSOB 141	Ed Markey, MA	DSOB 25
Roger Wicker, MS	DSOB 555	Tammy Duckworth, IL	HSOB 52
Richard Shelby, AL	RSOB 304	Chris Van Hollen, MD	HSOB 11
Joni Ernst, IA	HSOB 730		

Majority CoS: Richard Mather Russell **Minority CoS:** Mary Frances Repko
Minority Sched: Carolyn Mack

--- Subcommittees ---

CLEAN AIR & NUCLEAR SAFETY
Room:

Majority:		Minority:	
C: Mike Braun, IN	RSOB B85	**RM: Sheldon Whitehouse, RI**	HSOB 53
James Inhofe, OK	RSOB 205		
Shelley Capito, WV	RSOB 172	Ben Cardin, MD	HSOB 50
Kevin Cramer, ND	DSOB B40-C	Bernie Sanders, VT	DSOB 33
Mike Rounds, SD	HSOB 502	Jeff Merkley, OR	HSOB 31
Dan Sullivan, AK	HSOB 302	Kirsten Gillibrand, NY	RSOB 47
John Boozman, AR	HSOB 141	Cory Booker, NJ	HSOB 7
Roger Wicker, MS	DSOB 555	Ed Markey, MA	DSOB 25
Joni Ernst, IA	HSOB 730	Tammy Duckworth, IL	HSOB 52

FISHERIES, WATER, AND WILDLIFE
Room:

Majority:		Minority:	
C: Kevin Cramer, ND	DSOB B40-C	**RM: Tammy Duckworth, IL**	HSOB 52
Shelley Capito, WV	RSOB 172		
Mike Braun, IN	RSOB B85	Ben Cardin, MD	HSOB 5
Dan Sullivan, AK	HSOB 302	Bernie Sanders, VT	DSOB 3
John Boozman, AR	HSOB 141	Sheldon Whitehouse, RI	HSOB 5
Roger Wicker, MS	DSOB 555	Jeff Merkley, OR	HSOB 3
Richard Shelby, AL	RSOB 304	Chris Van Hollen, MD	HSOB 1

SUPERFUND, WASTE MANAGEMENT, & REGULATORY OVERSIGHT
Room:

Majority:		Minority:	
C: Mike Rounds, SD	HSOB 502	**RM: Cory Booker, NJ**	HSOB 7
James Inhofe, OK	RSOB 205	Kirsten Gillibrand, NY	RSOB 4
Richard Shelby, AL	RSOB 304	Ed Markey, MA	DSOB 2
Joni Ernst, IA	HSOB 730		

TRANSPORTATION & INFRASTRUCTURE

Room:

Majority:		Minority:	
C: Shelley Capito, WV	RSOB 172	**RM: Ben Cardin, MD**	HSOB 509
James Inhofe, OK	RSOB 205	Bernie Sanders, VT	DSOB 332
Kevin Cramer, ND	DSOB B40-C	Sheldon Whitehouse, RI	HSOB 530
Mike Braun, IN	RSOB B85	Jeff Merkley, OR	HSOB 313
Mike Rounds, SD	HSOB 502	Kirsten Gillibrand, NY	RSOB 478
Dan Sullivan, AK	HSOB 302	Cory Booker, NJ	HSOB 717
John Boozman, AR	HSOB 141	Ed Markey, MA	DSOB 255
Roger Wicker, MS	DSOB 555	Chris Van Hollen, MD	HSOB 110
Richard Shelby, AL	RSOB 304		

FINANCE

Room: DSOB 219
Website: www.finance.senate.gov
Phone: 202.224.4515
Ratio: 15 Republicans/13 Democrats
Subcommittees: 6

Majority:		Minority:	
C: Chuck Grassley, IA	HSOB 135	**RM: Ron Wyden, OR**	DSOB 221
Mike Crapo, ID	DSOB 239	Debbie Stabenow, MI	HSOB 731
Pat Roberts, KS	HSOB 109	Maria Cantwell, WA	HSOB 511
Mike Enzi, WY	RSOB 379 A	Bob Menendez, NJ	HSOB 528
John Cornyn, TX	HSOB 517	Tom Carper, DE	HSOB 513
John Thune, SD	DSOB 511	Ben Cardin, MD	HSOB 509
Richard Burr, NC	RSOB 217	Sherrod Brown, OH	HSOB 503
Johnny Isakson, GA	RSOB 131	Michael Bennet, CO	RSOB 261
Rob Portman, OH	RSOB 448	Bob Casey, PA	RSOB 393
Pat Toomey, PA	RSOB 248	Mark Warner, VA	HSOB 703
Tim Scott, SC	HSOB 104	Sheldon Whitehouse, RI	HSOB 530
Bill Cassidy, LA	HSOB 520	Maggie Hassan, NH	HSOB 330
James Lankford, OK	HSOB 316	Catherine Cortez Masto,	HSOB 516
Steve Daines, MT	HSOB 320	NV	
Todd Young, IN	RSOB 400		

Majority CoS: Kolan L. Davis   **Minority CoS:** Joshua L. Sheinkman

――――――――― Subcommittees ―――――――――

ENERGY, NATURAL RESOURCES & INFRASTRUCTURE
Room:

Majority:		Minority:	
C: Tim Scott, SC	HSOB 104	**RM: Michael Bennet, CO**	RSOB 261
Chuck Grassley, IA	HSOB 135	Ron Wyden, OR	DSOB 221
Mike Crapo, ID	DSOB 239	Maria Cantwell, WA	HSOB 511
Pat Roberts, KS	HSOB 109	Tom Carper, DE	HSOB 513
Mike Enzi, WY	RSOB 379-A	Sheldon Whitehouse, RI	HSOB 530
John Cornyn, TX	HSOB 517	Maggie Hassan, NH	HSOB 330
Richard Burr, NC	RSOB 217		
Steve Daines, MT	HSOB 320		

FISCAL RESPONSIBILITY & ECONOMIC GROWTH
Room:

Majority:		Minority:	
C: Bill Cassidy, LA	HSOB 520	**RM: Maggie Hassan, NH**	HSOB 330
Tim Scott, SC	HSOB 104	Ron Wyden, OR	DSOB 221
James Lankford, OK	HSOB 316		
Chuck Grassley, IA	HSOB 135		

HEALTH CARE
Room:

Majority:		Minority:	
C: Pat Toomey, PA	RSOB 248	**RM: Debbie Stabenow, MI**	HSOB 731
Chuck Grassley, IA	HSOB 135	Maria Cantwell, WA	HSOB 511
Pat Roberts, KS	HSOB 109	Bob Menendez, NJ	HSOB 528
Mike Enzi, WY	RSOB 379-A	Tom Carper, DE	HSOB 513
John Thune, SD	DSOB 511	Ben Cardin, MD	HSOB 509
Richard Burr, NC	RSOB 217	Sherrod Brown, OH	HSOB 503
Johnny Isakson, GA	RSOB 131	Bob Casey, PA	RSOB 393
Tim Scott, SC	HSOB 104	Mark Warner, VA	HSOB 703
Bill Cassidy, LA	HSOB 520	Sheldon Whitehouse, RI	HSOB 530
James Lankford, OK	HSOB 316	Maggie Hassan, NH	HSOB 330
Steve Daines, MT	HSOB 320	Catherine Cortez Masto,	HSOB 516
Todd Young, IN	RSOB 400	NV	
		Ron Wyden, OR	DSOB 221

INTERNATIONAL TRADE, CUSTOMS & GLOBAL COMPETITIVENESS
Room:

SENATE COMMITTEES

Majority:		Minority:	
C: John Cornyn, TX	HSOB 517	**RM: Bob Casey, PA**	RSOB 393
Mike Crapo, ID	DSOB 239	Ron Wyden, OR	DSOB 221
Pat Roberts, KS	HSOB 109	Debbie Stabenow, MI	HSOB 731
John Thune, SD	DSOB 511	Maria Cantwell, WA	HSOB 511
Johnny Isakson, GA	RSOB 131	Bob Menendez, NJ	HSOB 528
Rob Portman, OH	RSOB 448	Ben Cardin, MD	HSOB 509
Pat Toomey, PA	RSOB 248	Sherrod Brown, OH	HSOB 503
Tim Scott, SC	HSOB 104	Mark Warner, VA	HSOB 703
Bill Cassidy, LA	HSOB 520	Catherine Cortez Masto,	HSOB 516
Todd Young, IN	RSOB 400	NV	
Chuck Grassley, IA	HSOB 135		

SOCIAL SECURITY, PENSIONS & FAMILY POLICY
Room:

Majority:		Minority:	
C: Rob Portman, OH	RSOB 448	**RM: Sherrod Brown, OH**	HSOB 503
Chuck Grassley, IA	HSOB 135	Michael Bennet, CO	RSOB 261
Bill Cassidy, LA	HSOB 520	Bob Casey, PA	RSOB 393
James Lankford, OK	HSOB 316	Catherine Cortez Masto,	HSOB 516
Todd Young, IN	RSOB 400	NV	
		Ron Wyden, OR	DSOB 221

TAXATION & IRS OVERSIGHT
Room:

Majority:		Minority:	
C: John Thune, SD	DSOB 511	**RM: Mark Warner, VA**	HSOB 703
Mike Crapo, ID	DSOB 239	Bob Menendez, NJ	HSOB 528
Mike Enzi, WY	RSOB 379-A	Tom Carper, DE	HSOB 514
John Cornyn, TX	HSOB 517	Ben Cardin, MD	HSOB 509
Richard Burr, NC	RSOB 217	Michael Bennet, CO	RSOB 261
Johnny Isakson, GA	RSOB 131	Sheldon Whitehouse, RI	HSOB 530
Rob Portman, OH	RSOB 448	Ron Wyden, OR	DSOB 221
Pat Toomey, PA	RSOB 248		
Chuck Grassley, IA	HSOB 135		

FOREIGN RELATIONS

Room: DSOB 423
Website: www.foreign.senate.gov
Phone: 202.224.4651
Ratio: 12 Republicans/10 Democrats
Subcommittees: 14

Majority:		Minority:	
C: James Risch, ID	RSOB 483	**RM: Bob Menendez, NJ**	HSOB 528
Marco Rubio, FL	RSOB 284	Ben Cardin, MD	HSOB 509
Ron Johnson, WI	HSOB 328	Jeanne Shaheen, NH	HSOB 506
Cory Gardner, CO	RSOB 354	Christopher Coons, DE	RSOB 127
Mitt Romney, UT	RSOB B33	Tom Udall, NM	HSOB 531
Lindsey Graham, SC	RSOB 290	Chris Murphy, CT	HSOB 136
Johnny Isakson, GA	RSOB 131	Tim Kaine, VA	RSOB 231
John Barrasso, WY	DSOB 307	Ed Markey, MA	DSOB 255
Rob Portman, OH	RSOB 448	Jeff Merkley, OR	HSOB 313
Rand Paul, KY	RSOB 167	Cory Booker, NJ	HSOB 717
Todd Young, IN	RSOB 400		
Ted Cruz, TX	RSOB 404		

Majority CoS: Chris Socha   **Minority CoS:** Jessica Lewis

—————————— Subcommittees ——————————

AFRICA & GLOBAL HEALTH POLICY
Room:

Majority:		Minority:	
C: Lindsey Graham, SC	RSOB 290	**RM: Tim Kaine, VA**	RSOB 2
Johnny Isakson, GA	RSOB 131	Christopher Coons, DE	RSOB 127
Rob Portman, OH	RSOB 448	Cory Booker, NJ	HSOB 7
Ron Johnson, WI	HSOB 328	Chris Murphy, CT	HSOB 1
Ted Cruz, TX	RSOB 404		

AFRICA AND GLOBAL HEALTH POLICY
Room: DSOB 423

Majority:		Minority:	
Tim Kaine, VA	RSOB 231	Lindsey Graham, SC	RSOB 2
Chris Murphy, CT	HSOB 136	Johnny Isakson, GA	RSOB 1
Christopher Coons, DE	RSOB 127-A	Rob Portman, OH	RSOB 4
Cory Booker, NJ	HSOB 717	Ron Johnson, WI	HSOB 3
		Ted Cruz, TX	RSOB 4

EAST ASIA, THE PACIFIC & INTERNATIONAL CYBERSECURITY POLICY
Room:

Majority:		Minority:	
C: Cory Gardner, CO	RSOB 354	RM: Ed Markey, MA	DSOB 255
Marco Rubio, FL	RSOB 284	Christopher Coons, DE	RSOB 127-A
Ron Johnson, WI	HSOB 328	Jeff Merkley, OR	HSOB 313
Johnny Isakson, GA	RSOB 131	Tom Udall, NM	HSOB 531
Todd Young, IN	RSOB 400		

EAST ASIA, THE PACIFIC, AND INTERNATIONAL CYBERSECURITY POLICY
Room: DSOB 423

Majority:		Minority:	
Ed Markey, MA	DSOB 255	Cory Gardner, CO	RSOB 354
Tom Udall, NM	HSOB 531	Johnny Isakson, GA	RSOB 131
Jeff Merkley, OR	HSOB 313	Todd Young, IN	RSOB 400
Christopher Coons, DE	RSOB 127-A	Marco Rubio, FL	RSOB 284
		Ron Johnson, WI	HSOB 328

EUROPE & REGIONAL SECURITY COOPERATION
Room:

Majority:		Minority:	
C: Ron Johnson, WI	HSOB 328	RM: Jeanne Shaheen, NH	HSOB 506
John Barrasso, WY	DSOB 307	Chris Murphy, CT	HSOB 136
Rob Portman, OH	RSOB 448	Ben Cardin, MD	HSOB 509
Rand Paul, KY	RSOB 167	Christopher Coons, DE	RSOB 127-A
Mitt Romney, UT	RSOB B33		

EUROPE AND REGIONAL SECURITY COOPERATION
Room: DSOB 423

Majority:		Minority:	
Jeanne Shaheen, NH	HSOB 506	Ron Johnson, WI	HSOB 328
Ben Cardin, MD	HSOB 509	John Barrasso, WY	DSOB 307
Chris Murphy, CT	HSOB 136	Rand Paul, KY	RSOB 167
Christopher Coons, DE	RSOB 127-A	Rob Portman, OH	RSOB 448
		Mitt Romney, UT	RSOB B33

INTERNAT'L DEV INSTIT & INTERNAT'L ECON, ENERGY & ENVIRON POLICY
Room:

Majority:		Minority:	
C: Todd Young, IN	RSOB 400	RM: Jeff Merkley, OR	HSOB 313
Mitt Romney, UT	RSOB B33	Tom Udall, NM	HSOB 531
Rand Paul, KY	RSOB 167	Ed Markey, MA	DSOB 255
John Barrasso, WY	DSOB 307	Cory Booker, NJ	HSOB 717
Lindsey Graham, SC	RSOB 290		

MULTILATERAL INTERNATIONAL DEVELOPMENT, MULTILATERAL INSTITUTIONS, AND INTERNATIONAL ECONOMIC, ENERGY, AND ENVIRONMENTAL POLICY
Room: DSOB 423

Majority:		Minority:	
Jeff Merkley, OR	HSOB 313	Todd Young, IN	RSOB 400
Ed Markey, MA	DSOB 255	John Barrasso, WY	DSOB 307
Tom Udall, NM	HSOB 531	Lindsey Graham, SC	RSOB 290
Cory Booker, NJ	HSOB 717	Rand Paul, KY	RSOB 167
		Mitt Romney, UT	RSOB B33

NEAR EAST, SOUTH ASIA, CENTRAL ASIA & COUNTERTERRORISM
Room:

Majority:		Minority:	
C: Mitt Romney, UT	RSOB B33	RM: Chris Murphy, CT	HSOB 136
Ted Cruz, TX	RSOB 404	Ben Cardin, MD	HSOB 509
Lindsey Graham, SC	RSOB 290	Jeanne Shaheen, NH	HSOB 506
Cory Gardner, CO	RSOB 354	Tim Kaine, VA	RSOB 231
Rand Paul, KY	RSOB 167		

NEAR EAST, SOUTH ASIA, CENTRAL ASIA, AND COUNTERTERRORISM
Room: DSOB 423

Majority:		Minority:	
Chris Murphy, CT	HSOB 136	Mitt Romney, UT	RSOB B33
Ben Cardin, MD	HSOB 509	Ted Cruz, TX	RSOB 404
Jeanne Shaheen, NH	HSOB 506	Lindsey Graham, SC	RSOB 290
Tim Kaine, VA	RSOB 231	Cory Gardner, CO	RSOB 354
		Rand Paul, KY	RSOB 167

STATE DEPARTMENT AND USAID MANAGEMENT, INTERNATIONAL OPERATIONS, AND BILATERAL INTERNATIONAL DEVELOPMENT

Room: DSOB 423

Majority:		Minority:	
Cory Booker, NJ	HSOB 717	Johnny Isakson, GA	RSOB 131
Ed Markey, MA	DSOB 255	Todd Young, IN	RSOB 400
Tom Udall, NM	HSOB 531	Marco Rubio, FL	RSOB 284
Jeff Merkley, OR	HSOB 313	Rand Paul, KY	RSOB 167
		Rob Portman, OH	RSOB 448

STATE DEPT & USAID MNGMNT, INTERNAT'L OPS & INTERNAT'L DEV

Room:

Majority:		Minority:	
C: Johnny Isakson, GA	RSOB 131	RM: Cory Booker, NJ	HSOB 71
Todd Young, IN	RSOB 400	Ed Markey, MA	DSOB 25
Rand Paul, KY	RSOB 167	Jeff Merkley, OR	HSOB 31
Rob Portman, OH	RSOB 448	Tom Udall, NM	HSOB 53
Marco Rubio, FL	RSOB 284		

WEST HEM CRIME CIV SEC DEM RIGHTS & WOMEN'S ISSUES

Room:

Majority:		Minority:	
C: Marco Rubio, FL	RSOB 284	RM: Ben Cardin, MD	HSOB 50
Rob Portman, OH	RSOB 448	Tom Udall, NM	HSOB 53
Ted Cruz, TX	RSOB 404	Jeanne Shaheen, NH	HSOB 50
Cory Gardner, CO	RSOB 354	Tim Kaine, VA	RSOB 23
John Barrasso, WY	DSOB 307		

WESTERN HEMISPHERE, TRANSNATIONAL CRIME, CIVILIAN SECURITY, DEMOCRACY, HUMAN RIGHTS, AND GLOBAL WOMEN'S ISSUES

Room: DSOB 423

Majority:		Minority:	
Ben Cardin, MD	HSOB 509	Marco Rubio, FL	RSOB 28
Tom Udall, NM	HSOB 531	John Barrasso, WY	DSOB 3
Jeanne Shaheen, NH	HSOB 506	Cory Gardner, CO	RSOB 3
Tim Kaine, VA	RSOB 231	Rob Portman, OH	RSOB 4
		Ted Cruz, TX	RSOB 4

HEALTH, EDUCATION, LABOR & PENSIONS

Room: DSOB 428
Website: www.help.senate.gov
Phone: 202.224.5375
Ratio: 12 Republicans/11 Democrats
Subcommittees: 3

Majority:		Minority:	
C: Lamar Alexander, TN	DSOB 455	RM: Patty Murray, WA	RSOB 1
Mike Enzi, WY	RSOB 379 A	Bernie Sanders, VT	DSOB 3
Richard Burr, NC	RSOB 217	Bob Casey, PA	RSOB 3
Johnny Isakson, GA	RSOB 131	Tammy Baldwin, WI	HSOB 7
Rand Paul, KY	RSOB 167	Chris Murphy, CT	HSOB 1
Susan Collins, ME	DSOB 413	Elizabeth Warren, MA	HSOB 3
Bill Cassidy, LA	HSOB 520	Tim Kaine, VA	RSOB 2
Pat Roberts, KS	HSOB 109	Maggie Hassan, NH	HSOB 3
Lisa Murkowski, AK	HSOB 522	Tina Smith, MN	HSOB 7
Tim Scott, SC	HSOB 104	Doug Jones, AL	RSOB 3
Mitt Romney, UT	RSOB B33	Jacklyn Rosen, NV	DSOB C
Mike Braun, IN	RSOB B85		

Majority CoS: David Cleary   **Minority CoS:** Evan Schatz

--- Subcommittees ---

CHILDREN & FAMILIES

Room: DSOB 428
Phone: 202.224.5375

Majority:		Minority:	
C: Rand Paul, KY	RSOB 167	RM: Bob Casey, PA	RSOB
Lisa Murkowski, AK	HSOB 522	Bernie Sanders, VT	DSOB
Richard Burr, NC	RSOB 217	Chris Murphy, CT	HSOB
Bill Cassidy, LA	HSOB 520	Tim Kaine, VA	RSOB
Pat Roberts, KS	HSOB 109	Maggie Hassan, NH	HSOB
Tim Scott, SC	HSOB 104	Tina Smith, MN	HSOB
Mitt Romney, UT	RSOB B33	Patty Murray, WA	RSOB
Lamar Alexander, TN	DSOB 455		

EMPLOYMENT & WORKPLACE SAFETY
Room: DSOB 428
Phone: 202.224.5375

Majority:		Minority:	
C: Johnny Isakson, GA	RSOB 131	RM: Tammy Baldwin, WI	HSOB 709
Tim Scott, SC	HSOB 104	Bob Casey, PA	RSOB 393
Rand Paul, KY	RSOB 167	Elizabeth Warren, MA	HSOB 317
Mitt Romney, UT	RSOB B33	Tina Smith, MN	HSOB 720
Mike Braun, IN	RSOB B85	Doug Jones, AL	RSOB 326
Richard Burr, NC	RSOB 217	Jacklyn Rosen, NV	DSOB G12
Bill Cassidy, LA	HSOB 520	Patty Murray, WA	RSOB 154
Lamar Alexander, TN	DSOB 455		

PRIMARY HEALTH & RETIREMENT SECURITY
Room: DSOB 428
Phone: 202.224.5375

Majority:		Minority:	
C: Mike Enzi, WY	RSOB 379-A	RM: Bernie Sanders, VT	DSOB 332
Richard Burr, NC	RSOB 217	Tammy Baldwin, WI	HSOB 709
Susan Collins, ME	DSOB 413	Chris Murphy, CT	HSOB 136
Bill Cassidy, LA	HSOB 520	Elizabeth Warren, MA	HSOB 317
Pat Roberts, KS	HSOB 109	Tim Kaine, VA	RSOB 231
Mitt Romney, UT	RSOB B33	Maggie Hassan, NH	HSOB 330
Mike Braun, IN	RSOB B85	Doug Jones, AL	RSOB 326
Lisa Murkowski, AK	HSOB 522	Jacklyn Rosen, NV	DSOB G12
Tim Scott, SC	HSOB 104	Patty Murray, WA	RSOB 154
Lamar Alexander, TN	DSOB 455		

HOMELAND SECURITY & GOVERNMENT AFFAIRS
Room: DSOB 340
Website: www.hsgac.senate.gov
Phone: 202.224.4751
Ratio: 8 Republicans/6 Democrats
Subcommittees: 3

Majority:		Minority:	
C: Ron Johnson, WI	HSOB 328	RM: Gary Peters, MI	HSOB 724
Rob Portman, OH	RSOB 448	Tom Carper, DE	HSOB 513
Rand Paul, KY	RSOB 167	Maggie Hassan, NH	HSOB 330
James Lankford, OK	HSOB 316	Kamala Harris, CA	HSOB 112
Mitt Romney, UT	RSOB B33	Kyrsten Sinema, AZ	HSOB 825B C
Rick Scott, FL	HSOB 716	Jacklyn Rosen, NV	DSOB G12
Mike Enzi, WY	RSOB 379 A		
Josh Hawley, MO	DSOB B40A		

Majority CoS: Gabrielle D'Adamo   **Minority CoS:** David Weinberg

―――――――― Subcommittees ――――――――

FEDERAL SPENDING OVERSIGHT & EMERGENCY MANAGEMENT
Room: HSOB 439
Phone: 202.224.7155

Majority:		Minority:	
C: Rand Paul, KY	RSOB 167	RM: Maggie Hassan, NH	HSOB 330
Rick Scott, FL	HSOB 716	Kamala Harris, CA	HSOB 112
Mike Enzi, WY	RSOB 379-A	Kyrsten Sinema, AZ	HSOB 825B-C
Josh Hawley, MO	DSOB B40A	Gary Peters, MI	HSOB 724
Ron Johnson, WI	HSOB 328		

INVESTIGATIONS
Room:

Majority:		Minority:	
C: Rob Portman, OH	RSOB 448	RM: Tom Carper, DE	HSOB 513
Rand Paul, KY	RSOB 167	Maggie Hassan, NH	HSOB 330
James Lankford, OK	HSOB 316	Kamala Harris, CA	HSOB 112
Mitt Romney, UT	RSOB B33	Jacklyn Rosen, NV	DSOB G12
Josh Hawley, MO	DSOB B40A	Gary Peters, MI	HSOB 724
Ron Johnson, WI	HSOB 328		

REGULATORY AFFAIRS & FEDERAL MANAGEMENT
Room: HSOB 601
Phone: 202.224.4551

Majority:		Minority:	
C: James Lankford, OK	HSOB 316	RM: Kyrsten Sinema, AZ	HSOB 825B-C
Rob Portman, OH	RSOB 448	Tom Carper, DE	HSOB 513
Mitt Romney, UT	RSOB B33	Jacklyn Rosen, NV	DSOB G12
Rick Scott, FL	HSOB 716	Gary Peters, MI	HSOB 724
Mike Enzi, WY	RSOB 379-A		
Ron Johnson, WI	HSOB 328		

INDIAN AFFAIRS

Room: HSOB 838
Website: www.indian.senate.gov
Phone: 202.224.2251
Ratio: 7 Republicans/6 Democrats
Subcommittees: 0

Majority:		Minority:	
C: John Hoeven, ND	RSOB 338	Tom Udall, NM	HSOB 53
John Barrasso, WY	DSOB 307	Maria Cantwell, WA	HSOB 51
Lisa Murkowski, AK	HSOB 522	Jon Tester, MT	HSOB 31
James Lankford, OK	HSOB 316	Brian Schatz, HI	HSOB 72
Steve Daines, MT	HSOB 320	Catherine Cortez Masto,	HSOB 51
Martha McSally, AZ	DSOB B40D	NV	
Jerry Moran, KS	DSOB 521	Tina Smith, MN	HSOB 72

Majority CoS: Mike Andrews   **Minority CoS:** Jennifer Romero

JUDICIARY

Room: DSOB 224
Website: www.judiciary.senate.gov
Phone: 202.224.5225
Ratio: 12 Republicans/10 Democrats
Subcommittees: 8

Majority:		Minority:	
C: Lindsey Graham, SC	RSOB 290	**RM: Dianne Feinstein, CA**	HSOB 33
Chuck Grassley, IA	HSOB 135	Patrick Leahy, VT	RSOB 43
John Cornyn, TX	HSOB 517	Dick Durbin, IL	HSOB 71
Mike Lee, UT	RSOB 361 A	Sheldon Whitehouse, RI	HSOB 53
Ted Cruz, TX	RSOB 404	Amy Klobuchar, MN	DSOB 42
Ben Sasse, NE	RSOB 136	Christopher Coons, DE	RSOB 127
Josh Hawley, MO	DSOB B40A	Richard Blumenthal, CT	HSOB 70
Thom Tillis, NC	DSOB 185	Mazie Hirono, HI	HSOB 71
Joni Ernst, IA	HSOB 730	Cory Booker, NJ	HSOB 71
Mike Crapo, ID	DSOB 239	Kamala Harris, CA	HSOB 1
John Kennedy, LA	RSOB 416		
Marsha Blackburn, TN	DSOB 357		

Majority CoS: Rita Jochum   **Minority CoS:** Jennifer Duck

--- Subcommittees ---

ANTITRUST, COMPETITION POLICY & CONSUMER RIGHTS
Room: RSOB 361A
Phone: 202.224.5444

Majority:		Minority:	
C: Mike Lee, UT	RSOB 361-A	**RM: Amy Klobuchar, MN**	DSOB 4
Chuck Grassley, IA	HSOB 135	Patrick Leahy, VT	RSOB 4
Josh Hawley, MO	DSOB B40A	Richard Blumenthal, CT	HSOB 7
Mike Crapo, ID	DSOB 239	Cory Booker, NJ	HSOB 7
Marsha Blackburn, TN	DSOB 357		

BORDER SECURITY & IMMIGRATION
Room:

Majority:		Minority:	
C: John Cornyn, TX	HSOB 517	**RM: Dick Durbin, IL**	HSOB 7
Lindsey Graham, SC	RSOB 290	Dianne Feinstein, CA	HSOB 3
Chuck Grassley, IA	HSOB 135	Patrick Leahy, VT	RSOB 4
Mike Lee, UT	RSOB 361-A	Amy Klobuchar, MN	DSOB 4
Ted Cruz, TX	RSOB 404	Christopher Coons, DE	RSOB 12
Josh Hawley, MO	DSOB B40A	Richard Blumenthal, CT	HSOB 7
Thom Tillis, NC	DSOB 185	Mazie Hirono, HI	HSOB 7
Joni Ernst, IA	HSOB 730	Cory Booker, NJ	HSOB 7
John Kennedy, LA	RSOB 416		

BORDER SECURITY AND IMMIGRATION
Room: DSOB 224
Phone: 202.224.7840

Majority:		Minority:	
Dick Durbin, IL	HSOB 711	John Cornyn, TX	HSOB
Dianne Feinstein, CA	HSOB 331	Chuck Grassley, IA	HSOB
Mazie Hirono, HI	HSOB 713	Lindsey Graham, SC	RSOB
Amy Klobuchar, MN	DSOB 425	Mike Lee, UT	RSOB 36
Patrick Leahy, VT	RSOB 437	Ted Cruz, TX	RSOB
Christopher Coons, DE	RSOB 127-A	Joni Ernst, IA	HSOB
Richard Blumenthal, CT	HSOB 706	Thom Tillis, NC	DSOB
Cory Booker, NJ	HSOB 717	John Kennedy, LA	RSOB
		Josh Hawley, MO	DSOB B

CONSTITUTION
Room: RSOB 404
Phone: 202.224.5922

Majority:		Minority:	
C: Ted Cruz, TX	RSOB 404	RM: Mazie Hirono, HI	HSOB 713
John Cornyn, TX	HSOB 517	Dick Durbin, IL	HSOB 711
Mike Lee, UT	RSOB 361-A	Sheldon Whitehouse, RI	HSOB 530
Ben Sasse, NE	RSOB 136	Christopher Coons, DE	RSOB 127-A
Mike Crapo, ID	DSOB 239	Kamala Harris, CA	HSOB 112
Marsha Blackburn, TN	DSOB 357		

CRIME & TERRORISM
Room: DSOB B40A
Phone: 202.224.6154

Majority:		Minority:	
C: Josh Hawley, MO	DSOB B40A	RM: Sheldon Whitehouse,	HSOB 530
Lindsey Graham, SC	RSOB 290	RI	
John Cornyn, TX	HSOB 517	Dianne Feinstein, CA	HSOB 331
Ted Cruz, TX	RSOB 404	Dick Durbin, IL	HSOB 711
Thom Tillis, NC	DSOB 185	Amy Klobuchar, MN	DSOB 425
Joni Ernst, IA	HSOB 730	Christopher Coons, DE	RSOB 127-A
John Kennedy, LA	RSOB 416	Cory Booker, NJ	HSOB 717

INTELLECTUAL PROPERTY
Room: DSOB 224
Phone: 202.224.6342

Majority:		Minority:	
Christopher Coons, DE	RSOB 127-A	Thom Tillis, NC	DSOB 185
Sheldon Whitehouse, RI	HSOB 530	Marsha Blackburn, TN	DSOB 357
Dick Durbin, IL	HSOB 711	Chuck Grassley, IA	HSOB 135
Mazie Hirono, HI	HSOB 713	John Cornyn, TX	HSOB 517
Patrick Leahy, VT	RSOB 437	Lindsey Graham, SC	RSOB 290
Richard Blumenthal, CT	HSOB 706	Mike Crapo, ID	DSOB 239
Kamala Harris, CA	HSOB 112	Mike Lee, UT	RSOB 361-A
		Ben Sasse, NE	RSOB 136

OVERSIGHT, AGENCY ACTION, FEDERAL RIGHTS & FEDERAL COURTS
Room: RSOB 136
Phone: 202.224.4224

Majority:		Minority:	
C: Ben Sasse, NE	RSOB 136	RM: Richard Blumenthal,	HSOB 706
Chuck Grassley, IA	HSOB 135	CT	
Thom Tillis, NC	DSOB 185	Patrick Leahy, VT	RSOB 437
Joni Ernst, IA	HSOB 730	Sheldon Whitehouse, RI	HSOB 530
Mike Crapo, ID	DSOB 239	Amy Klobuchar, MN	DSOB 425
John Kennedy, LA	RSOB 416	Mazie Hirono, HI	HSOB 713

SUBCOMMITTEE ON INTELLECTUAL PROPERTY
Room: DSOB 185
Phone: 202.224.6342

Majority:		Minority:	
C: Thom Tillis, NC	DSOB 185	RM: Christopher Coons,	RSOB 127-A
Lindsey Graham, SC	RSOB 290	DE	
Chuck Grassley, IA	HSOB 135	Patrick Leahy, VT	RSOB 437
John Cornyn, TX	HSOB 517	Dick Durbin, IL	HSOB 711
Mike Lee, UT	RSOB 361-A	Sheldon Whitehouse, RI	HSOB 530
Ben Sasse, NE	RSOB 136	Richard Blumenthal, CT	HSOB 706
Mike Crapo, ID	DSOB 239	Mazie Hirono, HI	HSOB 713
Marsha Blackburn, TN	DSOB 357	Kamala Harris, CA	HSOB 112

Room: RSOB 305
Website: www.rules.senate.gov
Phone: 202.224.6352
Ratio: 10 Republicans/9 Democrats
Subcommittees: 0

Majority:		Minority:	
C: Roy Blunt, MO	RSOB 260	RM: Amy Klobuchar, MN	DSOB 425
Mitch McConnell, KY	RSOB 317	Dianne Feinstein, CA	HSOB 331
Lamar Alexander, TN	DSOB 455	Charles Schumer, NY	HSOB 322
Pat Roberts, KS	HSOB 109	Dick Durbin, IL	HSOB 711
Richard Shelby, AL	RSOB 304	Tom Udall, NM	HSOB 531
Ted Cruz, TX	RSOB 404	Mark Warner, VA	HSOB 703
Shelley Capito, WV	RSOB 172	Patrick Leahy, VT	RSOB 437
Roger Wicker, MS	DSOB 555	Angus King, ME	HSOB 133
Deb Fischer, NE	RSOB 454		

Cindy Hyde-Smith, MS	HSOB 702	Catherine Cortez Masto, NV	HSOB 516

Majority CoS: Fitzhugh Elder IV   **Minority CoS:** Travis Talvitie

SMALL BUSINESS & ENTREPRENEURSHIP

Room: RSOB 428A
Website: www.sbc.senate.gov
Phone: 202.224.5175
Ratio: 10 Republicans/9 Democrats
Subcommittees: 0

Majority:		Minority:	
C: Marco Rubio, FL	RSOB 284	**RM: Ben Cardin, MD**	HSOB 509
James Risch, ID	RSOB 483	Maria Cantwell, WA	HSOB 511
Rand Paul, KY	RSOB 167	Jeanne Shaheen, NH	HSOB 506
Tim Scott, SC	HSOB 104	Ed Markey, MA	DSOB 255
Joni Ernst, IA	HSOB 730	Cory Booker, NJ	HSOB 717
James Inhofe, OK	RSOB 205	Christopher Coons, DE	RSOB 127 A
Todd Young, IN	RSOB 400	Mazie Hirono, HI	HSOB 713
John Kennedy, LA	RSOB 416	Tammy Duckworth, IL	HSOB 524
Mitt Romney, UT	RSOB B33	Jacklyn Rosen, NV	DSOB G12
Josh Hawley, MO	DSOB B40A		

Majority CoS: Mike Needham   **Minority CoS:** Sean Moore

VETERANS' AFFAIRS

Room: RSOB- Russell Senate Office Building 412
Website: www.veterans.senate.gov
Phone: 202.224.9126
Ratio: 9 Republicans/8 Democrats
Subcommittees: 0

Majority:		Minority:	
C: Johnny Isakson, GA	RSOB 131	**RM: Jon Tester, MT**	HSOB 31
Jerry Moran, KS	DSOB 521	Patty Murray, WA	RSOB 15
John Boozman, AR	HSOB 141	Bernie Sanders, VT	DSOB 33
Bill Cassidy, LA	HSOB 520	Sherrod Brown, OH	HSOB 50
Mike Rounds, SD	HSOB 502	Richard Blumenthal, CT	HSOB 70
Thom Tillis, NC	DSOB 185	Mazie Hirono, HI	HSOB 71
Dan Sullivan, AK	HSOB 302	Joe Manchin, WV	HSOB 30
Marsha Blackburn, TN	DSOB 357	Kyrsten Sinema, AZ	HSOB 825B
Kevin Cramer, ND	DSOB B40 C		

Minority CoS: Tony McClain

SELECT AND SPECIAL COMMITTEES

AGING

Room: DSOB G-31
Website: www.aging.senate.gov
Phone: 202.224.5364
Ratio: 8 Republicans/8 Democrats
Subcommittees: 0

Majority:		Minority:	
C: Susan Collins, ME	DSOB 413	**RM: Bob Casey, PA**	RSOB 393
Tim Scott, SC	HSOB 104	Kirsten Gillibrand, NY	RSOB 478
Richard Burr, NC	RSOB 217	Richard Blumenthal, CT	HSOB 706
Martha McSally, AZ	DSOB B40D	Elizabeth Warren, MA	HSOB 317
Marco Rubio, FL	RSOB 284	Catherine Cortez Masto,	HSOB 516
Josh Hawley, MO	DSOB B40A	NV	
Mike Braun, IN	RSOB B85	Doug Jones, AL	RSOB 326
Rick Scott, FL	HSOB 716	Kyrsten Sinema, AZ	HSOB 825B C
		Jacklyn Rosen, NV	DSOB G12

Majority CoS: Kevin L. Kelley   **Minority CoS:** Kathryn Mevis

ETHICS

Room: HSOB 220
Website: www.ethics.senate.gov
Phone: 202.224.2981
Ratio: 3 Republicans/3 Democrats
Subcommittees: 0

Majority:		Minority:	
C: Johnny Isakson, GA	RSOB 131	**RM: Christopher Coons,**	RSOB 127 A
Pat Roberts, KS	HSOB 109	**DE**	
James Risch, ID	RSOB 483	Brian Schatz, HI	HSOB 722
		Jeanne Shaheen, NH	HSOB 506

INTELLIGENCE

Room: HSOB 211
Website: www.intelligence.senate.gov
Phone: 202.224.1700
Ratio: 8 Republicans/7 Democrats
Subcommittees: 0

Majority:		Minority:	
C: Richard Burr, NC	RSOB 217	**RM: Mark Warner, VA**	HSOB 703
James Risch, ID	RSOB 483	Dianne Feinstein, CA	HSOB 331
Marco Rubio, FL	RSOB 284	Ron Wyden, OR	DSOB 221
Susan Collins, ME	DSOB 413	Martin Heinrich, NM	HSOB 303
Roy Blunt, MO	RSOB 260	Angus King, ME	HSOB 133
Tom Cotton, AR	RSOB 124	Kamala Harris, CA	HSOB 112
John Cornyn, TX	HSOB 517	Michael Bennet, CO	RSOB 261
Ben Sasse, NE	RSOB 136		

Majority CoS: Chris A. Joyner   **Minority CoS:** Michael Colin Casey

JOINT COMMITTEES

JOINT CONGRESSIONAL-EXECUTIVE COMMISSION ON CHINA

Website: www.cecc.gov
Information for this committee, including membership, was not finalized as of the publication date and is therefore subject to change.

JOINT ECONOMIC

Website: www.jec.senate.gov

Majority U.S. Senate:		Minority U.S. Senate:	
Mike Lee, UT	RSOB 361 A	RM: Martin Heinrich, NM	HSOB 303
Tom Cotton, AR	RSOB 124	Amy Klobuchar, MN	DSOB 425
Ben Sasse, NE	RSOB 136	Gary Peters, MI	HSOB 724
Rob Portman, OH	RSOB 448	Maggie Hassan, NH	HSOB 330
Bill Cassidy, LA	HSOB 520		
Ted Cruz, TX	RSOB 404		
Majority U.S. House:		**Minority U.S. House:**	
C: Carolyn Maloney, NY-12	RHOB 2308	Information not available as of press time.	
Joyce Beatty, OH-03	RHOB 2303		
Don Beyer, VA-08	LHOB 1119		
Lois Frankel, FL-21	RHOB 2305		
Denny Heck, WA-10	RHOB 2452		
David Trone, MD-06	LHOB 1213		

Minority CoS: Harry Gural

JOINT SECURITY & COOPERATION IN EUROPE

Website: www.csce.gov
Information for this committee, including membership, was not finalized as of the publication date and is therefore subject to change.

JOINT TAXATION

Website: www.jct.gov

Majority U.S. Senate:		Minority U.S. Senate:	
VC: Chuck Grassley, IA	HSOB 135	Ron Wyden, OR	DSOB 22
Mike Crapo, ID	DSOB 239	Debbie Stabenow, MI	HSOB 73
Mike Enzi, WY	RSOB 379 A		
Majority U.S. House:		**Minority U.S. House:**	
C: Richard Neal, MA-01	RHOB 2309	Kevin Brady, TX-08	LHOB 101
John Lewis, GA-05	CHOB 300	Devin Nunes, CA-22	LHOB 101
Lloyd Doggett, TX-35	RHOB 2307		

HOUSE COMMITTEES

Committee rosters are listed in order of ranking membership with the Chairman and Ranking Member indicated with "C" and "RM" respectively. The chairman and ranking member of each committee usually have membership status on all subcommittees of which they are not members. This is referred to as ex officio membership. These memberships are subject to the rules of the individual committees.

ADMINISTRATION

Room: LHOB 1309
Website: www.cha.house.gov
Phone: 202.225.2061
Ratio: 6 Democrats/3 Republicans
Subcommittees: 0

Majority:		Minority:	
C: Zoe Lofgren, CA-19	LHOB 1401	RM: Rodney Davis, IL-13	LHOB 1740
Jamie Raskin, MD-08	CHOB 412	Mark Walker, NC-06	LHOB 1725
Susan Davis, CA-53	LHOB 1214	Barry Loudermilk, GA-11	CHOB 422
G.K. Butterfield, NC-01	RHOB 2080		
Marcia Fudge, OH-11	RHOB 2344		
Peter Aguilar, CA-31	CHOB 109		

Majority CoS: Jamie Fleet

Minority CoS: Jen Daulby
Minority Sched: Janet G. Schwalb

AGRICULTURE

Room: LHOB 1301
Website: www.agriculture.house.gov
Phone: 202.225.2171
Ratio: 26 Democrats/21 Republicans
Subcommittees: 6

Majority:		Minority:	
C: Collin Peterson, MN-07	RHOB 2204	RM: Mike Conaway, TX-11	RHOB 2469
David Scott, GA-13	CHOB 225	Glenn Thompson, PA-15	CHOB 124
Jim Costa, CA-16	RHOB 2081	Austin Scott, GA-08	RHOB 2417
Marcia Fudge, OH-11	RHOB 2344	Rick Crawford, AR-01	RHOB 2422
Jim McGovern, MA-02	CHOB 408	Scott DesJarlais, TN-04	RHOB 2301
Filemon Vela, TX-34	CHOB 307	Vicky Hartzler, MO-04	RHOB 2235
Stacey Plaskett, VI-01	RHOB 2404	Doug LaMalfa, CA-01	CHOB 322
Alma Adams, NC-12	RHOB 2436	Rodney Davis, IL-13	LHOB 1740
Abigail Spanberger, VA-07	LHOB 1239	Theodore Yoho, FL-03	LHOB 1730
Jahana Hayes, CT-05	LHOB 1415	Rick Allen, GA-12	RHOB 2400
Antonio Delgado, NY-19	LHOB 1007	Mike Bost, IL-12	LHOB 1440
T.J. Cox, CA-21	LHOB 1728	David Rouzer, NC-07	RHOB 2439
Angela Craig, MN-02	LHOB 1523	Ralph Abraham, LA-05	CHOB 417
Anthony Brindisi, NY-22	CHOB 329	Trent Kelly, MS-01	LHOB 1005
Jeff Van Drew, NJ-02	CHOB 331	James Comer, KY-01	LHOB 1037
Josh Harder, CA-10	CHOB 131	Roger Marshall, KS-01	CHOB 312
Kim Schrier, WA-08	LHOB 1123	Don Bacon, NE-02	LHOB 1024
Chellie Pingree, ME-01	RHOB 2162	Neal Dunn, FL-02	CHOB 316
Cheri Bustos, IL-17	LHOB 1233	Dusty Johnson, SD-01	LHOB 1508
Sean Maloney, NY-18	RHOB 2331	Jim Baird, IN-04	CHOB 532
Salud Carbajal, CA-24	LHOB 1431	James Hagedorn, MN-01	CHOB 325
Alfred Lawson, FL-05	LHOB 1406		
Tom O'Halleran, AZ-01	CHOB 324		
Jimmy Panetta, CA-20	CHOB 212		
Ann Kirkpatrick, AZ-02	CHOB 309		
Cindy Axne, IA-03	CHOB 330		

Majority CoS: Anne L. Simmons   **Minority CoS:** Matt Schertz
—————————— Subcommittees ——————————

BIOTECHNOLOGY, HORTICULTURE & RESEARCH
Room: LHOB 1301
Phone: 202.225.2171

Majority:		Minority:	
C: Stacey Plaskett, VI-01	RHOB 2404	RM: Neal Dunn, FL-02	CHOB 316
Antonio Delgado, NY-19	LHOB 1007	Glenn Thompson, PA-15	CHOB 124
T. Cox, CA-21	LHOB 1728	Vicky Hartzler, MO-04	RHOB 2235
Josh Harder, CA-10	CHOB 131	Doug LaMalfa, CA-01	CHOB 322
Anthony Brindisi, NY-22	CHOB 329	Rodney Davis, IL-13	LHOB 1740
Jeff Van Drew, NJ-02	CHOB 331	Theodore Yoho, FL-03	LHOB 1730
Kim Schrier, WA-08	LHOB 1123	Mike Bost, IL-12	LHOB 1440
Chellie Pingree, ME-01	RHOB 2162	James Comer, KY-01	LHOB 1037
Salud Carbajal, CA-24	LHOB 1431	Jim Baird, IN-04	CHOB 532
Jimmy Panetta, CA-20	CHOB 212	Mike Conaway, TX-11	RHOB 2469

Sean Maloney, NY-18 — RHOB 2331
Alfred Lawson, FL-05 — LHOB 1406
Collin Peterson, MN-07 — RHOB 2204

COMMODITY EXCHANGES, ENERGY & CREDIT

Room: LHOB 1301
Phone: 202.225.2171

Majority:		Minority:	
C: David Scott, GA-13	CHOB 225	RM: Austin Scott, GA-08	RHOB 2417
Jeff Van Drew, NJ-02	CHOB 331	Rick Crawford, AR-01	RHOB 2422
Filemon Vela, TX-34	CHOB 307	Mike Bost, IL-12	LHOB 1440
Stacey Plaskett, VI-01	RHOB 2404	David Rouzer, NC-07	RHOB 2439
Abigail Spanberger, VA-07	LHOB 1239	Roger Marshall, KS-01	CHOB 312
Antonio Delgado, NY-19	LHOB 1007	Neal Dunn, FL-02	CHOB 316
Angela Craig, MN-02	LHOB 1523	Dusty Johnson, SD-01	LHOB 1508
Sean Maloney, NY-18	RHOB 2331	Jim Baird, IN-04	CHOB 532
Ann Kirkpatrick, AZ-02	CHOB 309	Mike Conaway, TX-11	RHOB 2469
Cindy Axne, IA-03	CHOB 330		
Collin Peterson, MN-07	RHOB 2204		

CONSERVATION & FORESTRY

Room: LHOB 1301
Phone: 202.225.2171

Majority:		Minority:	
C: Abigail Spanberger, VA-07	LHOB 1239	RM: Doug LaMalfa, CA-01	CHOB 32
		Rick Allen, GA-12	RHOB 240
Marcia Fudge, OH-11	RHOB 2344	Ralph Abraham, LA-05	CHOB 41
Tom O'Halleran, AZ-01	CHOB 324	Trent Kelly, MS-01	LHOB 100
Chellie Pingree, ME-01	RHOB 2162	Mike Conaway, TX-11	RHOB 246
Cindy Axne, IA-03	CHOB 330		
Collin Peterson, MN-07	RHOB 2204		

GENERAL FARM COMMODITIES & RISK MANAGEMENT

Room: LHOB 1301
Phone: 202.225.2171

Majority:		Minority:	
C: Filemon Vela, TX-34	CHOB 307	RM: Glenn Thompson, PA-15	CHOB 12
Angela Craig, MN-02	LHOB 1523		
David Scott, GA-13	CHOB 225	Austin Scott, GA-08	RHOB 241
Alfred Lawson, FL-05	LHOB 1406	Rick Crawford, AR-01	RHOB 242
Jeff Van Drew, NJ-02	CHOB 331	Rick Allen, GA-12	RHOB 240
Collin Peterson, MN-07	RHOB 2204	Ralph Abraham, LA-05	CHOB 41
		Mike Conaway, TX-11	RHOB 246

LIVESTOCK & FOREIGN AGRICULTURE

Room: LHOB 1301
Phone: 202.225.2171

Majority:		Minority:	
C: Jim Costa, CA-16	RHOB 2081	RM: David Rouzer, NC-07	RHOB 24
Anthony Brindisi, NY-22	CHOB 329	Glenn Thompson, PA-15	CHOB 1
Jahana Hayes, CT-05	LHOB 1415	Scott DesJarlais, TN-04	RHOB 23
T.J. Cox, CA-21	LHOB 1728	Vicky Hartzler, MO-04	RHOB 22
Angela Craig, MN-02	LHOB 1523	Trent Kelly, MS-01	LHOB 10
Josh Harder, CA-10	CHOB 131	James Comer, KY-01	LHOB 10
Filemon Vela, TX-34	CHOB 307	Roger Marshall, KS-01	CHOB 3
Stacey Plaskett, VI-01	RHOB 2404	Don Bacon, NE-02	LHOB 10
Salud Carbajal, CA-24	LHOB 1431	James Hagedorn, MN-01	CHOB 3
Cheri Bustos, IL-17	LHOB 1233	Mike Conaway, TX-11	RHOB 24
Collin Peterson, MN-07	RHOB 2204		

SUBCOMMITTEE NUTRITION, OVERSIGHT & DEPARTMENT OPERATIONS

Room: LHOB 1010
Phone: 202.225.0317

Majority:		Minority:	
C: Marcia Fudge, OH-11	RHOB 2344	RM: Dusty Johnson, SD-01	LHOB 15
Jim McGovern, MA-02	CHOB 408		
Alma Adams, NC-12	RHOB 2436	Scott DesJarlais, TN-04	RHOB 23
Jahana Hayes, CT-05	LHOB 1415	Rodney Davis, IL-13	LHOB 17
Kim Schrier, WA-08	LHOB 1123	Theodore Yoho, FL-03	LHOB 17
Jeff Van Drew, NJ-02	CHOB 331	Don Bacon, NE-02	LHOB 10
Alfred Lawson, FL-05	LHOB 1406	James Hagedorn, MN-01	CHOB 3
Jimmy Panetta, CA-20	CHOB 212	Mike Conaway, TX-11	RHOB 24
Collin Peterson, MN-07	RHOB 2204		

APPROPRIATIONS

Room: The Capitol H-307
Website: www.appropriations.house.gov
Phone: 202.225.2771
Ratio: 30 Democrats/23 Republicans
Subcommittees: 12

Majority:		Minority:	
C: Nita Lowey, NY-17	RHOB 2365	RM: Kay Granger, TX-12	LHOB 1026
Marcy Kaptur, OH-09	RHOB 2186	Hal Rogers, KY-05	RHOB 2406
Pete Visclosky, IN-01	RHOB 2328	Robert Aderholt, AL-04	LHOB 1203
Jose Serrano, NY-15	RHOB 2354	Mike Simpson, ID-02	RHOB 2084
Rosa DeLauro, CT-03	RHOB 2413	John Carter, TX-31	RHOB 2110
David Price, NC-04	RHOB 2108	Ken Calvert, CA-42	RHOB 2205
Lucille Roybal-Allard, CA-40	RHOB 2083	Tom Cole, OK-04	RHOB 2207
		Mario Diaz-Balart, FL-25	CHOB 404
Sanford Bishop, GA-02	RHOB 2407	Tom Graves, GA-14	RHOB 2078
Barbara Lee, CA-13	RHOB 2470	Steve Womack, AR-03	RHOB 2412
Betty McCollum, MN-04	RHOB 2256	Jeff Fortenberry, NE-01	LHOB 1514
Tim Ryan, OH-13	LHOB 1126	Chuck Fleischmann, TN-03	RHOB 2410
Dutch Ruppersberger, MD-02	RHOB 2206	Jaime Herrera Beutler, WA-03	RHOB 2352
Debbie Wasserman Schultz, FL-23	LHOB 1114	Dave Joyce, OH-14	LHOB 1124
		Andy Harris, MD-01	RHOB 2334
Henry Cuellar, TX-28	RHOB 2372	Martha Roby, AL-02	CHOB 504
Chellie Pingree, ME-01	RHOB 2162	Mark Amodei, NV-02	CHOB 104
Mike Quigley, IL-05	RHOB 2458	Chris Stewart, UT-02	RHOB 2242
Derek Kilmer, WA-06	LHOB 1410	Steven Palazzo, MS-04	RHOB 2349
Matthew Cartwright, PA-08	LHOB 1034	Dan Newhouse, WA-04	LHOB 1414
Grace Meng, NY-06	RHOB 2209	John Moolenaar, MI-04	CHOB 117
Mark Pocan, WI-02	LHOB 1421	John Rutherford, FL-04	LHOB 1711
Catherine Clark, MA-05	RHOB 2448	Will Hurd, TX-23	CHOB 317
Peter Aguilar, CA-31	CHOB 109		
Cheri Bustos, IL-17	LHOB 1233		
Ed Case, HI-01	RHOB 2443		
Charles Crist, FL-13	CHOB 215		
Lois Frankel, FL-21	RHOB 2305		
Ann Kirkpatrick, AZ-02	CHOB 309		
Brenda Lawrence, MI-14	RHOB 2463		
Norma Torres, CA-35	RHOB 2444		
Bonnie Watson Coleman, NJ-12	RHOB 2442		

Majority CoS: Shalanda Young   **Minority CoS:** Anne Marie Chotvacs

--- Subcommittees ---

AGRICULTURE, RURAL DEVELOPMENT, FDA & RELATED AGENCIES

Room: The Capitol 2362-A
Phone: 202.225.2638

Majority:		Minority:	
C: Sanford Bishop, GA-02	RHOB 2407	RM: Jeff Fortenberry, NE-01	LHOB 1514
Rosa DeLauro, CT-03	RHOB 2413		
Chellie Pingree, ME-01	RHOB 2162	Robert Aderholt, AL-04	LHOB 1203
Mark Pocan, WI-02	LHOB 1421	Andy Harris, MD-01	RHOB 2334
Barbara Lee, CA-13	RHOB 2470	John Moolenaar, MI-04	CHOB 117
Betty McCollum, MN-04	RHOB 2256		
Henry Cuellar, TX-28	RHOB 2372		
Nita Lowey, NY-17	RHOB 2365		

COMMERCE, JUSTICE, SCIENCE & RELATED AGENCIES

Room: The Capitol H-307
Phone: 202.225.3351

Majority:		Minority:	
C: Jose Serrano, NY-15	RHOB 2354	RM: Robert Aderholt, AL-04	LHOB 1203
Matthew Cartwright, PA-08	LHOB 1034		
Grace Meng, NY-06	RHOB 2209	Martha Roby, AL-02	CHOB 504
Brenda Lawrence, MI-14	RHOB 2463	Steven Palazzo, MS-04	RHOB 2349
Charles Crist, FL-13	CHOB 215	Tom Graves, GA-14	RHOB 2078
Ed Case, HI-01	RHOB 2443		
Marcy Kaptur, OH-09	RHOB 2186		
Nita Lowey, NY-17	RHOB 2365		

DEFENSE

Room: The Capitol H-307
Phone: 202.225.2847

Majority:		Minority:	
C: Pete Visclosky, IN-01	RHOB 2328	RM: Ken Calvert, CA-42	RHOB 2205
Betty McCollum, MN-04	RHOB 2256	Hal Rogers, KY-05	RHOB 2406
Tim Ryan, OH-13	LHOB 1126	Tom Cole, OK-04	RHOB 2207

Dutch Ruppersberger, MD-02	RHOB 2206	Steve Womack, AR-03	RHOB 2412
		Robert Aderholt, AL-04	LHOB 1203
Marcy Kaptur, OH-09	RHOB 2186	John Carter, TX-31	RHOB 2110
Henry Cuellar, TX-28	RHOB 2372	Mario Diaz-Balart, FL-25	CHOB 404
Derek Kilmer, WA-06	LHOB 1410		
Peter Aguilar, CA-31	CHOB 109		
Cheri Bustos, IL-17	LHOB 1233		
Charles Crist, FL-13	CHOB 215		
Ann Kirkpatrick, AZ-02	CHOB 309		
Nita Lowey, NY-17	RHOB 2365		

Majority CoS: Sherry Young 202.225.2847

Minority CoS: Sherry Young 202.225.2847

ENERGY & WATER DEVELOPMENT & RELATED AGENCIES
Room: The Capitol H-307
Phone: 202.225.3421

Majority:		Minority:	
C: Marcy Kaptur, OH-09	RHOB 2186	RM: Mike Simpson, ID-02	RHOB 2084
Pete Visclosky, IN-01	RHOB 2328	Ken Calvert, CA-42	RHOB 2205
Debbie Wasserman Schultz, FL-23	LHOB 1114	Chuck Fleischmann, TN-03	RHOB 2410
		Dan Newhouse, WA-04	LHOB 1414
Ann Kirkpatrick, AZ-02	CHOB 309		
Derek Kilmer, WA-06	LHOB 1410		
Mark Pocan, WI-02	LHOB 1421		
Lois Frankel, FL-21	RHOB 2305		
Nita Lowey, NY-17	RHOB 2365		

FINANCIAL SERVICES & GENERAL GOVERNMENT
Room: RHOB 2000
Phone: 202.225.7245

Majority:		Minority:	
C: Mike Quigley, IL-05	RHOB 2458	RM: Tom Graves, GA-14	RHOB 2078
Jose Serrano, NY-15	RHOB 2354	Mark Amodei, NV-02	CHOB 104
Matthew Cartwright, PA-08	LHOB 1034	Chris Stewart, UT-02	RHOB 224
Sanford Bishop, GA-02	RHOB 2407	Dave Joyce, OH-14	LHOB 112
Norma Torres, CA-35	RHOB 2444		
Charles Crist, FL-13	CHOB 215		
Ann Kirkpatrick, AZ-02	CHOB 309		
Nita Lowey, NY-17	RHOB 2365		

HOMELAND SECURITY
Room: RHOB 2006
Phone: 202.225.5834

Majority:		Minority:	
C: Lucille Roybal-Allard, CA-40	RHOB 2083	RM: Chuck Fleischmann, TN-03	RHOB 2410
Henry Cuellar, TX-28	RHOB 2372	Steven Palazzo, MS-04	RHOB 2349
Dutch Ruppersberger, MD-02	RHOB 2206	Dan Newhouse, WA-04	LHOB 1414
		John Rutherford, FL-04	LHOB 1711
David Price, NC-04	RHOB 2108		
Debbie Wasserman Schultz, FL-23	LHOB 1114		
Grace Meng, NY-06	RHOB 2209		
Peter Aguilar, CA-31	CHOB 109		
Nita Lowey, NY-17	RHOB 2365		

INTERIOR, ENVIRONMENT & RELATED AGENCIES
Room: RHOB 2007
Phone: 202.225.3081

Majority:		Minority:	
C: Betty McCollum, MN-04	RHOB 2256	RM: Dave Joyce, OH-14	LHOB 11
Chellie Pingree, ME-01	RHOB 2162	Mike Simpson, ID-02	RHOB 20
Derek Kilmer, WA-06	LHOB 1410	Chris Stewart, UT-02	RHOB 22
Jose Serrano, NY-15	RHOB 2354	Mark Amodei, NV-02	CHOB 1
Mike Quigley, IL-05	RHOB 2458		
Bonnie Watson Coleman, NJ-12	RHOB 2442		
Brenda Lawrence, MI-14	RHOB 2463		
Nita Lowey, NY-17	RHOB 2365		

LABOR, HEALTH & HUMAN SERVICES, EDUCATION & RELATED AGENCIES
Room: RHOB 2358-B
Phone: 202.225.3508

Majority:		Minority:	
C: Rosa DeLauro, CT-03	RHOB 2413	RM: Tom Cole, OK-04	RHOB 22
Lucille Roybal-Allard, CA-40	RHOB 2083	Andy Harris, MD-01	RHOB 23

Barbara Lee, CA-13	RHOB 2470	Jaime Herrera Beutler,	RHOB 2352
Mark Pocan, WI-02	LHOB 1421	WA-03	
Katherine Clark, MA-05	RHOB 2448	John Moolenaar, MI-04	CHOB 117
Lois Frankel, FL-21	RHOB 2305	Tom Graves, GA-14	RHOB 2078
Cheri Bustos, IL-17	LHOB 1233		
Bonnie Watson Coleman, NJ-12	RHOB 2442		
Nita Lowey, NY-17	RHOB 2365		

LEGISLATIVE BRANCH
Room: The Capitol H-306
Phone: 202.225.7252

Majority:		Minority:	
C: Tim Ryan, OH-13	LHOB 1126	**RM: Jaime Herrera**	RHOB 2352
Dutch Ruppersberger, MD-02	RHOB 2206	**Beutler, WA-03**	
		Dan Newhouse, WA-04	LHOB 1414
Katherine Clark, MA-05	RHOB 2448		
Ed Case, HI-01	RHOB 2443		
Nita Lowey, NY-17	RHOB 2365		

MILITARY CONSTRUCTION, VETERANS AFFAIRS & RELATED AGENCIES
Room: The Capitol HT-2
Phone: 202.225.3047

Majority:		Minority:	
C: Debbie Wasserman Schultz, FL-23	LHOB 1114	**RM: John Carter, TX-31**	RHOB 2110
		Martha Roby, AL-02	CHOB 504
Sanford Bishop, GA-02	RHOB 2407	John Rutherford, FL-04	LHOB 1711
Ed Case, HI-01	RHOB 2443	Will Hurd, TX-23	CHOB 317
Tim Ryan, OH-13	LHOB 1126		
Chellie Pingree, ME-01	RHOB 2162		
Matthew Cartwright, PA-08	LHOB 1034		
Cheri Bustos, IL-17	LHOB 1233		
Nita Lowey, NY-17	RHOB 2365		

STATE, FOREIGN OPERATIONS & RELATED PROGRAMS
Room: The Capitol H-307
Phone: 202.225.2041

Majority:		Minority:	
C: Nita Lowey, NY-17	RHOB 2365	**RM: Hal Rogers, KY-05**	RHOB 2406
Barbara Lee, CA-13	RHOB 2470	Jeff Fortenberry, NE-01	LHOB 1514
Grace Meng, NY-06	RHOB 2209	Martha Roby, AL-02	CHOB 504
David Price, NC-04	RHOB 2108		
Lois Frankel, FL-21	RHOB 2305		
Norma Torres, CA-35	RHOB 2444		

TRANSPORTATION, HUD & RELATED AGENCIES
Room: RHOB 2358-A
Phone: 202.225.2141

Majority:		Minority:	
C: David Price, NC-04	RHOB 2108	**RM: Mario Diaz-Balart,**	CHOB 404
Mike Quigley, IL-05	RHOB 2458	**FL-25**	
Katherine Clark, MA-05	RHOB 2448	Steve Womack, AR-03	RHOB 2412
Bonnie Watson Coleman, NJ-12	RHOB 2442	John Rutherford, FL-04	LHOB 1711
		Will Hurd, TX-23	CHOB 317
Brenda Lawrence, MI-14	RHOB 2463		
Norma Torres, CA-35	RHOB 2444		
Peter Aguilar, CA-31	CHOB 109		
Nita Lowey, NY-17	RHOB 2365		

ARMED SERVICES
Room: RHOB 2216
Website: www.armedservices.house.gov
Phone: 202.225.4151
Ratio: 31 Democrats/26 Republicans
Subcommittees: 6

Majority:		Minority:	
C: Adam Smith, WA-09	RHOB 2264	**RM: Mac Thornberry,**	RHOB 2208
Susan Davis, CA-53	LHOB 1214	**TX-13**	
Jim Langevin, RI-02	RHOB 2077	Joe Wilson, SC-02	LHOB 1436
Rick Larsen, WA-02	RHOB 2113	Rob Bishop, UT-01	CHOB 123
Jim Cooper, TN-05	LHOB 1536	Michael Turner, OH-10	RHOB 2082
Joe Courtney, CT-02	RHOB 2332	Mike Rogers, AL-03	RHOB 2184
John Garamendi, CA-03	RHOB 2368	Mike Conaway, TX-11	RHOB 2469
Jackie Speier, CA-14	RHOB 2465	Doug Lamborn, CO-05	RHOB 2371
Tulsi Gabbard, HI-02	LHOB 1433	Rob Wittman, VA-01	RHOB 2055
Donald Norcross, NJ-01	RHOB 2437	Vicky Hartzler, MO-04	RHOB 2235

HOUSE COMMITTEES

Ruben Gallego, AZ-07	LHOB 1131	Austin Scott, GA-08	RHOB 2417
Seth Moulton, MA-06	LHOB 1127	Mo Brooks, AL-05	RHOB 2246
Salud Carbajal, CA-24	LHOB 1431	Paul Cook, CA-08	LHOB 1027
Anthony Brown, MD-04	LHOB 1323	Bradley Byrne, AL-01	CHOB 119
Ro Khanna, CA-17	CHOB 221	Sam Graves, MO-06	LHOB 1135
Bill Keating, MA-09	RHOB 2351	Elise Stefanik, NY-21	CHOB 318
Filemon Vela, TX-34	CHOB 307	Scott DesJarlais, TN-04	RHOB 2301
Andrew Kim, NJ-03	LHOB 1516	Ralph Abraham, LA-05	CHOB 417
Kendra Horn, OK-05	CHOB 415	Trent Kelly, MS-01	LHOB 1005
Gilbert Cisneros, CA-39	CHOB 431	Michael Gallagher, WI-08	LHOB 1230
Chrissy Houlahan, PA-06	LHOB 1218	Matt Gaetz, FL-01	LHOB 1721
Jason Crow, CO-06	LHOB 1229	Don Bacon, NE-02	LHOB 1024
Xochitl Liana Torres-Small, NM-02	CHOB 430	Jim Banks, IN-03	LHOB 1713
Elissa Slotkin, MI-08	LHOB 1531	Liz Cheney, WY-01	CHOB 416
Mikie Sherrill, NJ-11	LHOB 1208	Paul Mitchell, MI-10	CHOB 211
Katherine Hill, CA-25	LHOB 1130	Jack Bergman, MI-01	CHOB 414
Veronica Escobar, TX-16	LHOB 1505	Michael Waltz, FL-06	CHOB 216
Debra Haaland, NM-01	LHOB 1237		
Jared Golden, ME-02	LHOB 1223		
Lori Trahan, MA-03	LHOB 1616		
Elaine Luria, VA-02	CHOB 534		

Majority CoS: Paul Arcangeli   **Minority CoS:** Jennifer M. Stewart

——————————— Subcommittees ———————————

INTELLIGENCE, EMERGING THREATS & CAPABILITIES
Room: RHOB 2340
Phone: 202.225.4151

Majority:		Minority:	
C: Jim Langevin, RI-02	RHOB 2077	**RM: Elise Stefanik, NY-21**	CHOB 318
Rick Larsen, WA-02	RHOB 2113	Sam Graves, MO-06	LHOB 1135
Jim Cooper, TN-05	LHOB 1536	Ralph Abraham, LA-05	CHOB 417
Tulsi Gabbard, HI-02	LHOB 1433	Mike Conaway, TX-11	RHOB 2469
Anthony Brown, MD-04	LHOB 1323	Austin Scott, GA-08	RHOB 241
Ro Khanna, CA-17	CHOB 221	Scott DesJarlais, TN-04	RHOB 230
Bill Keating, MA-09	RHOB 2351	Michael Gallagher, WI-08	LHOB 123
Andrew Kim, NJ-03	LHOB 1516	Michael Waltz, FL-06	CHOB 21
Chrissy Houlahan, PA-06	LHOB 1218	Don Bacon, NE-02	LHOB 102
Jason Crow, CO-06	LHOB 1229	Jim Banks, IN-03	LHOB 171
Elissa Slotkin, MI-08	LHOB 1531		
Lori Trahan, MA-03	LHOB 1616		

MILITARY PERSONNEL
Room: RHOB 2340
Phone: 202.225.4151

Majority:		Minority:	
C: Jackie Speier, CA-14	RHOB 2465	**RM: Trent Kelly, MS-01**	LHOB 100
Susan Davis, CA-53	LHOB 1214	Ralph Abraham, LA-05	CHOB 41
Ruben Gallego, AZ-07	LHOB 1131	Liz Cheney, WY-01	CHOB 41
Gilbert Cisneros, CA-39	CHOB 431	Paul Mitchell, MI-10	CHOB 21
Veronica Escobar, TX-16	LHOB 1505	Jack Bergman, MI-01	CHOB 41
Debra Haaland, NM-01	LHOB 1237	Matt Gaetz, FL-01	LHOB 172
Lori Trahan, MA-03	LHOB 1616		
Elaine Luria, VA-02	CHOB 534		

READINESS
Room: RHOB 2340
Phone: 202.225.4151

Majority:		Minority:	
C: John Garamendi, CA-03	RHOB 2368	**RM: Doug Lamborn, CO-05**	RHOB 23
Tulsi Gabbard, HI-02	LHOB 1433	Austin Scott, GA-08	RHOB 24
Andrew Kim, NJ-03	LHOB 1516	Joe Wilson, SC-02	LHOB 14
Kendra Horn, OK-05	CHOB 415	Rob Bishop, UT-01	CHOB 1
Chrissy Houlahan, PA-06	LHOB 1218	Mike Rogers, AL-03	RHOB 21
Jason Crow, CO-06	LHOB 1229	Mo Brooks, AL-05	RHOB 22
Xochitl Liana Torres-Small, NM-02	CHOB 430	Elise Stefanik, NY-21	CHOB 3
Elissa Slotkin, MI-08	LHOB 1531	Jack Bergman, MI-01	CHOB 4
Veronica Escobar, TX-16	LHOB 1505		
Debra Haaland, NM-01	LHOB 1237		

SEAPOWER & PROJECTION FORCES
Room: RHOB 2340
Phone: 202.225.4151

Majority:		Minority:	
C: Joe Courtney, CT-02	RHOB 2332	**RM: Rob Wittman, VA-01**	RHOB 20
Jim Langevin, RI-02	RHOB 2077	Mike Conaway, TX-11	RHOB 24

Jim Cooper, TN-05	LHOB 1536	Michael Gallagher, WI-08	LHOB 1230
Donald Norcross, NJ-01	RHOB 2437	Jack Bergman, MI-01	CHOB 414
Seth Moulton, MA-06	LHOB 1127	Michael Waltz, FL-06	CHOB 216
Filemon Vela, TX-34	CHOB 307	Vicky Hartzler, MO-04	RHOB 2235
Gilbert Cisneros, CA-39	CHOB 431	Paul Cook, CA-08	LHOB 1027
Mikie Sherrill, NJ-11	LHOB 1208	Bradley Byrne, AL-01	CHOB 119
Katherine Hill, CA-25	LHOB 1130	Trent Kelly, MS-01	LHOB 1005
Jared Golden, ME-02	LHOB 1223		
Elaine Luria, VA-02	CHOB 534		

STRATEGIC FORCES
Room: RHOB 2340
Phone: 202.225.4151

Majority:		Minority:	
C: Jim Cooper, TN-05	LHOB 1536	RM: Michael Turner, OH-10	RHOB 2082
Susan Davis, CA-53	LHOB 1214		
Rick Larsen, WA-02	RHOB 2113	Joe Wilson, SC-02	LHOB 1436
John Garamendi, CA-03	RHOB 2368	Rob Bishop, UT-01	CHOB 123
Jackie Speier, CA-14	RHOB 2465	Mike Rogers, AL-03	RHOB 2184
Seth Moulton, MA-06	LHOB 1127	Mo Brooks, AL-05	RHOB 2246
Salud Carbajal, CA-24	LHOB 1431	Bradley Byrne, AL-01	CHOB 119
Ro Khanna, CA-17	CHOB 221	Scott DesJarlais, TN-04	RHOB 2301
Bill Keating, MA-09	RHOB 2351	Liz Cheney, WY-01	CHOB 416
Kendra Horn, OK-05	CHOB 415		

TACTICAL AIR & LAND FORCES
Room: RHOB 2340
Phone: 202.225.4151

Majority:		Minority:	
C: Donald Norcross, NJ-01	RHOB 2437	RM: Vicky Hartzler, MO-04	RHOB 2235
Jim Langevin, RI-02	RHOB 2077	Paul Cook, CA-08	LHOB 1027
Joe Courtney, CT-02	RHOB 2332	Matt Gaetz, FL-01	LHOB 1721
Ruben Gallego, AZ-07	LHOB 1131	Don Bacon, NE-02	LHOB 1024
Salud Carbajal, CA-24	LHOB 1431	Jim Banks, IN-03	LHOB 1713
Anthony Brown, MD-04	LHOB 1323	Paul Mitchell, MI-10	CHOB 211
Filemon Vela, TX-34	CHOB 307	Michael Turner, OH-10	RHOB 2082
Xochitl Liana Torres-Small, NM-02	CHOB 430	Doug Lamborn, CO-05	RHOB 2371
		Rob Wittman, VA-01	RHOB 2055
Mikie Sherrill, NJ-11	LHOB 1208		
Katherine Hill, CA-25	LHOB 1130		
Jared Golden, ME-02	LHOB 1223		

BUDGET

Room: CHOB 204-E
Website: www.budget.house.gov
Phone: 202.226.7200
Ratio: 21 Democrats/14 Republicans
Subcommittees: 0

Majority:		Minority:	
C: John Yarmuth, KY-03	CHOB 402	RM: Steve Womack, AR-03	RHOB 2412
Seth Moulton, MA-06	LHOB 1127	Rob Woodall, GA-07	LHOB 1724
Hakeem Jeffries, NY-08	RHOB 2433	Bill Johnson, OH-06	RHOB 2336
Brian Higgins, NY-26	RHOB 2459	Jason Smith, MO-08	RHOB 2418
Brendan Boyle, PA-02	LHOB 1133	Bill Flores, TX-17	RHOB 2228
Ro Khanna, CA-17	CHOB 221	George Holding, NC-02	LHOB 1110
Rosa DeLauro, CT-03	RHOB 2413	Chris Stewart, UT-02	RHOB 2242
David Price, NC-04	RHOB 2108	Ralph Norman, SC-05	CHOB 319
Jan Schakowsky, IL-09	RHOB 2367	Chip Roy, TX-21	LHOB 1319
Dan Kildee, MI-05	CHOB 203	Daniel Meuser, PA-09	CHOB 326
Jimmy Panetta, CA-20	CHOB 212	William Timmons, SC-04	CHOB 313
Joseph Morelle, NY-25	LHOB 1317	Daniel Crenshaw, TX-02	CHOB 413
Steven Horsford, NV-04	LHOB 1330	Kevin Hern, OK-01	LHOB 1019
Bobby Scott, VA-03	LHOB 1201	Tim Burchett, TN-02	LHOB 1122
Sheila Jackson Lee, TX-18	RHOB 2079		
Barbara Lee, CA-13	RHOB 2470		
Pramila Jayapal, WA-07	LHOB 1510		
Ilhan Omar, MN-05	LHOB 1517		
Albio Sires, NJ-08	RHOB 2268		
Scott Peters, CA-52	RHOB 2338		
Jim Cooper, TN-05	LHOB 1536		

Majority CoS: Ellen J. Balis
Majority Sched: Sheila A. McDowell

Minority CoS: Dan Keniry

COMMISSION CONGRESSIONAL MAILING STANDARDS

Room: LHOB 1307
Website: www.cha.house.gov
Phone: 202.225.9337
Ratio: 3 Democrats/2 Republicans
Subcommittees: 0

Majority:		Minority:	
Susan Davis, CA-53	LHOB 1214	**RM: Rodney Davis, IL-13**	LHOB 1740
Brad Sherman, CA-30	RHOB 2181	Robert Latta, OH-05	RHOB 2467
A. Donald McEachin, VA-04	CHOB 314		

Majority CoS: Matthew DeFreitas   **Minority CoS:** Tim Sullivan

EDUCATION & LABOR

Room: RHOB 2176
Website: www.edlabor.house.gov
Phone: 202.225.3725
Ratio: 28 Democrats/22 Republicans
Subcommittees: 5

Majority:		Minority:	
C: Bobby Scott, VA-03	LHOB 1201	RM: Virginia Foxx, NC-05	RHOB 2462
Andy Levin, MI-09	CHOB 228	Phil Roe, TN-01	CHOB 102
Susan Davis, CA-53	LHOB 1214	Glenn Thompson, PA-15	CHOB 124
Raul Grijalva, AZ-03	LHOB 1511	Tim Walberg, MI-07	RHOB 2266
Joe Courtney, CT-02	RHOB 2332	Brett Guthrie, KY-02	RHOB 2434
Marcia Fudge, OH-11	RHOB 2344	Bradley Byrne, AL-01	CHOB 119
Gregorio Sablan, MP-01	RHOB 2411	Glenn Grothman, WI-06	LHOB 1427
Frederica Wilson, FL-24	RHOB 2445	Elise Stefanik, NY-21	CHOB 318
Suzanne Bonamici, OR-01	RHOB 2231	Rick Allen, GA-12	RHOB 2400
Mark Takano, CA-41	CHOB 420	Francis Rooney, FL-19	CHOB 120
Alma Adams, NC-12	RHOB 2436	Lloyd Smucker, PA-11	CHOB 127
Mark DeSaulnier, CA-11	CHOB 503	Mark Walker, NC-06	LHOB 1725
Donald Norcross, NJ-01	RHOB 2437	Jim Banks, IN-03	LHOB 1713
Pramila Jayapal, WA-07	LHOB 1510	James Comer, KY-01	LHOB 1037
Joseph Morelle, NY-25	LHOB 1317	Benjamin Cline, VA-06	LHOB 1009
Susan Wild, PA-07	LHOB 1607	Russell Fulcher, ID-01	LHOB 1520
Josh Harder, CA-10	CHOB 131	Van Taylor, TX-03	LHOB 1404
Lucy McBath, GA-06	LHOB 1513	Steve Watkins, KS-02	LHOB 120
Kim Schrier, WA-08	LHOB 1123	Ronald Wright, TX-06	CHOB 428
Lauren Underwood, IL-14	LHOB 1118	Daniel Meuser, PA-09	CHOB 326
Jahana Hayes, CT-05	LHOB 1415	William Timmons, SC-04	CHOB 31
Donna Shalala, FL-27	LHOB 1320	Dusty Johnson, SD-01	LHOB 1508
Ilhan Omar, MN-05	LHOB 1517		
David Trone, MD-06	LHOB 1213		
Haley Stevens, MI-11	CHOB 227		
Susie Lee, NV-03	CHOB 522		
Lori Trahan, MA-03	LHOB 1616		
Joaquin Castro, TX-20	RHOB 2241		

Majority CoS: Veronique Pluviose   **Minority CoS:** Brandon Renz

--- Subcommittees ---

CIVIL RIGHTS & HUMAN SERVICES
Room: RHOB 2176
Phone: 202.225.3725

Majority:		Minority:	
C: Suzanne Bonamici, OR-01	RHOB 2231	RM: James Comer, KY-01	LHOB 103
		Glenn Thompson, PA-15	CHOB 12
Raul Grijalva, AZ-03	LHOB 1511	Elise Stefanik, NY-21	CHOB 31
Marcia Fudge, OH-11	RHOB 2344	Dusty Johnson, SD-01	LHOB 150
Kim Schrier, WA-08	LHOB 1123		
Jahana Hayes, CT-05	LHOB 1415		
David Trone, MD-06	LHOB 1213		
Susie Lee, NV-03	CHOB 522		

EARLY CHILDHOOD, ELEMENTARY & SECONDARY EDUCATION
Room: RHOB 2176
Phone: 202.225.3725

Majority:		Minority:	
C: Gregorio Sablan, MP-01	RHOB 2411	RM: Rick Allen, GA-12	RHOB 24
		Glenn Thompson, PA-15	CHOB 1
Kim Schrier, WA-08	LHOB 1123	Glenn Grothman, WI-06	LHOB 14
Jahana Hayes, CT-05	LHOB 1415	Van Taylor, TX-03	LHOB 14
Donna Shalala, FL-27	LHOB 1320	William Timmons, SC-04	CHOB 3
Susan Davis, CA-53	LHOB 1214		
Frederica Wilson, FL-24	RHOB 2445		
Mark DeSaulnier, CA-11	CHOB 503		
Joseph Morelle, NY-25	LHOB 1317		

HEALTH, EMPLOYMENT, LABOR & PENSIONS

Room: RHOB 2176
Phone: 202.225.3725

Majority:		Minority:	
C: Frederica Wilson, FL-24	RHOB 2445	RM: Tim Walberg, MI-07	RHOB 2266
		Phil Roe, TN-01	CHOB 102
Joe Courtney, CT-02	RHOB 2332	Rick Allen, GA-12	RHOB 2400
Marcia Fudge, OH-11	RHOB 2344	Francis Rooney, FL-19	CHOB 120
Donald Norcross, NJ-01	RHOB 2437	Jim Banks, IN-03	LHOB 1713
Joseph Morelle, NY-25	LHOB 1317	Russell Fulcher, ID-01	LHOB 1520
Susan Wild, PA-07	LHOB 1607	Van Taylor, TX-03	LHOB 1404
Josh Harder, CA-10	CHOB 131	Steve Watkins, KS-02	LHOB 1205
Lucy McBath, GA-06	LHOB 1513	Ronald Wright, TX-06	CHOB 428
Lauren Underwood, IL-14	LHOB 1118	Daniel Meuser, PA-09	CHOB 326
Donna Shalala, FL-27	LHOB 1320	Dusty Johnson, SD-01	LHOB 1508
Andy Levin, MI-09	CHOB 228		
Haley Stevens, MI-11	CHOB 227		
Lori Trahan, MA-03	LHOB 1616		

HIGHER EDUCATION & WORKFORCE INVESTMENT

Room: RHOB 2176
Phone: 202.225.3725

Majority:		Minority:	
C: Susan Davis, CA-53	LHOB 1214	RM: Lloyd Smucker, PA-11	CHOB 127
Raul Grijalva, AZ-03	LHOB 1511	Brett Guthrie, KY-02	RHOB 2434
Gregorio Sablan, MP-01	RHOB 2411	Glenn Grothman, WI-06	LHOB 1427
Suzanne Bonamici, OR-01	RHOB 2231	Elise Stefanik, NY-21	CHOB 318
Mark Takano, CA-41	CHOB 420	Jim Banks, IN-03	LHOB 1713
Alma Adams, NC-12	RHOB 2436	Mark Walker, NC-06	LHOB 1725
Donald Norcross, NJ-01	RHOB 2437	James Comer, KY-01	LHOB 1037
Pramila Jayapal, WA-07	LHOB 1510	Benjamin Cline, VA-06	LHOB 1009
Josh Harder, CA-10	CHOB 131	Russell Fulcher, ID-01	LHOB 1520
Andy Levin, MI-09	CHOB 228	Steve Watkins, KS-02	LHOB 1205
Ilhan Omar, MN-05	LHOB 1517	Daniel Meuser, PA-09	CHOB 326
David Trone, MD-06	LHOB 1213	William Timmons, SC-04	CHOB 313
Susie Lee, NV-03	CHOB 522		
Lori Trahan, MA-03	LHOB 1616		
Joaquin Castro, TX-20	RHOB 2241		

WORKFORCE PROTECTIONS

Room: RHOB 2176
Phone: 202.225.3725

Majority:		Minority:	
C: Alma Adams, NC-12	RHOB 2436	RM: Bradley Byrne, AL-01	CHOB 119
Mark DeSaulnier, CA-11	CHOB 503	Francis Rooney, FL-19	CHOB 120
Pramila Jayapal, WA-07	LHOB 1510	Mark Walker, NC-06	LHOB 1725
Susan Wild, PA-07	LHOB 1607	Benjamin Cline, VA-06	LHOB 1009
Lucy McBath, GA-06	LHOB 1513	Ronald Wright, TX-06	CHOB 428
Ilhan Omar, MN-05	LHOB 1517		
Haley Stevens, MI-11	CHOB 227		

ENERGY & COMMERCE

Room: RHOB 2322A
Website: www.energycommerce.house.gov
Phone: 202.225.2927
Ratio: 31 Democrats/24 Republicans
Subcommittees: 6

Majority:		Minority:	
C: Frank Pallone, NJ-06	RHOB 2107	RM: Greg Walden, OR-02	RHOB 2185
Yvette Clarke, NY-09	RHOB 2058	Fred Upton, MI-06	RHOB 2183
Bobby Rush, IL-01	RHOB 2188	John Shimkus, IL-15	RHOB 2217
Anna Eshoo, CA-18	CHOB 202	Michael Burgess, TX-26	RHOB 2161
Eliot Engel, NY-16	RHOB 2426	Steve Scalise, LA-01	RHOB 2049
Diana DeGette, CO-01	RHOB 2111	Robert Latta, OH-05	RHOB 2467
Mike Doyle, PA-18	CHOB 306	Cathy McMorris Rodgers, WA-05	LHOB 1035
Jan Schakowsky, IL-09	RHOB 2367		
G.K. Butterfield, NC-01	RHOB 2080	Brett Guthrie, KY-02	RHOB 2434
Doris Matsui, CA-06	RHOB 2311	Pete Olson, TX-22	RHOB 2133
Kathy Castor, FL-14	RHOB 2052	David McKinley, WV-01	RHOB 2239
John Sarbanes, MD-03	RHOB 2370	Adam Kinzinger, IL-16	RHOB 2245
Jerry McNerney, CA-09	RHOB 2265	Morgan Griffith, VA-09	RHOB 2202
Peter Welch, VT-01	RHOB 2187	Gus Bilirakis, FL-12	RHOB 2227
Ben Lujan, NM-03	RHOB 2323	Bill Johnson, OH-06	RHOB 2336
Paul Tonko, NY-20	RHOB 2369	Billy Long, MO-07	RHOB 2454
Dave Loebsack, IA-02	LHOB 1211	Larry Bucshon, IN-08	RHOB 2313
Kurt Schrader, OR-05	RHOB 2431	Bill Flores, TX-17	RHOB 2228
Joe Kennedy, MA-04	CHOB 304	Susan Brooks, IN-05	LHOB 2211

Tony Cardenas, CA-29	RHOB 2438	Markwayne Mullin, OK-02	RHOB 2421
Raul Ruiz, CA-36	RHOB 2342	Richard Hudson, NC-08	RHOB 2112
Scott Peters, CA-52	RHOB 2338	Tim Walberg, MI-07	RHOB 2266
Debbie Dingell, MI-12	CHOB 116	Buddy Carter, GA-01	RHOB 2432
Marc Veasey, TX-33	RHOB 2348	Jeff Duncan, SC-03	RHOB 2229
Ann Kuster, NH-02	CHOB 320	Greg Gianforte, MT-01	LHOB 1222
Robin Kelly, IL-02	RHOB 2416		
Nanette Barragan, CA-44	LHOB 1030		
Lisa Blunt Rochester, DE-01	LHOB 1519		
Darren Soto, FL-09	LHOB 1507		
Tom O'Halleran, AZ-01	CHOB 324		
A. Donald McEachin, VA-04	CHOB 314		

Majority CoS: Jeffrey C. Carroll   **Minority CoS:** Michael D. Bloomquist
Majority Sched: Elizabeth B. Ertel

─────────────── Subcommittees ───────────────

COMMUNICATIONS & TECHNOLOGY
Room: RHOB 2125
Phone: 202.225.2927

Majority:		**Minority:**	
C: Mike Doyle, PA-18	CHOB 306	**RM: Robert Latta, OH-05**	RHOB 2467
Jerry McNerney, CA-09	RHOB 2265	John Shimkus, IL-15	RHOB 2217
Yvette Clarke, NY-09	RHOB 2058	Steve Scalise, LA-01	RHOB 2049
Dave Loebsack, IA-02	LHOB 1211	Pete Olson, TX-22	RHOB 2133
Marc Veasey, TX-33	RHOB 2348	Adam Kinzinger, IL-16	RHOB 2245
A. Donald McEachin, VA-04	CHOB 314	Gus Bilirakis, FL-12	RHOB 2227
Darren Soto, FL-09	LHOB 1507	Bill Johnson, OH-06	RHOB 2336
Tom O'Halleran, AZ-01	CHOB 324	Billy Long, MO-07	RHOB 2454
Anna Eshoo, CA-18	CHOB 202	Bill Flores, TX-17	RHOB 2228
Diana DeGette, CO-01	RHOB 2111	Susan Brooks, IN-05	LHOB 221
G.K. Butterfield, NC-01	RHOB 2080	Tim Walberg, MI-07	RHOB 2266
Doris Matsui, CA-06	RHOB 2311	Greg Gianforte, MT-01	LHOB 1222
Peter Welch, VT-01	RHOB 2187	Greg Walden, OR-02	RHOB 2183
Ben Lujan, NM-03	RHOB 2323		
Kurt Schrader, OR-05	RHOB 2431		
Tony Cardenas, CA-29	RHOB 2438		
Debbie Dingell, MI-12	CHOB 116		
Frank Pallone, NJ-06	RHOB 2107		

CONSUMER PROTECTION & COMMERCE
Room: RHOB 2322A
Phone: 202.225.2927

Majority:		**Minority:**	
C: Jan Schakowsky, IL-09	RHOB 2367	**RM: Cathy McMorris**	LHOB 103
Kathy Castor, FL-14	RHOB 2052	**Rodgers, WA-05**	
Marc Veasey, TX-33	RHOB 2348	Fred Upton, MI-06	RHOB 218
Robin Kelly, IL-02	RHOB 2416	Michael Burgess, TX-26	RHOB 216
Tom O'Halleran, AZ-01	CHOB 324	Robert Latta, OH-05	RHOB 246
Ben Lujan, NM-03	RHOB 2323	Larry Bucshon, IN-08	RHOB 231
Tony Cardenas, CA-29	RHOB 2438	Richard Hudson, NC-08	RHOB 21
Lisa Blunt Rochester, DE-01	LHOB 1519	Buddy Carter, GA-01	RHOB 243
Darren Soto, FL-09	LHOB 1507	Greg Gianforte, MT-01	LHOB 122
Bobby Rush, IL-01	RHOB 2188	Greg Walden, OR-02	RHOB 218
Doris Matsui, CA-06	RHOB 2311		
Jerry McNerney, CA-09	RHOB 2265		
Debbie Dingell, MI-12	CHOB 116		
Frank Pallone, NJ-06	RHOB 2107		

ENERGY
Room: RHOB 2125
Phone: 202.225.2927

Majority:		**Minority:**	
C: Bobby Rush, IL-01	RHOB 2188	**RM: Fred Upton, MI-06**	RHOB 21
Scott Peters, CA-52	RHOB 2338	Robert Latta, OH-05	RHOB 24
Mike Doyle, PA-18	CHOB 306	Cathy McMorris Rodgers,	LHOB 10
John Sarbanes, MD-03	RHOB 2370	WA-05	
Jerry McNerney, CA-09	RHOB 2265	Pete Olson, TX-22	RHOB 21
Paul Tonko, NY-20	RHOB 2369	David McKinley, WV-01	RHOB 22
Dave Loebsack, IA-02	LHOB 1211	Adam Kinzinger, IL-16	RHOB 22
G.K. Butterfield, NC-01	RHOB 2080	Morgan Griffith, VA-09	RHOB 22
Peter Welch, VT-01	RHOB 2187	Bill Johnson, OH-06	RHOB 23
Kurt Schrader, OR-05	RHOB 2431	Larry Bucshon, IN-08	RHOB 23
Joe Kennedy, MA-04	CHOB 304	Bill Flores, TX-17	RHOB 22
Marc Veasey, TX-33	RHOB 2348	Richard Hudson, NC-08	RHOB 21
Ann Kuster, NH-02	CHOB 320	Tim Walberg, MI-07	RHOB 22
Robin Kelly, IL-02	RHOB 2416	Jeff Duncan, SC-03	RHOB 22
Nanette Barragan, CA-44	LHOB 1030	Greg Walden, OR-02	RHOB 21
A. Donald McEachin, VA-04	CHOB 314		

Tom O'Halleran, AZ-01	CHOB 324
Lisa Blunt Rochester, DE-01	LHOB 1519
Frank Pallone, NJ-06	RHOB 2107

ENVIRONMENT & CLIMATE CHANGE
Room: RHOB 2322A
Phone: 202.225.2927

Majority:		Minority:	
C: Paul Tonko, NY-20	RHOB 2369	RM: John Shimkus, IL-15	RHOB 2217
Yvette Clarke, NY-09	RHOB 2058	Cathy McMorris Rodgers, WA-05	LHOB 1035
Scott Peters, CA-52	RHOB 2338		
Nanette Barragan, CA-44	LHOB 1030	David McKinley, WV-01	RHOB 2239
A. Donald McEachin, VA-04	CHOB 314	Bill Johnson, OH-06	RHOB 2336
Lisa Blunt Rochester, DE-01	LHOB 1519	Billy Long, MO-07	RHOB 2454
Darren Soto, FL-09	LHOB 1507	Bill Flores, TX-17	RHOB 2228
Diana DeGette, CO-01	RHOB 2111	Markwayne Mullin, OK-02	RHOB 2421
Jan Schakowsky, IL-09	RHOB 2367	Buddy Carter, GA-01	RHOB 2432
Doris Matsui, CA-06	RHOB 2311	Jeff Duncan, SC-03	RHOB 2229
Jerry McNerney, CA-09	RHOB 2265	Greg Walden, OR-02	RHOB 2185
Raul Ruiz, CA-36	RHOB 2342		
Debbie Dingell, MI-12	CHOB 116		
Frank Pallone, NJ-06	RHOB 2107		

HEALTH
Room: RHOB 2322A
Phone: 202.225.2927

Majority:		Minority:	
C: Anna Eshoo, CA-18	CHOB 202	RM: Michael Burgess, TX-26	RHOB 2161
Eliot Engel, NY-16	RHOB 2426		
G.K. Butterfield, NC-01	RHOB 2080	Fred Upton, MI-06	RHOB 2183
Doris Matsui, CA-06	RHOB 2311	John Shimkus, IL-15	RHOB 2217
Kathy Castor, FL-14	RHOB 2052	Brett Guthrie, KY-02	RHOB 2434
John Sarbanes, MD-03	RHOB 2370	Morgan Griffith, VA-09	RHOB 2202
Ben Lujan, NM-03	RHOB 2323	Gus Bilirakis, FL-12	RHOB 2227
Kurt Schrader, OR-05	RHOB 2431	Billy Long, MO-07	RHOB 2454
Joe Kennedy, MA-04	CHOB 304	Larry Bucshon, IN-08	RHOB 2313
Tony Cardenas, CA-29	RHOB 2438	Susan Brooks, IN-05	LHOB 2211
Peter Welch, VT-01	RHOB 2187	Markwayne Mullin, OK-02	RHOB 2421
Raul Ruiz, CA-36	RHOB 2342	Richard Hudson, NC-08	RHOB 2112
Debbie Dingell, MI-12	CHOB 116	Buddy Carter, GA-01	RHOB 2432
Ann Kuster, NH-02	CHOB 320	Greg Gianforte, MT-01	LHOB 1222
Robin Kelly, IL-02	RHOB 2416	Greg Walden, OR-02	RHOB 2185
Nanette Barragan, CA-44	LHOB 1030		
Lisa Blunt Rochester, DE-01	LHOB 1519		
Bobby Rush, IL-01	RHOB 2188		
Frank Pallone, NJ-06	RHOB 2107		

OVERSIGHT & INVESTIGATIONS
Room: RHOB 2322A
Phone: 202.225.2927

Majority:		Minority:	
C: Diana DeGette, CO-01	RHOB 2111	RM: Brett Guthrie, KY-02	RHOB 2434
Jan Schakowsky, IL-09	RHOB 2367	Michael Burgess, TX-26	RHOB 2161
Joe Kennedy, MA-04	CHOB 304	David McKinley, WV-01	RHOB 2239
Raul Ruiz, CA-36	RHOB 2342	Morgan Griffith, VA-09	RHOB 2202
Ann Kuster, NH-02	CHOB 320	Susan Brooks, IN-05	LHOB 2211
Kathy Castor, FL-14	RHOB 2052	Markwayne Mullin, OK-02	RHOB 2421
John Sarbanes, MD-03	RHOB 2370	Jeff Duncan, SC-03	RHOB 2229
Paul Tonko, NY-20	RHOB 2369	Greg Walden, OR-02	RHOB 2185
Yvette Clarke, NY-09	RHOB 2058		
Scott Peters, CA-52	RHOB 2338		
Frank Pallone, NJ-06	RHOB 2107		

ETHICS
Room: LHOB 1015
Website: www.ethics.house.gov
Phone: 202.225.7103
Ratio: 5 Democrats/5 Republicans
Subcommittees: 0

Majority:		Minority:	
C: Ted Deutch, FL-22	RHOB 2447	RM: Kenny Marchant, TX-24	RHOB 2304
Grace Meng, NY-06	RHOB 2209		
Susan Wild, PA-07	LHOB 1607	John Ratcliffe, TX-04	CHOB 223
Dean Phillips, MN-03	LHOB 1305	George Holding, NC-02	LHOB 1110
Anthony Brown, MD-04	LHOB 1323	Jackie Walorski, IN-02	CHOB 419
		Michael Guest, MS-03	CHOB 230

FINANCIAL SERVICES

Room: RHOB 2129
Website: www.financialservices.house.gov
Phone: 202.225.4247
Ratio: 34 Democrats/26 Republicans
Subcommittees: 6

Majority:		Minority:	
C: Maxine Waters, CA-43	RHOB 2221	**RM: Patrick McHenry, NC-10**	RHOB 2004
Carolyn Maloney, NY-12	RHOB 2308		
Nydia Velazquez, NY-07	RHOB 2302	Ann Wagner, MO-02	RHOB 2350
Brad Sherman, CA-30	RHOB 2181	Pete King, NY-02	CHOB 302
Gregory Meeks, NY-05	RHOB 2310	Frank Lucas, OK-03	RHOB 2405
Wm. Lacy Clay, MO-01	RHOB 2428	Bill Posey, FL-08	RHOB 2150
David Scott, GA-13	CHOB 225	Blaine Luetkemeyer, MO-03	RHOB 2230
Al Green, TX-09	RHOB 2347		
Emanuel Cleaver, MO-05	RHOB 2335	Bill Huizenga, MI-02	RHOB 2232
Ed Perlmutter, CO-07	LHOB 1226	Sean Duffy, WI-07	RHOB 1714
Jim Himes, CT-04	LHOB 1227	Steve Stivers, OH-15	RHOB 2234
Bill Foster, IL-11	LHOB 2366	Andy Barr, KY-06	RHOB 2430
Joyce Beatty, OH-03	RHOB 2303	Scott Tipton, CO-03	CHOB 218
Denny Heck, WA-10	RHOB 2452	Roger Williams, TX-25	LHOB 1708
Juan Vargas, CA-51	RHOB 2244	French Hill, AR-02	LHOB 1533
Josh Gottheimer, NJ-05	CHOB 213	Thomas Emmer, MN-06	CHOB 315
Vicente Gonzalez, TX-15	CHOB 113	Lee Zeldin, NY-01	RHOB 2441
Alfred Lawson, FL-05	LHOB 1406	Barry Loudermilk, GA-11	CHOB 422
Michael San Nicolas, GU-01	LHOB 1632	Alex Mooney, WV-02	RHOB 2440
Rashida Tlaib, MI-13	LHOB 1628	Warren Davidson, OH-08	LHOB 1107
Katherine Porter, CA-45	LHOB 1117	Ted Budd, NC-13	CHOB 118
Cindy Axne, IA-03	CHOB 330	David Kustoff, TN-08	CHOB 523
Sean Casten, IL-06	CHOB 429	Trey Hollingsworth, IN-09	LHOB 1641
Ayanna Pressley, MA-07	LHOB 1108	Anthony Gonzalez, OH-16	LHOB 1023
Ben McAdams, UT-04	CHOB 130	John Rose, TN-06	LHOB 1233
Alexandria Ocasio-Cortez, NY-14	CHOB 229	Bryan Steil, WI-01	LHOB 1408
		Lance Gooden, TX-05	CHOB 423
Jennifer Wexton, VA-10	LHOB 1217	Denver Riggleman, VA-05	LHOB 1023
Stephen Lynch, MA-08	RHOB 2109		
Tulsi Gabbard, HI-02	LHOB 1433		
Alma Adams, NC-12	RHOB 2436		
Madeleine Dean, PA-04	CHOB 129		
Jesus Garcia, IL-04	CHOB 530		
Sylvia Garcia, TX-29	LHOB 1620		
Dean Phillips, MN-03	LHOB 1305		

Majority CoS: Charla G. Ouertatani   **Minority CoS:** Edward G. Skala

──────────── Subcommittees ────────────

CONSUMER PROTECTION & FINANCIAL INSTITUTIONS

Room: RHOB 2129
Phone: 202.225.4247

Majority:		Minority:	
C: Gregory Meeks, NY-05	RHOB 2310	**RM: Blaine Luetkemeyer, MO-03**	RHOB 223
David Scott, GA-13	CHOB 225		
Nydia Velazquez, NY-07	RHOB 2302	Scott Tipton, CO-03	CHOB 21
Wm. Lacy Clay, MO-01	RHOB 2428	Frank Lucas, OK-03	RHOB 240
Denny Heck, WA-10	RHOB 2452	Bill Posey, FL-08	RHOB 215
Bill Foster, IL-11	LHOB 2366	Andy Barr, KY-06	RHOB 243
Alfred Lawson, FL-05	LHOB 1406	Roger Williams, TX-25	LHOB 170
Rashida Tlaib, MI-13	LHOB 1628	Barry Loudermilk, GA-11	CHOB 42
Katherine Porter, CA-45	LHOB 1117	Ted Budd, NC-13	CHOB 11
Ayanna Pressley, MA-07	LHOB 1108	David Kustoff, TN-08	CHOB 5
Ben McAdams, UT-04	CHOB 130	Denver Riggleman, VA-05	LHOB 10
Alexandria Ocasio-Cortez, NY-14	CHOB 229		
Jennifer Wexton, VA-10	LHOB 1217		

HOUSING, COMMUNITY DEVELOPMENT & INSURANCE

Room: RHOB 2129
Phone: 202.225.4247

Majority:		Minority:	
C: Wm. Lacy Clay, MO-01	RHOB 2428	**RM: Sean Duffy, WI-07**	RHOB 17
Nydia Velazquez, NY-07	RHOB 2302	Lance Gooden, TX-05	CHOB 4
Emanuel Cleaver, MO-05	RHOB 2335	Blaine Luetkemeyer, MO-03	RHOB 22
Brad Sherman, CA-30	RHOB 2181		
Joyce Beatty, OH-03	RHOB 2303	Bill Huizenga, MI-02	RHOB 22
Al Green, TX-09	RHOB 2347	Scott Tipton, CO-03	CHOB 2
Vicente Gonzalez, TX-15	CHOB 113	Lee Zeldin, NY-01	RHOB 24
Carolyn Maloney, NY-12	RHOB 2308	David Kustoff, TN-08	CHOB 5
Denny Heck, WA-10	RHOB 2452	Anthony Gonzalez, OH-16	LHOB 10

Juan Vargas, CA-51	RHOB 2244	John Rose, TN-06	LHOB 1232
Alfred Lawson, FL-05	LHOB 1406	Bryan Steil, WI-01	LHOB 1408
Rashida Taib, MI-13	LHOB 1628		
Cindy Axne, IA-03	CHOB 330		

INVESTOR PROTECTION, ENTREPRENEURSHIP & CAPITAL MARKETS
Room: RHOB 2129
Phone: 202.225.4247

Majority:		Minority:	
C: Carolyn Maloney, NY-12	RHOB 2308	RM: Bill Huizenga, MI-02	RHOB 2232
		Trey Hollingsworth, IN-09	LHOB 1641
Brad Sherman, CA-30	RHOB 2181	Pete King, NY-02	CHOB 302
David Scott, GA-13	CHOB 225	Sean Duffy, WI-07	RHOB 1714
Jim Himes, CT-04	LHOB 1227	Steve Stivers, OH-15	RHOB 2234
Bill Foster, IL-11	LHOB 2366	Ann Wagner, MO-02	RHOB 2350
Gregory Meeks, NY-05	RHOB 2310	French Hill, AR-02	LHOB 1533
Juan Vargas, CA-51	RHOB 2244	Thomas Emmer, MN-06	CHOB 315
Josh Gottheimer, NJ-05	CHOB 213	Alex Mooney, WV-02	RHOB 2440
Vicente Gonzalez, TX-15	CHOB 113	Warren Davidson, OH-08	LHOB 1107
Michael San Nicolas, GU-01	LHOB 1632		
Katherine Porter, CA-45	LHOB 1117		
Cindy Axne, IA-03	CHOB 330		
Sean Casten, IL-06	CHOB 429		
Alexandria Ocasio-Cortez, NY-14	CHOB 229		

NAT'L SECURITY, INTERNATIONAL DEVELOPMENT & MONETARY POLICY
Room: RHOB 2129
Phone: 202.225.4247

Majority:		Minority:	
C: Emanuel Cleaver, MO-05	RHOB 2335	RM: Steve Stivers, OH-15	RHOB 2234
		Denver Riggleman, VA-05	LHOB 1022
Ed Perlmutter, CO-07	LHOB 1226	Pete King, NY-02	CHOB 302
Jim Himes, CT-04	LHOB 1227	Frank Lucas, OK-03	RHOB 2405
Denny Heck, WA-10	RHOB 2452	Roger Williams, TX-25	LHOB 1708
Brad Sherman, CA-30	RHOB 2181	French Hill, AR-02	LHOB 1533
Juan Vargas, CA-51	RHOB 2244	Thomas Emmer, MN-06	CHOB 315
Josh Gottheimer, NJ-05	CHOB 213	Anthony Gonzalez, OH-16	LHOB 1023
Michael San Nicolas, GU-01	LHOB 1632	John Rose, TN-06	LHOB 1232
Ben McAdams, UT-04	CHOB 130		
Jennifer Wexton, VA-10	LHOB 1217		
Stephen Lynch, MA-08	RHOB 2109		
Tulsi Gabbard, HI-02	LHOB 1433		
Jesus Garcia, IL-04	CHOB 530		

OVERSIGHT & INVESTIGATIONS
Room: RHOB 2129
Phone: 202.225.4247

Majority:		Minority:	
C: Al Green, TX-09	RHOB 2347	RM: Andy Barr, KY-06	RHOB 2430
Joyce Beatty, OH-03	RHOB 2303	Lee Zeldin, NY-01	RHOB 2441
Stephen Lynch, MA-08	RHOB 2109	Bill Posey, FL-08	RHOB 2150
Lydia Velazquez, NY-07	RHOB 2302	Barry Loudermilk, GA-11	CHOB 422
Ed Perlmutter, CO-07	LHOB 1226	Warren Davidson, OH-08	LHOB 1107
Juan Vargas, CA-51	RHOB 2244	John Rose, TN-06	LHOB 1232
Sean Casten, IL-06	CHOB 429	Bryan Steil, WI-01	LHOB 1408
Madeleine Dean, PA-04	CHOB 129		
Sylvia Garcia, TX-29	LHOB 1620		
Dean Phillips, MN-03	LHOB 1305		

SUBCOMMITTEE ON DIVERSITY & INCLUSION
Room: RHOB 2129
Phone: 202.225.4247

Majority:		Minority:	
C: Joyce Beatty, OH-03	RHOB 2303	RM: Ann Wagner, MO-02	RHOB 2350
Wm. Lacy Clay, MO-01	RHOB 2428	Anthony Gonzalez, OH-16	LHOB 1023
Al Green, TX-09	RHOB 2347	Frank Lucas, OK-03	RHOB 2405
Josh Gottheimer, NJ-05	CHOB 213	Alex Mooney, WV-02	RHOB 2440
Vicente Gonzalez, TX-15	CHOB 113	Ted Budd, NC-13	CHOB 118
Fred Lawson, FL-05	LHOB 1406	David Kustoff, TN-08	CHOB 523
Ayanna Pressley, MA-07	LHOB 1108	Trey Hollingsworth, IN-09	LHOB 1641
Tulsi Gabbard, HI-02	LHOB 1433	Bryan Steil, WI-01	LHOB 1408
Alma Adams, NC-12	RHOB 2436	Lance Gooden, TX-05	CHOB 425
Madeleine Dean, PA-04	CHOB 129		
Sylvia Garcia, TX-29	LHOB 1620		
Dean Phillips, MN-03	LHOB 1305		

FOREIGN AFFAIRS

Room: RHOB 2170
Website: www.foreignaffairs.house.gov
Phone: 202.225.5021
Ratio: 26 Democrats/21 Republicans
Subcommittees: 6

Majority:		Minority:	
C: Eliot Engel, NY-16	RHOB 2426	**RM: Michael McCaul,**	RHOB 2001
Joaquin Castro, TX-20	RHOB 2241	**TX-10**	
Brad Sherman, CA-30	RHOB 2181	Ann Wagner, MO-02	RHOB 2350
Gregory Meeks, NY-05	RHOB 2310	Chris Smith, NJ-04	RHOB 2373
Albio Sires, NJ-08	RHOB 2268	Steve Chabot, OH-01	RHOB 2408
Gerry Connolly, VA-11	RHOB 2238	Joe Wilson, SC-02	LHOB 1436
Ted Deutch, FL-22	RHOB 2447	Scott Perry, PA-10	LHOB 1207
Karen Bass, CA-37	RHOB 2059	Theodore Yoho, FL-03	LHOB 1730
Bill Keating, MA-09	RHOB 2351	Adam Kinzinger, IL-16	RHOB 2245
David Cicilline, RI-01	RHOB 2233	Lee Zeldin, NY-01	RHOB 2441
Ami Bera, CA-07	LHOB 1727	Jim Sensenbrenner, WI-05	RHOB 2449
Dina Titus, NV-01	RHOB 2464	Brian Mast, FL-18	RHOB 2182
Adriano Espaillat, NY-13	LHOB 1630	Francis Rooney, FL-19	CHOB 120
Ted Lieu, CA-33	CHOB 403	Brian Fitzpatrick, PA-01	LHOB 1722
Susan Wild, PA-07	LHOB 1607	John Curtis, UT-03	CHOB 125
Dean Phillips, MN-03	LHOB 1305	Kenneth Buck, CO-04	RHOB 2455
Ilhan Omar, MN-05	LHOB 1517	Ronald Wright, TX-06	CHOB 428
Colin Allred, TX-32	CHOB 328	Guy Reschenthaler, PA-14	CHOB 531
Andy Levin, MI-09	CHOB 228	Tim Burchett, TN-02	LHOB 1122
Abigail Spanberger, VA-07	LHOB 1239	Gregory Pence, IN-06	CHOB 222
Chrissy Houlahan, PA-06	LHOB 1218	Steve Watkins, KS-02	LHOB 1205
Tom Malinowski, NJ-07	CHOB 426	Michael Guest, MS-03	CHOB 230
David Trone, MD-06	LHOB 1213		
Jim Costa, CA-16	RHOB 2081		
Juan Vargas, CA-51	RHOB 2244		
Vicente Gonzalez, TX-15	CHOB 113		

Majority CoS: Jason B. Steinbaum   **Minority CoS:** Brendan P. Shields

––––––––––––– Subcommittees –––––––––––––

AFRICA, GLOBAL HEALTH, GLOBAL HUMAN RIGHTS & INTERNAT'I ORGS
Room: RHOB 2170
Phone: 202.225.5021

Majority:		Minority:	
C: Karen Bass, CA-37	RHOB 2059	**RM: Chris Smith, NJ-04**	RHOB 237.
Susan Wild, PA-07	LHOB 1607	Jim Sensenbrenner, WI-05	RHOB 244
Dean Phillips, MN-03	LHOB 1305	Ronald Wright, TX-06	CHOB 42.
Ilhan Omar, MN-05	LHOB 1517	Tim Burchett, TN-02	LHOB 112
Chrissy Houlahan, PA-06	LHOB 1218		

ASIA, THE PACIFIC & NONPROLIFERATION
Room: RHOB 2170
Phone: 202.225.5021

Majority:		Minority:	
C: Brad Sherman, CA-30	RHOB 2181	**RM: Theodore Yoho,**	LHOB 173
Dina Titus, NV-01	RHOB 2464	**FL-03**	
Chrissy Houlahan, PA-06	LHOB 1218	Scott Perry, PA-10	LHOB 120
Gerry Connolly, VA-11	RHOB 2238	Ann Wagner, MO-02	RHOB 235
Ami Bera, CA-07	LHOB 1727	Brian Mast, FL-18	RHOB 218
Andy Levin, MI-09	CHOB 228	John Curtis, UT-03	CHOB 12
Abigail Spanberger, VA-07	LHOB 1239		

EUROPE, EURASIA, ENERGY & THE ENVIRONMENT
Room: RHOB 2170
Phone: 202.225.5021

Majority:		Minority:	
C: Bill Keating, MA-09	RHOB 2351	**RM: Adam Kinzinger,**	RHOB 22
Abigail Spanberger, VA-07	LHOB 1239	**IL-16**	
Gregory Meeks, NY-05	RHOB 2310	Joe Wilson, SC-02	LHOB 14.
Albio Sires, NJ-08	RHOB 2268	Ann Wagner, MO-02	RHOB 23
Ted Deutch, FL-22	RHOB 2447	Jim Sensenbrenner, WI-05	RHOB 24
David Cicilline, RI-01	RHOB 2233	Francis Rooney, FL-19	CHOB 1.
Joaquin Castro, TX-20	RHOB 2241	Brian Fitzpatrick, PA-01	LHOB 17
Dina Titus, NV-01	RHOB 2464	Gregory Pence, IN-06	CHOB 2
Susan Wild, PA-07	LHOB 1607	Ronald Wright, TX-06	CHOB 4
David Trone, MD-06	LHOB 1213	Michael Guest, MS-03	CHOB 2
Jim Costa, CA-16	RHOB 2081	Tim Burchett, TN-02	LHOB 11
Vicente Gonzalez, TX-15	CHOB 113		

MIDDLE EAST, NORTH AFRICA & INTERNATIONAL TERRORISM
Room: RHOB 2170
Phone: 202.225.5021

Majority:		Minority:	
C: Ted Deutch, FL-22	RHOB 2447	RM: Joe Wilson, SC-02	LHOB 1436
Gerry Connolly, VA-11	RHOB 2238	Steve Chabot, OH-01	RHOB 2408
David Cicilline, RI-01	RHOB 2233	Adam Kinzinger, IL-16	RHOB 2245
Ted Lieu, CA-33	CHOB 403	Lee Zeldin, NY-01	RHOB 2441
Colin Allred, TX-32	CHOB 328	Brian Mast, FL-18	RHOB 2182
Tom Malinowski, NJ-07	CHOB 426	Brian Fitzpatrick, PA-01	LHOB 1722
David Trone, MD-06	LHOB 1213	Guy Reschenthaler, PA-14	CHOB 531
Brad Sherman, CA-30	RHOB 2181	Steve Watkins, KS-02	LHOB 1205
Bill Keating, MA-09	RHOB 2351		
Juan Vargas, CA-51	RHOB 2244		

OVERSIGHT & INVESTIGATIONS
Room: RHOB 2170
Phone: 202.225.5021

Majority:		Minority:	
C: Ami Bera, CA-07	LHOB 1727	RM: Lee Zeldin, NY-01	RHOB 2441
Ilhan Omar, MN-05	LHOB 1517	Scott Perry, PA-10	LHOB 1207
Adriano Espaillat, NY-13	LHOB 1630	Kenneth Buck, CO-04	RHOB 2455
Ted Lieu, CA-33	CHOB 403	Guy Reschenthaler, PA-14	CHOB 531
Tom Malinowski, NJ-07	CHOB 426		
David Cicilline, RI-01	RHOB 2233		

WESTERN HEMISPHERE, CIVILIAN SECURITY, & TRADE
Room: RHOB 2170
Phone: 202.225.5021

Majority:		Minority:	
C: Albio Sires, NJ-08	RHOB 2268	RM: Francis Rooney, FL-19	CHOB 120
Gregory Meeks, NY-05	RHOB 2310		
Joaquin Castro, TX-20	RHOB 2241	Chris Smith, NJ-04	RHOB 2373
Adriano Espaillat, NY-13	LHOB 1630	Theodore Yoho, FL-03	LHOB 1730
Dean Phillips, MN-03	LHOB 1305	John Curtis, UT-03	CHOB 125
Andy Levin, MI-09	CHOB 228	Kenneth Buck, CO-04	RHOB 2455
Vicente Gonzalez, TX-15	CHOB 113	Michael Guest, MS-03	CHOB 230
Juan Vargas, CA-51	RHOB 2244		

HOMELAND SECURITY

Room: FHOB H2-176
Website: www.homeland.house.gov
Phone: 202.226.2616
Ratio: 18 Democrats/13 Republicans
Subcommittees: 6

Majority:		Minority:	
C: Bennie Thompson, MS-02	RHOB 2466	RM: Mike Rogers, AL-03	RHOB 2184
		Michael McCaul, TX-10	RHOB 2001
Lauren Underwood, IL-14	LHOB 1118	Pete King, NY-02	CHOB 302
Sheila Jackson Lee, TX-18	RHOB 2079	John Katko, NY-24	RHOB 2457
Jim Langevin, RI-02	RHOB 2077	John Ratcliffe, TX-04	CHOB 223
Cedric Richmond, LA-02	CHOB 506	Clay Higgins, LA-03	CHOB 424
Donald Payne, NJ-10	CHOB 103	Mark Walker, NC-06	LHOB 1725
Kathleen Rice, NY-04	RHOB 2181	Debbie Lesko, AZ-08	LHOB 1113
Lou Correa, CA-46	LHOB 1039	Mark Green, TN-07	CHOB 533
Xochitl Liana Torres-Small, NM-02	CHOB 430	Van Taylor, TX-03	LHOB 1404
		John Joyce, PA-13	LHOB 1337
Max Rose, NY-11	LHOB 1529	Daniel Crenshaw, TX-02	CHOB 413
Elissa Slotkin, MI-08	LHOB 1531	Michael Guest, MS-03	CHOB 230
Emanuel Cleaver, MO-05	RHOB 2335		
Al Green, TX-09	RHOB 2347		
Yvette Clarke, NY-09	RHOB 2058		
Dina Titus, NV-01	RHOB 2464		
Bonnie Watson Coleman, NJ-12	RHOB 2442		
Nanette Barragan, CA-44	LHOB 1030		
Valdez Demings, FL-10	CHOB 217		

Majority CoS: Hope E. Goins   **Minority CoS:** Christopher Vieson
Majority Sched: Amanda S. Mims

――――――――― Subcommittees ―――――――――

BORDER SECURITY, FACILITATION & OPERATIONS
Room: FHOB H2-176
Phone: 202.226.2616

Majority:		Minority:	
C: Kathleen Rice, NY-04	RHOB 2435	RM: Clay Higgins, LA-03	CHOB 424
Donald Payne, NJ-10	CHOB 103	Debbie Lesko, AZ-08	LHOB 1113

Lou Correa, CA-46	LHOB 1039	John Joyce, PA-13	LHOB 1337
Xochitl Liana Torres-Small, NM-02	CHOB 430	Michael Guest, MS-03	CHOB 230
		Mike Rogers, AL-03	RHOB 2184
Al Green, TX-09	RHOB 2347		
Yvette Clarke, NY-09	RHOB 2058		
Bennie Thompson, MS-02	RHOB 2466		

CYBERSECURITY, INFRASTRUCTURE PROTECTION & INNOVATION
Room: FHOB H2-176
Phone: 202.226.2616

Majority:		Minority:	
C: Cedric Richmond, LA-02	CHOB 506	RM: John Katko, NY-24	RHOB 2457
		John Ratcliffe, TX-04	CHOB 223
Sheila Jackson Lee, TX-18	RHOB 2079	Mark Walker, NC-06	LHOB 1725
Jim Langevin, RI-02	RHOB 2077	Van Taylor, TX-03	LHOB 1404
Kathleen Rice, NY-04	RHOB 2435	Mike Rogers, AL-03	RHOB 2184
Lauren Underwood, IL-14	LHOB 1118		
Elissa Slotkin, MI-08	LHOB 1531		
Bennie Thompson, MS-02	RHOB 2466		

EMERGENCY PREPAREDNESS, RESPONSE & RECOVERY
Room: FHOB H2-176
Phone: 202.226.2616

Majority:		Minority:	
C: Donald Payne, NJ-10	CHOB 103	RM: Pete King, NY-02	CHOB 30
Cedric Richmond, LA-02	CHOB 506	John Joyce, PA-13	LHOB 133
Max Rose, NY-11	LHOB 1529	Daniel Crenshaw, TX-02	CHOB 41
Lauren Underwood, IL-14	LHOB 1118	Michael Guest, MS-03	CHOB 23
Al Green, TX-09	RHOB 2347	Mike Rogers, AL-03	RHOB 218
Yvette Clarke, NY-09	RHOB 2058		
Bennie Thompson, MS-02	RHOB 2466		

INTELLIGENCE & COUNTERTERRORISM
Room: FHOB H2-176
Phone: 202.226.2616

Majority:		Minority:	
C: Max Rose, NY-11	LHOB 1529	RM: Mark Walker, NC-06	LHOB 172
Sheila Jackson Lee, TX-18	RHOB 2079	Pete King, NY-02	CHOB 30
Jim Langevin, RI-02	RHOB 2077	Mark Green, TN-07	CHOB 53
Elissa Slotkin, MI-08	LHOB 1531	Mike Rogers, AL-03	RHOB 218
Bennie Thompson, MS-02	RHOB 2466		

OVERSIGHT, MANAGEMENT & ACCOUNTABILITY
Room: FHOB H2-176
Phone: 202.226.2616

Majority:		Minority:	
C: Xochitl Liana Torres-Small, NM-02	CHOB 430	RM: Daniel Crenshaw, TX-02	CHOB 41
Dina Titus, NV-01	RHOB 2464	Clay Higgins, LA-03	CHOB 4
Bonnie Watson Coleman, NJ-12	RHOB 2442	Van Taylor, TX-03	LHOB 140
		Mike Rogers, AL-03	RHOB 218
Nanette Barragan, CA-44	LHOB 1030		
Bennie Thompson, MS-02	RHOB 2466		

TRANSPORTATION & MARITIME SECURITY
Room: FHOB H2-176
Phone: 202.226.2616

Majority:		Minority:	
C: Lou Correa, CA-46	LHOB 1039	RM: Debbie Lesko, AZ-08	LHOB 11
Emanuel Cleaver, MO-05	RHOB 2335	John Katko, NY-24	RHOB 24
Dina Titus, NV-01	RHOB 2464	John Ratcliffe, TX-04	CHOB 2
Bonnie Watson Coleman, NJ-12	RHOB 2442	Mark Green, TN-07	CHOB 5
		Mike Rogers, AL-03	RHOB 2
Nanette Barragan, CA-44	LHOB 1030		
Valdez Demings, FL-10	CHOB 217		
Bennie Thompson, MS-02	RHOB 2466		

JUDICIARY

Room: RHOB 2138
Website: www.judiciary.house.gov
Phone: 202.225.3951
Ratio: 24 Democrats/17 Republicans
Subcommittees: 5

Majority:		Minority:	
C: Jerry Nadler, NY-10	RHOB 2132	RM: Doug Collins, GA-09	LHOB 1
Mary Scanlon, PA-05	LHOB 1535	Jim Sensenbrenner, WI-05	RHOB 2
Zoe Lofgren, CA-19	LHOB 1401	Steve Chabot, OH-01	RHOB 2
Sheila Jackson Lee, TX-18	RHOB 2079	Louie Gohmert, TX-01	RHOB 2

Steve Cohen, TN-09	RHOB 2104	Jim Jordan, OH-04	RHOB 2056
Hank Johnson, GA-04	RHOB 2240	Kenneth Buck, CO-04	RHOB 2455
Ted Deutch, FL-22	RHOB 2447	John Ratcliffe, TX-04	CHOB 223
Karen Bass, CA-37	RHOB 2059	Martha Roby, AL-02	CHOB 504
Cedric Richmond, LA-02	CHOB 506	Matt Gaetz, FL-01	LHOB 1721
Hakeem Jeffries, NY-08	RHOB 2433	Mike Johnson, LA-04	CHOB 418
David Cicilline, RI-01	RHOB 2233	Andy Biggs, AZ-05	LHOB 1318
Eric Swalwell, CA-15	CHOB 407	Tom McClintock, CA-04	RHOB 2312
Ted Lieu, CA-33	CHOB 403	Debbie Lesko, AZ-08	LHOB 1113
Jamie Raskin, MD-08	CHOB 412	Guy Reschenthaler, PA-14	CHOB 531
Pramila Jayapal, WA-07	LHOB 1510	Benjamin Cline, VA-06	LHOB 1009
Valdez Demings, FL-10	CHOB 217	Kelly Armstrong, ND-01	LHOB 1004
Lou Correa, CA-46	LHOB 1039	Greg Steube, FL-17	CHOB 521
Sylvia Garcia, TX-29	LHOB 1620		
Joseph Neguse, CO-02	LHOB 1419		
Lucy McBath, GA-06	LHOB 1513		
Greg Stanton, AZ-09	CHOB 128		
Madeleine Dean, PA-04	CHOB 129		
Debbie Mucarsel-Powell, FL-26	CHOB 114		
Veronica Escobar, TX-16	LHOB 1505		

Majority CoS: Perry H. Apelbaum   **Minority CoS:** Brendan Belair
——————————— Subcommittees ———————————

ANTITRUST, COMMERCIAL & ADMINISTRATIVE LAW
Room: Thomas P. O'Neill Federal Bldg. 6240
Phone: 202.226.7680

Majority:		**Minority:**	
: David Cicilline, RI-01	RHOB 2233	**RM: Jim Sensenbrenner,**	RHOB 2449
Hank Johnson, GA-04	RHOB 2240	**WI-05**	
Jamie Raskin, MD-08	CHOB 412	Matt Gaetz, FL-01	LHOB 1721
Pramila Jayapal, WA-07	LHOB 1510	Kenneth Buck, CO-04	RHOB 2455
Valdez Demings, FL-10	CHOB 217	Kelly Armstrong, ND-01	LHOB 1004
Mary Scanlon, PA-05	LHOB 1535	Greg Steube, FL-17	CHOB 521
Joseph Neguse, CO-02	LHOB 1419		
Lucy McBath, GA-06	LHOB 1513		

CONSTITUTION, CIVIL RIGHTS & CIVIL LIBERTIES
Room: RHOB 2138
Phone: 202.225.3951

Majority:		**Minority:**	
: Steve Cohen, TN-09	RHOB 2104	**RM: Mike Johnson, LA-04**	CHOB 418
Jamie Raskin, MD-08	CHOB 412	Louie Gohmert, TX-01	RHOB 2267
Eric Swalwell, CA-15	CHOB 407	Jim Jordan, OH-04	RHOB 2056
Mary Scanlon, PA-05	LHOB 1535	Guy Reschenthaler, PA-14	CHOB 531
Madeleine Dean, PA-04	CHOB 129	Benjamin Cline, VA-06	LHOB 1009
Sylvia Garcia, TX-29	LHOB 1620	Kelly Armstrong, ND-01	LHOB 1004
Veronica Escobar, TX-16	LHOB 1505		
Sheila Jackson Lee, TX-18	RHOB 2079		

COURTS, INTELLECTUAL PROPERTY & INTERNET
Room: Thomas P. O'Neill Federal Bldg. 6310
Phone: 202.225.5741

Majority:		**Minority:**	
: Hank Johnson, GA-04	RHOB 2240	**RM: Martha Roby, AL-02**	CHOB 504
Ted Deutch, FL-22	RHOB 2447	Steve Chabot, OH-01	RHOB 2408
Cedric Richmond, LA-02	CHOB 506	Jim Jordan, OH-04	RHOB 2056
Hakeem Jeffries, NY-08	RHOB 2433	John Ratcliffe, TX-04	CHOB 223
Ted Lieu, CA-33	CHOB 403	Matt Gaetz, FL-01	LHOB 1721
Greg Stanton, AZ-09	CHOB 128	Mike Johnson, LA-04	CHOB 418
Zoe Lofgren, CA-19	LHOB 1401	Andy Biggs, AZ-05	LHOB 1318
Steve Cohen, TN-09	RHOB 2104	Guy Reschenthaler, PA-14	CHOB 531
Karen Bass, CA-37	RHOB 2059	Benjamin Cline, VA-06	LHOB 1009
Eric Swalwell, CA-15	CHOB 407		
Lou Correa, CA-46	LHOB 1039		

CRIME, TERRORISM & HOMELAND SECURITY
Room: Thomas P. O'Neill Federal Bldg. B-336
Phone: 202.225.5727

Majority:		**Minority:**	
: Karen Bass, CA-37	RHOB 2059	**RM: John Ratcliffe, TX-04**	CHOB 223
Sheila Jackson Lee, TX-18	RHOB 2079	Jim Sensenbrenner, WI-05	RHOB 2449
Valdez Demings, FL-10	CHOB 217	Steve Chabot, OH-01	RHOB 2408
Lucy McBath, GA-06	LHOB 1513	Louie Gohmert, TX-01	RHOB 2267
Ted Deutch, FL-22	RHOB 2447	Tom McClintock, CA-04	RHOB 2312
Cedric Richmond, LA-02	CHOB 506	Debbie Lesko, AZ-08	LHOB 1113
Hakeem Jeffries, NY-08	RHOB 2433	Guy Reschenthaler, PA-14	CHOB 531
David Cicilline, RI-01	RHOB 2233		

Ted Lieu, CA-33	CHOB 403	
Madeleine Dean, PA-04	CHOB 129	
Debbie Mucarsel-Powell, FL-26	CHOB 114	
Steve Cohen, TN-09	RHOB 2104	

IMMIGRATION & CITIZENSHIP

Room: Thomas P. O'Neill Federal Bldg. 6320
Phone: 202.225.3926

Majority:		Minority:	
C: Zoe Lofgren, CA-19	LHOB 1401	RM: Kenneth Buck, CO-04	RHOB 245
Pramila Jayapal, WA-07	LHOB 1510	Andy Biggs, AZ-05	LHOB 131
Lou Correa, CA-46	LHOB 1039	Tom McClintock, CA-04	RHOB 231
Sylvia Garcia, TX-29	LHOB 1620	Debbie Lesko, AZ-08	LHOB 111
Joseph Neguse, CO-02	LHOB 1419	Kelly Armstrong, ND-01	LHOB 100
Debbie Mucarsel-Powell, FL-26	CHOB 114	Greg Steube, FL-17	CHOB 52
Veronica Escobar, TX-16	LHOB 1505		
Sheila Jackson Lee, TX-18	RHOB 2079		
Mary Scanlon, PA-05	LHOB 1535		

NATURAL RESOURCES

Room: LHOB 1324
Website: www.naturalresources.house.gov
Phone: 202.225.6065
Ratio: 25 Democrats/19 Republicans
Subcommittees: 5

Majority:		Minority:	
C: Raul Grijalva, AZ-03	LHOB 1511	RM: Rob Bishop, UT-01	CHOB 12
Debra Haaland, NM-01	LHOB 1237	Don Young, AK-01	RHOB 231
Gregorio Sablan, MP-01	RHOB 2411	Louie Gohmert, TX-01	RHOB 22
Grace Napolitano, CA-32	LHOB 1610	Doug Lamborn, CO-05	RHOB 23
Jim Costa, CA-16	RHOB 2081	Rob Wittman, VA-01	RHOB 20
Jared Huffman, CA-02	LHOB 1527	Tom McClintock, CA-04	RHOB 23
Alan Lowenthal, CA-47	CHOB 108	Paul Gosar, AZ-04	RHOB 20
Ruben Gallego, AZ-07	LHOB 1131	Paul Cook, CA-08	LHOB 10
T.J. Cox, CA-21	LHOB 1728	Bruce Westerman, AR-04	CHOB 2
Joseph Neguse, CO-02	LHOB 1419	Garret Graves, LA-06	RHOB 24
Mike Levin, CA-49	LHOB 1626	Jody Hice, GA-10	CHOB 4
Jeff Van Drew, NJ-02	CHOB 331	Aumua Radewagen, AS-01	LHOB 13
Joe Cunningham, SC-01	CHOB 423	Daniel Webster, FL-11	LHOB 12
Nydia Velazquez, NY-07	RHOB 2302	Liz Cheney, WY-01	CHOB 4
Diana DeGette, CO-01	RHOB 2111	Mike Johnson, LA-04	CHOB 4
Wm. Lacy Clay, MO-01	RHOB 2428	Jenniffer Gonzalez-Colon, PR-01	LHOB 16
Debbie Dingell, MI-12	CHOB 116		
Anthony Brown, MD-04	LHOB 1323	John Curtis, UT-03	CHOB 1
A. Donald McEachin, VA-04	CHOB 314	Kevin Hern, OK-01	LHOB 10
Darren Soto, FL-09	LHOB 1507	Russell Fulcher, ID-01	LHOB 15
Ed Case, HI-01	RHOB 2443		
Steven Horsford, NV-04	LHOB 1330		
Michael San Nicolas, GU-01	LHOB 1632		
Matthew Cartwright, PA-08	LHOB 1034		
Paul Tonko, NY-20	RHOB 2369		

Majority CoS: David Watkins　　　**Minority CoS:** Parish M. Braden

———————— Subcommittees ————————

ENERGY & MINERAL RESOURCES

Room: FHOB 1324
Phone: 202.225.6065

Majority:		Minority:	
C: Alan Lowenthal, CA-47	CHOB 108	RM: Paul Gosar, AZ-04	RHOB 2
Mike Levin, CA-49	LHOB 1626	Doug Lamborn, CO-05	RHOB 2
Joe Cunningham, SC-01	CHOB 423	Bruce Westerman, AR-04	CHOB
A. Donald McEachin, VA-04	CHOB 314	Garret Graves, LA-06	RHOB 2
Diana DeGette, CO-01	RHOB 2111	Liz Cheney, WY-01	CHOB
Anthony Brown, MD-04	LHOB 1323	Kevin Hern, OK-01	LHOB 1
Jared Huffman, CA-02	LHOB 1527	Rob Bishop, UT-01	CHOB
Raul Grijalva, AZ-03	LHOB 1511		

INDIGENOUS PEOPLES OF THE UNITED STATES

Room: LHOB 1324
Phone: 202.225.6065

Majority:		Minority:	
C: Ruben Gallego, AZ-07	LHOB 1131	RM: Paul Cook, CA-08	LHOB 1
Darren Soto, FL-09	LHOB 1507	Don Young, AK-01	RHOB 2
Michael San Nicolas, GU-01	LHOB 1632	Rob Wittman, VA-01	RHOB 2
Debra Haaland, NM-01	LHOB 1237	Aumua Radewagen, AS-01	LHOB 1

Ed Case, HI-01	RHOB 2443	John Curtis, UT-03	CHOB 125
Raul Grijalva, AZ-03	LHOB 1511	Kevin Hern, OK-01	LHOB 1019
		Rob Bishop, UT-01	CHOB 123

NATIONAL PARKS, FORESTS & PUBLIC LANDS

Room: FHOB H2-186
Phone: 202.225.6065

Majority:		Minority:	
C: Debra Haaland, NM-01	LHOB 1237	RM: Don Young, AK-01	RHOB 2314
Joseph Neguse, CO-02	LHOB 1419	Louie Gohmert, TX-01	RHOB 2267
Diana DeGette, CO-01	RHOB 2111	Tom McClintock, CA-04	RHOB 2312
Debbie Dingell, MI-12	CHOB 116	Paul Cook, CA-08	LHOB 1027
Steven Horsford, NV-04	LHOB 1330	Bruce Westerman, AR-04	CHOB 209
Jared Huffman, CA-02	LHOB 1527	Jody Hice, GA-10	CHOB 409
Ruben Gallego, AZ-07	LHOB 1131	Daniel Webster, FL-11	LHOB 1210
Alan Lowenthal, CA-47	CHOB 108	John Curtis, UT-03	CHOB 125
Ed Case, HI-01	RHOB 2443	Russell Fulcher, ID-01	LHOB 1520
Raul Grijalva, AZ-03	LHOB 1511	Rob Bishop, UT-01	CHOB 123

OVERSIGHT & INVESTIGATIONS

Room: LHOB 1324
Phone: 202.225.6065

Majority:		Minority:	
C: T.J. Cox, CA-21	LHOB 1728	RM: Louie Gohmert, TX-01	RHOB 2267
Debbie Dingell, MI-12	CHOB 116		
A. Donald McEachin, VA-04	CHOB 314	Paul Gosar, AZ-04	RHOB 2057
Michael San Nicolas, GU-01	LHOB 1632	Mike Johnson, LA-04	CHOB 418
Raul Grijalva, AZ-03	LHOB 1511	Jenniffer Gonzalez-Colon, PR-01	LHOB 1609
		Rob Bishop, UT-01	CHOB 123

WATER, OCEANS & WILDLIFE

Room: LHOB 1522
Phone: 202.225.6065

Majority:		Minority:	
C: Jared Huffman, CA-02	LHOB 1527	RM: Tom McClintock, CA-04	RHOB 2312
Grace Napolitano, CA-32	LHOB 1610	Doug Lamborn, CO-05	RHOB 2371
Jim Costa, CA-16	RHOB 2081	Rob Wittman, VA-01	RHOB 2055
Gregorio Sablan, MP-01	RHOB 2411	Garret Graves, LA-06	RHOB 2402
Jeff Van Drew, NJ-02	CHOB 331	Jody Hice, GA-10	CHOB 409
Nydia Velazquez, NY-07	RHOB 2302	Aumua Radewagen, AS-01	LHOB 1339
Anthony Brown, MD-04	LHOB 1323	Daniel Webster, FL-11	LHOB 1210
Ed Case, HI-01	RHOB 2443	Mike Johnson, LA-04	CHOB 418
Alan Lowenthal, CA-47	CHOB 108	Jenniffer Gonzalez-Colon, PR-01	LHOB 1609
T.J. Cox, CA-21	LHOB 1728		
Joseph Neguse, CO-02	LHOB 1419		
Mike Levin, CA-49	LHOB 1626	Russell Fulcher, ID-01	LHOB 1520
Joe Cunningham, SC-01	CHOB 423	Rob Bishop, UT-01	CHOB 123
Raul Grijalva, AZ-03	LHOB 1511		

OVERSIGHT & REFORM

Room: RHOB 2157
Website: www.oversight.house.gov
Phone: 202.225.5051
Ratio: 24 Democrats/18 Republicans
Subcommittees: 5

Majority:		Minority:	
C: Elijah Cummings, MD-07	RHOB 2163	RM: Jim Jordan, OH-04	RHOB 2056
		Justin Amash, MI-03	CHOB 106
Katherine Hill, CA-25	LHOB 1130	Paul Gosar, AZ-04	RHOB 2057
Carolyn Maloney, NY-12	RHOB 2308	Virginia Foxx, NC-05	RHOB 2462
Eleanor Norton, DC-01	RHOB 2136	Thomas Massie, KY-04	RHOB 2453
Wm. Lacy Clay, MO-01	RHOB 2428	Mark Meadows, NC-11	LHOB 2160
Stephen Lynch, MA-08	RHOB 2109	Jody Hice, GA-10	CHOB 409
Jim Cooper, TN-05	LHOB 1536	Glenn Grothman, WI-06	LHOB 1427
Gerry Connolly, VA-11	RHOB 2238	James Comer, KY-01	LHOB 1037
Raja Krishnamoorthi, IL-08	CHOB 115	Michael Cloud, TX-27	RHOB 1314
Jamie Raskin, MD-08	CHOB 412	Bob Gibbs, OH-07	RHOB 2446
Harley Rouda, CA-48	RHOB 2300	Clay Higgins, LA-03	CHOB 424
Debbie Wasserman Schultz, FL-23	LHOB 1114	Ralph Norman, SC-05	CHOB 319
		Chip Roy, TX-21	LHOB 1319
John Sarbanes, MD-03	RHOB 2370	Carol Miller, WV-03	LHOB 1605
Peter Welch, VT-01	RHOB 2187	Mark Green, TN-07	CHOB 533
Jackie Speier, CA-14	RHOB 2465	Kelly Armstrong, ND-01	LHOB 1004
Robin Kelly, IL-02	RHOB 2416	Greg Steube, FL-17	CHOB 521
Mark DeSaulnier, CA-11	CHOB 503		
Brenda Lawrence, MI-14	RHOB 2463		

Stacey Plaskett, VI-01	RHOB 2404		
Ro Khanna, CA-17	CHOB 221		
Jimmy Gomez, CA-34	LHOB 1530		
Alexandria Ocasio-Cortez, NY-14	CHOB 229		
Ayanna Pressley, MA-07	LHOB 1108		
Rashida Tlaib, MI-13	LHOB 1628		

Majority CoS: David P. Rapallo   **Minority CoS:** Christopher Hixon
――――――――――――――――――――― Subcommittees ―――――――――――――――――――――

GOVERNMENT OPERATIONS
Room: RHOB 2471
Phone: 202.225.5051

Majority:		Minority:	
C: Gerry Connolly, VA-11	RHOB 2238	**RM: Mark Meadows, NC-11**	LHOB 216●
Eleanor Norton, DC-01	RHOB 2136		
John Sarbanes, MD-03	RHOB 2370	Thomas Massie, KY-04	RHOB 245
Jackie Speier, CA-14	RHOB 2465	Jody Hice, GA-10	CHOB 40●
Brenda Lawrence, MI-14	RHOB 2463	Glenn Grothman, WI-06	LHOB 142●
Stacey Plaskett, VI-01	RHOB 2404	James Comer, KY-01	LHOB 103
Ro Khanna, CA-17	CHOB 221	Ralph Norman, SC-05	CHOB 31
Stephen Lynch, MA-08	RHOB 2109	Greg Steube, FL-17	CHOB 52
Jamie Raskin, MD-08	CHOB 412		

NATIONAL SECURITY
Room: RHOB 2471
Phone: 202.225.5051

Majority:		Minority:	
C: Stephen Lynch, MA-08	RHOB 2109	**RM: Jody Hice, GA-10**	CHOB 4C
Jim Cooper, TN-05	LHOB 1536	Justin Amash, MI-03	CHOB 1C
Peter Welch, VT-01	RHOB 2187	Paul Gosar, AZ-04	RHOB 205
Harley Rouda, CA-48	RHOB 2300	Virginia Foxx, NC-05	RHOB 246
Debbie Wasserman Schultz, FL-23	LHOB 1114	Mark Meadows, NC-11	LHOB 216
		Michael Cloud, TX-27	RHOB 131
Robin Kelly, IL-02	RHOB 2416	Mark Green, TN-07	CHOB 53
Mark DeSaulnier, CA-11	CHOB 503		
Stacey Plaskett, VI-01	RHOB 2404		
Brenda Lawrence, MI-14	RHOB 2463		

SUBCOMMITTEE ON CIVIL RIGHTS & CIVIL LIBERTIES
Room: RHOB 2471
Phone: 202.225.5051

Majority:		Minority:	
C: Jamie Raskin, MD-08	CHOB 412	**RM: Chip Roy, TX-21**	LHOB 13
Carolyn Maloney, NY-12	RHOB 2308	Justin Amash, MI-03	CHOB 1●
Wm. Lacy Clay, MO-01	RHOB 2428	Thomas Massie, KY-04	RHOB 24
Debbie Wasserman Schultz, FL-23	LHOB 1114	Mark Meadows, NC-11	LHOB 21●
		Jody Hice, GA-10	CHOB 4●
Robin Kelly, IL-02	RHOB 2416	Michael Cloud, TX-27	RHOB 13●
Jimmy Gomez, CA-34	LHOB 1530	Carol Miller, WV-03	LHOB 16
Alexandria Ocasio-Cortez, NY-14	CHOB 229		
Ayanna Pressley, MA-07	LHOB 1108		
Eleanor Norton, DC-01	RHOB 2136		

SUBCOMMITTEE ON ECONOMIC & CONSUMER POLICY
Room: RHOB 2471
Phone: 202.225.5051

Majority:		Minority:	
C: Raja Krishnamoorthi, IL-08	CHOB 115	**RM: Michael Cloud, TX-27**	RHOB 13
		Glenn Grothman, WI-06	LHOB 14
Mark DeSaulnier, CA-11	CHOB 503	James Comer, KY-01	LHOB 1●
Katherine Hill, CA-25	LHOB 1130	Chip Roy, TX-21	LHOB 13
Ro Khanna, CA-17	CHOB 221	Carol Miller, WV-03	LHOB 1●
Ayanna Pressley, MA-07	LHOB 1108		
Rashida Tlaib, MI-13	LHOB 1628		
Gerry Connolly, VA-11	RHOB 2238		

SUBCOMMITTEE ON ENVIRONMENT
Room: RHOB 2471
Phone: 202.225.5051

Majority:		Minority:	
C: Harley Rouda, CA-48	RHOB 2300	**RM: James Comer, KY-01**	LHOB 1●
Katherine Hill, CA-25	LHOB 1130	Paul Gosar, AZ-04	RHOB 2●
Rashida Tlaib, MI-13	LHOB 1628	Bob Gibbs, OH-07	RHOB 2●
Raja Krishnamoorthi, IL-08	CHOB 115	Clay Higgins, LA-03	CHOB
Jackie Speier, CA-14	RHOB 2465	Kelly Armstrong, ND-01	LHOB 1
Jimmy Gomez, CA-34	LHOB 1530		

Alexandria Ocasio-Cortez, CHOB 229
NY-14

RULES

Room: The Capitol H-312
Website: www.rules.house.gov
Phone: 202.225.9091
Ratio: 9 Democrats/4 Republicans
Subcommittees: 2

Majority:		Minority:	
C: Jim McGovern, MA-02	CHOB 408	RM: Tom Cole, OK-04	RHOB 2207
Alcee Hastings, FL-20	RHOB 2353	Rob Woodall, GA-07	LHOB 1724
Norma Torres, CA-35	RHOB 2444	Michael Burgess, TX-26	RHOB 2161
Ed Perlmutter, CO-07	LHOB 1226	Debbie Lesko, AZ-08	LHOB 1113
Jamie Raskin, MD-08	CHOB 412		
Mary Scanlon, PA-05	LHOB 1535		
Joseph Morelle, NY-25	LHOB 1317		
Donna Shalala, FL-27	LHOB 1320		
Mark DeSaulnier, CA-11	CHOB 503		

Majority CoS: Donald C. Sisson   **Minority CoS:** Kelly A. Dixon
Chambers
—————————— Subcommittees ——————————

LEGISLATIVE & BUDGET PROCESS
Room: The Capitol H-312
Phone: 202.225.9091

Information for this committee, including membership, was not finalized as of the publication date and is therefore subject to change.

RULES & ORGANIZATION OF THE HOUSE
Room: The Capitol H-312
Phone: 202.225.9091

Information for this committee, including membership, was not finalized as of the publication date and is therefore subject to change.

SCIENCE, SPACE & TECHNOLOGY

Room: RHOB 2321
Website: www.science.house.gov
Phone: 202.225.6375
Ratio: 22 Democrats/15 Republicans
Subcommittees: 5

Majority:		Minority:	
C: Eddie Johnson, TX-30	RHOB 2306	RM: Frank Lucas, OK-03	RHOB 2405
Ami Bera, CA-07	LHOB 1727	Mo Brooks, AL-05	RHOB 2246
Zoe Lofgren, CA-19	LHOB 1401	Bill Posey, FL-08	RHOB 2150
Daniel Lipinski, IL-03	RHOB 2346	Randy Weber, TX-14	CHOB 107
Suzanne Bonamici, OR-01	RHOB 2231	Brian Babin, TX-36	RHOB 2236
Conor Lamb, PA-17	RHOB 1224	Andy Biggs, AZ-05	LHOB 1318
Elizabeth Fletcher, TX-07	LHOB 1429	Roger Marshall, KS-01	CHOB 312
Haley Stevens, MI-11	CHOB 227	Neal Dunn, FL-02	CHOB 316
Kendra Horn, OK-05	CHOB 415	Ralph Norman, SC-05	CHOB 319
Mikie Sherrill, NJ-11	LHOB 1208	Michael Cloud, TX-27	RHOB 1314
Brad Sherman, CA-30	RHOB 2181	Troy Balderson, OH-12	LHOB 1221
Steve Cohen, TN-09	RHOB 2104	Pete Olson, TX-22	RHOB 2133
Jerry McNerney, CA-09	RHOB 2265	Anthony Gonzalez, OH-16	LHOB 1023
Ed Perlmutter, CO-07	LHOB 1226	Michael Waltz, FL-06	CHOB 216
Paul Tonko, NY-20	RHOB 2369	Jim Baird, IN-04	CHOB 532
Bill Foster, IL-11	LHOB 2366		
Don Beyer, VA-08	LHOB 1119		
Charles Crist, FL-13	CHOB 215		
Sean Casten, IL-06	CHOB 429		
Katherine Hill, CA-25	LHOB 1130		
Ben McAdams, UT-04	CHOB 130		
Jennifer Wexton, VA-10	LHOB 1217		

Majority CoS: Dick Obermann   **Minority CoS:** Josh Mathis
—————————— Subcommittees ——————————

ENERGY
Room: RHOB 2321
Phone: 202.225.6375

Majority:		Minority:	
C: Conor Lamb, PA-17	RHOB 1224	RM: Randy Weber, TX-14	CHOB 107
Daniel Lipinski, IL-03	RHOB 2346	Andy Biggs, AZ-05	LHOB 1318
Elizabeth Fletcher, TX-07	LHOB 1429	Neal Dunn, FL-02	CHOB 316
Haley Stevens, MI-11	CHOB 227	Ralph Norman, SC-05	CHOB 319
Kendra Horn, OK-05	CHOB 415	Michael Cloud, TX-27	RHOB 1314
Jerry McNerney, CA-09	RHOB 2265		

Bill Foster, IL-11	LHOB 2366		
Sean Casten, IL-06	CHOB 429		

ENVIRONMENT
Room: RHOB 2321
Phone: 202.225.6375

Majority:		Minority:	
C: Elizabeth Fletcher, TX-07	LHOB 1429	**RM: Roger Marshall, KS-01**	CHOB 312
Suzanne Bonamici, OR-01	RHOB 2231	Brian Babin, TX-36	RHOB 2236
Conor Lamb, PA-17	RHOB 1224	Anthony Gonzalez, OH-16	LHOB 1023
Paul Tonko, NY-20	RHOB 2369	Jim Baird, IN-04	CHOB 532
Charles Crist, FL-13	CHOB 215		
Sean Casten, IL-06	CHOB 429		
Ben McAdams, UT-04	CHOB 130		
Don Beyer, VA-08	LHOB 1119		

INVESTIGATIONS & OVERSIGHT
Room: RHOB 2321
Phone: 202.225.6375

Majority:		Minority:	
C: Mikie Sherrill, NJ-11	LHOB 1208	**RM: Ralph Norman, SC-05**	CHOB 31
Suzanne Bonamici, OR-01	RHOB 2231	Andy Biggs, AZ-05	LHOB 131
Steve Cohen, TN-09	RHOB 2104	Michael Waltz, FL-06	CHOB 21
Don Beyer, VA-08	LHOB 1119		
Jennifer Wexton, VA-10	LHOB 1217		

RESEARCH & TECHNOLOGY
Room: RHOB 2321
Phone: 202.225.6375

Majority:		Minority:
C: Haley Stevens, MI-11	CHOB 227	Information not available as of press time.
Daniel Lipinski, IL-03	RHOB 2346	
Mikie Sherrill, NJ-11	LHOB 1208	
Brad Sherman, CA-30	RHOB 2181	
Paul Tonko, NY-20	RHOB 2369	
Ben McAdams, UT-04	CHOB 130	
Steve Cohen, TN-09	RHOB 2104	
Bill Foster, IL-11	LHOB 2366	

SPACE & AERONAUTICS
Room: RHOB 2321
Phone: 202.225.6375

Majority:		Minority:
C: Kendra Horn, OK-05	CHOB 415	Information not available as of press time.
Zoe Lofgren, CA-19	LHOB 1401	
Ami Bera, CA-07	LHOB 1727	
Ed Perlmutter, CO-07	LHOB 1226	
Don Beyer, VA-08	LHOB 1119	
Charles Crist, FL-13	CHOB 215	
Katherine Hill, CA-25	LHOB 1130	
Jennifer Wexton, VA-10	LHOB 1217	

SMALL BUSINESS

Room: RHOB 2357
Website: www.smallbusiness.house.gov
Phone: 202.225.4038
Ratio: 13 Democrats/10 Republicans
Subcommittees: 5

Majority:		Minority:	
Abby Finkenauer, IA-01	CHOB 124	**RM: Steve Chabot, OH-01**	RHOB 24
Jared Golden, ME-02	LHOB 1223	Aumua Radewagen, AS-01	LHOB 13
Andrew Kim, NJ-03	LHOB 1516	Trent Kelly, MS-01	LHOB 1(
Jason Crow, CO-06	LHOB 1229	Troy Balderson, OH-12	LHOB 12
Sharice Davids, KS-03	LHOB 1541	Kevin Hern, OK-01	LHOB 1(
Judy Chu, CA-27	RHOB 2423	James Hagedorn, MN-01	CHOB 3
Marc Veasey, TX-33	RHOB 2348	Peter Stauber, MN-08	CHOB
Dwight Evans, PA-03	LHOB 1105	Tim Burchett, TN-02	LHOB 1
Bradley Schneider, IL-10	LHOB 1432	Ross Spano, FL-15	CHOB 2
Adriano Espaillat, NY-13	LHOB 1630	John Joyce, PA-13	LHOB 1
Antonio Delgado, NY-19	LHOB 1007		
Chrissy Houlahan, PA-06	LHOB 1218		
Angela Craig, MN-02	LHOB 1523		

Majority CoS: Melissa Jung	**Minority CoS:** Kevin W. Fitzpatrick
Majority Sched: Mory Garcia	

––––––––––– Subcommittees –––––––––––

CONTRACTING & INFRASTRUCTURE

Room: RHOB 2361
Phone: 202.225.4038

Majority:		Minority:	
C: Jared Golden, ME-02	LHOB 1223	RM: Peter Stauber, MN-08	CHOB 126
		James Hagedorn, MN-01	CHOB 325
		Troy Balderson, OH-12	LHOB 1221

ECONOMIC GROWTH, TAX & CAPITAL ACCESS

Room: RHOB 2361
Phone: 202.225.4038

Majority:		Minority:	
C: Andrew Kim, NJ-03	LHOB 1516	RM: Kevin Hern, OK-01	LHOB 1019
		Ross Spano, FL-15	CHOB 224
		Aumua Radewagen, AS-01	LHOB 1339
		Peter Stauber, MN-08	CHOB 126

INNOVATION & WORKFORCE DEVELOPMENT

Room: RHOB 2361
Phone: 202.225.4038

Majority:		Minority:	
C: Jason Crow, CO-06	LHOB 1229	RM: Troy Balderson, OH-12	LHOB 1221
		Tim Burchett, TN-02	LHOB 1122
		Kevin Hern, OK-01	LHOB 1019
		John Joyce, PA-13	LHOB 1337

INVESTIGATIONS, OVERSIGHT & REGULATIONS

Room: RHOB 2361
Phone: 202.225.4038

Majority:		Minority:	
C: Judy Chu, CA-27	RHOB 2423	RM: Ross Spano, FL-15	CHOB 224
		Trent Kelly, MS-01	LHOB 1005
		Tim Burchett, TN-02	LHOB 1122

RURAL DEVELOPMENT, AGRICULTURE, TRADE & ENTREPRENEURSHIP

Room: RHOB 2361
Phone: 202.225.4038

Majority:		Minority:	
C: Abby Finkenauer, IA-01	CHOB 124	RM: John Joyce, PA-13	LHOB 1337
		Aumua Radewagen, AS-01	LHOB 1339
		Trent Kelly, MS-01	LHOB 1005
		James Hagedorn, MN-01	CHOB 325

TRANSPORTATION & INFRASTRUCTURE

Room: RHOB 2165
Website: www.transportation.house.gov
Phone: 202.225.4472
Ratio: 37 Democrats/30 Republicans
Subcommittees: 6

Majority:		Minority:	
C: Pete DeFazio, OR-04	RHOB 2134	RM: Sam Graves, MO-06	LHOB 1135
Salud Carbajal, CA-24	LHOB 1431	Don Young, AK-01	RHOB 2314
Eleanor Norton, DC-01	RHOB 2136	Rick Crawford, AR-01	RHOB 2422
Eddie Johnson, TX-30	RHOB 2306	Bob Gibbs, OH-07	RHOB 2446
Elijah Cummings, MD-07	RHOB 2163	Daniel Webster, FL-11	LHOB 1210
Rick Larsen, WA-02	RHOB 2113	Thomas Massie, KY-04	RHOB 2453
Grace Napolitano, CA-32	LHOB 1610	Mark Meadows, NC-11	RHOB 2160
Daniel Lipinski, IL-03	RHOB 2346	Scott Perry, PA-10	LHOB 1207
Steve Cohen, TN-09	RHOB 2104	Rodney Davis, IL-13	LHOB 1740
Albio Sires, NJ-08	RHOB 2268	Rob Woodall, GA-07	LHOB 1724
John Garamendi, CA-03	RHOB 2368	John Katko, NY-24	RHOB 2457
Hank Johnson, GA-04	RHOB 2240	Brian Babin, TX-36	RHOB 2236
Andre Carson, IN-07	RHOB 2135	Garret Graves, LA-06	RHOB 2402
Dina Titus, NV-01	RHOB 2464	David Rouzer, NC-07	RHOB 2439
Sean Maloney, NY-18	RHOB 2331	Mike Bost, IL-12	LHOB 1440
Fred Huffman, CA-02	LHOB 1527	Randy Weber, TX-14	CHOB 107
Julia Brownley, CA-26	RHOB 2262	Doug LaMalfa, CA-01	CHOB 322
Frederica Wilson, FL-24	RHOB 2445	Bruce Westerman, AR-04	CHOB 209
Donald Payne, NJ-10	CHOB 103	Lloyd Smucker, PA-11	CHOB 127
Alan Lowenthal, CA-47	CHOB 108	Paul Mitchell, MI-10	CHOB 211
Mark DeSaulnier, CA-11	CHOB 503	Brian Mast, FL-18	RHOB 2182
Stacey Plaskett, VI-01	RHOB 2404	Michael Gallagher, WI-08	LHOB 1230
Stephen Lynch, MA-08	RHOB 2109	Gary Palmer, AL-06	CHOB 207
Anthony Brown, MD-04	LHOB 1323	Brian Fitzpatrick, PA-01	LHOB 1722
Adriano Espaillat, NY-13	LHOB 1630		

Tom Malinowski, NJ-07	CHOB 426	Jennifer Gonzalez-Colon, PR-01	LHOB 1609
Greg Stanton, AZ-09	CHOB 128		
Debbie Mucarsel-Powell, FL-26	CHOB 114	Troy Balderson, OH-12	LHOB 1221
		Ross Spano, FL-15	CHOB 224
Elizabeth Fletcher, TX-07	LHOB 1429	Peter Stauber, MN-08	CHOB 126
Colin Allred, TX-32	CHOB 328	Carol Miller, WV-03	LHOB 1605
Sharice Davids, KS-03	LHOB 1541	Gregory Pence, IN-06	CHOB 222
Abby Finkenauer, IA-01	CHOB 124		
Jesus Garcia, IL-04	CHOB 530		
Antonio Delgado, NY-19	LHOB 1007		
Christopher Pappas, NH-01	CHOB 323		
Angela Craig, MN-02	LHOB 1523		
Harley Rouda, CA-48	RHOB 2300		

Majority CoS: Kathy Dedrick   **Minority CoS:** Paul J. Sass

───────────── Subcommittees ─────────────

AVIATION

Room: RHOB 2165
Phone: 202.225.4472

Majority:		Minority:	
C: Rick Larsen, WA-02	RHOB 2113	RM: Garret Graves, LA-06	RHOB 2402
Andre Carson, IN-07	RHOB 2135	Don Young, AK-01	RHOB 231
Stacey Plaskett, VI-01	RHOB 2404	Daniel Webster, FL-11	LHOB 121
Stephen Lynch, MA-08	RHOB 2109	Thomas Massie, KY-04	RHOB 245
Eleanor Norton, DC-01	RHOB 2136	Scott Perry, PA-10	LHOB 120
Daniel Lipinski, IL-03	RHOB 2346	Rob Woodall, GA-07	LHOB 172
Steve Cohen, TN-09	RHOB 2104	John Katko, NY-24	RHOB 245
Hank Johnson, GA-04	RHOB 2240	David Rouzer, NC-07	RHOB 243
Dina Titus, NV-01	RHOB 2464	Lloyd Smucker, PA-11	CHOB 12
Julia Brownley, CA-26	RHOB 2262	Paul Mitchell, MI-10	CHOB 21
Anthony Brown, MD-04	LHOB 1323	Brian Mast, FL-18	RHOB 218
Greg Stanton, AZ-09	CHOB 128	Michael Gallagher, WI-08	LHOB 123
Colin Allred, TX-32	CHOB 328	Brian Fitzpatrick, PA-01	LHOB 172
Jesus Garcia, IL-04	CHOB 530	Troy Balderson, OH-12	LHOB 122
Eddie Johnson, TX-30	RHOB 2306	Peter Stauber, MN-08	CHOB 12
Sean Maloney, NY-18	RHOB 2331	Sam Graves, MO-06	LHOB 113
Donald Payne, NJ-10	CHOB 103		
Sharice Davids, KS-03	LHOB 1541		
Angela Craig, MN-02	LHOB 1523		
Grace Napolitano, CA-32	LHOB 1610		
Salud Carbajal, CA-24	LHOB 1431		
Pete DeFazio, OR-04	RHOB 2134		

COAST GUARD & MARITIME TRANSPORTATION

Room: RHOB 2165
Phone: 202.225.4472

Majority:		Minority:	
C: Sean Maloney, NY-18	RHOB 2331	RM: Bob Gibbs, OH-07	RHOB 24
Elijah Cummings, MD-07	RHOB 2163	Don Young, AK-01	RHOB 23
Rick Larsen, WA-02	RHOB 2113	Randy Weber, TX-14	CHOB 1
Stacey Plaskett, VI-01	RHOB 2404	Brian Mast, FL-18	RHOB 21
John Garamendi, CA-03	RHOB 2368	Michael Gallagher, WI-08	LHOB 12
Alan Lowenthal, CA-47	CHOB 108	Carol Miller, WV-03	LHOB 16
Anthony Brown, MD-04	LHOB 1323	Sam Graves, MO-06	LHOB 11
Christopher Pappas, NH-01	CHOB 323		
Pete DeFazio, OR-04	RHOB 2134		

ECONOMIC DEV'T, PUBLIC BUILDINGS & EMERGENCY MANAGEMENT

Room: RHOB 2165
Phone: 202.225.4472

Majority:		Minority:	
C: Dina Titus, NV-01	RHOB 2464	RM: Mark Meadows, NC-11	LHOB 2
Debbie Mucarsel-Powell, FL-26	CHOB 114	Gary Palmer, AL-06	CHOB 2
Sharice Davids, KS-03	LHOB 1541	Jennifer Gonzalez-Colon, PR-01	LHOB 16
Eleanor Norton, DC-01	RHOB 2136	Carol Miller, WV-03	LHOB 16
Hank Johnson, GA-04	RHOB 2240	Gregory Pence, IN-06	CHOB 2
John Garamendi, CA-03	RHOB 2368	Sam Graves, MO-06	LHOB 1
Anthony Brown, MD-04	LHOB 1323		
Elizabeth Fletcher, TX-07	LHOB 1429		
Pete DeFazio, OR-04	RHOB 2134		

HIGHWAYS & TRANSIT

Room: RHOB 2165
Phone: 202.225.4472

Majority:		Minority:	
C: Eleanor Norton, DC-01	RHOB 2136	RM: Rodney Davis, IL-13	LHOB 1

Eddie Johnson, TX-30	RHOB 2306	Don Young, AK-01	RHOB 2314
Steve Cohen, TN-09	RHOB 2104	Rick Crawford, AR-01	RHOB 2422
John Garamendi, CA-03	RHOB 2368	Bob Gibbs, OH-07	RHOB 2446
Hank Johnson, GA-04	RHOB 2240	Daniel Webster, FL-11	LHOB 1210
Jared Huffman, CA-02	LHOB 1527	Thomas Massie, KY-04	RHOB 2453
Julia Brownley, CA-26	RHOB 2262	Mark Meadows, NC-11	LHOB 2160
Frederica Wilson, FL-24	RHOB 2445	Rob Woodall, GA-07	LHOB 1724
Alan Lowenthal, CA-47	CHOB 108	John Katko, NY-24	RHOB 2457
Mark DeSaulnier, CA-11	CHOB 503	Brian Babin, TX-36	RHOB 2236
Salud Carbajal, CA-24	LHOB 1431	David Rouzer, NC-07	RHOB 2439
Anthony Brown, MD-04	LHOB 1323	Mike Bost, IL-12	LHOB 1440
Adriano Espaillat, NY-13	LHOB 1630	Doug LaMalfa, CA-01	CHOB 322
Tom Malinowski, NJ-07	CHOB 426	Bruce Westerman, AR-04	CHOB 209
Greg Stanton, AZ-09	CHOB 128	Lloyd Smucker, PA-11	CHOB 127
Colin Allred, TX-32	CHOB 328	Paul Mitchell, MI-10	CHOB 211
Sharice Davids, KS-03	LHOB 1541	Michael Gallagher, WI-08	LHOB 1230
Abby Finkenauer, IA-01	CHOB 124	Gary Palmer, AL-06	CHOB 207
Jesus Garcia, IL-04	CHOB 530	Brian Fitzpatrick, PA-01	LHOB 1722
Antonio Delgado, NY-19	LHOB 1007	Troy Balderson, OH-12	LHOB 1221
Christopher Pappas, NH-01	CHOB 323	Ross Spano, FL-15	CHOB 224
Angela Craig, MN-02	LHOB 1523	Peter Stauber, MN-08	CHOB 126
Harley Rouda, CA-48	RHOB 2300	Carol Miller, WV-03	LHOB 1605
Grace Napolitano, CA-32	LHOB 1610	Gregory Pence, IN-06	CHOB 222
Albio Sires, NJ-08	RHOB 2268	Sam Graves, MO-06	LHOB 1135
Sean Maloney, NY-18	RHOB 2331		
Donald Payne, NJ-10	CHOB 103		
Daniel Lipinski, IL-03	RHOB 2346		
Dina Titus, NV-01	RHOB 2464		
Stacey Plaskett, VI-01	RHOB 2404		
Pete DeFazio, OR-04	RHOB 2134		

RAILROADS, PIPELINES & HAZARDOUS MATERIALS

Room: RHOB 2165
Phone: 202.225.4472

Majority:		Minority:	
C: Daniel Lipinski, IL-03	RHOB 2346	RM: Rick Crawford, AR-01	RHOB 2422
Albio Sires, NJ-08	RHOB 2268	Scott Perry, PA-10	LHOB 1207
Donald Payne, NJ-10	CHOB 103	Rodney Davis, IL-13	LHOB 1740
Elizabeth Fletcher, TX-07	LHOB 1429	Brian Babin, TX-36	RHOB 2236
Elijah Cummings, MD-07	RHOB 2163	Mike Bost, IL 12	LHOB 1440
Andre Carson, IN-07	RHOB 2135	Randy Weber, TX-14	CHOB 107
Frederica Wilson, FL-24	RHOB 2445	Doug LaMalfa, CA-01	CHOB 322
Mark DeSaulnier, CA-11	CHOB 503	Lloyd Smucker, PA-11	CHOB 127
Stephen Lynch, MA-08	RHOB 2109	Paul Mitchell, MI-10	CHOB 211
Tom Malinowski, NJ-07	CHOB 426	Brian Fitzpatrick, PA-01	LHOB 1722
Grace Napolitano, CA-32	LHOB 1610	Troy Balderson, OH-12	LHOB 1221
Steve Cohen, TN-09	RHOB 2104	Ross Spano, FL-15	CHOB 224
Jesus Garcia, IL-04	CHOB 530	Peter Stauber, MN-08	CHOB 126
Eleanor Norton, DC-01	RHOB 2136	Gregory Pence, IN-06	CHOB 222
Hank Johnson, GA-04	RHOB 2240	Sam Graves, MO-06	LHOB 1135
Alan Lowenthal, CA-47	CHOB 108		
Colin Allred, TX 32	CHOB 328		
Angela Craig, MN-02	LHOB 1523		
Pete DeFazio, OR-04	RHOB 2134		

WATER RESOURCES & ENVIRONMENT

Room: RHOB 2165
Phone: 202.225.4472

Majority:		Minority:	
C: Grace Napolitano, CA-32	LHOB 1610	RM: Bruce Westerman, AR-04	CHOB 209
Debbie Mucarsel-Powell, FL-26	CHOB 114	Daniel Webster, FL-11	LHOB 1210
		Thomas Massie, KY-04	RHOB 2453
Eddie Johnson, TX-30	RHOB 2306	Rob Woodall, GA-07	LHOB 1724
John Garamendi, CA-03	RHOB 2368	Brian Babin, TX-36	RHOB 2236
Jared Huffman, CA-02	LHOB 1527	Garret Graves, LA-06	RHOB 2402
Alan Lowenthal, CA-47	CHOB 108	David Rouzer, NC-07	RHOB 2439
Salud Carbajal, CA-24	LHOB 1431	Mike Bost, IL-12	LHOB 1440
Adriano Espaillat, NY-13	LHOB 1630	Randy Weber, TX-14	CHOB 107
Elizabeth Fletcher, TX-07	LHOB 1429	Doug LaMalfa, CA-01	CHOB 322
Abby Finkenauer, IA-01	CHOB 124	Brian Mast, FL-18	RHOB 2182
Antonio Delgado, NY-19	LHOB 1007	Gary Palmer, AL-06	CHOB 207
Christopher Pappas, NH-01	CHOB 323	Jenniffer Gonzalez-Colon, PR-01	LHOB 1609
Angela Craig, MN-02	LHOB 1523	Sam Graves, MO-06	LHOB 1135
Harley Rouda, CA-48	RHOB 2300		
Frederica Wilson, FL-24	RHOB 2445		
Stephen Lynch, MA-08	RHOB 2109		

Tom Malinowski, NJ-07	CHOB 426		
Pete DeFazio, OR-04	RHOB 2134		

VETERANS' AFFAIRS

Room: LHOB B234
Website: veterans.house.gov
Phone: 202.225.9756
Ratio: 16 Democrats/12 Republicans
Subcommittees: 5

Majority:		Minority:	
C: Mark Takano, CA-41	CHOB 420	**RM: Phil Roe, TN-01**	CHOB 102
Conor Lamb, PA-17	RHOB 1224	Aumua Radewagen, AS-01	LHOB 1339
Mike Levin, CA-49	LHOB 1626	Gus Bilirakis, FL-12	RHOB 2227
Julia Brownley, CA-26	RHOB 2262	Mike Bost, IL-12	LHOB 1440
Kathleen Rice, NY-04	RHOB 2435	Neal Dunn, FL-02	CHOB 316
Anthony Brindisi, NY-22	CHOB 329	Jack Bergman, MI-01	CHOB 414
Max Rose, NY-11	LHOB 1529	Jim Banks, IN-03	LHOB 1713
Christopher Pappas, NH-01	CHOB 323	Andy Barr, KY-06	RHOB 2430
Elaine Luria, VA-02	CHOB 534	Daniel Meuser, PA-09	CHOB 326
Susie Lee, NV-03	CHOB 522	Steve Watkins, KS-02	LHOB 1205
Joe Cunningham, SC-01	CHOB 423	Chip Roy, TX-21	LHOB 1319
Gilbert Cisneros, CA-39	CHOB 431	Greg Steube, FL-17	CHOB 521
Collin Peterson, MN-07	RHOB 2204		
Gregorio Sablan, MP-01	RHOB 2411		
Colin Allred, TX-32	CHOB 328		
Lauren Underwood, IL-14	LHOB 1118		

Majority CoS: Raymond C. Kelley   **Minority CoS:** Jonathan A. Towers
Majority Sched: Carol Murray

——————————— Subcommittees ———————————

DISABILITY ASSISTANCE & MEMORIAL AFFAIRS
Room: Thomas P. O'Neill Federal Bldg. B234
Phone: 202.225.9756

Majority:		Minority:	
C: Elaine Luria, VA-02	CHOB 534	**RM: Mike Bost, IL-12**	LHOB 144
Gilbert Cisneros, CA-39	CHOB 431	Gus Bilirakis, FL-12	RHOB 222
Gregorio Sablan, MP-01	RHOB 2411	Steve Watkins, KS-02	LHOB 120
Colin Allred, TX-32	CHOB 328	Greg Steube, FL-17	CHOB 52
Lauren Underwood, IL-14	LHOB 1118		

ECONOMIC OPPORTUNITY
Room: Thomas P. O'Neill Federal Bldg. B234
Phone: 202.225.9756

Majority:		Minority:	
C: Mike Levin, CA-49	LHOB 1626	**RM: Gus Bilirakis, FL-12**	RHOB 222
Kathleen Rice, NY-04	RHOB 2435	Jack Bergman, MI-01	CHOB 41
Anthony Brindisi, NY-22	CHOB 329	Jim Banks, IN-03	LHOB 171
Christopher Pappas, NH-01	CHOB 323	Andy Barr, KY-06	RHOB 243
Elaine Luria, VA-02	CHOB 534	Daniel Meuser, PA-09	CHOB 32
Susie Lee, NV-03	CHOB 522		
Joe Cunningham, SC-01	CHOB 423		

HEALTH
Room: Thomas P. O'Neill Federal Bldg. B234
Phone: 202.225.9756

Majority:		Minority:	
C: Julia Brownley, CA-26	RHOB 2262	**RM: Neal Dunn, FL-02**	CHOB 3
Conor Lamb, PA-17	RHOB 1224	Aumua Radewagen, AS-01	LHOB 13
Mike Levin, CA-49	LHOB 1626	Andy Barr, KY-06	RHOB 24
Anthony Brindisi, NY-22	CHOB 329	Daniel Meuser, PA-09	CHOB 3
Max Rose, NY-11	LHOB 1529	Greg Steube, FL-17	CHOB 5
Gilbert Cisneros, CA-39	CHOB 431		
Collin Peterson, MN-07	RHOB 2204		

OVERSIGHT & INVESTIGATIONS
Room: LHOB B234
Phone: 202.225.9756

Majority:		Minority:	
C: Christopher Pappas, NH-01	CHOB 323	**RM: Jack Bergman, MI-01**	CHOB 4
		Aumua Radewagen, AS-01	LHOB 1
Kathleen Rice, NY-04	RHOB 2435	Mike Bost, IL-12	LHOB 1
Max Rose, NY-11	LHOB 1529	Chip Roy, TX-21	LHOB 1
Gilbert Cisneros, CA-39	CHOB 431		
Collin Peterson, MN-07	RHOB 2204		

TECHNOLOGY MODERNIZATION
Room: LHOB B234
Phone: 202.225.9756

Majority:		Minority:	
C: Susie Lee, NV-03	CHOB 522	RM: Jim Banks, IN-03	LHOB 1713
Julia Brownley, CA-26	RHOB 2262	Steve Watkins, KS-02	LHOB 1205
Conor Lamb, PA-17	RHOB 1224	Chip Roy, TX-21	LHOB 1319
Joe Cunningham, SC-01	CHOB 423		

WAYS & MEANS

Room: LHOB 1102
Website: www.waysandmeans.house.gov
Phone: 202.225.3625
Ratio: 25 Democrats/17 Republicans
Subcommittees: 6

Majority:		Minority:	
C: Richard Neal, MA-01	RHOB 2309	RM: Kevin Brady, TX-08	LHOB 1011
John Lewis, GA-05	CHOB 300	Devin Nunes, CA-22	LHOB 1013
Lloyd Doggett, TX-35	RHOB 2307	Vern Buchanan, FL-16	RHOB 2427
Mike Thompson, CA-05	CHOB 406	Adrian Smith, NE-03	CHOB 502
John Larson, CT-01	LHOB 1501	Kenny Marchant, TX-24	RHOB 2304
Earl Blumenauer, OR-03	LHOB 1111	Tom Reed, NY-23	RHOB 2263
Ron Kind, WI-03	LHOB 1502	Mike Kelly, PA-16	LHOB 1707
Bill Pascrell, NJ-09	RHOB 2409	George Holding, NC-02	LHOB 1110
Danny Davis, IL-07	RHOB 2159	Jason Smith, MO-08	RHOB 2418
Linda Sanchez, CA-38	RHOB 2329	Tom Rice, SC-07	CHOB 512
Brian Higgins, NY-26	RHOB 2459	David Schweikert, AZ-06	LHOB 1526
Terri Sewell, AL-07	RHOB 2201	Jackie Walorski, IN-02	CHOB 419
Suzan DelBene, WA-01	RHOB 2330	Darin LaHood, IL-18	LHOB 1424
Judy Chu, CA-27	RHOB 2423	Brad Wenstrup, OH-02	RHOB 2419
Gwen Moore, WI-04	RHOB 2252	Jodey Arrington, TX-19	LHOB 1029
Dan Kildee, MI-05	CHOB 203	Drew Ferguson, GA-03	LHOB 1032
Brendan Boyle, PA-02	LHOB 1133	Ron Estes, KS-04	LHOB 1524
Don Beyer, VA-08	LHOB 1119		
Dwight Evans, PA-03	LHOB 1105		
Bradley Schneider, IL-10	LHOB 1432		
Thomas Suozzi, NY-03	CHOB 214		
Jimmy Panetta, CA-20	CHOB 212		
Stephanie Murphy, FL-07	LHOB 1710		
Jimmy Gomez, CA-34	LHOB 1530		
Steven Horsford, NV-04	LHOB 1330		

Majority CoS: Brandon Casey   **Minority CoS:** Gary J. Andres

---- Subcommittees ----

HEALTH

Room: LHOB 1102
Phone: 202.225.3625

Majority:		Minority:	
C: Lloyd Doggett, TX-35	RHOB 2307	RM: Devin Nunes, CA-22	LHOB 1013
Mike Thompson, CA-05	CHOB 406	Vern Buchanan, FL-16	RHOB 2427
Earl Blumenauer, OR-03	LHOB 1111	Adrian Smith, NE-03	CHOB 502
Ron Kind, WI-03	LHOB 1502	Kenny Marchant, TX-24	RHOB 2304
Brian Higgins, NY-26	RHOB 2459	Tom Reed, NY-23	RHOB 2263
Terri Sewell, AL-07	RHOB 2201	Mike Kelly, PA-16	LHOB 1707
Judy Chu, CA-27	RHOB 2423	George Holding, NC-02	LHOB 1110
Dwight Evans, PA-03	LHOB 1105		
Bradley Schneider, IL-10	LHOB 1432		
Jimmy Gomez, CA-34	LHOB 1530		
Steven Horsford, NV-04	LHOB 1330		

OVERSIGHT

Room: LHOB 1102
Phone: 202.225.4021

Majority:		Minority:	
C: John Lewis, GA-05	CHOB 300	RM: Mike Kelly, PA-16	LHOB 1707
Linda Sanchez, CA-38	RHOB 2329	Jackie Walorski, IN-02	CHOB 419
Suzan DelBene, WA-01	RHOB 2330	Darin LaHood, IL-18	LHOB 1424
Judy Chu, CA-27	RHOB 2423	Brad Wenstrup, OH-02	RHOB 2419
Gwen Moore, WI-04	RHOB 2252		
Brendan Boyle, PA-02	LHOB 1133		
Thomas Suozzi, NY-03	CHOB 214		

SELECT REVENUE MEASURES

Room: LHOB 1102
Phone: 202.225.3625

Majority:		Minority:	
C: Mike Thompson, CA-05	CHOB 406	RM: Adrian Smith, NE-03	CHOB 502
Lloyd Doggett, TX-35	RHOB 2307	Tom Rice, SC-07	CHOB 512
John Larson, CT-01	LHOB 1501	David Schweikert, AZ-06	LHOB 1526
Linda Sanchez, CA-38	RHOB 2329	Darin LaHood, IL-18	LHOB 1424

Suzan DelBene, WA-01	RHOB 2330	Jodey Arrington, TX-19	LHOB 1029
Gwen Moore, WI-04	RHOB 2252	Drew Ferguson, GA-03	LHOB 1032
Brendan Boyle, PA-02	LHOB 1133		
Don Beyer, VA-08	LHOB 1119		
Thomas Suozzi, NY-03	CHOB 214		

SOCIAL SECURITY
Room: LHOB 1102
Phone: 202.225.3625

Majority:		Minority:	
C: John Larson, CT-01	LHOB 1501	**RM: Tom Reed, NY-23**	RHOB 2263
Bill Pascrell, NJ-09	RHOB 2409	Jodey Arrington, TX-19	LHOB 1029
Linda Sanchez, CA-38	RHOB 2329	Drew Ferguson, GA-03	LHOB 1032
Brian Higgins, NY-26	RHOB 2459	Ron Estes, KS-04	LHOB 1524
Dan Kildee, MI-05	CHOB 203		
Brendan Boyle, PA-02	LHOB 1133		
Bradley Schneider, IL-10	LHOB 1432		

TRADE
Room: LHOB 1102
Phone: 202.225.3625

Majority:		Minority:	
C: Earl Blumenauer, OR-03	LHOB 1111	**RM: Vern Buchanan, FL-16**	RHOB 2427
Bill Pascrell, NJ-09	RHOB 2409	Devin Nunes, CA-22	LHOB 1013
Ron Kind, WI-03	LHOB 1502	George Holding, NC-02	LHOB 111
Danny Davis, IL-07	RHOB 2159	Tom Rice, SC-07	CHOB 512
Brian Higgins, NY-26	RHOB 2459	Kenny Marchant, TX-24	RHOB 2304
Terri Sewell, AL-07	RHOB 2201	Jason Smith, MO-08	RHOB 2418
Suzan DelBene, WA-01	RHOB 2330	David Schweikert, AZ-06	LHOB 1524
Don Beyer, VA-08	LHOB 1119		
Dan Kildee, MI-05	CHOB 203		
Jimmy Panetta, CA-20	CHOB 212		
Stephanie Murphy, FL-07	LHOB 1710		

WORKER & FAMILY SUPPORT
Room: LHOB 1102
Phone: 202.225.3625

Majority:		Minority:	
C: Danny Davis, IL-07	RHOB 2159	**RM: Jackie Walorski, IN-02**	CHOB 41
Judy Chu, CA-27	RHOB 2423		
Terri Sewell, AL-07	RHOB 2201	Brad Wenstrup, OH-02	RHOB 241
Gwen Moore, WI-04	RHOB 2252	Ron Estes, KS-04	LHOB 152
Dwight Evans, PA-03	LHOB 1105	Darin LaHood, IL-18	LHOB 142
Stephanie Murphy, FL-07	LHOB 1710		
Jimmy Gomez, CA-34	LHOB 1530		

SELECT AND SPECIAL COMMITTEES

PERMANENT SELECT ON INTELLIGENCE

Room: The Capitol Visitors Center HVC-304
Website: www.intelligence.house.gov
Phone: 202.225.7690
Ratio: 13 Democrats/9 Republicans
Subcommittees: 4

Majority:		Minority:	
C: Adam Schiff, CA-28	RHOB 2269	RM: Devin Nunes, CA-22	LHOB 1013
Peter Welch, VT-01	RHOB 2187	Mike Conaway, TX-11	RHOB 2469
Jim Himes, CT-04	LHOB 1227	Michael Turner, OH-10	RHOB 2082
Terri Sewell, AL-07	RHOB 2201	Brad Wenstrup, OH-02	RHOB 2419
Andre Carson, IN-07	RHOB 2135	Chris Stewart, UT-02	RHOB 2242
Jackie Speier, CA-14	RHOB 2465	Rick Crawford, AR-01	RHOB 2422
Mike Quigley, IL-05	RHOB 2458	Elise Stefanik, NY-21	CHOB 318
Eric Swalwell, CA-15	CHOB 407	Will Hurd, TX-23	CHOB 317
Joaquin Castro, TX-20	RHOB 2241	John Ratcliffe, TX-04	CHOB 223
Denny Heck, WA-10	RHOB 2452		
Sean Maloney, NY-18	RHOB 2331		
Valdez Demings, FL-10	CHOB 217		
Raja Krishnamoorthi, IL-08	CHOB 115		

Majority CoS: Timothy Bergreen

--- Subcommittees ---

COUNTERTERRORISM, COUNTERINTELLIGENCE & COUNTERPROLIFERATION
Room: Capitol Visitor Center HVC-304
Phone: 202.225.7690

Majority:		Minority:	
C: Andre Carson, IN-07	RHOB 2135	RM: Rick Crawford, AR-01	RHOB 2422
Jackie Speier, CA-14	RHOB 2465	Mike Conaway, TX-11	RHOB 2469
Mike Quigley, IL-05	RHOB 2458	Brad Wenstrup, OH-02	RHOB 2419
Joaquin Castro, TX-20	RHOB 2241	Chris Stewart, UT-02	RHOB 2242
Peter Welch, VT-01	RHOB 2187		
Sean Maloney, NY-18	RHOB 2331		

DEFENSE INTELLIGENCE & WARFIGHTER SUPPORT
Room: Capitol Visitor Center HVC-304
Phone: 202.225.7690

Majority:		Minority:	
C: Terri Sewell, AL-07	RHOB 2201	RM: Brad Wenstrup, OH-02	RHOB 2419
Jim Himes, CT-04	LHOB 1227		
Denny Heck, WA-10	RHOB 2452	Michael Turner, OH-10	RHOB 2082
Peter Welch, VT-01	RHOB 2187	Mike Conaway, TX-11	RHOB 2469
Sean Maloney, NY-18	RHOB 2331	Will Hurd, TX-23	CHOB 317
Valdez Demings, FL-10	CHOB 217		

INTELLIGENCE MODERNIZATION & READINESS
Room: Capitol Visitor Center HVC-304
Phone: 202.225.7690

Majority:		Minority:	
C: Eric Swalwell, CA-15	CHOB 407	RM: Will Hurd, TX-23	CHOB 317
Terri Sewell, AL-07	RHOB 2201	Rick Crawford, AR-01	RHOB 2422
Jackie Speier, CA-14	RHOB 2465	Elise Stefanik, NY-21	CHOB 318
Joaquin Castro, TX-20	RHOB 2241	John Ratcliffe, TX-04	CHOB 223
Valdez Demings, FL-10	CHOB 217		
Raja Krishnamoorthi, IL-08	CHOB 115		

STRATEGIC TECHNOLOGIES & ADVANCED RESEARCH
Room: Capitol Visitor Center HVC-304
Phone: 202.225.7690

Majority:		Minority:	
C: Jim Himes, CT-04	LHOB 1227	RM: Chris Stewart, UT-02	RHOB 2242
Andre Carson, IN-07	RHOB 2135	Elise Stefanik, NY-21	CHOB 318
Mike Quigley, IL-05	RHOB 2458	John Ratcliffe, TX-04	CHOB 223
Denny Heck, WA-10	RHOB 2452	Michael Turner, OH-10	RHOB 2082
Eric Swalwell, CA-15	CHOB 407		
Raja Krishnamoorthi, IL-08	CHOB 115		

SELECT COMMITTEE ON THE CLIMATE CRISIS

Room: RHOB 2052
Website:
Phone: 202.225.3376
Ratio: 9 Democrats/6 Republicans
Subcommittees: 0

Majority:		Minority:	
C: Kathy Castor, FL-14	RHOB 2052	RM: Garret Graves, LA-06	RHOB 2402
Ben Lujan, NM-03	RHOB 2323	Morgan Griffith, VA-09	RHOB 2202
Suzanne Bonamici, OR-01	RHOB 2231	Gary Palmer, AL-06	CHOB 207

HOUSE COMMITTEES

Julia Brownley, CA-26	RHOB 2262	Buddy Carter, GA-01	RHOB 2432
Jared Huffman, CA-02	LHOB 1527	Carol Miller, WV-03	LHOB 1605
A. Donald McEachin, VA-04	CHOB 314	Kelly Armstrong, ND-01	LHOB 1004
Mike Levin, CA-49	LHOB 1626		
Sean Casten, IL-06	CHOB 429		
Joseph Neguse, CO-02	LHOB 1419		

SELECT COMMITTEE ON THE MODERNIZATION OF CONGRESS

Room: LHOB 1410
Website: www.newdemocratcoalition-himes.house.gov
Phone: 202.225.5916
Ratio: 6 Democrats/6 Republicans
Subcommittees: 0

Majority:		Minority:	
C: Derek Kilmer, WA-06	LHOB 1410	**RM: Tom Graves, GA-14**	RHOB 2078
Emanuel Cleaver, MO-05	RHOB 2335	Rob Woodall, GA-07	LHOB 1724
Suzan DelBene, WA-01	RHOB 2330	Susan Brooks, IN-05	LHOB 2211
Zoe Lofgren, CA-19	LHOB 1401	Rodney Davis, IL-13	LHOB 1740
Mark Pocan, WI-02	LHOB 1421	Dan Newhouse, WA-04	LHOB 1414
Mary Scanlon, PA-05	LHOB 1535	William Timmons, SC-04	CHOB 313

EXECUTIVE BRANCH

The Executive Branch of the U.S. government was formed through Article II of the U.S. Constitution. The Executive Branch is primarily composed of the President (who is also the Commander-in-Chief of the armed services), the White House staff, the Executive Office of the President, the Vice President, as well as the 14 Federal departments, the heads of which form the President's Cabinet.

Also included under the purview of the Executive Branch are the various subordinate divisions of the Federal departments, independent Federal agencies, the independent Federal reserve system, and several permanent and ad hoc agencies, boards, commissions and committees. The Executive Branch is responsible for carrying out and enforcing the federal laws and protecting the people of the United States.

President of the United States **Donald J. Trump (R)**   p **202.456.1414**

1600 Pennsylvania Ave. NW
Washington, DC 20500
Bio. 06/14/1946 • New York , NY • University of Pennsylvania Wharton School of Business (PA), B.A. • Presbyterian • M. Melania Trump, 5 ch (4 from previous marriages), 8 gr-ch
Salary $400,000

Vice President **Mike Pence (R)**   p

,
Bio. 06/07/1959 • Columbus, IN, IN • Attorney • Hanover College, B.A., 1981; Indiana University School of Law, J.D., 1986 • Disciples of Christ • M. Karen Pence, 3 ch
Salary $230,700

THE OFFICE OF THE PRESIDENT

www.whitehouse.gov

President
Donald J. Trump

Chief of Staff (Acting)
Hon. John Michael Mulvaney   202.456.1414

Counselor to the President
Kellyanne Conway   202.456.1414

National Security Advisor
John R. Bolton   202.456.1414

Press Secretary
Sarah Huckabee Sanders   202.456.1111

Senior Adviser to the President for Strategic Planning
Jared Kushner   202.456.1414

Senior Counselor to the President for Policy
Stephen Miller   202.224.4124

THE OFFICE OF THE VICE PRESIDENT

www.whitehouse.gov/vicepresident

Vice President
Mike Pence

Second Lady
Karen Pence   202.456.1111

Chief of Staff
Nick Ayers   202.456.1111

Chief of Staff to the Second Lady
Jana Toner   202.456.1111

National Security Advisor
Lt. Gen. (Ret) Keith Kellogg   202.456.1111

THE OFFICE OF THE FIRST LADY

www.whitehouse.gov/firstlady

First Lady
Melania Trump

Chief of Staff
Lindsay Reynolds   202.456.1111

EXECUTIVE OFFICE OF THE PRESIDENT

www.whitehouse.gov

Through the U.S. Code's Reorganization Act of 1939, authority over a variety of Federal agencies was transferred to the Executive Branch, which has since formed the Executive Office of the President. The composition of the Executive Office customarily changes with each administration to reflect the policy goals of the President.

The President, through the Office of Management and Budget (OMB), manages the Executive Office of the President. It is through the OMB that the Executive Branch's departments, agency programs, policies and expenditures are shaped. In addition to OMB, the following agencies comprise the Executive Office of the President.

Council of Economic Advisers (CEA)
EEOB
1650 Pennsylvania Ave. NW
Washington, DC 20504
Chairman: Kevin Hassett   **202.456.1111**

Council on Environmental Quality
722 Jackson Pl. NW
Washington, DC 20506
Vacant at time of printing.   **202.395.5750**

Domestic Policy Council
1600 Pennsylvania Ave. NW
Washington, DC 20500
Director: Andrew Bremburg   **202.456.1111**

National Economic Council
EEOB
West of White House
Washington, DC 20500
Director: Larry Kudlow   **202.456.1111**

National Security Council (NSC)
1600 Pennsylvania Ave. NW
Washington, DC 20500
Chairman: John R. Bolton   **202.456.1414**

Office of Administration
1600 Pennsylvania Ave. NW
Washington, DC 20500
Director: Marcia Lee Kelly   **202.442.9094**

Office of National Drug Control Policy
750 17th St. NW
Washington, DC 20006
Director (acting): James W. Carroll   **202.395.6700**

Office of Science and Technology Policy
EEOB
1650 Pennsylvania Ave.
Washington, DC 20504
Vacant at time of printing.   **202.456.4444**

THE CABINET

The Executive Branch's 14 department Secretaries form the President's Cabinet. The President appoints each Secretary, who must be confirmed by the Senate. The Cabinet advises the President on various aspects of the Executive Branch and then proceed as the president directs. The annual salary for Department Secretaries is $203,700.

The President also has the authority to appoint members of the Executive Office of the President and other officials to Cabinet-level rank, The Vice President and the President's chief of staff are considered members of the Cabinet. Under the Trump administration, the following administrators also are considered members of the Cabinet.

Chief of Staff (acting)
Hon. John Michael Mulvaney

Director, Office of Management and Budget
Hon. John Michael Mulvaney   202.395.4840

Trade Representative
Robert E. Lighthizer   202.395.6850

Administrator, Environmental Protection Agency
Andrew Wheeler   202.564.4700

U.S Ambassador to the United Nations (acting)
Jonathan Cohen

Administrator, Small Business Administration
Linda McMahon

Department of Agriculture (USDA)
Sonny Perdue (PUR-doo)   p **202.720.3935**

1400 Independence Ave
Washington, DC 20250
Bio. 12/20/1946 • Perry, GA • Governor • University of Georgia, Bach. Deg.; University of Georgia, D.V.M. • Baptist • M. Mary Ruff, 4 ch, 14 grch

Department of Commerce (DOC)
Wilbur Ross (rawss)   p **202.482.2000**

1401 Constitution Ave.
Washington, DC 20230
Website commerce.gov
Bio. 11/28/1937 • Weehawken , NJ • Yale University (CT), B.A.; Harvard Business School (MA), M.B.A. • M. Hilary Geary, 2 ch (from previous marriage)
Chief of Staff Ryan Zinke
Deputy Secretary Matthew G. Whitaker (acting)

Department of Defense (DOD)
Patrick M. Shanahan (acting)   p

1400 Defense Pentagon
Washington, DC 20301
Bio. 06/27/1962 • Aberdeen, WA • University of Washington, B.S.; Massachusetts Institute of Technology, M.S.; Massachusetts Institute of Technology, M.B.A. • Not Known • S.

Department of Education (ED)
Betsy DeVos (duh-VAWSS)   p **202.401.3000**

400 Maryland Ave. SW
Washington, DC 20202
Website ed.gov
Bio. 06/08/1958 • Holland, MI • Philanthropist • Calvin College (MI), B.A. • Christian Reformed Church • M. Dick Devos, 4 ch

Department of Energy (DOE)
Rick Perry (PAIR-ree)   p **202.586.5000**

1000 Independence Ave.
Washington, DC 20585
Website energy.gov
Bio. 03/04/1950 • Paint Creek, TX • Member, TX State House; TX Commissioner of Agriculture; Lt. Governor, TX • U.S. Air Force Captain • Methodist • M. Anita Thigpen, 2 ch
Chief of Staff Ryan Zinke
Deputy Secretary Matthew G. Whitaker (acting)

Department of Health and Human Services (HHS)
Alex M. Azar (AY zur)   p **202.690.7000**

330 C St SW
Washington, DC 20416
Email Secretary@HHS.gov
Website hhs.gov
Bio. 06/17/1967 • Johnstown, PA • Dartmouth College, B.A., 1988; Yale Law School (CT), J.D, 1991 • Not Known • M. Jennifer Azar, 2 ch

Department of Homeland Security (DHS)
Kirstjen M. Nielsen (NEEL-suhn)   p **202.786.9900**

Secretary of Homeland Security
Washington, DC 20528
Website dhs.gov
Bio. 05/14/1972 • Georgetown University (DC), B.S.; University of Virginia School of Law, J.D • .

Department of Housing and Urban Development (HUD)
Ben Carson (KAR-suhn)   p **202.708.0417**

451 7th St. SW
Washington, DE 20410
Website hud.gov
Bio. 09/18/1951 • Detriot , MI • Yale University (CT), B.A.; University of Michigan, D.M.S. • Seventh-Day Adventist • M. Candy Carson, 3 ch

Department of Justice (DOJ)
Matthew G. Whitaker (acting)   p **202.514.2000**

950 Pennsylvania Ave. NW
Washington, DC 20530
Bio. 10/29/1969 • Des Moines, IA • University of Iowa, B.A.; University of Iowa, M.B.A.; University of Iowa, J.D • Lutheran • M. Marci Whitaker, 3 ch

Department of Labor (DOL)
Alex Acosta (uh-KAW-stuh)   p **866.487.2365**

200 Constitution Ave. NW
Washington, DC 20210
Website dol.gov
Bio. 01/16/1969 • , FL • Attorney • Harvard College (MA), B.A.; Harvard University Law School (MA), J.D. • M. Jan Williams
Chief of Staff Ryan Zinke
Deputy Secretary Matthew G. Whitaker (acting)

Department of State (DOS)
Hon. Michael R. Pompeo (PAHM pay oh)   p **202.647.6575**

2201 C St. NW
Washington, DC 20520
Website state.gov
Bio. 12/30/1963 • Orange, CA • U.S. Army Captain
(1986-1991) • U.S. Military Academy - West Point (NY),
B.S., 1986; Harvard University Law School (MA), J.D., 1994 •
Presbyterian • M. Susan Pompeo, 1 ch

Department of the Interior (DOI)
David Bernhardt (acting)   p **202.208.3100**

1849 C St. NW
Washington, DC 20240
Website doi.gov
Bio. 08/17/1969 • Rifle, CO • University of Northern
Colorado, B.A.; George Washington University School of Law
(DC), J.D • M. Gena Bernhardt, 2 ch

Department of Transportation (DOT)
Elaine Chao (chou)   p **202.366.4000**

West Building, 1200 New Jersey Ave. SE
Washington, DC 20590
Website dot.gov
Bio. 03/26/1953 • Taipei Mount Holyoke College (MA), B.A.;
Harvard Business School (MA), M.B.A. • Baptist • M. Sen.
Mitch McConnell, 3 ch (from previous marriage)

Department of Treasury
Steven Mnuchin (muh-NOO-chin)   p **202.622.2000**

1500 Pennsylvania Ave. NW
Washington, DC 20220
Website treasury.gov
Bio. 12/21/1962 • New York, NY • Goldman Sachs • Yale
University (CT), B.A. • Jewish • E. Louise Linton, 3 ch (from
previous marriage)
Chief of Staff Ryan Zinke
Deputy Secretary Matthew G. Whitaker (acting)

Department of Veterans Affairs (VA)
Robert L. Wilkie (WIL kee)   p **800.827.1000**

810 Vermont Ave. NW
Washington, DC 20220
Website va.gov
Bio. 08/02/1962 • FrankfurtU.S. Navy Reserve, U.S. Air Force
Reserve (Lt. Colonel) • Wake Forest University (NC), B.A.;
Loyola University, New Orleans (LA), J.D; Georgetown
University (DC), LL.M.; U.S. Army War College (PA), M.S. • M.

SELECTED FEDERAL AGENCIES

American Battle Monuments Commission   abmc.gov
2300 Clarendon Blvd.   703.696.6900
Courthouse Plaza II., Suite 500
Arlington, VA 22201

AMTRAK - Natl Railroad Passenger Corporation   amtrak.com
60 Massachusetts Ave. NE   202.906.3000
Washington, DC 20002

Bureau of Alcohol, Tobacco, Firearms and   atf.gov
Explosives (ATF)   202.648.8500
99 New York Ave. NE
Washington, DC 20226

Bureau of Indian Affairs (BIA) bia.gov
1849 C St. NW 202.208.5116
MS-4606-MIB
Washington, DC 20240

Bureau of Land Management (BLM) blm.gov
1849 C St. NW 202.208.3801
Room 5665
Washington, DC 20240

Bureau of Ocean Energy Management boem.gov
1849 C St. NW 202.208.6474
Office of Public Affairs
Washington, DC 20240

Central Intelligence Agency cia.gov
Office of Public Affairs 703.482.0623
Washington, DC 20505

Commodity Futures Trading Commission (CFTC) cftc.gov
1155 21st St. NW 202.418.5000
Three Lafayette Centre
Washington, DC 20581

Congressional Budget Office (CBO) cbo.gov
Second & D St. SW 202.226.2602
Fourth Floor
Washington, DC 20515-6925

Corporation for National & Community Service nationalservice.gov
250 E St. SW 800.833.3722
Washington, DC 20525

Director of National Intelligence (ODNI) dni.gov
Office of the Director of National Intelligence 703.733.8600
Washington, DC 20511

Election Assistance Commission (EAC) eac.gov
1335 East West Hwy. 301.563.3919
Suite 4300
Silver Spring, MD 20910

Export-Import Bank of the United States exim.gov
811 Vermont Ave. NW 212.809.2650
Washington, DC 20571

Farm Credit Administration fca.gov
1501 Farm Credit Dr. 703.883.4056
McLean, VA 22102-5090

Federal Accounting Standards Advisory Board fasab.gov
(FASAB) 202.512.7350
441 G St. NW
Suite 6814
Washington, DC 20548

Federal Aviation Administration (FAA) faa.gov
Department of Transportation (DOT) 202.366.4000
800 Independence Ave. SW
Washington, DC 20591

Federal Bureau of Investigation (FBI) fbi.gov
935 Pennsylvania Ave. NW 202.324.3000
Washington, DC 20535-0001

Federal Communications Commission fcc.gov
445 12th St. SW 888.225.5322
Washington, DC 20554

Federal Deposit Insurance Corporation fdic.gov
550 17th St. NW 877.275.3342
Washington, DC 20429-9990

Federal Election Commission fec.gov
999 E St. NW 202.694.1000
Washington, DC 20463

Federal Energy Regulatory Commission ferc.gov
888 First St. NE 202.502.6088
Washington, DC 20426

Federal Highway Administration (FHA) fhwa.dot.gov
Department of Transportation (DOT) 202.366.4000
1200 New Jersey Ave. SE
Washington, DC 20590

Federal Housing Finance Agency fhfa.gov
400 Seventh St. SW 202.649.3800
Constitution Center
Washington, DC 20219

Federal Labor Relations Authority (FLRA) flra.gov
1400 K St. NW 202.218.7777
Washington, DC 20424

Federal Maritime Commission fmc.gov
800 N. Capitol St. NW 202.523.5800
Washington, DC 20573

Federal Mediation & Conciliation Service
fmcs.gov
202.606.8100
2100 K St. NW
Washington, DC 20427

Federal Railroad Administration
fra.dot.gov
202.366.4000
Department of Transportation (DOT)
1200 New Jersey Ave. SE
Washington, DC 20590

Federal Reserve System
federalreserve.gov
202.974.7008
20th St. & Constitution Ave. NW
Washington, DC 20551

Federal Trade Commission (FTC)
ftc.gov
202.326.2395
600 Pennsylvania Ave. NW
Washington, DC 20580

Federal Transit Administration
fta.dot.gov
202.366.4040
Department of Transportation (DOT)
1200 New Jersey Ave. SE
Washington, DC 20590

Government Accountability Office
gao.gov
202.512.4800
441 G St. NW
Washington, DC 20548

Government National Mortgage Association
ginniemae.gov
202.708.1535
451 7th Street, SW
Room B-133
Washington, DC 20410

Government Printing Office (GPO)
gpo.gov
202.512.1800
732 N. Capitol St. NW
Washington, DC 20401-0001

Institute of Museum and Library Services (IMLS)
imls.gov
202.653.4657
955 L'Enfant Plaza North SW
Suite 4000
Washington, DC 20024-2135

Inter-American Foundation
iaf.gov
202.360.4530
1331 Pennsylvania Ave. NW
Suite 1200 North
Washington, DC 20004

Internal Revenue Service (IRS)
irs.gov
410.224.5000
Department of Treasury
190 Admiral Cochrane Dr.
Annapolis, MD 21401

Legal Services Corporation
lsc.gov
202.295.1500
3333 K St. NW
Washington, DC 20007

Library of Congress (LOC)
loc.gov
202.707.5000
101 Independence Ave. SE
Washington, DC 20540

Medicare Payment Advisory Commission (MedPAC)
medpac.gov
202.220.3700
425 I St. NW
Suite 701
Washington, DC 20001

Merit Systems Protection Board
mspb.gov
202.254.4475
1615 M St. NW
Washington, DC 20419

National Aeronautics and Space Administration (NASA)
nasa.gov
202.358.0001
300 E St. SW
Suite 5R30
Washington, DC 20546

National Archives and Records Administration
archives.gov
866.272.6272
8601 Adelphi Rd.
College Park, MD 20740

National Council on Disability
ncd.gov
202.272.2004
1331 F St. NW
Suite 850
Washington, DC 20004

National Credit Union Administration
ncua.gov
703.518.6300
1775 Duke St.
Alexandria, VA 22314

National Endowment For the Arts
arts.gov
202.682.5400
400 Seventh St. SW
Washington, DC 20506-0001

National Highway Traffic Safety Administration (NHTSA)
nhtsa.gov
202.366.9550
Department of Transportation (DOT)
1200 New Jersey Ave. SE
Washington, DC 20590

National Indian Gaming Commission
90 K St. NE
Suite 200
Washington, DC 20005

nigc.gov
202.632.7003

National Labor Relations Board
1015 Half St. SE
Washington, DC 20570-0001

nlrb.gov
202.273.1000

National Mediation Board
1301 K St. NW
Suite 250 East
Washington, DC 20005

nmb.gov
202.692.5000

National Park Service (NPS)
1849 C St. NW
Washington, DC 20240

nps.gov
202.208.6843

National Science Foundation
4201 Wilson Blvd.
Arlington, VA 22230

nsf.gov
703.292.5111

National Transportation Safety Board
490 L'Enfant Plaza SW
Washington, DC 20594

ntsb.gov
202.314.6000

Occupational Safety and Health Administration
Department of Labor (DOL)
200 Constitution Ave. NW
Room Number N3626
Washington, DC 20210

osha.gov
800.321.6742

Office of Government Ethics (OGE)
1201 New York Ave. NW
Suite 500
Washington, DC 20005

oge.gov
202.482.9300

Office of Housing
451 Seventh St. SW
Washington, DC 20410

hud.gov
202.645.0585

Office of Special Counsel
1730 M St. NW
Suite 218
Washington, DC 20036

osc.gov
202.254.3600

Office of the Comptroller of the Currency
Department of Treasury
400 Seventh St. SW
Washington, DC 20219

occ.gov
202.649.6800

Overseas Private Investment Corp (OPIC)
1100 New York Ave. NW
Washington, DC 20527

opic.gov
202.336.8799

Peace Corps
1111 20th St. NW
Washington, DC 20526

peacecorps.gov
206.553.5490

Pension Benefit Guaranty Corporation
P.O. Box 151750
Alexandria, VA 22315-1750

pbgc.gov
202.326.4000

Postal Regulatory Commission
901 New York Ave. NW
Suite 200
Washington, DC 20268

prc.gov
202.789.6800

Selective Service System
P.O. Box 94638
Palatine, IL 60094-4638

sss.gov
847.688.6888

Smithsonian Institution
P.O. Box 37012
Room 153, MRC 010
Washington, DC 20013

si.edu
202.633.1000

Social Security Administration
6401 Security Blvd.
1100 W. High Rise
Baltimore, MD 21235

ssa.gov
800.7721213

Trade & Development Agency (TDA)
1000 Wilson Blvd.
Suite 1600
Arlington, VA 22209

ustda.gov
206.389.7301

U.S. Agency for International Development
1300 Pennsylvania Ave. NW
Washington, DC 20523

usaid.gov
202.712.4300

U.S. Census Bureau
4600 Silver Hill Road
Washington, DC 20233

census.gov
301.763.4636

U.S. Chemical Safety & Hazard Investigation Board
csb.gov
202.261.7600
1750 Pennsylvania Ave. NW
Suite 910
Washington, DC 20006

U.S. Commission of Fine Arts
cfa.gov
202.504.2200
401 F St. NW
Suite 312
Washington, DC 20001

U.S. Commission on Civil Rights
usccr.gov
202.376.8105
1331 Pennsylvania Ave. NW
Suite 1150
Washington, DC 20425

U.S. Consumer Product Safety Commission
cpsc.gov
301.504.7923
4330 East West Hwy.
Bethesda, MD 20814

U.S. Copyright Office
copyright.gov
202.707.3000
101 Independence Ave. SE
Washington, DC 20559-6000

U.S. Drug Enforcement Administration
dea.gov
202.305.8500
800 K St. NW
Suite 500
Washington, DC 20001

U.S. Environmental Protection Agency
epa.gov
202.564.4700
1200 Pennsylvania Ave. NW
Washington, DC 20460

U.S. Equal Employment Opportunity Commission
eeoc.gov
800.669.4000
131 M St. NE
Washington, DC 20507

U.S. Fish and Wildlife Service
fws.gov
252.946.3361
5275 Leesburg Pike
Falls Church, VA 22041

U.S. General Services Administration
gsa.gov
202.708.5841
1800 F St. NW
Washington, DC 20405

U.S. Institute of Peace
usip.gov
202.457.1700
2301 Constitution Ave. NW
Washington, DC 20037

U.S. International Trade Commission
usitc.gov
202.205.2000
500 E St. SW
Washington, DC 20436

U.S. Marshals Service
usmarshals.gov
202.353.0600
Third & Constitution Ave. NW
Room 1103
Washington, DC 20001

U.S. Mint
usmint.gov
800.872.6468
Department of Treasury
801 Ninth St. NW
Washington, DC 20220-0012

U.S. Nuclear Regulatory Commission
nrc.gov
301.415.7000
11555 Rockville Pike
One Flint North
Rockville, MD 20852-2738

U.S. Office of Personnel Management
opm.gov
202.606.1800
1900 E St. NW
Washington, DC 20415

U.S. Postal Service
usps.gov
202.268.2608
475 L'Enfant Plaza SW
Room 1P830
Washington, DC 20260-1101

U.S. Securities and Exchange Commission
sec.gov
800.732.0330
100 F St. NE
Washington, DC 20549

U.S. Small Business Administration
sba.gov
202.205.8800
409 Third St. SW
Washington, DC 20416

Veterans Employment & Training Service
dol.gov
202.693.4700
Department of Labor (DOL)
200 Constitution Ave. NW
Room S-1325
Washington, DC 20210

Violence Against Women Program
ovw.usdoj.gov
509.684.9800
145 N St. NE
Suite 10W.121
Washington, DC 20530

THE SUPREME COURT OF THE UNITED STATES

One First St. NE
Washington, DC 20543
202.479.3000
www.supremecourt.gov

Court Officers
Clerk — Scott Harris
Counselor to the Chief Justice — Jeffrey P. Minear
Court Counsel — Ethan Torrey
Curator — Catherine Fitts
Director of Information Technology — Robert J. Hawkins
Librarian — Linda Maslow
Marshal — Pamela Talkin
Public Information Officer — Kathleen L. Arberg
Reporter of Decisions — Christine L. Fallon

U.S. Supreme Court and Federal Court Resources
Federal Judicial Center — **fjc.gov**
Federal Judiciary — **uscourts.gov**
Supreme Court Historical Society — **supremecourthistory.org**
U.S. Court of Appeals for the Federal Circuit — **cafc.uscourts.gov**
U.S. Supreme Court Opinion Announcements — **202.479.3360**
U.S. Supreme Court Public Information Office — **202.479.3211**
U.S. Supreme Court Visitor Information Line — **202.479.3030**

2019 UNITED STATES SUPREME COURT

Chief Justice John G. Roberts (RAH bertz)

Nominated by George W. Bush, 2005
Bio. 01/27/1955 • Buffalo, NY • United States Court of Appeals for the District of Columbia Circuit; Private Practicing Attorney; U.S. Department of Justice; Office of the White House Counsel • Harvard College (MA), A.B, 1976; Harvard University Law School (MA), J.D., 1979 • Catholic • M. Jane Marie Sullivan Roberts, 2 ch
Law Clerks Evelyn Babcock • Cole T. Carter • Julie M. Karaba • Michael Clemente • Zaki Anwar • David Beylik • Joseph Falvey • Megan Braun
Salary $263,300
Jurisdiction United States Court of Appeals for the District of Columbia, Fourth and Federal Circuits

Associate Justice Clarence Thomas (TOM as)

Nominated by George H.W. Bush, 1991
Bio. 06/23/1948 • Pin Point, GA • Judge, U.S. Court of Appeals for the DC Circuit; Chair, U.S. Equal Opportunity Employment Commission; Assistant Secretary, U.S. Department of Education; Assistant Attorney General of Missouri • College of The Holy Cross (MA), A.B; Yale University Law School (CT), J.D., 1974 • Catholic • M. Virginia 'Ginni' Lamp Thomas, 1 ch
Law Clerks Kathryn Anne Kimball • Christopher Ernest Mills • Russell Balikian • Madeline Lansky • Brian Lipshutz • Caroline A. Cook • James Matthew Rice • Laura Wolk
Salary $251,800
Jurisdiction U.S. Court of Appeals for the Eleventh Circuit

Associate Justice Ruth Bader Ginsburg (GINNS berg)

Nominated by William J. Clinton, 1993
Bio. 03/15/1933 • Brooklyn, NY • Judge, U.S. Court of Appeals for the DC Circuit; Member, National Board of Directors and General Counsel, American Civil Liberties Union; Law Professor • Cornell University (NY), B.A.; Columbia University Law School (NY), LL.B.; Harvard University Law School (MA), B.A. • Jewish • W. , 2 ch; 4 gr-ch
Law Clerks Kathryn Barber • Rachel Bayefsky • Rebecc Lee • Matthew Jacob Rubenstein • Alyssa Marie Barnare • Marco P. Basile • Susan M. Pelletier • Michael Qian • Jack Boeglin • David Louk
Salary $251,800
Jurisdiction U.S. Court of Appeals for the Second Circuit

Associate Justice Stephen G. Breyer (BRY er)

Nominated by William J. Clinton, 1994
Bio. 08/15/1938 • San Francisco, CA • Chief Judge and Judge, U.S. Court of Appeals for the First District; Law Professor, Harvard University • Stanford University (CA), A.B; Oxford University (England), B.A.; Harvard University, LL.B. • Jewish • M. Joanna Hare Breyer, 3 ch; 5 gr-ch
Law Clerks Alec Warren Schierenbeck • Celia Choy • Dalia Mignouna • Eugene Sokoloff • Janine Mrie Lopez • Jo-Ann Tamila Karhson • Nicholas Roberts Rosellini • William Ernest Havemann
Salary $251,800
Jurisdiction U.S. Court of Appeals for the First Circuit

Associate Justice Samuel A. Alito (Ah LEE tow)

Nominated by George W. Bush, 2006
Bio. 04/01/1950 • Trenton, NJ • Judge, U.S. Court of Appeals for the Third District; Law Professor; U.S. Attorney; Deputy Assistant Attorney General; Assistant to the Solicitor General; Assistant U.S. Attorney; Law Clerk • Princeton University (NJ), A.B; Yale University Law School (CT), J.D. • Catholic • M. Martha-Ann Bomgardner Alito, 2 ch
Law Clerks Jorge Benjamin Aguinaga • David Casazza • Whitney Downs Hermandorfer • Sherif Girgis • Aimee W. Brown
Salary $251,800
Jurisdiction U.S. Court of Appeals for the Third and Fifth Circuits

Associate Justice Sonia M. Sotomayor (so-"toe"-my-YOR)

Nominated by Barack H. Obama, 2009
Bio. 06/25/1954 • The Bronx, NY • Judge, U.S. District Court of Appeals for the Second District; Judge, U.S. District Court for the Southern District of New York • Princeton University (NJ), A.B, 1976; Yale University Law School (CT), J.D., 1979 • Catholic • D.
Law Clerks Samiyyah Ali • Michael Skocpol • Rachel Wilf-Townsend • Michael Zuckerman
Salary $251,800
Jurisdiction U.S. Court of Appeals for the Sixth and Tenth Circuits

Associate Justice Elena Kagan (KAY-guhn)

Nominated by Barack H. Obama, 2010
Bio. 04/28/1960 • New York, NY • Law Professor and Dean, Harvard Law School; US Solicitor General • Princeton Universtiy, A.B, 1981; Oxford University (England), M.Phil, 1983; Harvard University Law School (MA), J.D., 1986 • Jewish • S.
Law Clerks Robert B. Niles • Ashley Robertson • Zachary B. Savage • Reema Shaw • Mica Moore • Zayn Siddique • Jordan Brock • Alex Miller • Peter Davis
Salary $251,800
Jurisdiction U.S. Court of Appeals for the Ninth Circuit

Associate Justice Neil M. Gorsuch (GOR-such)

Nominated by Donald J. Trump, 2017
Bio. 08/29/1967 • Denver, CO • United States Court of Appeals for the Tenth Circuit; Judicial Clerk (1991-1994); Attorney • Oxford University (England), DPhil; Columbia University (NY), B.A., 1988; Harvard University Law School (MA), J.D, 1991 • Episcopalian • M. Louise Gorsuch, 2 ch
Law Clerks Tobi Merrit Edwards • Ethan Price Davis • Paul Alessio Mezzina • Jeffrey T. Quilici • Kelly C. Holt • Trevor W. Ezell
Salary $251,800
Jurisdiction U.S. Court of Appeals for the Eighth Circuit

Associate Justice Brett M. Kavanaugh (cah vuh NAW)

Nominated by Donald J. Trump, 2018
Bio. 02/12/1965 • Washington, DC • Yale University (CT), B.A.; Yale University (CT), J.D • Catholic • M. Ashley Estes Kavanaugh, 2 ch
Law Clerks Shannon Grammel • Kimberly J. Jackson • Megan Marie Lacy • Sarah Shaw Nommensen
Salary $251,800
Jurisdiction U.S. Court of Appeals for the Seventh Circuits

The Electoral College was established in Article II of the U.S. Constitution. The Electoral College requires that the President and Vice President be elected through a group of electors based on state population rather than by popular vote. This ensures that less populated states, such as Vermont and North Dakota, will have a bearing on the results of the national election, rather than the election being determined primarily by the more populated states such as California and New York.

For example, the Electoral College ensures that candidates must visit all of the states, as an election cannot be won based on winning only the most populated states. A candidate must therefore make an effort to visit and win a majority of states in order to win an election.

Each state has an amount of electors equal to the number of their Members in Congress. Therefore, each state has at least three electors (the District of Columbia also receives three electors for a national total of 538 electors). Though laws vary from state to state, the state parties typically choose electors. Electors in some states cast their ballot based on the popular vote of the state and others cast their vote based on the party candidate. However, rarely will an elector vote opposite of the vote of the people.

Electors in each state meet in their respective state capitals in December to cast their votes for President and Vice President. Once these ballots have been cast, they are sent to Congress, where they are counted by the President of the Senate on January 6 (or the following day if January 6 falls on a Sunday). The candidate with an absolute majority prevails. If no candidate receives an absolute majority of electoral votes, the House of Representatives selects the next President and the Senate selects the next Vice President.

For more information on the Electoral College, contact the National Archives and Records Administration at **www.archives.gov**.

The Electoral College

Total: 538
Majority Needed to Elect: 270

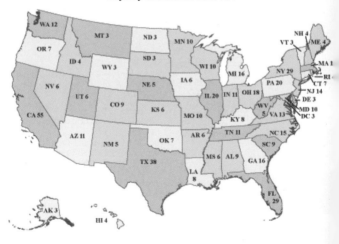

NOTES

NOTES

ERRATA

The following errors have been discovered since the initial printing of this directory; appropriate corrections are provided here.

PAGE	ERROR
p. 24	The room number for Sen. Kyrsten Sinema is incorrect. The correct room number is HSOB 317.
p. 82	The room number for Sen. Ben Sasse is incorrect. The correct room number is RSOB 107.
p. 106	The map for Pennsylvania excludes District 7. Corrected map pictured below:

p. 154

There is a duplicate record with Majority and Minority membership switched for Senate Subcommittee on Africa and Global Health Policy. The correct listing is as follows:

AFRICA AND GLOBAL HEALTH POLICY
Room: DSOB 423   Phone: 202.224.4651

Majority:		Minority:	
C: Lindsey Graham, SC	RSOB 290	**RM: Tim Kaine, VA**	RSOB 231
Johnny Isakson, GA	RSOB 131	Christopher Coons, DE	RSOB 127-A
Rob Portman, OH	RSOB 448		
Ron Johnson, WI	HSOB 328	Cory Booker, NJ	HSOB 717
Ted Cruz, TX	RSOB 404	Chris Murphy, CT	HSOB 136

p. 155

1. There is a duplicate record with Majority and Minority membership switched for Subcommittee on East Asia, the Pacific, and International Cybersecurity Policy. The correct listing is as follows:

EAST ASIA, THE PACIFIC, AND INTERNATIONAL CYBERSECURITY POLICY
Room: DSOB 423   Phone: 202.224.4651

Majority:		Minority:	
C: Cory Gardner, CO	RSOB 354	**RM: Ed Markey, MA**	DSOB 255
Marco Rubio, FL	RSOB 284	Christopher Coons, DE	RSOB 127-A
Ron Johnson, WI	HSOB 328	Jeff Merkley, OR	HSOB 313
Johnny Isakson, GA	RSOB 131	Tom Udall, NM	HSOB 531
Todd Young, IN	RSOB 400		

2. There is a duplicate record with Majority and Minority membership switched for Subcommittee on Europe and Regional Security Cooperation. The correct listing is as follows:

EUROPE AND REGIONAL SECURITY COOPERATION
Room: DSOB 423   Phone: 202.224.4651

Majority:		Minority:	
C: Ron Johnson, WI	HSOB 328	**RM: Jeanne Shaheen, NH**	HSOB 506
John Barrasso, WY	DSOB 307	Chris Murphy, CT	HSOB 136
Rob Portman, OH	RSOB 448	Ben Cardin, MD	HSOB 509
Rand Paul, KY	RSOB 167	Christopher Coons, DE	RSOB 127-A
Mitt Romney, UT	RSOB B33		

3. Majority and Minority membership switched for Senate Subcommittee on Multilateral, International Development, and International Economic, Energy, and Environmental Policy. The correct listing is as follows:

MULTILATERAL INTERNATIONAL DEVELOPMENT, MULTILATERAL INSTITUTIONS, AND INTERNATIONAL ECONOMIC, ENERGY, AND ENVIRONMENTAL POLICY
Room: DSOB 423   Phone: 202.224.4651

Majority:		Minority:	
C: Todd Young, IN	RSOB 400	**RM: Jeff Merkley, OR**	HSOB 313
John Barrasso, WY	DSOB 307	Ed Markey, MA	DSOB 255
Lindsey Graham, SC	RSOB 290	Tom Udall, NM	HSOB 531
Rand Paul, KY	RSOB 167	Cory Booker, NJ	HSOB 717
Mitt Romney, UT	RSOB B33		

ERRATA

p. 155

4. There is a duplicate record with Majority and Minority membership switched for Subcommittee on the Near East, South Asia, Central Asia, and Counterterrorism. The correct listing is as follows:

NEAR EAST, SOUTH ASIA, CENTRAL ASIA, AND COUNTERTERRORISM
Room: DSOB 423   **Phone:** 202.224.4651

Majority:		Minority:	
C: Mitt Romney, UT	RSOB B33	**RM: Chris Murphy, CT**	HSOB 136
Ted Cruz, TX	RSOB 404	Ben Cardin, MD	HSOB 509
Lindsey Graham, SC	RSOB 290	Jeanne Shaheen, NH	HSOB 506
Cory Gardner, CO	RSOB 354	Tim Kaine, VA	RSOB 231
Rand Paul, KY	RSOB 167		

p. 156

1. There is a duplicate record with Majority and Minority membership switched for Subcommittee on the State Department and USAID Management, International Operations, and Bilateral International Development. The correct listing is as follows:

STATE DEPT AND USAID MGMT, INT'L OPS, AND INT'L DEVELOPMENT
Room: DSOB 423   **Phone:** 202.224.4651

Majority:		Minority:	
C: Johnny Isakson, GA	RSOB 131	**RM: Cory Booker, NJ**	HSOB 717
Todd Young, IN	RSOB 400	Ed Markey, MA	DSOB 255
Rand Paul, KY	RSOB 167	Jeff Merkley, OR	HSOB 313
Rob Portman, OH	RSOB 448	Tom Udall, NM	HSOB 531
Marco Rubio, FL	RSOB 284		

2. There is a duplicate record for Senate Subcommittee on the Western Hemisphere, Transnational Crime, Civilian Security, Democracy, Human Rights, and Global Women's Issues with Majority and Minority membership switched. The correct listing is as follows:

WEST HEM CRIME CIV SEC DEM RIGHTS & WOMEN'S ISSUES
Room: DSOB 423   **Phone:** 202.224.4651

Majority:		Minority:	
C: Marco Rubio, FL	RSOB 284	**RM: Ben Cardin, MD**	HSOB 509
Rob Portman, OH	RSOB 448	Tom Udall, NM	HSOB 531
Ted Cruz, TX	RSOB 404	Jeanne Shaheen, NH	HSOB 506
Cory Gardner, CO	RSOB 354	Tim Kaine, VA	RSOB 231
John Barrasso, WY	DSOB 307		

p. 158

There is a duplicate record for Senate Subcommittee on Border Security and Immigration with Majority and Minority membership switched. The correct listing is as follows:

BORDER SECURITY AND IMMIGRATION
Room: DSOB 224   **Phone:** 202.224.7840

Majority:		Minority:	
C: John Cornyn, TX	HSOB 517	**RM: Dick Durbin, IL**	HSOB 711
Lindsey Graham, SC	RSOB 290	Dianne Feinstein, CA	HSOB 331
Chuck Grassley, IA	HSOB 135	Patrick Leahy, VT	RSOB 437
Mike Lee, UT	RSOB 361-A	Amy Klobuchar, MN	DSOB 425
Ted Cruz, TX	RSOB 404	Christopher Coons, DE	RSOB 127-A
Josh Hawley, MO	DSOB B40A	Richard Blumenthal, CT	HSOB 706
Thom Tillis, NC	DSOB 185	Mazie Hirono, HI	HSOB 713
Joni Ernst, IA	HSOB 730	Cory Booker, NJ	HSOB 717
John Kennedy, LA	RSOB 416		

p. 159

Majority and Minority membership are switched for Subcommittee on Intellectual Property. The correct listing is as follows:

INTELLECTUAL PROPERTY
Room: DSOB 224   **Phone:** 202.224.6342

Majority:		Minority:	
C: Thom Tillis, NC	DSOB 185	**RM: Christopher Coons, DE**	RSOB 127-A
Marsha Blackburn, TN	DSOB 357		
Chuck Grassley, IA	HSOB 135	Sheldon Whitehouse, RI	HSOB 530
John Cornyn, TX	HSOB 517	Dick Durbin, IL	HSOB 711
Lindsey Graham, SC	RSOB 290	Mazie Hirono, HI	HSOB 713
Mike Crapo, ID	DSOB 239	Patrick Leahy, VT	RSOB 437
Mike Lee, UT	RSOB 361-A	Richard Blumenthal, CT	HSOB 706
Ben Sasse, NE	RSOB 136	Kamala Harris, CA	HSOB 112

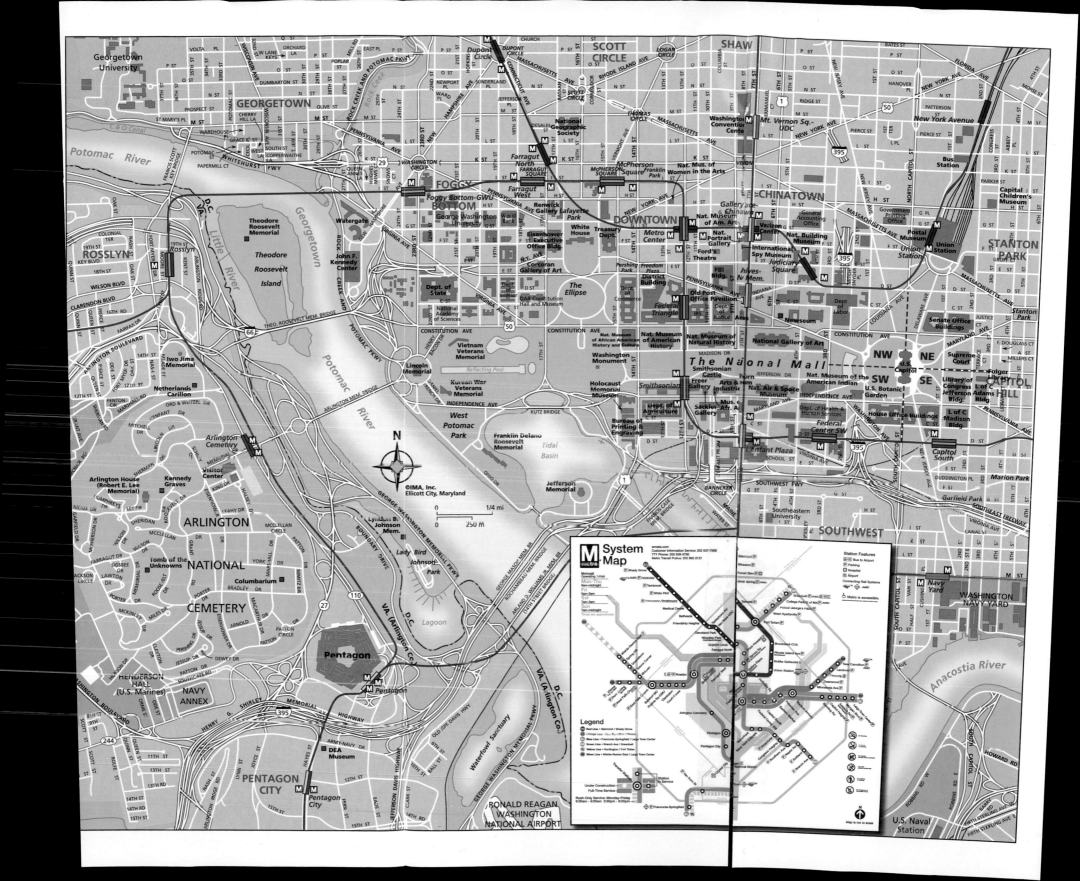

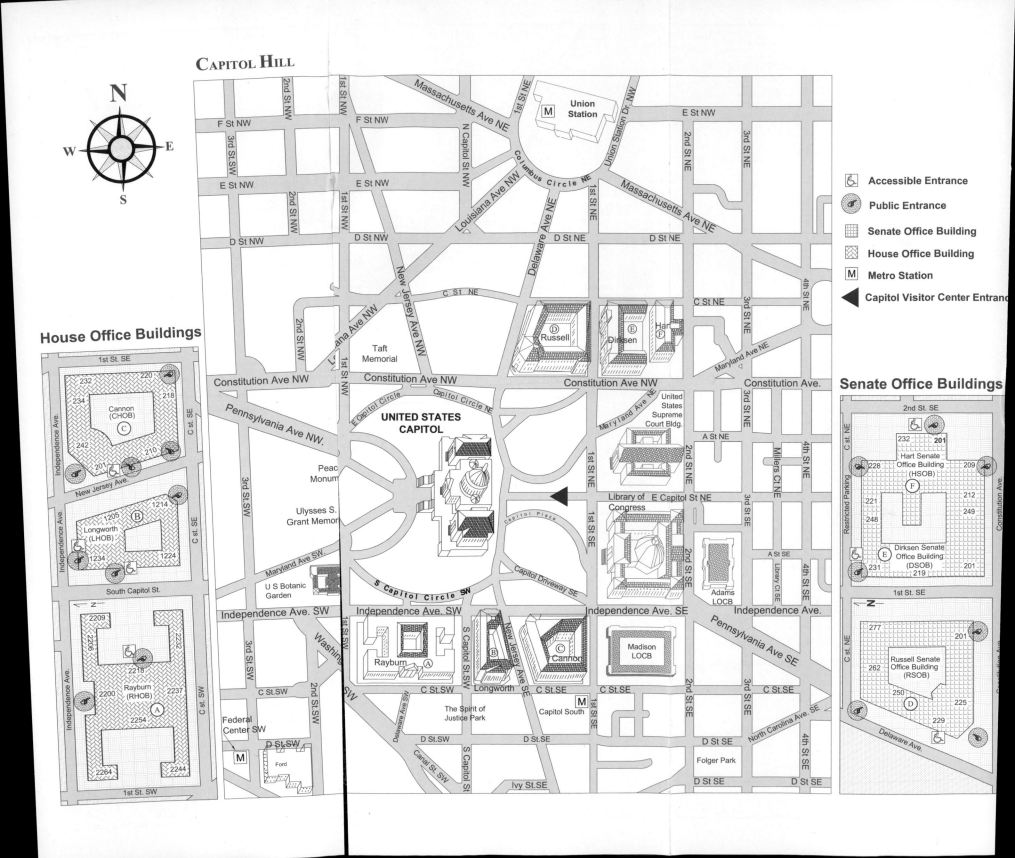

CAPITOL HILL

N
W E
S

House Office Buildings

1st St. SE

232
234
220
218
Cannon (CHOB)
C
242
201 210

New Jersey Ave.

Independence Ave.
C st. SE

Pennsylvania Ave. NW.

1205
1214
Longworth (LHOB)
B
1234
1224

Independence Ave.
C st. SE

South Capitol St.

N
2209
2206
2232
2218
Rayburn (RHOB)
A
2200
2237
2254
2264
2244

Independence Ave.
C st. SW

3rd St.SW

1st St. SW

2nd St NW
2nd St NW
1st St NW
1st St NW
N Capitol St NW

F St NW
F St NW
E St NW
E St NW
D St NW
D St NW

3rd St. SW

2nd St NW

Louisiana Ave NW

New Jersey Ave NW

1st St NW

Constitution Ave NW
Constitution Ave NW

Pennsylvania Ave. NW.

3rd St.SW

Maryland Ave. SW.

Washington SW

2nd St. SW

Taft Memorial

Peace Monument

Ulysses S. Grant Memorial

U S Botanic Garden

Federal Center SW

M

Ford

D St.SW

Massachusetts Ave NE

Union Station
M

Columbus Circle NE

Union Station Dr. NW

Massachusetts Ave NE

E St NW
E St NW

D St NE
D St NE

C St NE
C St NE

Constitution Ave NW
Constitution Ave.

Russell
D
Dirksen
E
Har
F

Delaware Ave NE

Louisiana Ave NW

Capitol Circle NE

E Capitol Circle
Capitol Circle NE

UNITED STATES CAPITOL

S Capitol Circle SW

Independence Ave. SW

Rayburn
A

B

Cannon
C

Longworth

C St.SW
C St SE
C St SE

D St.SW
D St SE

The Spirit of Justice Park

Capitol South
M

S Capitol St. SW

New Jersey Ave SE

Delaware Ave SW

Canal St. SW

Ivy St.SE

Capitol Plaza

Library of Congress

E Capitol St NE

Capitol Driveway SE

Madison LOCB

Adams LOCB

United States Supreme Court Bldg.

Maryland Ave NE

Maryland Ave NE

A St NE

Constitution Ave.

3rd St NE
4th St NE

Millers Ct NE

A St SE

2nd St SE
3rd St SE

Library Ct SE
4th St SE

Independence Ave. SE
Independence Ave.

Pennsylvania Ave SE

North Carolina Ave. SE

Folger Park

D St SE
D St SE

2nd St NE
3rd St NE

4th St NE

1st St NE
1st St SE

Legend

♿ **Accessible Entrance**

Public Entrance

▦ **Senate Office Building**

▨ **House Office Building**

M **Metro Station**

◀ **Capitol Visitor Center Entrance**

Senate Office Buildings

2nd St. SE

♿
232 **201**
Hart Senate Office Building (HSOB)
228
F
209
221
212
248
249
Dirksen Senate Office Building (DSOB)
E
231
219
201

Restricted Parking

C st. NE
Constitution Ave.

1st St. SE

N

C st. NE

277
201
Russell Senate Office Building (RSOB)
262
D
250
225
229

Delaware Ave.